Devotions to help you
stand strong 24/7

TYNDALE KiDS

Tyndale House Publishers, Inc.
Wheaton, IL

Young Believer™
365

*Devotions to help you
stand strong 24/7*

Stephen Arterburn
Jesse Florea

Today is the start of something big. It's the first day of a new year, another step into the twenty-first century, a bold leap into your future. Isn't that great!?! Aren't you totally excited?!?

Well, maybe you're not excited. Maybe you feel it's a little scary. And you're right. Getting ready for the first day of a new school year, moving to a different house, getting a new haircut, having a new baby brother or sister, trying a new food—any new beginning can be a bit frightening. You don't know what to expect. Your mind can race with questions. Is this the year I make first chair in the band? Is this the year I have to get braces? Is this the year I grow six inches? Is this the year I score big in soccer?

Only time will answer all of your questions. But you can answer one question today: Will you drift into the next 365 days timid and afraid about what's going to happen, or will you enter this year with a smile on your face expecting great things?

Check out 2 Timothy 1:7 in the *Young Believer Bible:*

In this verse the apostle Paul encourages his friend Timothy to rely on God's Spirit to make him powerful. As a believer in Jesus Christ, you have that same Spirit inside of you to help you be strong instead of afraid.

●●●

Did you know you were born with only two fears? The fear of falling and the fear of loud noises are all that scare babies. But as you grow, other fears enter your mind. Will you fit in at school? Will you be the best? What will happen tomorrow? A popular saying goes, "Let go and let God." It means don't worry about it. Trust God with your future. He wants to give you a life filled with his joy, power, and love. Will you step out in boldness and live for him?

Here are a couple of things I'm trusting God for boldness to accomplish this year:

1. _____

2. _____

Pray:

Ask God to fill you with his Spirit and make you bold as you begin a new year.

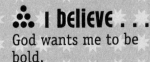

⁙ I believe . . .
God wants me to be bold.

Creak! Crack! BANG!

You just heard a loud noise that woke you up in the middle of the night. You peek around the room but don't see anything. You strain your ears, but the sound is gone. What should you do next?

a. Pull the covers over your head, curl up in a little ball, and try to sleep as scary thoughts race through your mind.
b. Jump out of bed and shout, "I've got a baseball bat in here. Don't mess with me!"
c. Sit up and holler for your mom or dad.
d. Calm down, start thinking straight, and ask God to help you fall back to sleep and have good dreams.

Creaks and squeaks in the night can be freaky. But those things can seem like no big deal compared to bigger scares such as threats of terrorism or wondering if your parents will ever get divorced. Life is full of uncertainties. But the Bible says over and over that there's no need to be afraid because God is always near. He's the most wonderful protector and friend you could ever find. The answer is *d*.

Check out Psalm 91:1-2 in the *Young Believer Bible:*

Although we don't know who wrote this psalm, it's obvious that person had figured out that trusting God equals safety. Whether this writer fought lions, braved stormy seas, led armies into battle, or simply faced questions about the future, he recognized that God kept him safe when he ran to him.

●●●

Have you ever had to run to God for safety? Maybe a bully was trying to pick a fight. Maybe you heard some noises at night. Maybe you were caught in a bad storm. God can comfort you in any situation—and better yet, he wants to. All you have to do is curl up in his loving arms. He will be a shelter in all of life's stormy situations.

Because I believe God keeps me safe, I'll memorize a couple of these verses so I can bring them to mind the next time I feel scared: Psalm 31:24, Psalm 56:11, and John 14:27.

Pray:

Thank God for being a safe place during scary times.

⁂ I believe . . .
God keeps me safe.

You have a lot of important decisions to make every day. What clothes will you wear? Will you practice the piano? What will you eat for breakfast? Should you take a shower? Will you be nice to your brother? Do you have to clean up after the dog?

The answers to those questions determine what kind of day you'll have. Then when the next morning comes, you have to make all the same choices again.

But can you guess what is the most important decision you'll make during your lifetime? Should you wear purple and orange socks to school? No, that's not it. Should you eat that hamburger in the back of the fridge with green stuff growing on it? Uh-uh. The most important decision you'll ever make is the decision to believe that Jesus is God's Son, who died for your sins, and to accept him as your personal Savior. It will bring a joy and peace to your life that will start now and last forever. Have you made the decision to let Jesus take control of your life?

Check out 1 John 1:8-9 in the *Young Believer Bible:*

In these verses, one of Jesus' best friends, John, writes that everybody messes up. But the good news is if we ask Jesus to forgive us, he does. Plus he cleans us up and makes us right with God like he is.

●●●

Do you know without a doubt that you'll go to heaven when you die? You can be sure of that. Jesus allows only perfect people in heaven with him. And since nobody is perfect, we all have a big problem. You, like everybody else, have messed up, whether it's been by lying, cheating, wanting your friends' stuff, disobeying your parents, or treating your friends badly. God calls those actions sin. God sees all of your sins, but he will forgive your sins through Jesus Christ. All you have to do is pray and ask Jesus into your life.

Pray:

"Dear God, please forgive me. I know I'm a sinner. I believe Jesus died and rose from the dead so I could be forgiven of my sins and live forever in heaven. Thank you for loving me and allowing me to have a personal relationship with you. Amen."

(If you just prayed that prayer for the first time, tell somebody—your parents, a children's pastor, the person who gave you this book. You just made the most important decision you'll ever make!)

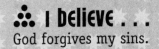

I believe . . .
God forgives my sins.

Imagine yourself standing at the starting line of a long race. You've trained hard and decided to run this race to the end. As you look at the runners around you, you notice you're in pretty good company. These athletes are fit and prepared to run. You do a couple of quick stretches to make sure you're ready. Right before the starter's pistol goes off, the kid next to you taps your shoulder.

You look over at him and see that he's wearing a bathrobe instead of shorts like everybody else. Not only that, he's wearing slippers instead of running shoes!

"I'm sure glad that's over," he says.

Over?!? you think. *It's not over. The race hasn't even begun!*

"Are you nutty?" you ask. "Don't you know the starter hasn't fired the gun yet?"

"Yeah, I don't care," the kid replies. "I decided to show up for the race, and that's enough for me. Boy, I'm tired. I think I'm going back to bed."

Just then the starter raises his hand. *BANG!*

You take off with the rest of the runners, leaving that kid in the dust.

He was a little confused, you think, as you race to the front.

Check out Hebrews 12:1 in the *Young Believer Bible:*

This verse tells you a lot about what it means to be a Christian. It says to get rid of the things that hold you back from living for God, learn from the actions of other Christians around you, and never give up as you run the race for Christ.

• • •

Many people think that once they make the decision to accept Christ into their hearts that's it. They've reached the end. They've done all they can do. And that's kind of true. Once you have a personal relationship with Jesus, you're guaranteed to live with him forever in heaven.

But praying to accept Christ is not the end of your Christian life. It's just the beginning. God has amazing plans for you. If you sit around instead of running the race, you will miss some incredible things.

Here are some ideas that will help me run a good race for God. (Hint: What about reading the Bible and going to church? Anything else?)

1. _____

2. _____

3. _____

Pray:
Ask God to help you in the training of becoming a great runner for him.

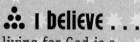

⁘ I believe . . .
living for God is a long, exciting race.

Sarah was a solid student. Her grades didn't all look like the first letter in the alphabet, but she paid attention in class, did her homework, studied hard, and tried her best. She had just one problem. Her grades didn't all look like the second letter in the alphabet, either. In fact, most of her marks were pretty average—could have been worse, but could have been much better.

Sarah's parents were disappointed because they knew she was smart enough to get better grades. Sarah was frustrated because she worked so hard. And Sarah's teachers didn't know what to do for her. Sarah couldn't figure out how to defeat her problem. Every time she got a test, her palms would start to sweat, her heart would beat faster, her eyes would get big, and her mind would go blank. She could barely remember her name, let alone the chief of the Incas. And asking her to multiply 10 by 12 was like telling her to figure out how many hamburgers McDonald's sells in a day—it was impossible. Sarah's test anxiety brought her brain to a halt.

Check out Psalm 118:6-7 in the *Young Believer Bible*:

These verses remind you that you have nothing to fear because you have the Lord with you. God will help you triumph over your enemies, whether those enemies are people, circumstances, or tests.

●●●

Most test anxiety comes from one thing: the fear of failure. Think about this question: Who is disappointed in you if you fail? God isn't. Your worth in his eyes doesn't depend on good grades or how much you succeed in sports or music or anything else. But he does want you to do your best. And worrying only holds you back from doing your best.

Next time I'm worried about failing, I'll remember these three *R*s:

1. Remember God loves me no matter what.

2. Relax.

3. Get ready to do my best.

Pray:

Tell God you're glad he loves you, no matter how you do in school.

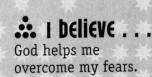

⁂ I believe . . .
God helps me overcome my fears.

What is the strangest Christmas present you've ever received?

a. A pink, full-body fluffy bunny suit
b. A doll that speaks only French and says, "Maman" and "Où est mon croissant?"
c. A football helmet without a face mask
d. Other (fill in the blank) _____
e. None of the above

The answer's certainly not *e*. You probably marked *d* and filled in the blank.

What is it that causes people to buy weird gifts? Their hearts are probably in the right place. They just want to do something nice for you. But the results can be quite odd, because they don't know you well enough to have a clue about the things you like.

Isn't it cool when relatives know what you want and get you the perfect gift? That's a lot more fun. Not only do you like the gift because it's something you wanted and it reflects your interests, but you also feel good because it shows that somebody knows you well.

Check out Matthew 2:11 in the *Young Believer Bible:*

The second part of this verse provides a list of what the wise men brought to Jesus. Their treasures included gold, frankincense, and myrrh.

● ● ●

At first, the wise men's gifts seem like the eight-foot scarf and foot-long mittens your aunt knitted for you last year—they just don't fit. What's a kid supposed to do with gold, incense, and myrrh? But each of the treasures had a special meaning.

• Gold stands for wealth. It's a gift fit for a king. And Jesus is the King of kings.
• Incense was used in worship services. It's a gift fit for a priest. And nobody knew God's Word or lived according to his rules better than Jesus.
• Myrrh was used as a pain killer or to prepare a dead person's body for burial. It's a gift for someone who will experience pain and death.

When I think about the fact that Jesus died for me, this is how I feel:

_____

_____

_____

The reason Jesus was born in the first place was to suffer and die for everyone's sins.

⁖ I believe . . .

the gifts that the wise men gave Jesus tell me a lot about his life.

Pray:

Thank Jesus for coming to the earth to suffer and die for you.

Scientists have been trying for years to figure out if aliens exist. Special satellite dishes point upward, listening for noises in outer space. The government has spent millions of dollars without finding a thing.

Hollywood also has a fascination with aliens. Lots of TV shows and movies feature extraterrestrial beings. Some aliens are pictured as friendly. Some of them try to take over the earth. And they all look a little different.

What do you think an alien would look like if one did exist? Do you think it would be green? In old movies most of them are. Maybe it would have a big head. Maybe it'd have several heads and lots of eyes. Cool! How about arms and hands? Perhaps it wouldn't need hands, because it would have big suctionlike tubes on the end of its arms that suck in everything it wanted. Would it walk on legs? float? fly through the air with a jet pack? The possibilities are endless.

Actually, if you want to figure out what an alien looks like, all you have to do is look in the mirror. It's no joke. The Bible calls you an alien.

Check out 1 Peter 2:11 in the *Young Believer Bible:*

In this verse Peter reminds us that as children of God we are aliens living in a strange land. Our true home is heaven. And because of this fact, we need to be careful to keep away from the harmful things of this world.

● ● ●

Because the devil was cast out of heaven and down to earth, he has a lot of power here. As a believer in Jesus Christ, you know heaven is your final home. So you're really an alien here on earth. You live here, but this isn't your final destination. And with God's power you can overcome the devil and make a difference for God while you're on this planet.

Does that make sense? It's a tricky concept—one you may want to talk about more with a parent or a youth pastor. But know this: Being an alien is exciting. You can help God bring others into his kingdom. You can set an example for others by living for God on earth.

Pray:

Ask God to help you be an effective "alien" on earth.

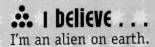

∴ I believe . . .
I'm an alien on earth.

Whoever invented the drive-thru window must've been a genius. You cruise up to it, babble a few words into the microphone, pull forward, and pick up your meal with the secret toy surprise. Anytime you're hungry, you can ask your parents to whip through the drive-thru for a quick bite to eat.

It's fast. It's fun. It's easy.

But have you noticed how simple it is to start treating God like a drive-thru window with your prayers? You have a test at school—so you pray to do well. You wreck on your bike—so you pray to feel better. Your cat runs away—so you pray it will come home.

Now there's nothing wrong with those prayers. God wants to hear from you and cares about everything that happens in your life. He's always listening, and you never have to wait to talk to him. But he wants to be much more than a drive-thru prayer window. He wants to hear about your good times and bad. Pray to him and thank him just for being him. Pray to him *all* the time, not just the times that you need something from him.

But just so you know, he probably won't ask, "Do you want fries with that?"

Check out Matthew 6:6 in the *Young Believer Bible:*
In this verse Jesus encourages you to go to a quiet place when you pray—a place where you won't be distracted and you can concentrate on talking to God. The verse also promises that God rewards this action.

●●●

Think of a time and place that would give you the best opportunity to talk to God without being interrupted. Start small (one or two minutes a day), then work your way up until praying to God is like speaking to a friend on the phone. Talk to God about your family, school, friends, church, pets . . . anything!

Here's the time and place I'm going to talk to God, as well as a few specific things I'm going to pray about:

Time: _____   Place: _____

Prayer Requests:

_____

_____

_____

Now get started and see what a difference it makes in your relationship with him.

Pray:
Tell God you want to be closer to him.

∴ I believe . . .
prayer is important.

Have you ever had a friend who lived far away—not just on the other side of town, but across the country?

It can be hard living so far from a friend, but it can also be fun to write letters, send e-mail, and talk on the phone. But nothing beats the excitement of finding out that friend is coming for a visit! You can do things together the whole time she's visiting—it will be like a party. It's easy to spend every second with your friend.

But what if you found out your friend was going to move next door? "Great!" you say.

And it would be great at first. But before you know it, the excitement you and your friend used to have would be gone. It would still be fun to hang out, but you wouldn't really do special things all the time. You'd usually do the same old thing when you were together—it would become just kind of ho-hum. Sometimes you might miss the way you felt when seeing your friend was not the norm. What would you do to bring back the excitement?

Check out Psalm 42:1-2 in the *Young Believer Bible:*

In these verses, the psalmist talks about wanting to be with God. He probably had times when his friendship with God was amazing; but he probably also had times when God was more like a next-door friend. His words show that he put effort into making his time with God special.

•••

Can you relate? Think of a time when you were especially hot, tired, and anxious for a cool drink. Remember how great it was when the drink finally flowed over your lips? Now remember a time when you were thirsty to know about God.

Here's how things are going now in my life. And here's what I'm thankful to God for. When things aren't going so great, I can write and tell Jesus what's making me feel ho-hum or tell him how I'd like things to be:

Pray:
Ask God to make you thirsty for him!

⁙ I believe . . .
I have to work on my relationship with Jesus.

Selfish Simon met a pie man going to the fair.

"Give me a blueberry pie, now!" Selfish Simon screamed at the pie man.

"That will be five dollars, young man," the pie man told Simon very calmly.

"I have no money," Simon said. "But I want that pie now!"

"A pie costs money to make," the pie man explained. "I have to pay for flour, eggs, and fruit. I need to sell my pies to make money for my family. I can't give them away."

"I don't care about you or your family," Selfish Simon said. "I just care about *me.*"

⁚⁚

Have you ever known a kid who was totally selfish like Simon—someone who thought the world revolved around him? That person probably had a lot of friends and was really happy all the time, right?

Wrong. Kids who only think of themselves drive other people away. And even when they get their way, selfish people never seem happy.

All of us can act selfishly from time to time. It's a natural way to behave and think. But how do you think God wants us to act?

Check out Philippians 2:3 in the *Young Believer Bible:*

In this verse, Paul writes something that goes directly against what a lot of people say in our world. Society will tell you to look out for number one—yourself. But Paul says to think of other people as more important than yourself.

●●●

Do you want your life to shine like a diamond and glow like a ruby for Jesus? Then you need to live like a GEM. The *G* stands for God. The *E* represents everybody. And the *M* stands for me. Think of it this way: put your relationship with *God* first in your life, *everybody* else second, and *me* last.

It's not easy to be a GEM for Jesus. You'll have to fight against what you naturally want to do. But if you can get your life in GEM order, it'll be super valuable to you, to God, and to other people.

Pray:

"Dear God, help me to put you first, everybody else second, and me last. Amen."

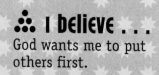

⁚⁚ I believe . . .
God wants me to put others first.

January 11

What goes best with peanut butter and jelly sandwiches, chocolate chip cookies, and a bowl of dry cereal? If you said milk, you're totally correct. (Getting hungry?)

Did you know that a couple of hundred years ago drinking an ice-cold glass of milk could make you really sick? Then in the mid-1800s, French scientist Louis Pasteur discovered that heating milk killed dangerous bacteria and made it safe for drinking. Milk is still "pasteurized" today—just go to the fridge and look at a carton if you don't believe it.

But if you travel to Paris, France, to look where Pasteur is buried, you won't find the words "Got Milk?" written on his grave. Instead his headstone reads: Joseph Meister Lived.

That's because on July 6, 1885, Joseph and his mother showed up at Pasteur's lab. Joseph had been bitten 14 times by a dog that had rabies. Back then catching the rabies disease was as good as being dead. Although Pasteur hadn't been able to properly test his vaccine for rabies, at Joseph's mother's urging he gave Joseph 13 shots. And Joseph Meister lived.

Check out Daniel 12:3 in the *Young Believer Bible:*

Daniel was an awesome man of God. He refused to stop praying to God even if that meant being thrown into a pit filled with lions. In this verse he says if you lead people to a belief in Christ, you will shine like the stars forever and ever.

●●●

As a believer in Christ, you have a permanent cure for eternal death. And best of all—it has been tested! Jesus Christ is a 100 percent effective remedy for sin. All you have to do is introduce him to your friends and let him do the work. When a person prays and commits her life to following Jesus, she has guaranteed eternal life. So get out there and start sharing your faith with your friends.

These are a few of my friends who don't know Christ:

1. _____

2. _____

3. _____

Pray:

Ask God for the boldness and opportunity to share him with the people on your list.

∴ I believe . . .
I should share Jesus with my friends.

PeeWee Smith couldn't wait for football tryouts. He started doing sit-ups and push-ups during the summer to get stronger. But PeeWee never seemed to get bigger.

At the first day of practice, PeeWee was the smallest kid on the field. But when the coach said run, he ran as fast as he could. When the coach talked, he listened. And when Coach handed out the playbook, he memorized everything the first night. By the end of the week, PeeWee felt pretty good . . . until Coach said to line up for tackling drills. Two lines formed about 10 yards apart. The player at the front of one line carried a football, while the first person in the other line tried to tackle him. Coach yelled out instructions and encouragement after each hit.

When it was PeeWee's turn to tackle, he looked at the other line and saw "Mountain" Mike Manly—the biggest kid in school—staring at him. Rumors said Mike brushed his teeth with a pine tree and used a rake to comb his hair. PeeWee ran at Mike and tried to tackle him with all his might. But the Mountain just dragged PeeWee yard after yard, through the mud, over prickly weeds, and into the end zone.

Check out Psalm 63:8 in the *Young Believer Bible:*

David was a mighty king of Israel. But he had a lot of troubles in his life and had to overcome a lot of obstacles to become king. In this verse, he says he's going to hang on to God because God lifts him up.

●●●

Just like PeeWee clung to "Mountain" Mike's leg, you need to cling to God. To finish the story, PeeWee made the football team because his determination and never-give-up attitude impressed the coach. You need to have the same attitude when it comes to your belief in Jesus Christ. Even when times are difficult, when you feel like you're being dragged through the mud and people are making fun of your faith, you need to stick close to Christ. If you don't let go of him, he will lift you up.

Pray:

Ask God to give you the determination to cling to him.

⠿ I believe . . .
I need to stay close to God.

January 13

How long do you think you could balance on one foot? Try timing yourself. Did you reach one minute? two minutes? ten minutes? *Not bad.*

In 1997 a man in Sri Lanka (that's in Asia) balanced on one foot for 76 hours and 40 minutes. That's more than three whole days standing on one leg! What an amazing feat. What an unbelievable showcase of skill. What an . . . incredible waste of time! And all Arulanantham Suresh Joachim (any guesses on how to pronounce that?) earned was getting his name in the *Guinness Book of World Records* and a long foot massage.

As impressive a balancing act as standing on one foot for days is, you do some pretty awesome balancing every day too. You have to balance school, homework, friends, sports, hobbies, music, chores, and more. *Whew.* That's a lot. And don't forget about reading your Bible and praying to God. Sometimes you probably feel overwhelmed. The key is to maintain a proper balance in your daily plans between family, friends, faith, and fun. How's your balance today?

Check out Ecclesiastes 7:8 in the *Young Believer Bible:*

During his day, King Solomon was considered the wisest man in the world. In this verse Solomon says finishing a project is better than starting one. He adds that having patience is better than being proud.

●●●

Do you start things but don't have time to finish them? Do you feel that days are too short because you can't get everything done? You might be too busy. If your life is out of whack because you're hanging out with friends too much or spending a lot of time playing sports, you may want to ask your parents to help you bring your life back in balance. And if you're too busy to spend a little time with God every day, it's time for a balance check.

Here's what I spend most of my time doing every day. Do I have a balanced life? Do I make time for God?

1. _____
2. _____
3. _____
4. _____
5. _____

Pray:

Ask God to show you where you can make more time for him every day.

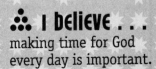

∴ I believe . . .
making time for God every day is important.

January 14

Bill couldn't wait for school to start after Christmas break. This semester he was going to join the band. Bill loved music, and he wanted to do his best. Following the first day of class, he took his new trumpet home and just started making noise on it. He didn't look at his music book. He didn't peek at the teacher's instructions. He didn't even know what those three little buttons on top were supposed to do. All Bill knew was that he was excited to be part of the band . . . and he liked his trumpet.

After a few weeks, Bill stopped blasting as long and loud as he used to. He was discouraged because he wasn't getting any better. His music teacher even said Bill might be booted out of band. Sure, he still hadn't cracked open his music book, but Bill was trying his best.

Can you figure out Bill's problem?

Check out Psalm 119:9-16 in the *Young Believer Bible:*

In these verses the psalmist says again and again how important it is to read God's Word. If you read more of this psalm, you'll see he keeps saying that following God's Word, rules, commands, principles, and laws is the best way to live.

● ● ●

Some people think being a Christian means they have to be nice to everybody, give away all their possessions, and move to Africa to be a missionary. But as a believer in Jesus Christ, you don't have to guess what it means to be a Christian. You can *know* what it means. All you have to do is open the Bible.

The Bible explains everything. Sure, some of the words are hard to pronounce. But if you try to read the Bible yourself, you'll probably be surprised how much of it is easy to understand. Plus there are tons of youth Bibles made just for you. Pick one up and get into God's Word!

Pray:

Tell God you're going to read his Word every day, even if it's just for a couple of minutes.

⁘ I believe . . .

I should follow God's instructions in the Bible.

January 15

The Constitution of the United States says, "We hold these truths to be self-evident that all men are created equal." But when Martin Luther King Jr. was born in Georgia on January 15, 1929, all people were not treated equally. African-Americans didn't have the same privileges as white people—especially in the southern part of the United States. There were different schools for white children and for black children. African-Americans weren't allowed in certain restaurants. They had different bathrooms and drinking fountains.

Martin Luther King Jr. wanted to change that. He wanted all people to be treated like it says in the Constitution. When Martin Luther King Jr. was a child, he was smart, well-spoken, and thoughtful. His dad was a pastor who taught his son about God's Word. Martin Luther King Jr. entered Morehouse College in Atlanta in a special program for gifted students when he was 15 years old. By the time he was 28, he was traveling the country making speeches. In 1963, he made one of his most famous speeches when he said he dreamed that his four children would "one day live in a nation where they will not be judged by the color of their skin but by the content of their character." Do you think his dream has come true?

Check out Matthew 17:20 in the Young Believer Bible:

In this verse Jesus tells his disciples that they need to have more faith. With just a little faith, his children can do mind-blowing things—like moving mountains.

● ● ●

Can one person change the world? In just thirteen years, Martin Luther King Jr. did a lot to change how people of all skin colors were treated in the United States. What do you dream about? Do any of your goals include serving God? What will it take to make your dreams reality?

These are some of my dreams:

1. _____

2. _____

3. _____

Pray:

Ask God to give you the faith to make your dreams come true.

⁘ I believe . . .
God can change the world through me.

Why do you think the pilgrims sailed across the ocean and landed in North America?

a. Things were getting a little too crowded in England.
b. They were tired of playing soccer and wanted to compete in American football.
c. It was an accident. They booked a three-hour tour, but then their tiny ship was tossed and ran aground on this uncharted continent.

All good answers. But all are wrong.

The pilgrims left England to find a place where they could worship God freely. In their country, the government told them how and where to worship. They wanted to worship God their own way—without government rules.

When the founding fathers of the United States wrote the Constitution, they made sure the pilgrims' dream was kept alive. Amendment 1 in the Bill of Rights says: "Congress shall make no law respecting an establishment of religion, or prohibiting the free exercise thereof. . . ."

That's a fancy way of saying the government can't tell you what religion you have to follow or stop you from worshiping any way you want.

Check out Romans 13:3 in the *Young Believer Bible:*

In this verse Paul tells Christians to follow the rules of society. He says the best way to stay out of trouble is to do what is right.

●●●

Do you think it's okay to talk about God at school? Some kids think they can't. They've heard something about the separation of church and state, and think it's against the law to mention Jesus Christ on school grounds.

The truth is if you live in the United States, you have the right to talk about God at school. You can even hand out invitations to a special church activity without breaking any rules. Plus if your school permits other groups to meet on campus, it has to allow you to organize a prayer group or a Bible study at school, or even bring a Bible to lunch or recess if you want.

I won't hide my faith. Here are some ways that I can bring God to school:

1. _____

2. _____

3. _____

Pray:
Ask God to help you tell kids about him at school.

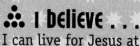

⁘ I believe . . .
I can live for Jesus at school.

What can you buy with a penny? Not much. A gum ball . . . maybe. Pennies are pretty worthless.

Robert, a kid in Florida, would disagree. He collects pennies. Sometimes he finds them on the sidewalk. Other times he picks up pennies and other coins near vending machines or in the grocery store. Neighbors, church members, and family members also give him their two cents worth. Robert has discovered if you put enough pennies and other coins together, you can end up with a pretty sizable chunk of money. One year he collected $30. Another year he tallied $42. And another year, after a story about him appeared in a local newspaper, he collected $127.

You might be thinking, *Robert must be really rich.* And you're right. But he's not rich in money, he's rich in good will. That's because every Christmas, Robert takes the money he's collected and buys gifts for people in hospitals, nursing homes, or children's homes. He even tucks in a Scripture verse with each present.

"What I do is for the glory of God," Robert says. "Everything I do in public represents God."

Spreading God's love for a penny—now that's a good deal.

Check out Matthew 5:14-16 in the *Young Believer Bible*:

When you were younger, did you ever sing "This Little Light of Mine"? It's based on these verses. This is where Jesus says we are the light of the world. When we let our light shine and people see the good things we do, then they praise God.

●●●

Which is brighter, a 40-watt, a 75-watt, or a 100-watt lightbulb? If you guessed the 100-watt bulb, you're right. The main difference between the bulbs is the amount of energy they use. It costs more to light up the brightest one. And it will cost you to be a 100-watt bulb for God. You'll have to put in time and energy to get closer to Jesus. That means reading your Bible and praying. Once you're plugged into the ultimate power source—Jesus Christ—you'll shine brightly for him.

These are a few ways I can shine for God at school, at home, and in my neighborhood:

1. _____

2. _____

3. _____

Pray:

Ask God to give you the opportunity to shine for him—
then see what happens.

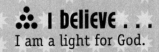
∴ I believe . . .
I am a light for God.

Ever watch professional wrestling on television? You've probably noticed there are some pretty big and strong guys who climb into the ring. But there's a guy in the Bible who makes modern wrestlers look like wimps. His name was Samson, and one time he killed a thousand men using just the jawbone of a donkey. *Whoa!* What would it be like to interview this biblical strongman?

Reporter: So what makes you so strong?

Samson: My mother told me that before I was born an angel appeared to her and told her I'd be God's servant. I've never drunk any wine or cut my hair. Hi, Mom!

Reporter: Okay. But when did you know God had given you this amazing strength?

Samson: A lion attacked me when I was just a young man. But I was able to kill it with my bare hands.

Reporter: What's your greatest feat of strength?

Samson: Once I lifted a city's gates with their posts and bars right out of the ground and dragged them all the way up a hill.

Reporter: Why do you think God gave you this power?

Samson: He's using me to help deliver his people from the Philistines.

Check out Ephesians 6:10 in the Young Believer Bible:

Paul wrote this verse from prison—he actually wrote a lot of the New Testament from prison. Here he tells Christians to be strong in the Lord and gain their power from God.

● ● ●

Where do you turn when things are difficult in your life? Samson turned to God. He'd been tricked, captured, and blinded by the Philistines. Then in Judges 16:28, he called to God to give him strength one more time. God heard Samson's cries and gave him the power to knock down the Philistine temple.

And God still answers the prayers of his people today. With his strength you can overcome any obstacle.

These are some situations in which I need God's help:

1. _____

2. _____

3. _____

When you're in a bind, turn to God for his strength. You may be amazed at the results.

⁙ I believe . . .

God is my ultimate power source.

Pray:
Thank God that he's a pillar of strength that you can lean against.

Atlanta Braves pitcher John Smoltz has won more games in the play-offs and World Series than any other pitcher in his team's history.

Just think if that were you. Think about the pressure of millions of people watching on televisions around the world and tens of thousands of people screaming in the stadium. Your team's success would sit squarely on your shoulders.

Pretty scary, huh?

John used to think so. "I used to pitch to please everybody else," he says. "But I don't do that anymore. If you're constantly worried about other people, you're not going to perform to the best of your ability."

When this all-star switched his focus from the people watching on TV and in the stands to playing for God, his career really took off.

"I was freed up from trying to get public acceptance," John explains. "I began playing for an audience of One, not of millions."

So now when John steps on the pitcher's mound, he tries his hardest and wants to please just one person: Jesus Christ.

"Above all," John says, "seek godly acceptance, not worldly acceptance. Worldly acceptance is temporary. Godly acceptance is eternal."

Check out John 15:5 in the *Young Believer Bible:*

In this verse, Jesus says he's the vine and we are the branches. If we stay connected to Christ, we'll grow strong in our faith. But if we break away from Jesus, we'll wither and accomplish nothing.

●●●

Have you ever tried to do everything to make a friend happy, only to find out one day that she decided not to be your friend anymore? If so, that didn't make you feel very good, did it? People can change their minds and do things to hurt your feelings.

God never changes. And his mind is made up: He loves you always and forever. So next time you have to make a choice between pleasing a friend and pleasing God, why not choose to stick close to God? After all, he's the only one who will never let you down!

Pray:

Commit to God that you will try to please him more than other people.

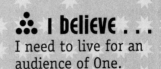

∴ I believe . . .
I need to live for an audience of One.

Aren't babies amazing? Maybe you have a little brother or sister you've watched grow up. You yourself grew from a tiny infant into who you are today. And even before you were born, you did some pretty phenomenal growing.

Did you know that your heart started beating only three weeks after your life began inside your mother? At about the same time, your brain began working. When you were eight weeks old, your muscle system was complete. Your mom couldn't feel you move because you were smaller than a golf ball, but you could kick and swim. At two and a half months, your hands were totally formed. You even had fingerprints! A week later your taste buds began to form. You could smile and hear. Perhaps you even started recognizing your mother's and father's voices.

For the next six months, you kept growing and developing until you were ready to be born. Now look at you. You're a masterpiece, created in God's image. And there's nobody else in the whole world who's exactly like you.

Check out Psalm 139:13-14 in the Young Believer Bible:

Sometimes David just liked to sit, think, and write about God. In these verses he recognizes God's awesome creative powers. It's God who forms each one of us, and all of his works are wonderful.

● ● ●

You are fearfully and wonderfully made. Doesn't that make you feel special? When God made Earth, stars, planets, plants, and animals, he "saw that it was good" (Genesis 1:25). But when God made the first man and woman, the Bible says "it was excellent in every way" (Genesis 1:31). All people are created in God's image—no matter the color of their skin or if they're mentally or physically challenged.

You might know someone with a disability. Maybe you try to avoid that person. Next time, why not make a point of saying hi and treating him like one of God's amazing creations?

Pray:

Ask God to help you treat all people as his special creations.

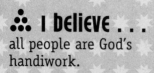

⸪ I believe . . .

all people are God's handiwork.

You can learn a lot from reading a book. You're probably thinking I'm talking about the Bible, right? You can learn everything you need to know about life by reading God's Word, because it contains more wisdom than all the other books in the world. But you can learn a little something from most books you read.

Have you ever read *The Adventures of Tom Sawyer* by Mark Twain? It's a classic. There's one scene in that story where Tom is asked to paint the fence—something he dreads doing. He's grumbling and groaning as he starts, but then he sees some of his friends walking by. He puts a smile on his face and acts like he's having a great time working. His friends see Tom having fun and ask to help. Tom hesitates. Finally, his friends start giving him stuff—an apple, a dead rat, marbles—to let them paint the fence. After all, it looks like fun.

In no time flat the fence is painted, and Tom has a pocketful of goodies.

Check out Ecclesiastes 4:9 in the Young Believer Bible:

The Bible contains lots of verses that are very practical and helpful in everyday life. This is one of them. It explains how working together helps get things done more quickly.

●●●

Tom Sawyer tricked his friends into helping him, which isn't a kind thing to do. But he knew something you can learn from: If you work together with others, you can get more done.

When you need help, don't be afraid to ask somebody to come to your aid. Be honest that you need help. If your math homework is too hard, ask your teacher for some tips. If you're having difficulty fixing your bike, ask a friend to share his mechanical know-how. If digging a hole in the backyard isn't working, ask your dad to use his strength. You'll be less frustrated, and you'll get more done. And the next time somebody asks you for help . . . well, you know what to do.

Pray:

Ask God to make you more willing to help others and to be helped.

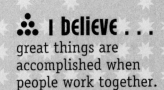

∴ I believe . . .
great things are accomplished when people work together.

Question: Ten cats were in a boat and one jumped out. How many were left?
Answer: None. They were copycats.

Does it bother you when people are copycats? Maybe your little brothers or sisters dress like you, talk like you, and play the same sports you play. Maybe they even walk around mimicking you all day. Watching them is like looking in a mirror.

Maybe this scene sounds familiar:

You: Can you stop copying me?
Your brother: Can you stop copying me?
You: I mean it.
Your brother: I mean it.
You: I'm a little pest.
Your brother: I'm a little pest.
You: Ha, ha!
Your brother: Ha, ha!
You: I'm telling Mom.
Your brother: I'm telling Mom.

Frustrating, huh?

But do you know why your little brothers or sisters copy you? They *really* want to be like you. They love you. They look up to you. They think you're so cool that they want to be your little clones. If they act like you, they're actually showing you how much they respect you and want to be like you.

Check out Ephesians 5:1-2 in the *Young Believer Bible:*

These verses say we should copy God. Do what he does. Say what he says. And the perfect way to imitate God is by loving others.

●●●

You've probably heard it said tons of times that Jesus is your example. Maybe you even wear a "What Would Jesus Do?" bracelet to remind yourself to act like him.

But the apostle Paul explained what it means to follow Jesus Christ. To become a mirror image of God, you have to live a life of love. And that's not always easy. Sometimes it's hard to show love to a school bully or an annoying little sister or a parent who's just punished you. But Jesus will give you the ability to act with love. And the best part is God will never get mad at you for copying him!

Pray:

Thank Jesus for being such a great example of love.

 **I believe . . .**
to live like God means
I need to love others.

Has anyone ever told you that you look like your mom or dad? You may have the smile, walk, or even laugh of one of them. That's because you bear your parents' image—you came from them, so naturally you're going to resemble them.

Maybe you get tired of your aunt always saying, "You look just like your dad did when he was your age," or your grandma saying, "Your eyes are just like your mother's." You want to be an individual, right? And you are! You're uniquely you, but you also share characteristics with your parents. Everyone you meet can see the reflection of your parents in you—which, if you think about it, is kind of cool.

But if you could be like anyone, who would it be? A movie star? Your parents? A famous scientist? A president? The Bible says that all human beings share the image of one Person—Someone more powerful than the greatest president and more brilliant than the smartest scientist. Humans bear the image of the perfect, loving God.

Check out Genesis 1:27 in the *Young Believer Bible:*

God created both men and women in his image. When God made Adam and Eve, the first man and woman, he carefully designed them to reflect his emotions and character.

●●●

All of God's wonderful qualities—his creativity, compassion, and intelligence—are reflected in his creation: you! Because of that, you are incredibly special. The image of the all-powerful, loving Creator shines brightly through you.

How do you reflect God? What abilities has he given you? Maybe you're kind to everyone you meet. Maybe you're able to get good grades in difficult subjects like math and science. Maybe you can create beautiful drawings or paintings. When you use the talents God has given you, you are reflecting him and bringing him glory.

These are three talents or characteristics I have that reflect God:

1. _____

2. _____

3. _____

Pray:

Ask God to make you a true reflection of him today!

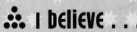

∴ I believe . . .

God created people and patterned them after himself.

I have trouble keeping my room clean. It seems like it takes hours to clean it up, but only seconds until it's messy again. Can you help me?
Sloppy Joe
Messy, France

Dear Sloppy,
Wanting a clean room is a good thing, but it takes some work. You might want to develop a system. Try picking up all your dirty clothes first. Second, straighten up your closet. Next, put your toys where they belong and stack your books back on the shelves. Finally, throw away any papers you don't need and tidy up your desk. You could also try developing a checklist to keep yourself on track. That might help you be able to go a hundred miles an hour and still do a great job!

As far as rooms being easier to mess up than clean up, you're right! The key is to put things away as soon as you're done with them. Do a little neatening up every day. That way your room stays clean. And if your parents are like most, they probably want you to have a tidy room before you do something fun.

Check out 1 Samuel 2:8 in the *Young Believer Bible*:
In the second part of this verse, the prophet Samuel's mother, Hannah, praises God for creating the earth and setting it in order.

●●●

Is an organized person a better Christian than someone who's unorganized? Probably not. But if your life is organized, you may end up with more time to spend with God. A lot of adults carry daily planners so they know what they're supposed to do every minute of the day.

And you need to make sure you're doing well in school, helping out around the house, growing closer to God, enjoying a hobby, and spending time with friends and family. Taking responsibility now for the things you need to do will help create some good habits when you do grow up and have to carry a Palm Pilot everywhere.

Pray:
Ask God to bring to mind ideas that will help you be more organized.

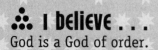

∴ I believe . . .
God is a God of order.

"Oh, and it's Jake versus sin!" the announcer shouts into the microphone. A hush falls over the crowd. "Jake is thinking about telling a lie. He's forming a good story in his mind right now. That's it! He *forgot* to do his homework. It had nothing to do with the seventy-three rounds of Skate Shed he played instead.

"And sin takes the lead! It's down to the last few seconds. Looks like sin is going to win this match!

"And . . . wait a minute! Jake just said a prayer. Another contender has entered the ring. It's the Holy Sprit. I've seen this guy before. He's unbeatable!

"Jake's reconsidering. Wow! What a hit! The Holy Spirit just knocked out sin.

"Jake tells the truth and wins the victory!"

⁂

You may never see a boxing match like this one, but maybe you can relate to sin's power over you. Sometimes temptation feels like a knock-down-drag-out fight. It's hard to do what's right. But with God's help, you *can* beat sin.

Check out 1 John 4:4 in the *Young Believer Bible:*

The Bible says that Satan is the ruler of this world. But this verse says that the One who is in you, God's Holy Spirit, is more powerful than Satan, the one who is in the world.

●●●

Temptations come every day—the chance to cheat on a test, the irresistible urge to yell at an annoying sibling, or the opportunity to cover up the truth with a little lie. Sometimes it may seem impossible to resist temptation and do the right thing. But Jesus won the victory over sin when he rose again, and he gave you the power to overcome sin too.

Here are three temptations I need God's help to overcome:

1. _____

2. _____

3. _____

Pray:

Thank God that you can have victory over sin, and ask him to help you have victory today!

I believe . . .

Holy Spirit gives
power to win over

One afternoon at recess, Jenny noticed a boy named Pete standing in the middle of the soccer field. He wasn't running around. He wasn't playing with the other kids. He was just standing there.

Day after day, Jenny kept noticing this boy standing and staring at the ground. Finally, she couldn't take it anymore. She had to know what was going on.

"Why are you standing here?" she asked.

"Because my older brother told me to stand here at recess," Pete replied.

"But what are you doing?" Jenny asked.

"I'm standing at the spot I'm supposed to."

"But *why* do you have to stand here?"

"Because my brother told me to."

Jenny quickly decided this mystery wasn't going to be easily solved, so she waited after school to talk with his mom.

"Why does Pete stand in the middle of the soccer field during recess?" Jenny asked.

"That's what he's supposed to do," the boy's mom answered.

"But what is he doing?" Jenny asked, getting more frustrated.

"He's standing in the spot," the mom said matter-of-factly. "Somebody from our family always stands in that spot during recess. I stood at that same spot when I went to school here."

Check out Romans 14:12 in the *Young Believer Bible:*

In this verse Paul says every Christian will have to tell God what he did for him. Each will have to give an account to God for his or her actions.

●●●

Do you know why you go to church every Sunday? Is it because a parent told you to g Pete knew he was supposed to stand in that spot, but he didn't know why. His m didn't know why either. It was just something their family did. Doesn't it seem pr silly to keep doing something without knowing what the purpose is for doing it

God wants all of you—your heart, your mind, your actions. And the only wa can give him everything is to learn about him and what he wants from and for y you understand why going to church is a valuable way to spend your time?

Pray:

Commit to God that you're going to learn more about him.

"Sticks and stones may break my bones, but names can never hurt me." You probably heard that when you were younger. Do you think it's true?

The truth is, being called a name does hurt . . . deeply. A broken bone just takes a couple of months to heal, but it can take years to recover from stinging words. Ask your parents if they remember being called names as children. A lot of adults still have painful memories related to name-calling. And some kids can be especially cruel. If they find out that being called a certain name bothers you, they'll say it over and over again.

Experts say it takes five positive comments to counteract one negative one. Think about your own life. You've probably been on the receiving end of unkind remarks, but you've also probably dealt a few verbal jabs yourself. Do you think you say five times as many nice things as mean things to your brothers and sisters? Do you talk kindly to "outcast" kids at your school?

Check out Proverbs 12:18 in the *Young Believer Bible:*

This verse talks directly about the things we say. It says some people hurt others with what comes out of their mouths, but wise people use healing words.

●●●

Do you want your words to stab people or bring them healing? The choice is yours. Nobody can force you to say something. You have to think it and then open your lips to let it out. You can stop the message or change it anytime you want.

Think about what you said to people this week. Did you tease your little sister or talk back to your parents? Did you join other kids in making fun of a student at school? It's easy to say something but impossible to take it back. And while you can't take back words, you can work to make things better with people you may have hurt.

These are some people I've hurt with my words. Because I want to bring healing, I'll go to them this week, tell them I'm sorry, and ask for forgiveness.

Person: _____   What I said: _____

Person: _____   What I said: _____

Person: _____   What I said: _____

Pray:

Ask God to bring to mind people to whom you should apologize. Then pray you'll have the courage to make things right.

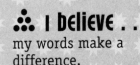

⁘ I believe . . .
my words make a difference.

It's the heart of the winter. The days are short. The sun goes down early. And if you live anywhere besides Florida or southern California, you're probably sick of snow, cold, and ice.

Or maybe you're just plain sick. Winter is a popular time to catch the cold or flu. There's probably plenty of coughing and sore throats to go around at school, church, or the mall. And being sick isn't a lot of fun.

Your nose runs, you're too hot or too cold, your body aches, and you're tired but you can't sleep.

Doctors say the best way to avoid catching a cold is to wash your hands a lot. Staying away from large crowds of people also helps.

But if you're already sick, you're going to have to drink a lot and get a lot of rest. Sleep and fluids help your body get better fast. And believe it or not, chicken soup has also been known to help you feel better sooner.

Of course, it still takes a while to get well. It's not like you can snap your fingers and feel good again.

Check out Jeremiah 17:14 in the *Young Believer Bible:*
In this verse, God's prophet writes that God is the true Healer and Savior.

●●●

Do you think Jesus ever got sick? Maybe, maybe not. We do know that he could heal people with just a touch of his hand. One time somebody simply touched his robe and was healed—now that's power! And Jesus has the power to heal people today.

Just as Jeremiah wrote, you can pray to God and ask him to heal you and save you. A physician is another name for a doctor. God is known as the Great Physician. When you pray for God to save you from your sins—that's all it takes for him to do it. You just need to ask Jesus to come into your life once, and he does.

But when you ask him to help you get over a cold, he doesn't always answer immediately. And that's okay. Continue to trust him and his power.

Pray:
Thank God for his healing and protection in your life.

∴ I believe . . .
God is the Great
Physician.

Have you ever played laser tag? There are a lot of fun places where you can play. First you pick a code name—maybe one that sounds powerful like Ace, Sting, Yoda, Hammer, or Blaster. Then you go into a room, strap on some gear with flashing lights, and enter the arena.

Laser-tag arenas can be really cool. Loud music, black lights making things glow, fog machines, and sparkling lasers are all over. It's high-paced, frantic action. Bodies move quickly in the dark, trying to stay away from little beams of red light. You try to shoot other people's sensors with your laser as you hide behind obstacles, pop out, duck down, and try to remain safe. You really have no idea who you're aiming at in the glowing lights or who's aiming at you. Then *wham-O!* Your laser shakes. Somebody's got you. You wait a few seconds, and you're back in the action.

And in the end, you exit the arena, get your scorecards, see how you played, and laugh with your friends. Then it's time for round two!

Check out John 8:12 in the *Young Believer Bible:*
This verse says Jesus lights up the darkness so we can follow him.

●●●

As fun as laser tag can be, the flashing lights, fog, and lasers sometimes make it difficult to figure out where you are in the arena. Thank God your relationship with Jesus isn't the same way. You're not shooting in the dark with him. Jesus is the light. He's a glowing beacon, a lighthouse, an ever fixed mark. If you aim at him and strive to follow him, then you know you're going the right way.

And following Jesus is fun. Every moment of your life won't be a high-action adventure, but God promises an abundant life. And there's nothing more exciting than living for God.

Pray:
Thank God that following him isn't confusing—he lights your way.

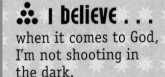
⁘ I believe . . .
when it comes to God, I'm not shooting in the dark.

Do you like playing with clay? Most kids mess around with Play-Doh when they are little (some kids even try eating it—yuck!). And most children love smashing clay into different shapes.

Some kids are very artistic and learn to make complicated things such as houses, animals, and people. Many other kids stick with making simpler things like pancakes, balls, and snakes.

No matter what your skill level, you probably have had to make a project with clay in art class at school. The teacher asked you to get your hands dirty trying to mold your best creation. And when you were done, the teacher took it away, cooked it to make it hard, and gave it back to you to admire.

Doesn't it feel great to hold something you made with your own hands? It doesn't matter if your vase tilts a little bit to one side or isn't totally round—you still like it just the way it is. It's perfect in your eyes because you made it.

Check out Ephesians 1:4 in the *Young Believer Bible:*
This verse points out that even before God created the world, it was his plan that we would be blameless in his sight. God knew he'd have to send his Son, Jesus Christ, to accomplish this plan.

●●●

Do you know what God thinks when he looks at you? He thinks you are prized, precious, and valued. Think about that for a minute. Have you ever been to a fair and wanted to win a huge, orange stuffed animal? You plopped down dollar after dollar, trying to win that animal and bring it home. And when you finally won it, you hugged it so hard that some of the stuffing almost popped out.

God sees you like that big stuffed animal at the fair. He's willing to pay a huge price to get you. And you cost a lot more than the ten dollars it can take to win a prize at a fair. God sent his greatest treasure—his Son, Jesus—to earth to die for you. Through Jesus, you're perfect in God's eyes.

Pray:
Thank God for his love and sacrifice.

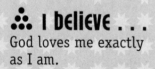

∴ I bEliEvE . . .
God loves me exactly
as I am.

If you've picked up your Bible recently, you've probably noticed that Jesus Christ is known by a lot of names. In fact, you can find nearly two hundred different names for Jesus. Here are just a few:

- Door of salvation
- Author of life
- Image of the invisible God
- Messiah
- Judge of all men
- Good Shepherd

- Excellent One
- Voice of God
- Savior of the world
- Promise of paradise
- Master

And that's only a short list.

Why do you think Jesus has so many names? Did people forget his real name and just make up something? Probably not. Jesus' names describe different parts of his mission. He's our judge and savior. He's the voice and image of God. He's your master and shepherd. And the more you learn about him, the more you'll find that you still have so much to discover.

Check out Philippians 2:9-10 in the Young Believer Bible:

These verses say Jesus is "a name that is above every other name." Every knee shall bow—in heaven, on earth, and under the earth—to Jesus.

● ● ●

Jesus was called by a lot of names. Of course, his enemies didn't call him nice things. Maybe you know what that feels like. Perhaps you have some nicknames you'd like to forget. Or you may have some ideas of what you'd like to be called.

Here are some nicknames I'd like to be known as:

1. _____

2. _____

3. _____

Now think about this: If you know Jesus personally as your Savior, then you're called God's child. You're directly related to the "name that is above every other name." And there's no name cooler than Jesus. Study Jesus' many names, and try to learn more about him—the name above all others.

Pray:

Commit to God that you're going to learn more of Jesus' names.

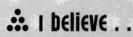

⁘ I believe . . .
Jesus is the name above all others.

February 1

Put your hand on your chest. Do you feel anything? I hope so, because if your heart isn't beating, you're in trouble! God created your heart to do some important work. Without your heart pumping blood to all parts of your body, you'd quickly cease living. February is Heart Month, so check out these heart-stopping facts:

- Your heart is about the same size as your fist.
- About 100,000 times: That's how many times your heart beats every day.
- About a gallon and a half of blood circulates through your body every 20 seconds. That means at the end of the day, your blood has traveled 12,000 miles—almost halfway around the world.
- Blood pulses through your body in rubbery tubes called blood vessels. The largest of these is the aorta, which is as big around as a garden hose. The smallest are called capillaries, which are so tiny that it takes 10 of them to equal the thickness of a human hair.
- Your heart is located in the center of your chest, where your ribs can best protect it.
- Even when you're just watching TV, your heart is working twice as hard as the leg muscles of a person sprinting.

Check out 1 Samuel 16:7 in the *Young Believer Bible:*
This verse says people judge who you are by what you look like, but God cares more about your character and heart.

●●●

You've probably already figured this out, but the above verse isn't talking about your physical heart. Sure, God cares about that heart, but it's just a muscle. He cares much more about your spiritual heart: your character and personality. God sees everything you do. Your outward actions make a big difference to him and to other people.

However, God cares even more about *why* you do the things you do. What's your motivation? Do you do chores because your parents *make* you or because you love your family? Do you help an elderly neighbor so you can earn a Boy Scout badge, or do you do it to share God's love?

Just something to think about, because God knows your heart.

Pray:
Tell God you want to have a pure heart.

∴ I believe . . .
God cares about my heart.

February 2

Today is a special day for groundhogs. It's special because outside a small Pennsylvania town, a furry, four-legged weather forecaster is about to predict how many days of winter remain.

Don't laugh. This is serious business for the folks of Punxsutawney. Although the event does look a little silly, some people believe the groundhog's predictions are for real. Residents say he's never been wrong, and that's pretty impressive considering the world's most famous groundhog, Punxsutawney Phil, has been forecasting the length of winter for almost 120 years.

Ceremonies take place at Gobbler's Knob. A crowd gathers and waits for Phil to emerge from his electrically heated burrow. Once he steps outside and looks for his shadow, a representative of the Groundhog Club picks up Phil and holds him to his ear. Tradition says Phil whispers his prediction in "groundhogese" to the representative who then translates it for the people.

In truth, the groundhog's prediction is based on the weather. If it's a sunny day and Punxsutawney Phil sees his shadow, it means six more weeks of winter are coming. If it's cloudy and no shadow can be found, winter will end a couple of weeks sooner.

It's all just tradition and superstition, but as you can see, Phil's shadow means a lot to many people.

Check out Acts 5:14-15 in the *Young Believer Bible:*

God did many miracles through Peter. These verses tell how Peter preached in Jerusalem and many people gave their lives to Christ. God healed people through Peter's shadow.

●●●

Punxsutawney Phil's shadow supposedly predicts the weather. God healed people through Peter's shadow. Although shadows themselves don't have power, they do reflect an image.

What do kids think when they see your shadow coming? Do they run away and hide because you have an icy personality? Or do they warm up when you're around?

God wants your shadow, or your life, to represent him. He wants kids to be drawn to your life and what it stands for. For some kids you'll be the closest thing to God that they'll ever see. Do your actions and words cast a beautiful image of your Savior?

Pray:
Ask God to help make your shadow meaningful in other kids' lives.

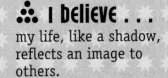

⁛ I believe . . .
my life, like a shadow, reflects an image to others.

What are some of your most valuable possessions?

1. _____   2. _____   3. _____

Look at your list. What do you have on it? Maybe you have an important video game or a comic book or a doll your grandmother gave you. Different things are important to different people. Your most valuable possession might be worth a whole lot of money. But that's not always the case. Maybe your most valuable possession has a lot of value because of who gave it to you or how you got it.

Is your Bible on that list? It's valuable in a lot of ways. It's worth a ton of money. People in some countries would give everything they have to own a Bible. And other people risk their lives to sneak Bibles to them. God's Word is also valuable because of who gave it to you—God himself. God inspired every word in the Bible. It's the perfect gift from the perfect Savior.

However, a lot of the time it's easy to look at the Bible like any old book. But it's much more than that.

Check out Psalm 19:9-10 in the *Young Believer Bible:*
These verses say the rules God gives you in the Bible are totally valuable. They're more precious and desirable than gold. And his Word is also sweet—sweeter than honey. You can enjoy it!

●●●

It's kind of funny to compare a book to candy or money. But that's exactly what King David did in the above verses. Maybe King David had gone nutty from hiding and fighting too much?

Got your Bible handy? (Hopefully, you have it opened up right next to you because you just looked up those verses.) Good. Now lick the cover.

Just kidding. But if you did, it probably wouldn't taste sweeter than honey. And if you took it to a store, you most likely couldn't buy a skateboard with it, even though it's worth more than gold.

Open up God's Word, savor what he's saying to you, and look for ways to "spend" that knowledge every day. You'll find out that King David was right.

Pray:
Ask God to help you treat his Word like a precious gift.

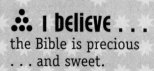

∴ I believe . . .
the Bible is precious
. . . and sweet.

February 4

How big is your family? You probably have a brother or sister, at least one parent, and maybe a pet or two living in your home. Perhaps a grandparent stays with you too, which is pretty neat. Some families have twenty or more kids living in the same house—now that's huge!

But what would you say if you found out that your family actually has more than 2 billion members? That number would look exactly like this: 2,000,000,000. Do you believe it? You should. Because if you have prayed and asked Jesus into your life, then you're part of God's family. Two billion people—that's one out of every three people living on earth—say they're Christians. Did you know if every Christian held hands, we could circle the globe more than 60 times without stopping? Pretty cool, huh?

It feels good to be part of a big family. And just like you have chores to do in your family, you have a job to do in God's family.

Check out Romans 12:4-8 in the
Young Believer Bible:

These verses talk about the family of God. They say that the members together form one body, and everybody has a certain gift to use to serve God. Everybody in God's family does not have the same job.

•••

Think about what you like to do. If you like helping people, you can use that to spread God's love to others. Maybe you're good at inviting your friends to church and getting them to come to Sunday school.

Do you like talking about God with your friends? That's another great way to serve him. God has created you with certain gifts that can be used to make his church body strong. Have you discovered where you best fit in God's body? There's always work to do and ways you can help.

Here are three ideas of how I might best serve in God's family:

1. _____

2. _____

3. _____

Pray:

Ask God to help make you an active and useful part of his body.

⁞ I believe . . .
I'm an important part of God's family.

February 5

In a *TV Guide* poll, one out of every four Americans said they would *not* give up watching television for one million dollars. This fact might make you think, *Are those people crazy!?! A million bucks is a ton of money.*

But that poll just shows you how important television is to a lot of people.

An average kid spends more time watching television every year than going to school. *Wow!* The numbers look like this: 900 hours of schooling versus 1,144 hours watching TV. A person who watches an average of a little more than three hours of television a day will see 20,000 commercials this year!

That's no big deal, you may be thinking. *I could be doing worse things with my time.*

Maybe that's true, but filling your mind with violent images—not to mention other inappropriate pictures—from TV shows and commercials isn't a great idea. Plus being a couch potato can make your body look like one. Check out these facts:

• Playing basketball for one hour burns as many calories as watching TV for six hours.
• Practicing the piano for an hour burns as many calories as watching three hours of TV.

Might be a good idea to take a look at your TV viewing and see if there are some changes you need to make.

Check out Colossians 3:5-6 in the Young Believer Bible:

These verses say you shouldn't do things that feed your earthly nature and cause you to sin. God doesn't like these things, which include evil and impure thoughts.

● ● ●

If you have asked Christ into your heart, then the Holy Spirit lives inside you. He's with you always, and he doesn't like when you let bad images into your brain. The above verses say you should kill any desires you have of acting like the person you were before you accepted Jesus. And that's not an easy thing to do. Maybe you need to get rid of some video games or stop watching shows at a friend's house. You know what you have to do to guard your mind. The hard—and important—part is doing it.

Pray:

Ask God to help you "put to death" things that would cause you to stumble in your relationship with him.

⁞ I believe . . .
I should protect my mind.

Sometimes the referees aren't very good during my basketball games. When they make bad calls, I get really mad and take it out on other people. Can you help?
Upset
Fairplay, Kentucky

Dear Upset,
People make mistakes. And believe it or not, all referees are bound to make bad calls every now and then. But it's good to remember that a ref's mistake usually doesn't decide the outcome of a game. Players win and lose games. So instead of worrying about a bad call, you should concentrate on how you and your teammates are performing. Let your coach talk with the refs about the bad calls—it'll take the pressure off you and help you play your best.

But you have more important issues to deal with here: anger and unforgiveness. There are much better ways to deal with your anger than taking it out on other people. Breathing deeply, counting to ten, and praying to God can help. And forgiving the person who made the mistake is a great way to let go of your anger. It's really hard to be mad at somebody you've just forgiven. By realizing that everybody makes mistakes and by concentrating on having an attitude of forgiveness, you'll have more fun during your games.

Check out Ephesians 4:31-32 in the Young Believer Bible:

These verses say to get rid of all your bitterness, rage, and anger. God asks us to be kind to everybody and forgive them just as Jesus forgives you.

●●●

Isn't it nice to have Jesus as your example? He never asks you to do something that he hasn't already done. Think of a time when you needed forgiveness. Maybe you had a fight with a brother or sister and had to apologize to each other. Doesn't it feel good when somebody says, "I forgive you"? You feel better, and the person who forgave you feels better. It's a win-win situation.

That's what Jesus wants for you. He doesn't want you to walk around being bitter or angry. He wants you to be lighthearted and happy. Forgiving others can make you feel that way.

Pray:
Ask God to help you forgive people—even when you don't want to.

. I believe . . .
.eed to forgive
her people when
ey make mistakes.

For years Christians have been asking themselves the question "What would Jesus do?" before making a decision. You can probably still find books, baseball caps, and bracelets with "WWJD" printed on them.

But asking yourself "What would Jesus do?" isn't very hard. Things get much more difficult when you actually try to do what you think Jesus would do. You might even feel it's impossible. After all, Jesus was God's Son. He was perfect, sinless. Everything he did was great. You, on the other hand, make mistakes. Lots of them. We all do. If you don't mess up for 30 minutes, you start feeling pretty good about yourself, right? (Okay, some of you may even go a whole hour!)

And guess what? It's no surprise to God. He knows you're going to mess up. He knows all of your faults. He doesn't expect you to muster up the strength to act like him all the time. In fact, he knows you don't have the ability to act like him. You need help. And God gives you all the help you need.

Check out John 14:26 in the *Young Believer Bible:*
Before Jesus died on the cross, he gave his disciples a surefire plan for living like him. In this verse, Jesus says God will send the Holy Spirit to teach you and remind you about what Jesus would want you to do.

● ● ●

The Holy Spirit can be misunderstood. Everybody's heard of him, but God and Jesus can seem a lot more friendly. Some people call the Holy Spirit the Holy Ghost, and that sounds sort of frightening.

The truth is the Holy Spirit *is* God and has been around since before the universe was formed. That's what the Bible says in Genesis 1:2. His job is to help make it easier for you to follow in Jesus' steps. Living like Jesus is impossible if you're trying to do it on your own. But with God's power—and his perfect Helper—nothing is impossible.

Pray:
Ask the Holy Spirit to help guide you.

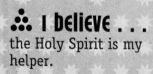

∴ I believe . . .
the Holy Spirit is my helper.

What do you think of when you hear the word *beauty*? Do you picture a pretty movie star or your own mom? Maybe you visualize a breathtaking piece of art or a glittering jewel. Or perhaps you picture a herd of wild horses running across a great plain.

How does it make you feel to see such beauty? Beautiful things make people happy. They lift their spirits and help them dream.

Have you ever seen a snowcapped mountain, a crystal-blue lake, or a wildflower? These beautiful things were each carefully imagined and then created by God. And in his power and love, he knew exactly what would bring you joy. God loves to delight his children, so he's filled this world with many beautiful things for you to enjoy. From dazzling rainbows to fluffy kittens to sleeping babies, God specializes in beauty.

Check out Psalm 8:3-4 in the *Young Believer Bible:*
In these verses David is thinking about all the amazing stuff that God created—and he's shocked that God did it all for him.

●●●

Why did God make his creation so beautiful? For one thing, the Bible says everything reflects God's own glory and majesty. When you look at the beauty of creation, you get a taste of the beauty of God himself.

But God the Father also wanted to create a world that his greatest creation—people—would enjoy.

You're so precious to him that he goes all out to bring joy into your life. And best of all, the beauty of this earth is just a taste of the glory of heaven and all the amazing things you'll see there.

These are some of my favorite parts of creation:

1. _____

2. _____

3. _____

Using old photographs or magazine pictures of creation, arrange pictures of your favorites on a sheet of paper and glue them down to make a collage. Now write the verses you just read on your collage and hang it in your room as a reminder of God's love and care.

Pray:
Thank God for his beautiful creation.

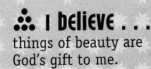

∴ I believe . . .
things of beauty are
God's gift to me.

There once was a boy named Reed whose job was to keep the cows out of the town's tomato field. Because cows are such big animals, they squashed this vegetable-like fruit into a mushy red pulp. Plus they splattered tomato juice all over the place. *Disgusting.*

Only two cows lived in the village, and their barns were miles away from the garden. So although Reed had an important job, it was a boring job. Nothing ever happened—except for the tomatoes getting bigger and redder.

Finally, Reed got so bored that he couldn't stand it. He had to do something to make it more fun. One afternoon he ran into town screaming, "The cows are in the tomato patch! The cows are in the tomato patch!"

The townspeople sprinted to their precious tomato garden only to find that everything was okay.

"*Ha, ha.* You should've seen your faces," Reed said, laughing.

A week went by, and Reed started getting bored again and remembered how much fun it was to trick the townspeople.

"The cows are smashing the tomatoes!" he screamed as he ran into town again.

The townspeople again ran to the garden to discover their tomatoes were safe.

"That was even funnier this time," Reed said.

The next week something horrible happened. One of the cows escaped from its house and ran into the tomato field.

Reed sprang into action. "A cow's crushing the tomatoes!" he shouted.

But nobody listened to him.

"I mean it this time. There really is a cow," he pleaded.

Nobody from the village believed him, and the tomatoes were ruined.

Check out Proverbs 15:29 in the
Young Believer Bible:

This verse says the Lord is far away from people who do wicked things. But God hears the prayers of those who follow him.

●●●

Reed thought it was fun to fool people, but in the end he realized there was a price to pay for his actions.

People who follow their wicked desires pay a big price—they stay far away from God. Unlike the townspeople, God can't be tricked. He only listens to the prayers of people who follow him.

Pray:

Ask God to help you follow him.

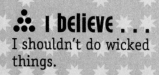

⁂ I believe . . .
I shouldn't do wicked things.

Do you have any older brothers or sisters in high school or college? If so, have you ever picked up one of their calculus books and started reading?

What's calculus?

Exactly. Nobody knows exactly what this high-level kind of math is used for. Opening a book certainly won't help you understand it—you'll barely be able to read it. Maybe it was invented just to torture high school seniors and college students! If you ever get your hands on a calculus text, just open it up and try to figure it out.

It's impossible to understand! Formulas, numbers, letters—none of it makes sense (except maybe to math teachers or guys wearing white coats and pocket protectors). Okay, maybe it's not that bad. But to a normal student your age, calculus appears to be gibberish.

Now do you want to hear something exciting? One day in the not-so-distant future, you might actually be able to figure out this crazy-looking math. *Really.* But you won't be able to do it on your own. It'll take some effort, and you'll need a good teacher. But if you want to, you can learn to understand calculus.

Check out 1 Corinthians 2:13-14 in the *Young Believer Bible:*

These verses say people without the Spirit of God in their lives think God's truth is foolishness. They can't understand it, because they don't have the Spirit. But if you know God, then you can understand his Word because the Spirit helps you.

●●●

Have you ever tried to show one of your non-Christian friends something cool in the Bible, but he just didn't get it? Now you know why. God's wisdom doesn't make sense to people who don't have the Holy Spirit. It's like trying to read a calculus book without having a good teacher. The Spirit is like your own personal tutor of heavenly truth. And if you ask him to help you understand a difficult section of the Bible, he can help you figure out what God is saying to you.

Pray:

Thank God for sending his Spirit to help you understand more about him.

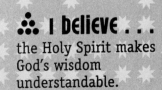

⁙ I believe . . .
the Holy Spirit makes God's wisdom understandable.

Getting in trouble is no fun. Parents can come up with some pretty painful punish-ments. One of the worst is being sent to your room. You're stuck inside those four walls with a little window. No TV. No video games. No Internet access. Sitting on your bed with just your thoughts is definitely not enjoyable.

As bad as being sent to your room is, being stuck in a jail cell would be worse. Sure, you have to do a lot worse stuff to be sent to jail than to your room—but jail would be a terrible punishment. Trapped behind bars. No chance for freedom. Pacing the same piece of pavement day after day. Unable to escape.

Actually, being sent to your room and going to jail are the same in that you're stuck in one place. You're not allowed out of your room until your parents give you permission. And prisoners stay trapped in jail until somebody comes and unlocks the door.

Check out Revelation 3:20 in the
Young Believer Bible:

This verse paints a neat picture of God. It says he stands at the door to your heart and knocks. If you hear him and open that door, God will come in and be your friend.

●●●

People who don't know God are living in a kind of prison. Many don't realize they're trapped, but without God nobody can live a full and meaningful life. And just like you couldn't get out of jail on your own, you can't escape a meaningless life without Jesus. A respected Christian man named Dietrich Bonhoeffer who lived during World War II said, "The door of freedom has to be opened 'from the outside.'"

Jesus holds the keys to everyone's heart. He unlocks the door, knocks, and waits to be invited inside. God doesn't force himself on anybody. He waits to be let inside. And once a person opens the door to his heart, God helps him understand the meaning of true freedom.

Pray:
Thank God for the true freedom that he gives to you.

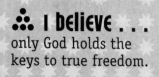

⁛ I believe . . .
only God holds the
keys to true freedom.

Want to hear something amazing?

About seven out of every ten Christians living in the United States prayed to follow Jesus before their twelfth birthday. That means most of Jesus Christ's followers committed their lives to him when they were around your age!

Pretty cool, huh? God's message isn't tricky. Jesus loves you. He died for you. He wants to forgive you. All you have to do is tell him you know you're a sinner, ask him to forgive you, and accept his gift of forgiveness. Simple.

Think back to when you first prayed to become a Christian. Do you remember who introduced you to Jesus Christ? Maybe your parents prayed with you to accept him. Maybe you had an inspiring youth pastor or Sunday school teacher. Maybe you read a Bible story about Jesus and prayed on your own. Maybe the Lord used a friend to lead you to him. Why not do the same for your friends?

Check out Philemon 1:6 in the *Young Believer Bible:*

This verse comes from one of the shortest books in the Bible. It says we should be generous because of our faith.

●●●

Are you ready for a challenge? It won't hurt. In fact, it will take only minutes (maybe less) every day. Choose three friends and pray for them every day until you're done reading this book. Ask the Lord to give you opportunities to talk about him with them. Pray that your speech, actions, and attitudes will be a reflection of Christ. Pray that your life will cause your friends to ask, "Why do you act the way you do?"

And while you're praying for your friends, you may want to ask God to give you the strength to live more like him. God can help you. He wants to use you. You can make a forever difference in your friends' lives. Take the challenge!

I will pray for these friends:

1. _____

2. _____

3. _____

Pray:

Ask God to bring to mind three friends for whom you can pray.

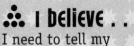

∴ I believe . . .
I need to tell my friends about Jesus.

February 13

It's almost Valentine's Day. You know what that means: cards, candy hearts, and lots of chocolate!

Did you know that chocolate started to gain popularity more than 480 years ago? In 1523, the Aztec Indians in Mexico gave Spanish explorer Hernando Cortes a drink made from cacao beans called *chocolatl*. Cortes added sugar and—*poof!*—hot chocolate was invented. But it took about 200 years for a chocolate craze to begin.

In the 1800s, a lot of businesses started making chocolate.

- John Cadbury opened a small factory in England to produce drinking chocolate in 1831. Today, Cadbury Limited is one of the world's largest chocolate producers.
- In 1852, Ghiradelli Chocolate Company opened in San Francisco, California. It's the oldest chocolate manufacturer in the United States.
- Daniel Peter created milk chocolate in Vevey, Switzerland, in 1876.
- Tootsie Rolls hit the market in 1896.

Today, chocolate is a favorite sweet around the world. And companies work hard to make it. Hershey Foods Corporation needs 50,000 cows to provide enough milk for one day of chocolate making. *Wow!* And that number probably goes up around Valentine's Day.

Check out Deuteronomy 8:10 in the Young Believer Bible:

This verse tells you that if you have enough to eat and are satisfied, then you should praise God—because he provides for you.

●●●

Okay, chocolate isn't a need (try telling that to a chocoholic). It's more of a want, because it's so delicious. But here's the great news: God not only provides for your needs, a lot of times he also takes care of some of your wants. He doesn't want you to live a boring, humdrum life. Living for God is exciting. It's like eating chocolate instead of plain bread. You can trust him to provide for you.

These are some exciting things I want to do for God:

1. _____
2. _____
3. _____

Now keep track of this list. Pray for God to help you live a special life for him by accomplishing these things. He can help you do it.

Pray:

Thank God for providing for your needs (and many of your wants—like chocolate).

⁂ I believe . . .
God provides for my needs.

The legend of St. Valentine can be confusing. A lot of different stories exist about this man. The most popular story says St. Valentine lived during the time that the cruel emperor Claudius II ruled Rome. Claudius liked to have a big army and loved to fight wars, but he saw something that bothered him. He believed young soldiers who were married didn't fight as well because they were concerned about their families. Claudius made a law that young people couldn't be married.

But St. Valentine kept performing wedding ceremonies after Claudius outlawed marriage. Claudius found out, arrested St. Valentine, and had him killed. But before he died, St. Valentine wrote a note to the jailer's daughter, who had become his friend. He signed the note, "From your Valentine." St. Valentine was killed on February 14, 269. About 230 years later, Pope Gelasius made February 14 a day to honor St. Valentine.

Other stories say St. Valentine was killed for attempting to help Christians escape harsh Roman prisons. Either way, he will always be remembered as somebody who helped and loved people.

Check out Galatians 5:14 in the *Young Believer Bible:*
This verse states clearly how we should treat people: "Love your neighbor as yourself." That's pretty simple to read, but it can be hard to do.

●●●

St. Valentine showed people he loved them. Sometimes that fact is missing on Valentine's Day. Some kids don't give cards to classmates who bother them, or they give them the "dumb card." Make sure to treat everybody with love on Valentine's Day—and throughout the year.

And while you're enjoying all of the candy, nice notes, and hugs from family and friends, how about doing something nice for the people around you?

People like to be cared for. One way to show your love would be to write a note to your mom, dad, brother, sister, or friend to say how you feel about him or her. You could also spend some of your money to buy flowers for your mom or do something special for your dad. And remember what Valentine's Day is really about.

Pray:
Ask God to help you care for other people as much as you care for yourself.

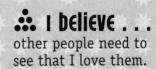

∴ I believe . . .
other people need to
see that I love them.

What do you think about when you hear the word *love*? Do you picture a couple sitting on a park bench, holding hands and gazing into each other's eyes? Maybe you think about a mother looking at her newborn baby. Or perhaps you see a soldier giving up his life to save his buddy. All of these images demonstrate love. And you can probably think of many more.

Think about the people who love you most. How do they show that they love you? They probably look for ways to do what's best for you. Maybe they give you hugs and kisses. They may also tell you that they love you.

Love comes in many forms. But no matter who it comes from, nothing feels as good as being loved. Love is God's idea. He came up with it. God's Word tells you about the source of true love.

Check out 1 John 4:16 in the *Young Believer Bible:*

God's love is dependable because God is love. All love comes from him. And if God lives in you, you will show love to others. Even when you don't feel like being loving, God's love will shine through you.

●●●

There are many kinds of love: romantic love, family love, and the love between friends. But all love comes from God. He loved you first and created you to love. As you know him better and better, you'll show love more.

Sometimes it's really hard to be loving. It's easy to love people who love you, but God calls us to love everyone, even our enemies. That may seem impossible. But with God's help, all things are possible.

How do you show love to others? Think about the people you know: Mom and Dad, brothers and sisters, friends at school, people at your church. God wants you to love those people.

These are some people I sometimes find hard to love. But I know that as I come to know God's love better, he'll help me act more loving, even when it's tough.

1. _____

2. _____

3. _____

Pray:

Ask God to help you show his love to others.

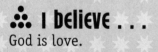

⁙ I believe . . .
God is love.

In movies, actors pull off some pretty amazing stunts. Special effects and computers can make people appear to fly or go back in time or wrestle a dinosaur or shoot a laser gun. All of that stuff could be awesome if it were real . . . well, except for wrestling dinosaurs. *Yikes.*

Maybe that's why movies are so popular. People spend billions—yes, billions—of dollars every year to watch people do the impossible. Movies can take you to imaginary places and show you unbelievable things.

But when you leave the theater, things are still normal in real life. Movies are make-believe. The amazing things you see on the big screen can't be duplicated in your own life.

The Bible is different. The amazing things you read in God's Word can be done again or will come true in your life. All you have to do is rely on God.

Check out Mark 10:25-27 in the *Young Believer Bible:*
In these verses Jesus is talking to his disciples about how hard it is for a person with a lot of money to go to heaven. He says it's easier for a camel to go through the eye of a needle than for a rich man to enter the kingdom of God. But then Jesus adds that nothing is impossible with God.

●●●

You might have discovered that you have limited abilities. You probably can't dunk a basketball or bring a dead person back to life. And unless God blesses you with height and excellent jumping ability, you may never dunk a basketball. However, faith in Jesus raised the dead. Jesus had the power to walk on water, calm storms, and feed thousands with one small lunch of fish and bread.

As amazing as that is, it's just as amazing to realize that because Jesus died and came back to life, you can live with God forever.

Pray:
Praise God that with him nothing is impossible.

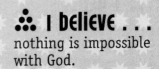

I believe . . .
nothing is impossible with God.

"I'll be at your recital on Saturday," Katie said before she hung up the phone. "I promise!"

Heather smiled. She had been reminding Katie of her piano recital for weeks. Heather had been practicing her difficult concerto for three months, and she was glad her best friend would be there.

On the day of the recital, Heather scanned the audience before sitting down to play her piece. Katie wasn't there. Heather tried to put it out of her mind, but inside she was fighting bitter disappointment.

Why isn't she here? Heather thought. *She promised.*

Heather sat down and played perfectly. She was really excited when she stood to take her bow. But she still wished she could've shared her achievement with her best friend.

Maybe you've experienced the same disappointment as Heather. People don't always keep their promises. Sometimes they forget. Sometimes they change their minds. And sometimes they deliberately go back on their word. But God *always* keeps his promises. His Word is perfectly reliable.

Check out Joshua 23:14 in the *Young Believer Bible:*

God made many promises to his people, the Israelites, when he led them into the Promised Land. He told them he would provide for them and help them to conquer other nations. Before Joshua, the leader of Israel, died he reminded the people that every promise God had made to them had come true.

●●●

You may wonder if you can trust God's Word. Will he really give you eternal life if you trust in his Son? Will he really help you to do what is right? Will he really be with you always? If you look back on the promises God has made in the past, you can see that he is faithful to do what he says. He promised his people a Savior would come to save them from their sins. And he sent Jesus to do just that!

These verses contain some of God's important promises to me. Here's what those promises are:

John 1:12 _____

Hebrews 13:5-6 _____

1 John 1:9 _____

Pray:
Ask God to help you trust his promises today!

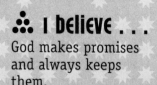

∴ I believe . . .
God makes promises and always keeps them.

Names can be funny. Sure, your parents gave you a name when you were born. But people don't always call you by what's written on your birth certificate.

Think about the name Robert. If that's your name, you may be called a lot of things. Maybe your parents call you Robert. Friends might call you Rob. And your grandma might prefer to shout out "Bobby!" when she sees you. Does that mean you're three different people? Of course not. It just may mean people focus on different parts of your character when they see you.

Your parents may prefer Robert because that's exactly what they named you. Friends usually like a simpler, more casual name—like Rob. And your grandma may focus on your childlike qualities by calling you Bobby.

The name Elizabeth is similar. If that's your name, friends might call you Liz, grandparents might like Lizzie, and your parents might prefer Eliza. All that means is that you're a complex, fun person. One name just isn't enough to describe who you are.

Check out 2 Corinthians 13:13 in the Young Believer Bible:

This verse talks about the three persons of God and some of the gifts they offer: grace from the Lord Jesus Christ, love from God the Father, and fellowship with the Holy Spirit.

●●●

Just like you may need more than one name to describe your personality, an infinite God needs more than one title. That kind of goes without saying, huh?

God has three distinct names. Each one describes a part of his character, and the above verse gives a good, short description of the differences. God the Father is loving. He loves you so much that he sent his Son to pay the penalty for your sins. God the Son, Jesus Christ, came to earth, and through his grace he restored your relationship with the Father. And God the Holy Spirit lives inside each person who believes in God. It's through his fellowship that you're united to other believers and to God himself.

Pray:

Ask God to help you learn about each of his names.

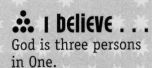

∴ I believe . . .
God is three persons in One.

Even if you haven't studied DNA in science class, you've probably heard a lot of talk about it. Crime shows on television and the nightly news often mention this building block of life.

DNA is like a microscopic supercomputer that tells your body's cells what to do. Your DNA determines how tall you are, the color of your eyes, and what you look like. It stores the same amount of information that can be held on hundreds of thousands of sheets of paper. Yet DNA is so small that all of the DNA from every human living today could fit on a dime.

Some scientists think DNA appeared by chance. But even under perfect conditions, scientists can't create DNA in a lab.

Studying the possibility of DNA being created by chance shows that it's impossible. If you painted a penny green, threw it along with millions of copper pennies into a swimming pool the size of the sun, mixed them all up, put on a blindfold, walked into the pool and pulled out a penny, what is the chance that you'd pick the single green penny on your first try? That would be about the same chance as DNA forming by accident. In other words, it can't happen.

Other scientists believe only an intelligent designer—God—could create something as perfect and complex as DNA.

Which scientists do you think are right?

Check out Isaiah 45:11-12 in the *Young Believer Bible:*
In these verses the Lord speaking through the prophet Isaiah says that his hands made the universe, earth, and people.

●●●

The first couple of chapters in the Bible talk about God creating the universe: light, darkness, sky, land, plants, sun, moon, stars, fish, animals, humans. For thousands of years, everybody agreed with the Bible. Then a little more than 140 years ago, some scientists tried to explain how things were created without mentioning God. Their ideas about creation occurring over time and by chance became popular. But today more and more evidence is being discovered that points back to God.

Look at yourself in the mirror. You're a unique combination of your mother's and father's DNA. Something as complex as you couldn't have been created by chance. Don't you agree?

Pray:
Thank God for his creative genius in making everything.

∴ I believe . . .
God created people.

If you took your first lick of a giant scoop of triple-chocolate-brownie-fudge ice cream and it slipped off the cone and fell to the ground, how would you feel?

Or if your little sister cut up your favorite shirt to make clothes for her dolls, what would be your reaction?

If you said "angry" or "I'd be mad," you're like most kids.

Anger is a strange emotion that comes out in different ways. Some kids get all red-faced and hot when they're mad. Others become really cold and quiet. Everybody reacts to anger differently. But the fact is everybody gets mad sometimes.

Think about how you feel when you get angry. Are you out of control or calm? Because everybody gets mad, it's good to have a plan of how to handle it when it comes along. Some kids like to hit a pillow when they're angry. Others find that counting backward from ten helps them calm down. The key is not to bottle up anger until it explodes.

After all, how would it look if someone accidentally dropped his books in the hall and suddenly started screaming, jumping around, and waving his hands in the air like a wild person? Sort of makes you laugh, right?

Check out Mark 11:15-17 in the *Young Believer Bible:*
In these verses you see a time when Jesus was angry. He turned over tables and chased people out of God's temple.

•••

Think about why Jesus got mad. People were selling things and thinking only about making money in God's house. They weren't worshiping him. The Bible says it's possible to get mad and not sin (Ephesians 4:26). Jesus got mad because God's holy place was being mistreated. That's a good reason to feel angry.

And since you know Jesus never sinned, you can try to follow his example when it comes to anger.

These are some things that are worth being mad about:

1. _____

2. _____

3. _____

Look at your list. Do you think you've experienced good anger like Jesus? (Maybe you feel mad when bullies pick on other kids.) Or do you think you've sinned when you've been mad? (Maybe you've gotten angry and pouted when your parents didn't rent a movie you wanted.)

God gives us the ability to feel. Will you work hard to use your feelings to be more like him?

Pray:
Ask God to help you control your anger and get mad about the right things.

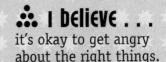

∴ I believe . . .
it's okay to get angry about the right things.

People are funny. Ever notice that they can always find something to complain about? This is especially true when people talk about themselves. If you asked people what they thought was wrong with them, they'd probably be able to give you a long list: "My nose is too skinny; I'm too tall; I look weird when I walk; my hair is too curly; I have too many freckles; my voice is too low; one of my feet is bigger than the other." Everybody thinks he or she is flawed.

You might feel the same way. Maybe you wish you were stronger or had longer hair or were better at math or could run faster.

Is there something you wish you could change about yourself? What would you do if that never changed? Would you be mad at God? Do you think it would hold you back from being successful in life?

Check out 2 Corinthians 12:7-9 in the Young Believer Bible:

Paul wrote most of the New Testament and helped bring thousands of people into God's kingdom. In these verses, he said there's something that really bothered him. He even asked God three times to change this "thorn" about himself. But God told him, "My power works best in your weakness." So Paul learned to live with his inadequacy—he even celebrated it.

● ● ●

God created you just as he wanted you. He gave you everything you need to serve him. And guess what? God doesn't make mistakes. Maybe you need to have a quiet personality instead of a loud one to bring a certain person to Christ. Maybe being short will help you be less noticed when you're handing out Bibles in a foreign country. Only God knows your future—and his plans are bigger for you than anything you could imagine.

Here's one thing I wish I could change about myself:

If you ask God to help you accept that characteristic about yourself and use it for him, he will! Remember, in your weakness you can learn to depend on his strength to help you.

Pray:

Thank God for creating you exactly as he did—flaws and all.

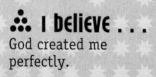

⠿ I believe . . .
God created me
perfectly.

February 22

Tammy knew she wasn't supposed to play soccer in the house, but the play-offs were coming up and she was excited. She grabbed her ball and started to juggle it.

"One [knee]—two [knee]—three [head]—four [knee]—five [left foot]—six [right foot]—seven—*Oops!*"

The ball bounced off Tammy's foot, sailed through the living room, and knocked into her mom's favorite vase.

Crash!

Mom said that vase was an antique, Tammy thought. *What am I going to do?*

Then it came to her . . . the perfect story.

When Mom got home from the store, Tammy was kneeling over the vase.

"Mom, you won't believe what happened!" she said excitedly. "When you were gone a gorilla broke into our house. I was totally scared so I ran upstairs. But I saw the gorilla come into the living room. And I guess he just didn't like this vase, because he picked it up and smashed it on the ground. I couldn't believe he did that because you really love this vase. And—"

"Did the gorilla also like playing soccer?" Mom interrupted.

"What?" Tammy asked, confused.

"I just wanted to know if the gorilla liked soccer, because I see your soccer ball in the corner over there."

Oops, Tammy thought. *I'm busted.*

Check out Jeremiah 23:24 in the Young Believer Bible:

In this verse God asks some questions with obvious answers. First, he says, "Can anyone hide from me?" Answer: *No.* Then he asks, "Am I not everywhere in all the heavens and earth?" Answer: *Yes.*

●●●

God sees everything. Trying to hide something from him is as crazy as the story Tammy made up to try to fool her mom. And because God sees everything, the best thing you can do is tell him the truth. Let him know when you fail. If you have a deep, dark secret, let the Lord know about it. (He already does anyway.) But he wants you to admit everything to him and then allow him to forgive you and make you stronger.

Pray:

Tell God you want to be honest with him all the time.

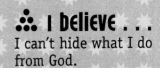

∴ I bεLiεvε . . .
I can't hide what I do from God.

King Solomon thought. He contemplated. He pondered. God had just made him an un-believable offer: "What do you want? Ask, and I will give it to you!" (1 Kings 3:5).

Anything? Solomon had a choice to make. What would he ask for? Would he ask for wealth? Would he ask for a long life? Would he ask for victory over his enemies? Would he ask for the new model chariot with spoked wheels and diamond-studded trim? Solomon thought and thought. What would he need to be a good king?

Then it hit him. Solomon knew exactly what to do. He asked God for wisdom to lead his people. He realized that wisdom was much more valuable than riches, long life, constant victories, and a cool ride.

God was pleased with Solomon's unselfish request. God granted Solomon his re-quest and gave him great insight and understanding. Later in his life, Solomon wrote down the wisdom God gave him. Many of his writings are included in the Bible in the book of Proverbs. Because Solomon asked for wisdom, God blessed him and made him the wisest king who ever lived!

Check out Proverbs 9:10 in the *Young Believer Bible:*

This verse tells you how to get the great treasure of wisdom—by fearing God. Fearing God means honoring him enough to obey him. When you obey God, you are being wise.

●●●

Wisdom is knowing the right thing to do and then doing it. It's making good choices. You can show wisdom in what you say and by the things you do. You have many choices every day. Sometimes it's hard to know what's right. But God will give you wisdom when-ever you ask. And because he knows everything, he always knows what's best for you.

When you obey God, you will behave wisely. You can learn more about how to be wise by reading the book of Proverbs. Wisdom is more valuable than money, toys, or popularity.

Here's how I can act wisely in each of the following areas:

How I'll treat my family: _____

My actions at school: _____

Spending my money: _____

Setting an example for my friends: _____

Other: _____

Pray:

Ask God to give you wisdom in each decision you make today and this week.

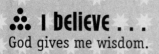

∴ I believe . . .
God gives me wisdom.

What is your reaction when your mom asks you to clean the kitchen?

a. I groan and remind her I did it last time.
b. I roll up my sleeves and grab a dishcloth.
c. I dance around the kitchen singing, "I'm the kitchen-cleaning fairy, and I've come to make the kitchen sparkling clean."
d. I say okay then find an opportunity to slip away.

If you jump for joy at the opportunity to clean or go right to work, you're a delight to your parents and an outstanding exception to the norm. But let's face it. Dancing with glee probably isn't your first reaction to a work order.

Most kids would probably go with option *a*. When you're asked to do something unpleasant, it's easy to grumble and complain. But guess what? For a Christian kid, complaining should never be an option. The correct choice is *b*. But you already knew that, huh?

Check out Philippians 2:14-15 in the Young Believer Bible:

"In everything you do, stay away from complaining and arguing." That's pretty clear. Why should you do it? People are watching to see how you respond to tough requests. When you choose to react without a complaint, you stand out and others notice your good attitude.

• • •

Curbing complaints takes practice. Sometimes a groan or a grumble comes out before you even think to stop it. Think about your own personal complaint department. Do you need to make any improvements?

Here's what I tend to complain about most:

1. _____
2. _____
3. _____

Now on a separate piece of paper, write down three grateful responses. For example, instead of saying, "Mom, you *always* make me clean the kitchen," say, "Mom, thanks for making dinner. I'd be glad to clean the kitchen."

Reacting cheerfully to unpleasant jobs may feel weird at first, but give it a try. A happy response pleases God. And you may be surprised by how much happier you feel—and how much faster the work gets done—when you kick out complaints.

Pray:

Ask God to help you do everything without complaining.

∴ I believe . . .

God wants me to do everything without complaining.

Animals are amazing.

You probably know the cheetah is the fastest land animal. Reaching speeds of 70 miles per hour (mph), the cheetah could get a speeding ticket on many U.S. highways.

But did you know an antelope can run 60 mph? And that's a good thing, because antelope often have to run away from cheetahs. A lion can reach up to 50 mph, which isn't bad for an animal that sleeps more than 20 hours a day.

Grizzly bears and elephants are pretty big animals. But both of them can run faster than humans. Grizzlies have been clocked at 30 mph, while elephants can ramble around at 25 mph, just slightly faster than the fastest human runners.

And speaking of big, fast animals, the blue whale swims 30 mph—which makes it the fastest marine mammal. However, the blue whale isn't the fastest creature in the water. That honor goes to the sailfish, which swims 68 mph.

Flying animals are the fastest things on earth. A dragonfly can fly 36 mph—not bad. But the peregrine falcon dives toward the earth at speeds of 100 to 200 mph.

Check out Genesis 1:20-25 in the *Young Believer Bible:*

These verses record God's creation of fish, birds, and animals. He dreamed up every living thing on earth.

●●●

As amazing as animals are, God is so much more amazing. His creativity is shown in every living creature. He gave the animals their personalities and special characteristics. He made chameleons to change colors to match their surroundings. And God created the basilisk lizard so it could run across the water. Animals didn't start by chance. They didn't crawl out of slimy goo in the ground and change over time.

Animals were designed to be amazing. They were created by an intelligent and awesome Designer—God—the same Designer who made you.

Pray:

Thank God for his creativity when he made the animals.

∴ I believe . . .
God created animals.

Rachel crawled back under her covers. She'd been sick all night. *Why do I have to have cancer?* she thought. *I'm only 10.*

Rachel had been fighting cancer for almost a year. It felt like she spent more time in the hospital than at home, and the chemotherapy kept making her sick. She couldn't even go to school anymore or play soccer, her favorite sport.

Why would God let this happen? she wondered.

One year later Rachel smiled as she ran onto the soccer field. Her hair was still short and choppy, but she didn't mind. Her cancer was in remission, and she was thankful to God. Through her sickness, she learned to trust him. She learned to say, *I'm willing to die if that's your plan.*

Through Rachel's sickness, God gave her greater compassion for others. She was able to visit the sick ward at the children's hospital and talk to other kids who had cancer. And she understood exactly how they were feeling.

Check out Genesis 50:20 in the *Young Believer Bible:*

Joseph was sold into slavery by his brothers, falsely accused of a crime he didn't commit, and imprisoned. He had a lot of reasons to question God for allowing these bad things to happen. Instead, when Joseph was able to save his family by giving them food, he understood that the hard times were all part of God's plan.

●●●

You may be going through a hard time right now. Maybe your parents are getting a divorce. Maybe you or someone you love is sick. Or maybe someone close to you has died. No matter what hard thing is happening in your life, God is with you. And he can use painful experiences to make you more kind and caring like Jesus.

Jesus experienced the greatest pain: He was falsely accused, betrayed by his friend, and died a painful death. He was even separated from God, his own Father, because of everybody's sin. Jesus knows what every hurt feels like. When tough times come, remember that he is with you.

Pray:

Ask God to use the tough times in your life for his good.

⁂ I believe . . .
I grow stronger with God's help during tough times.

One of my friends lies a lot. I don't think I can be her friend anymore. What should I do?
Tired
Truth or Consequences, New Mexico

Dear Tired,
Stick out your tongue and look at it in the mirror. Pretty small, huh? But the tongue is one of the most powerful muscles in the body. It helps you eat and talk. With our tongues, we can speak helpful words or cause harm. When something goes wrong with the tongue, it can cause huge problems. Lying is one of the biggest.

Have you ever asked yourself why your friend lies? Is she always looking for attention? What are her other friends like? If she doesn't have many friends (and most big-time liars don't), she may be trying to impress you so you'll keep being her friend.

One of the best things you can do is talk to her. Tell her you're her friend because of who she is—not because of the stories she makes up. Explain to her that you can't trust her because she tells so many lies. Your honesty with her will set a good example. But you also need to say that you want to surround yourself with people who tell the truth . . . so her slippery tongue needs to start shooting straight.

Check out Psalm 52:2-4 in the *Young Believer Bible:*
King David knew how hard it is to tame the tongue. Here he writes that the tongue can cut like a sharp razor with its lies.

●●●

People lie for different reasons. Some do it to stay out of trouble. Others stretch the truth to make themselves look better. And still others fib so they won't hurt people's feelings. The truth is a *lot* of people lie. But does that make it right? Of course not.

God wants you to speak the truth. But perhaps you've messed up in the past and told a lie.

Here's a time when I didn't tell the truth:

_____

_____

_____

Start by asking God to forgive you. Although it might be tough to do, explain the story to whoever you lied to, ask her to forgive you, and commit to telling the truth in the future.

❖ I believe . . .
I should speak the truth.

Pray:
Ask God to help you tame your tongue with honesty.

Do you like hiking? Now realize that hiking isn't just walking around a track or through a big city. No, this is about getting outside and discovering some of God's creation.

Hiking in the mountains is awesome because you can end up seeing some amazing sights. Perhaps a family of deer will stray across your path. Or maybe you'll end up at a deep-blue mountain lake or at the top of a huge cliff where you can see forever. Hiking on the beach, through a cave, or at a park can be equally fun. When you're hiking, you never know what you might see.

One of the most important things to bring with you on a hike is a map. A compass or Global Positioning System would also be helpful, especially if you're hiking in a place you've never been before. It's nice to have something that helps you stay on the right path, because getting lost is not good.

Check out Exodus 13:21 in the *Young Believer Bible:*

Just after Pharaoh let God's people leave Egypt, God began guiding the Israelites with a pillar of cloud during the day and a pillar of fire at night.

●●●

When the Israelites left Egypt, they had no idea where they were going. They just wanted to get out so they could be free from slavery. God led them in the desert along a safe path. And what a great way to lead them—all they had to do was follow a giant column of smoke or a huge pillar of fire. If you were an Israelite, you'd certainly feel you were in good hands if you were following something that obvious. It'd be impossible to get lost.

Today, God doesn't use cloud pillars to guide his people. But he still guides you through your parents and other people who know him. But your best map in following God is his Word: the Bible.

Pray:

Tell God you're going to look for him to lead you.

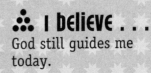

⁙ I believe . . .
God still guides me today.

- Why do your parents change the oil in their car every three thousand miles?
- Why do you go to the dentist at least once a year?
- Why do you clean your room several times during the week?
- Why do you pull weeds out of a garden?
- Why do you oil your bike chain and check the brakes before you ride it for the first time each spring?

The answer to all of these questions is the same: Preventative maintenance.

Huh?!? you may be thinking. *What's that?*

Preventative maintenance keeps the things you have in good working order. If you didn't do little checkups to take care of your things, they'd eventually fall apart.

Think if you didn't pull weeds out of a garden. Soon the weeds would choke out the other plants and flowers and completely take over. If your parents didn't change the oil in their car, the engine would be ruined and cost thousands of dollars to replace. And if you stopped cleaning your room, pretty soon you wouldn't be able to find your bed.

Check out Song of Songs 2:15 in the
Young Believer Bible:

Foxes are cute little animals, but they can quickly destroy a garden. This verse says the foxes need to be caught before they ruin a vineyard that's about to blossom.

●●●

It's easy to ignore "little foxes." They look cute and seem harmless. But sometimes if you neglect the little things, they can cause big problems. Doing preventative maintenance in your life is more important than doing it to your possessions.

Here are some ways I keep my life in good working order:

1. Exercise

2. Read the Bible to know God's Word

3. Make sure my language would please God

4. _____

5. _____

6. _____

7. _____

It's good to check your life often to make sure you're keeping out the "little foxes," so then you can bloom into something beautiful for God.

Pray:
Ask God to point out any little detail in your life that could pull you away from him.

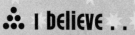 **I believe . . .**

I need to take care of the little things in my life.

March 1

Everyone knows the answer to 1 + 1. It's 2. Is the answer always 2? Yes. There's only one correct answer, one truth.

Some people try to say there are lots of different truths about the way to find God. But that's a lie. The Bible is clear. There is only one truth—God's truth. In the book of John, Jesus talks about truth in some interesting ways. First, he says the truth of his teachings can set you free (John 8:32). Later, Jesus says, "I am . . . the truth. . . . No one can come to the Father except through me" (John 14:6). Jesus also said if you're on the side of truth, you'll listen to him.

Obviously Jesus believed in one truth about who he was—the Son of God, the Savior. It wasn't a popular opinion. Some people didn't like him very much. But that didn't stop Jesus from speaking the truth.

Are you willing to speak the truth about Jesus too? You may lose some friends and be labeled narrow-minded. But being narrow-minded on issues of truth is a good thing.

Check out Matthew 7:14 in the *Young Believer Bible:*
In this verse Jesus says it's not easy to find the road in life that leads to him because the gateway is small and the road is narrow. In fact, only a few people find it.

●●●

Being a Christian means you're part of a family. You're one of God's chosen children. As Jesus said, not a lot of people find the road to him. But those who do, know there's only one truth. Sometimes living for God's truth hurts because God asks his children to live by his standards.

You may miss out on some parties and make some people mad at you. But following God's truth shows the world that you're a Christian. While many people around you wander through life trying to find truth, you can use your words, attitudes, and actions to point people to the one and only truth: Jesus Christ.

Pray:
Commit to Jesus that you're going to stand up for his truth.

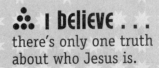

∴ I believe . . .
there's only one truth
about who Jesus is.

Buried deep inside a mountain in Colorado sits the North American Aerospace Defense Command (NORAD). This place is responsible for tracking all man-made objects in space and detecting an air attack against North America. NORAD currently keeps track of almost nine thousand objects orbiting Earth, including rocket bodies, satellites, and space junk. It's one of the most advanced and safest places in the world. Check out these facts:

- It took almost five years to build and took 1.5 million pounds of dynamite to dig out almost 700,000 tons of rock.
- The complex includes 15 buildings—12 are three stories high—built inside the mountain. The buildings rest on springs, each of which weighs 1,000 pounds. This way the buildings can sway if there's an earthquake or nuclear explosion.
- A natural spring provides 30,000 to 120,000 gallons of water a day to workers inside the mountain. Four tanks with a total capacity of 6 million gallons hold the water.

As amazing as this man-made marvel is, NORAD can only *track* objects. It can't control them. Only God, who made the mountain that NORAD is built inside, can control the objects around Earth . . . and in the entire universe.

Check out Job 37:15-16 in the *Young Believer Bible:*
In these verses one of Job's friends asks him if he knows how God controls storms and balances the clouds. Of course Job doesn't. But then in the next chapter God talks to Job about many of his marvels.

●●●

God knows everything. Just think about that. Nothing ever happens that makes God say, "Whoa! I didn't see that coming!" He put the planets in their orbits, formed the Earth, set the weather patterns, and controls the stars. He's the master Designer, and he's always in control.

Does your life ever feel out of control? Maybe you have so many things going on that your head starts to spin.

These things make me feel frantic (for example, school tests or basketball tryouts):

1. _____
2. _____
3. _____

God wants to take care of those things for you. When you give them to him, you can trust that he's in control.

Pray:
Tell God you're going to trust him and stay close to him when things seem to get out of control.

∴ I believe . . .
God is in control.

I have this friend who always wants to play with me. She asks to come to my house all of the time and gets upset when I'm with other friends. What should I do?
Smothered
Buddi, Ethiopia

Dear Smothered,
You won't find an easy answer to this problem. It sounds like this girl needs to find some other friends before she drives you batty. You may want to help her find a new friend or two by introducing her to some other kids. But you need to do something quick, before your patience runs out and you end up acting not very kindly to her. Before you lose your temper or decide to become a hermit by hiding in your room all the time, you may want to think about this advice: Sit down and have a serious and honest talk with this girl. Let her know that you enjoy playing with her, but you also need to play with other friends. And don't forget to be nice!

If this girl is a true friend, she'll understand that everyone needs space at times.

Check out Proverbs 27:6 in the *Young Believer Bible:*

This verse says you can trust a friend who tells you something to help you be a better person, even if her words hurt a little. On the other hand, a mean person may act nicely toward you, but if she only has bad intentions then she's no friend.

●●●

Do you ever find it difficult to tell somebody the truth when you think it might hurt her feelings? As a friend, you probably feel you have to be nice all the time. But being a true friend means being honest, even though honesty sometimes hurts. If your friends use language that makes you uncomfortable, you need to tell them. If you see a friend experimenting with smoking, you should let him know how bad it is for him. Don't be afraid to stand up for what you believe. In the end, it could make your friendship even stronger. And it could really help your friends.

Pray:

Ask God to give you the courage to be honest with your friends.

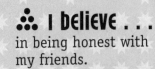
∴ I believe . . .
in being honest with
my friends.

Can you name the most widely read book in human history? Here are some clues: This book has been translated into more languages than any other. People have been reading it for centuries. And even though it was written thousands of years ago, people still eagerly read it today.

Think you have the answer? Here is one more clue: you may have sung a song about this book in Sunday school. That's right. It's the *B-I-B-L-E*.

At least 40 different people wrote the Bible over more than 1,500 years. But none of them were the true author. The true Author was God. The Holy Bible, also called God's Word and the Scriptures, is God's message to humans. But how is that possible if people wrote the Bible? God had a special plan to use all those writers to produce a masterpiece—his perfect Word.

Check out 2 Peter 1:19-21 in the *Young Believer Bible:*

God is the true author of the Bible. All Scripture comes from him. But he used people—prophets, disciples, and other faithful believers—to write down his words. The Holy Spirit guided these writers so they would write the words of God. They were inspired in such a way that absolutely no mistakes were made.

● ● ●

Because God was involved in the whole writing process, you can trust that every word of the Bible is true. Many historical writings from Bible times support the truth of the Scriptures. The Bible is God's special letter to people. It tells you what God is like and teaches you how to live for him. Most importantly, it explains God's great love for his creation and his plan of salvation for all who believe in his Son. You own the most popular book of all time! Open it today to read God's words to you!

Pray:

Thank God for giving you the Bible, and ask him to help you do what it says.

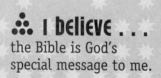

⋰ I believe . . .
the Bible is God's
special message to me.

March 5

Pretend you know a girl named Sandi. Sandi loves to go to the beach. She enjoys the sun and looking for shells and building sand castles. But Sandi's favorite activity is swimming. To her, there's nothing better than splashing around in the waves. Sandi's not a very strong swimmer, but that doesn't stop her from going a long way from shore. You see, the lifeguard is Sandi's friend. He watches over her. They met one time when Sandi accidentally went out too far in the waves and was pulled away from the shore by the riptide. The lifeguard saved her life when she couldn't swim back.

Now it seems as if the lifeguard has to go pull Sandi out of the water almost every day. She just can't get enough of swimming in the deep water.

Ask yourself these questions: Do you think Sandi's smart for going in the deep water every day? Do you think she's being fair to the lifeguard? What would you say to Sandi?

Check out Romans 6:1-2 in the *Young Believer Bible:*

These verses talk about sin. First, Paul asks if it's a good idea to keep sinning so God can keep forgiving you. Then he says, "Of course not!" When a person accepts Jesus into her life, she dies to sin and shouldn't keep doing the same wrong things.

●●●

Even though Sandi wasn't sinning by continuing to go out in deep water, she really wasn't being too smart. In a way, she's kind of like some people who think that, because God forgives them, they can keep sinning as much as they want. They know they're saved, so they keep making poor decisions. But God doesn't want you to live that way.

He wants you to repent and turn away from your sin. When you repent, you're asking for forgiveness from your past bad actions. But you're also committing to God that you're going to change in the future. If you don't plan on changing in the future and you continue doing the same bad things, you're not living out God's plan for your life. So when you mess up, turn to God, tell him you did something wrong, and try to act differently in the future.

Pray:

Thank God for forgiving you.

∴ I believe . . .
being forgiven doesn't make it okay to keep sinning.

Statistics show that the average family buys more than two video games every year. And these games can be a lot of fun. But sometimes it's easy to let Nintendo or PlayStation take too much of your time. Check out these warning signs to see if you're a video-game maniac.

You know you're playing too many video games when

- your thumbs bleed because all the skin has been rubbed off by the joystick;
- your eyes spin around in your head;
- you start every conversation with "What level are you on?";
- you can't remember your best friend's name, because you haven't seen him in months;
- you wake up in the middle of the night screaming, "Bonus round!";
- your couch has a permanent indent from where you sit.

Did you pass the test, or do you need to do some serious thinking about how often you play video games?

Check out Ecclesiastes 3:1 in the *Young Believer Bible:*
This verse says there's a time for every activity. One activity shouldn't take up all your time.

●●●

How long do you plan to live—80, 90, 100 years? God may bless you with a long and happy life. But while 80 years may seem like a long time, think how little space it would take on a line that showed the thousands and thousands of years the earth has existed and will exist. If you look at your life compared to that huge long line, your time on earth is just a dot—a speck.

But you don't need to let this fact worry you. You can do a lot with your "dot." The key is to make good choices about how you spend your time.

Pray:
Ask God to show you how to best use your time to serve him.

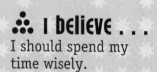

∴ I believe . . .
I should spend my
time wisely.

Are you an animal lover? Many kids are. They love looking at animals in zoos, holding them at pet stores, and living with them at home. Millions of animals are bought every year as pets. People are willing to spend thousands of dollars to house, take care of, and feed their animal friends.

Do you know what the most popular pet in the United States is? Dogs? No. Fish? Guess again. The answer is cats. Those furry, funny felines are tops in the pet world. Dogs are second—that's no surprise. Then come parakeets. Rabbits, gerbils, and hamsters get lumped together as the fourth most common pet. And finally come fish in the fifth spot.

The next five most popular pets fall in two categories: reptiles and birds. Reptiles (that's snakes, lizards, turtles) come in sixth. Then you'll find finches, cockatiels, canaries, and parrots.

But have you ever wondered why people love animals so much? Maybe it's because they're cute. Perhaps it's because pets are fun to play with. If people were totally honest, the real answer might be that they love their pets because their pets love them. It doesn't matter how you treated your dog yesterday because he still loves you today. Now that's pretty cool.

Check out 1 John 4:19 in the *Young Believer Bible:*
This verse says we love others because God first loved us. Our ability to love comes from God. He created love. And he loves you.

●●●

As cool as it is to have your cat brush against your leg and purr, it's so much greater to realize how much God loves you. Your dog may be quick to forgive and even quicker to love you, but God's love is so much better. It's unconditional, which means God loves you no matter what. He loves you when you forget about him. He loves you when your behavior isn't all that great. And he loves you when you're feeling lonely. There's nothing you can do to earn his love. Plus there's nothing you can do to make it go away. God's love is perfect and permanent.

Pray:
Thank God for his forever kind of love.

∴ I believe . . .
God loves me more
than my pet does.

Evan pounded the last nail into the tree house. He stood back and admired his work—two large windows in the front, a trapdoor in the floor, and a ladder fastened securely to the trunk of the tree. Evan smiled. It was perfect.

He'd been working on the tree house for months. Dad had helped him carefully cut the boards into even lengths and nail them onto a solid frame. Evan had selected just the right pieces for the ladder. Now the last board was in place, and the tree house was ready. He'd finished just in time. His cousin Lars was coming the next day for a visit. Evan couldn't wait for Lars to see it! The hours and hours of work would be worth it.

Lars will love it, he thought.

Did you know someone is hard at work preparing a place for you too? And it's going to be a lot better than a tree house. Jesus is preparing a place in heaven for all those who know him.

Check out John 14:2-3 in the *Young Believer Bible:*

Jesus told his disciples that he was going home to his Father in heaven to prepare a place for them. He promised to return when it was ready and take them home to be with him.

● ● ●

You're so special that Jesus is preparing a place just for you. That place is heaven, and he's making it just right. And when everything's ready, he's coming back to take you to be with him forever!

Are you ready for Jesus to come back? He could come any day. What are you doing each day to prepare for his return? He told his disciples to love each other, learn more about God, and tell others about him. The more you study God's Word, the more prepared you will be to spend eternity with him.

I want to be ready for Jesus to come back, so here are three things I can do to get to know him better:

1. _____

2. _____

3. _____

Pray:

Thank Jesus for making a place for you in heaven.

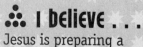

⁘ I believe . . .
Jesus is preparing a
place for me in heaven.

March 9

Danny spotted the kids at recess. Three of the older middle schoolers huddled behind some trees. He tried to sneak up and see what they were doing, but one of the boys saw Danny and called him over.

When Danny got within a few feet of the group, he could smell the smoke.

"Wanna try a cigarette?" one of the boys asked, coughing. "They're really awesome."

Danny didn't think it looked awesome. He remembered seeing television commercials and hearing his parents say how bad smoking is. But these were three of the biggest boys in school.

"Uh, I don't think so," Danny finally answered.

"What's the matter?" the biggest kid asked. "Chicken?"

"Yeah, you scared?" another chimed in.

"No!" Danny said, trying to sound tough.

"Then do it," one of them said, thrusting a lit cigarette in Danny's face.

Danny thought about it. *I don't want these kids to think I'm not cool. But I know I shouldn't smoke.*

"I won't smoke," Danny said firmly. "It's bad for me."

He turned and started running back to school as the other boys shouted names at him.

But Danny didn't care. He was too busy thanking God for helping him do the right thing.

Check out 2 Timothy 2:22 in the Young Believer Bible:

This verse shows the importance of running away from wrong things when you're young. Instead you should run toward right things, including faith, love, and peace.

● ● ●

At some point, somebody will try to get you to do things that you know are wrong. Maybe a friend will encourage you to steal something from a store. Or perhaps you'll be tempted to fit into the crowd by smoking or drinking. Growing up isn't easy. Temptations will come.

But with God's help and the power of the Holy Spirit, you can overcome the evil things that block your path from living for God. God wants you to pray to him with a pure heart and run away from temptation. That's not being a "chicken." It's being smart.

Pray:

Ask God to help you run away from temptation.

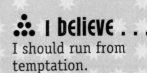

∴ I believe . . .
I should run from temptation.

Have you ever felt like your parents have too much power? They make the rules. They tell you what to do. They can stay up late and make you go to bed early. They can eat whatever and whenever they want—even if that means eating dessert before dinner. *(Hey, won't that ruin their appetites?)* They get to decide everything.

Sometimes it doesn't feel fair being a kid. You have to keep your room clean. You have to walk the dog and clean up after it goes to the bathroom. You have to go to school every day. What a bum deal!

But have you ever thought about all the responsibilities a parent has? Parents have to go to work so you can have food, clothing, and a place to live. Parents need to make sure you stay healthy and go to the doctor. Parents make sure you're filling your mind and body with good stuff instead of junk.

When you think about it, parents are the ones who brought you into the world. And now it's up to them to show you how to live right.

Check out Job 10:8 in the *Young Believer Bible:*

In this verse, Job feels abandoned by God. God has allowed a bunch of bad stuff to happen to him (sores on his body, the death of his children and animals, and trouble with friends). It's understandable that Job is confused about why God let those bad things happen.

●●●

If you think about it, God is the ultimate parent. He's even called your heavenly Father. But unlike your parents, God won't make mistakes. Parents can get mad, overreact, and yell. God never yells. He always understands, always does the right thing. But God also disciplines his children when they need it. Sometimes he does things that you might not understand—like he did in Job's life. It's important at those times to trust your Creator and know that he's got a great plan for you. After all, he's the One who made you. He will take care of you, even when it's hard to understand what he's doing.

Pray:

Tell God you're going to keep following him, even when you don't understand.

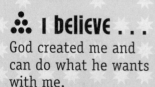

∴ I believe . . .
God created me and can do what he wants with me.

Climbing the world's highest mountains would be hard work. It'd take years of training, thousands of dollars of equipment, months of planning, and lots of people working together.

Just imagine yourself high up on Mt. Everest. Gusting winds nearly blow you off your feet. Every step takes all of the energy you can summon. The air is so thin at nearly five miles above sea level that you're sucking in oxygen from a tank in order to breathe. You're tied to eight other climbers as you hike slowly upward. Temperatures are so far below freezing that you can't remember the last time you took off your gloves. If your hands were exposed for a minute, they'd be totally numb. It's just one foot after the other.

Plod, plod, plod, plod.

When am I going to get there? you think as you look at the summit. *Is it possible that I'm going backward? It feels that way!*

For hours you continue your hike—nine people working together for one goal. And finally—you make it!

Check out Psalm 125:1-2 in the *Young Believer Bible:*

These verses say if you trust in the Lord, then you will be like a mountain: secure and unshakable, lasting forever. Not only that, but the Lord surrounds his people like a mountain. Now that's protection!

●●●

Ever wonder why mountain climbers tie themselves to each other? It's not so they can find their way home. It's for safety. If one stumbles, the others will catch him. Climbers know they're stronger together—as a team—than they are on their own.

The same thing is true with your relationship with Jesus Christ. You need to team up and tie yourself to him. Trusting in him makes you strong because he'll never slip. The cord between you and God will never break. He'll always be there to pick you up when you fall. And together you can reach great heights!

Pray:

Thank Jesus for being rock solid in your life and for surrounding and protecting you like a mountain.

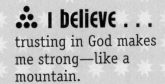

∴ I believe . . .
trusting in God makes me strong—like a mountain.

Have you ever played with a Magic 8-ball? You ask this plastic sphere a question, shake it up, and read its answer. It can seem kind of fun and funny to ask the 8-ball, "Will I ever drive a car?" only to have the 8-ball answer, "Things don't look good." But do you want to hear something scary? Some people take the Magic 8-ball seriously. They make decisions in their life based on what this piece of plastic says, instead of on what God and the Bible say.

There are other things that can pull people away from God. Horoscopes in newspapers, psychic hot-line commercials on television, and certain books that talk about witchcraft can all be a bad influence on kids and adults. It's a good idea to stay away from these things.

Check out 1 Peter 5:8 in the *Young Believer Bible:*
This verse says that you need to be on the lookout for the devil. He's like a lion prowling after someone to devour.

●●●

The Bible is clear: Satan is real, and he wants only evil for everybody on earth. His goal is for you to take your eyes off Jesus and focus them on something he made. Horoscopes, psychic hot lines, witchcraft, and Magic 8-balls may seem like games, but behind the fun you'll find their roots are wicked. The devil knows that if he showed you all of his evil, you'd turn away. So he makes things seem harmless. But once you're hooked on what seems harmless, you may start following harmful advice instead of God's Word.

Unfortunately, a lot of these bad things are very popular. Don't be fooled. People looking for wisdom from the stars started horoscopes and a lot of these other things. Why trust the stars when you can rely on the One who *made* the stars?

Pray:
Ask God to help you spot Satan's tricks and to stay close to Jesus.

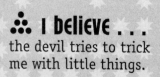

∴ I believe . . .
the devil tries to trick
me with little things.

How would you define "forever"?

a. A really long time
c. Longer than I live

b. As long as I live
d. A time with no end

If you chose *d,* you picked God's answer. Forever is an unending amount of time. God is eternal, meaning he has no beginning and no end. And in his Word, he has promised that those who believe in Jesus Christ will spend forever with him.

Forever is a very long time. You may have heard people say, "I'll love you forever." What they mean is that they will love you for as long as they live. But when God says forever, he means a time with no beginning and no end. And he invites you to spend eternity with him, because he truly loves you forever!

Check out 1 Thessalonians 4:17 in the *Young Believer Bible:*

Someday the Lord will return, and all who know him will go to heaven to spend eternity with God. On that day, believers who are living will join those who have already died to be with the Lord.

●●●

The Bible says believers will spend eternity with God. If you're a believer, heaven will be your forever home. You'll live in God's presence in the place Jesus is preparing for you. If forever never ends, what will you do during all that time?

Sometimes people picture heaven as a place where angels sit on clouds and strum harps. But that's not the description the Bible gives. When you get to heaven, you'll worship God and continue to learn more and more about him.

Think about the things you most enjoy doing on earth. The things you do in heaven will be so much more wonderful that they'll make earth seem really dull. Eternity will be a joyous time with God that lasts forever!

These verses tell me about heaven. Here's what each says believers will be doing in our forever home:

1. Revelation 3:21 _____

2. Revelation 7:9-12 _____

3. Revelation 7:15 _____

4. Revelation 14:13 _____

5. Revelation: 19:9 _____

Pray:
Thank God for inviting you to spend eternity with him.

∴ I believe . . .
eternity is forever.

Piper always acted perfect. Janelle couldn't stand it. Teachers always called on Piper. Parents all loved Piper. And even most of the kids were fooled. Piper acted as if she never did anything wrong, and she always looked, well . . . perfect.

The thing that bugged Janelle the most was that Piper seemed to think she was perfect too. She always had to do things better to make others look bad. And she thought her way was the best way.

Have you ever known someone like Piper? Maybe you've felt the same way as Janelle. People shouldn't pretend that they're perfect. Maybe that's why it's so annoying when somebody acts like she is. The truth is, nobody is perfect. There is only one person who lived a perfect life: Jesus Christ. Can you imagine how his friends and relatives might have felt? At times they may have wondered why he always did everything right. The good news is the Bible tells you that Jesus has passed on his perfect power to you.

Check out Titus 3:5 in the *Young Believer Bible:*

Even though you may stumble during your lifetime, if you believe in Jesus, he has made you perfect in his sight. Someday when you get to heaven, you will understand that perfection. Until then, the Holy Spirit gives you the power to be holy and pleasing to God.

●●●

Perfection is a desirable characteristic. Everybody wishes at one time or another to be perfect or to do something perfectly. But the Bible says only Jesus was perfect in every way.

When you get annoyed by people who act like they're perfect, you can focus on your own actions. Are you doing the right thing? Would Jesus behave the way you're behaving? Next time you feel bugged by "Miss Perfect," smile and remember that someday—with Christ's help—you will be perfect.

Pray:

Thank God for sacrificing his perfect Son for you and making you perfect.

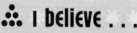

⸭ I Believe . . .

Jesus' mercy—not my actions—has made me perfect in his sight.

Picture yourself sitting on the stage at school. The auditorium is packed. People are even standing in the back. All eyes are locked on you. They can't wait to hear what you have to say. It's just you, a spotlight, and a microphone alone on the stage. What are you thinking?

- Choice #1: *Wow! I can't wait to speak. It's amazing so many people have shown up. I'm so glad they want to hear what I have to say.*
- Choice #2: *Duh. Ahhh. Duh. Hmmm. Brrrr. Duh.*
- Choice #3: *Help! What am I doing up here? How can I escape? Please, let there be a fire drill.*
- Choice #4: *This is boring. I wish I was at home playing Nintendo.*

If you're like a lot of people, you may agree most with choice two or three. Many people are afraid to speak in front of a crowd. Either they get totally freaked out (like #3) or their minds go blank (like #2). Either way, it's not a pretty picture.

Think of how you'd feel if you had to stand up for Jesus and let people know that you follow him. What's your answer now?

Check out Romans 1:16 in the *Young Believer Bible:*
This verse lets us know we shouldn't be ashamed about the Good News of Jesus Christ. Only Jesus has the power to save people who believe in him.

●●●

A lot of kids are shy when it comes to telling others they believe in Jesus. That's why some kids choose not to talk about Jesus to their friends or to be baptized. Speaking up can be scary, especially when you're not sure what people will think of you. And you may feel like everyone would be staring at you if you chose to be baptized. But being baptized is one of the best ways you can show the world that you are reborn as a believer in Christ. You do it to follow Jesus' example and to please God.

Whenever you get into situations where you feel shy about God, pray and ask him for power and strength as you stand up for him.

Pray:
Tell God you're not going to be shy when it comes to following him.

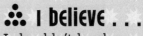

⠿ I believe . . .
I shouldn't be shy about my relationship with Jesus.

Here's a quick quiz.

Question: What makes you feel good, think more clearly, and sleep better?
1. A big, fluffy pillow
2. Eating a box of doughnuts every morning
3. Watching television
4. Exercising every day

The answer is number 4. Exercise is one of the best things you can do for your body, and it can be fun.

Write down some of your favorite activities:

1. _____ 2. _____ 3. _____

Perhaps you wrote down playing soccer, practicing piano, or laughing. Getting exercise doesn't have to be hard. But studies show that a lot of kids don't exercise, and many kids are overweight.

When you exercise you send more oxygen to all parts of your body, because you breathe deeper and your heart beats faster. You also burn calories, which helps keep you at a healthy weight. Check out these calorie-burning exercises:

• Bike riding—350 calories an hour
• Walking (slowly)—290 calories an hour
• Jogging—490 calories an hour
• Mowing the lawn—240 calories an hour

So whatever you like doing, get out there and do it. And remember, it's better to exercise a little bit each day instead of a whole lot at once.

Check out 1 Corinthians 6:19 in the
Young Believer Bible:

This verse says your body is a temple of the Holy Spirit. Because God's Spirit lives in you, your body is not your own.

●●●

If you're a believer, then God lives inside you. That's kind of awesome to think about. And because your body is a temple of his Spirit, it's important to treat it like one. Taking care of yourself, eating the right foods, and getting exercise are all ways you can keep your "temple" in tip-top condition.

And God's temples come in all shapes and sizes. His house doesn't always look the same. Just because you don't look like the stars on TV or the models in magazines, don't think that God doesn't like living in your temple. He loves you exactly as you are.

∴ I believe . . .
my body belongs to God.

Pray:
Tell God you're going to try to treat your body like his temple.

Are you a competitive person? Take this quiz and find out.

Scene 1: If you lose at something, you throw a fit and scream, "That's not fair!"

1. Yes   2. No   3. Sometimes

Scene 2: You refuse to do something unless there's a winner and a loser. That's why you don't like to make jewelry, build forts, organize clubs, or paint pictures.

1. Yes   2. No   3. Sometimes

Scene 3: You believe there's no such thing as second place, because that's just another name for first loser.

1. Yes   2. No   3. Sometimes

Scene 4: When you win a game, you dance around and sing, "I win. I win again. Nobody can beat me."

1. Yes   2. No   3. Sometimes

If you answered yes to two or more of the above statements, you're a competitive person.

Being competitive isn't bad. It's good to want to win and perform your best. But some kids get carried away with winning and losing. They're not happy unless they're victorious.

Did you know there's one contest you can never win on your own no matter how competitive you are? You'll never be able to overcome and triumph over your sins on your own. You're going to need help. The good news is, Jesus can provide that help.

Check out 1 Corinthians 15:57 in the *Young Believer Bible:*

This verse says God gives you the ultimate victory—victory over sin and death. By believing in Jesus Christ, you can live forever in heaven. Thank you, God!

● ● ●

Some kids' self-image is caught up in winning and losing. They feel bad about themselves if they don't get the highest test grade, or they feel like they're something special because they hit the winning basket. In the grand scheme of things, God cares about so much more than either one of those accomplishments. Sure, he wants you to try your hardest. But victories in sports and at school are not what matter most to God. The things he really wants you to triumph over are your sins—and you can't do that by yourself. Only Jesus can give you that victory.

Pray:

Think of any sins you haven't told God about lately. Then tell him about them and ask him to forgive you.

∴ I believe . . .

God gives me the ultimate victory— victory over sin and death.

Wouldn't it be funny if professional basketball players all dribbled the ball like four-year-olds? They'd be head down, ball bouncing high, totally out of control. NBA basketball would be a different game if everybody dribbled like a beginner. The players would be running into each other, smashing into the basket, and tripping over people in the audience. Now that's *fan*-tastic!

Do you remember when you first learned to dribble a basketball? You just stared at the ball as it bounced from your hand to the ground and back again. You never looked around because you were so focused on dribbling. But is dribbling the main idea of basketball? Of course not.

The point of basketball is shooting hoops to score points. You need to know how to pass and shoot. And you're not going to be very good at those two things if your eyes are always looking down at the ball. The goal is to be able to dribble with your head up. You want your eyes looking downcourt, so you can decide to pass or shoot. It takes lots of time to learn how to dribble without looking at the ball. But by keeping your eyes on the goal, you'll become a much better player.

Check out Hebrews 12:2 in the *Young Believer Bible:*
This verse talks about where we should put our attention. It says to look to Jesus. He makes our faith perfect. He died for us. And now he's in heaven at the right hand of God.

●●●

Do you remember when you first accepted Jesus into your life? Maybe that wasn't too long ago. When you're a new Christian, it's easy to get caught looking at your feet. You're just thinking about taking the next step. But if you're just looking at your feet, it's easy to get lost or bump into something.

God wants you to keep your head up and your eyes on Jesus. He's your ultimate goal. When you keep your eyes on him, he'll be able to guide you through life's troubles to the final victory of heaven!

Pray:
Tell God you're going to focus on him, because he's your true goal.

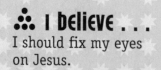

∴ I believe . . .
I should fix my eyes on Jesus.

March 19

Have you ever wanted to be a secret agent? You could carry spy gadgets and receive top-secret messages on your stealth phone. You could read important documents. And you could go on dangerous missions to exciting foreign countries. Secret agents are highly trained and have learned skills the average person doesn't have. That's why they're given the most important and dangerous jobs to keep the country safe and protect its citizens.

If you believe in Jesus Christ, you're his agent. You have a message the world can't understand: the Good News that Jesus offers salvation. Because you are his child, God gives you secret information that people who don't know him can't understand. He helps you understand important things about him. And he has an important, not-so-secret mission for you: telling others about Jesus. God gives you everything you need for the job. Do you accept his mission? You'll only succeed with his help. You can do it!

This message will self-destruct in ten, nine, eight, seven, six, five, four, three, two, one . . .

Check out 1 Corinthians 2:6-7, 10 in the *Young Believer Bible:*

As a believer in Jesus Christ, you understand the message of salvation. These verses say that the Good News is a mystery to those who don't know Christ. That's because the Holy Spirit helps believers understand. He reveals to you secrets about God.

●●●

Because God has revealed the mystery of his salvation to you, you have a special responsibility to share it with others. You may think it will be hard to tell others about God. But he'll give you the opportunities and the ability.

One easy way to talk about Jesus is to share your testimony. A testimony is your own personal story of what God has done in your life.

God is writing the story of my life, and part of that story includes when I became a believer in him. I'll write about when I decided to believe in Jesus as my Savior, or about something God has done for me since then. Then I'll find one person with whom to share my story.

Pray:

Ask the Holy Spirit to help you share God's wonderful secret with others!

⋰ I believe . . .
God reveals special secrets to believers.

What do you think your friends would say if you asked them who Jesus is? They might say he was a good person, a smart teacher, a famous man, or a religious leader.

But if you asked Jesus who he is, he'd say he's God. He said it in the Bible more than once. When you think about it, that's a pretty bold thing to say. Today if somebody said he was the son of God, you'd probably think he was crazy or trying to trick you. You definitely wouldn't say, "He's a good person."

Next time someone you know says Jesus was just a smart teacher, you can say, "That's impossible!" A good teacher doesn't say he is God. That would make that person a very bad teacher. But Jesus' life, death, and resurrection prove he is whom he says: God. As a Christian, you've made the smart choice and prayed for Jesus to come into your life and save you from your sins. Now you can help others make the same life-saving decision.

Check out John 10:30 in the *Young Believer Bible:*

There's no mistaking the message of this verse. Jesus says very clearly that he and God are one and the same.

● ● ●

Do you know why Jesus was killed on the cross? If you think, *So I could be forgiven of all the bad things I do*, you're correct. But the people who killed Jesus didn't know his death would mean forgiveness. They killed Jesus because he said he was God. They even gave him a chance to save his life by taking back what he said. But Jesus wouldn't deny the truth. He knew it was God's plan for him to die and then rise from the dead, so we could have a way to go to heaven to be with him. Nobody but Jesus Christ has ever risen from the dead by his own power—that fact alone shows Jesus is God.

Pray:

Ask God to help you understand and accept that Jesus is God.

∴ I believe . . .

Jesus is God.

The man stepped out of the tomb, his arms and legs wrapped in strips of cloth. A piece of linen covered his face. The crowd gasped as the man walked forward. He'd been dead for four days!

"Set him free," a strong voice commanded.

Men ran forward and began unwrapping the mummylike man, freeing him from his grave clothes. The man was no longer dead—but alive!

This probably sounds like a scene from a horror movie. Frankenstein or Egyptian mummies come to mind. But this story really happened, and it's recorded in John 11.

One of Jesus' best friends died. His name was Lazarus. Jesus knew Lazarus was sick, but he didn't go to him until after he died. At first, it's hard to understand why Jesus waited so long. If your best friend were dying and you had the power to save him, wouldn't you go right away? But Jesus had another plan. It was his Father's plan for Jesus to bring Lazarus back to life. That plan showed God's power and glory over death.

Check out John 11:25-26 in the *Young Believer Bible:*

Jesus claims that he is the resurrection and the life. He has the power over life and death. And more importantly, he has the power to offer you life forever with him when your life on earth is over.

● ● ●

Jesus made it clear that he would overcome death. First he brought Lazarus back to life. What an amazing miracle! But in the days that followed, Jesus was killed and laid in a tomb. He proved his final victory over death when he rose again three days later. Because Jesus overcame death, you can be sure that he has the power to save you and give you eternal life.

Maybe you know a Christian who has died. Even though it's sad to lose someone you love, as a believer in Jesus you have the hope that you will see that person again one day. Because Jesus provides salvation and life forever with him, that person will live for all eternity. And you don't need to be afraid when you die either.

Pray:

Thank God for sending Jesus to win the victory over death.

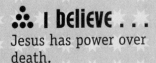

∴ I believe . . .
Jesus has power over death.

Have you ever seen an advice column in the newspaper? It might look something like this:

> *Dear Gabby,*
> *My mom makes me clean my room every day. I tell her that it's actually good to have clothes all over the floor, because if I had to escape my room in an emergency there would be a soft surface for my feet. She tells me to pick up my clothes anyway.*
> *What a Mess*

> *Dear What a Mess,*
> *You could tell your mom that your clothes actually provide a cozy home for all those dust bunnies under your bed. If that doesn't win her over, tell her you're doing a science project to see how much mold can grow under a wet towel in three months. Good luck!*
> *Gabby*

Sometimes advice in the newspaper can be silly. But God says asking for advice is serious business.

Check out Proverbs 15:22 in the *Young Believer Bible:*

If you make a plan by yourself, it may fail because you're basing your decision on one person's opinion—yours. But accepting the wisdom of others you trust can help you make better choices.

●●●

Have you ever heard the saying "Two heads are better than one"? Well, God's Word proves that saying is true. Whenever you have a problem to solve or an important decision to make, you should ask other Christians for advice. Parents and other grown-ups can give good advice because they've lived longer than you have, and they've faced many of the same problems. Christian friends can give good counsel too. Sometimes a friend can see more clearly than you can when you're making a bad decision.

Whether you're deciding what activity to get involved in after school or figuring out how to work out a problem with a friend, another person's advice can help. Whatever the situation, get in the habit of asking for the input of others. God uses people in your life to show you what's right. And don't forget to ask the Lord's opinion first!

Pray:
Ask God to help you to remember to seek godly advice.

⁂ I believe . . .
sometimes it's good to ask others for godly advice.

Have you ever been to an art museum? You know, the kind of place that displays the works of great artists from ages ago. Surprisingly, it's not boring. In fact, it can be fun.

People have painted some amazing things. Landscapes, night skies, bowls of fruit, portraits of themselves, epic battles—you name it, somebody has painted it. Artists have even painted what they believe happened at the birth of Christ or when Judas betrayed Jesus. You sometimes feel a lot of emotion from looking at a painting. Some make you feel relaxed, others make you uncomfortable, and still others cause you to smile.

Sometimes it's interesting to get really close to a painting and look at how the artist completed the work. Artists use all different kinds of brush strokes. Some paint using only dots, while others sweep across the canvas in wide strokes. And in the corner of most paintings, you'll also see something else that's very important: the artist's name.

Check out Nehemiah 9:6 in the Young Believer Bible:

This is one of many occasions when God's people turned back to him and asked for his forgiveness. They started by giving God credit for all of his amazing creations—and that's quite a list.

●●●

Wouldn't it be funny if God signed everything he created, just like great painters sign their work? You'd see an amazing sunset, and written across the sky in pink clouds would be one word: *God*. You could climb a high mountain, and scrawled across the top would be *God*. You'd pick up a puppy, turn it over, and sure enough: *God*.

If God put his name on everything he created, his name would be everywhere. That would actually be kind of cool, because then nobody could disagree that he is Lord of all. But God chose not to write his name on everything. However, he still deserves the credit. So next time you're amazed by something in creation, make sure to thank God.

Pray:

Ask God to make you more aware of everything that he made.

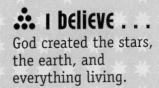

∴ I believe . . .
God created the stars, the earth, and everything living.

Sometimes it's easy to start feeling good about yourself. And that's okay. You probably do a lot of good things. But check the box if you do any of the following:

❑ Kick the neighbor's cat
❑ Hide your brother's baseball glove
❑ Feed the dog your green beans
❑ Look at your neighbor's paper during a test
❑ Think mean things about your mom
❑ Pretend to be sick so you can miss school

If you checked none or only one box, you really are a good person. But don't get carried away! No one's perfect.

That's where some kids can get off base in their thinking. It's great to have self-confidence—to believe in your abilities. But once you start thinking that you can do no wrong, it's easy to get wrapped up in your own high opinion of yourself. That's called being too proud or self-absorbed.

Nobody can live a perfect life. Well, nobody, that is, except for Jesus, the Son of God.

Check out Proverbs 20:9 in the *Young Believer Bible:*
This verse asks whether anyone has never sinned. The answer is nobody . . . except Jesus.

●●●

Jesus was the most extraordinary person to ever walk the earth. He was 100 percent human and 100 percent God. Nobody knows what things upset Jesus as a child or who his friends were when he was a teenager. But we do know that Jesus *was* sinless. He never lied, never cheated. And he *never* strayed from his Father's will for his life. If that's not perfect, nothing is.

Don't worry about trying to be perfect. God doesn't expect you to be. That's why Jesus came to earth. He was born to live the perfect life and die on the cross for the times you mess up. Believing in him and asking him to forgive your sins makes you perfect—even if you feel like kicking the neighbor's cat every once in a while.

Pray:
Thank Jesus that because of his perfect life you can also be perfect in God's eyes.

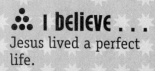

⁂ I believe . . .
Jesus lived a perfect life.

March 25

Imagine this scene. A man wearing a suit and tie knocks on your door and asks for you. He says he's from the Super Home Clearinghouse. In his hand he has one of those enormous cardboard checks made out to you for a huge amount. In addition to the money, he gives you tickets to your favorite amusement park, a lifetime supply of ice cream, and a $10,000 gift certificate to Toys"R"Us. What would you do?

a. Jump up and down, yelling, "Yes! Yes! Yes! All my dreams have come true!"
b. Give the man a bear hug while doing a little dance
c. Say "Thank You!" a billion, zillion times
d. All of the above

You probably answered *d*. If someone did something that generous for you, you'd probably be pretty excited and want to show your appreciation. But Someone did something a million times better for you than giving you toys and ice cream. God. And he deserves your praise and thanks.

Check out Isaiah 63:7 in the *Young Believer Bible:*

God is kind and compassionate toward you. He gives you many great things and is worthy of your praise. Just because he is God is reason enough for you to praise him. But on top of that, he showers you with good things.

●●●

God has given you life and a beautiful world to enjoy. But more importantly, in an ultimate act of love he gave his Son to die so you could have life forever with him. You have so many reasons to be thankful to him.

You have the privilege of being able to praise God directly. When you talk to him, he hears you. If you're a believer, there's nothing and no one standing in between you and God. And he loves to listen to his children thank him for all of the things he provides for them. Plus as you tell others about his kindness, they'll see that he is a good God.

These are three things I'm thankful for today:

1. _____
2. _____
3. _____

Pray:

Thank God for all the good things he's given you.

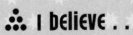

∴ I believe . . .
God deserves my praise and thanksgiving.

Do you ever have strange dreams? Dreams can be funny, scary, and exciting. Maybe you've dreamed you could fly. That would be cool, being able to zoom into the air whenever you wanted. Sometimes you might dream that your friends took something from you—and you might wake up mad at them. Dreams can seem so real . . . and sometimes they are.

The apostle John had one of the most famous dreams. He wrote about it in the last book of the Bible. In Revelation, John writes about the things he saw when an angel took him to heaven to see what's going to happen in the last days of Earth. John wrote about the future in Revelation, because God wants everybody to know what's going to happen in the final battle between God and Satan. Here's a hint: God wins!

Check out Revelation 5:6 in the *Young Believer Bible:*

In this verse John writes that he saw a Lamb standing in the center of the throne in heaven. He had seven horns and seven eyes, which were the seven spirits God had sent to Earth.

●●●

This verse is a little hard to figure out at first. In fact, a lot of Revelation can seem confusing. It's written with a lot of symbolism. That's when you use an image or a symbol to represent something else, such as when you refer to Jesus as a Lion or a Lamb. So when John sees a Lamb that looks like it's been killed, he's really talking about Jesus.

Now, this Lamb is anything but ordinary. It has seven horns, seven eyes, and seven spirits. The number seven has special meaning in the Bible. It stands for completion or perfection, just like Creation took seven days (including God's day number seven, the day God rested). But there's more symbolism in this verse. A horn stands for power. Eyes stand for sight. And spirits mean presence.

If you put all that together, it means this Lamb has complete power, perfect sight, and complete presence. In other words, Jesus Christ is all-powerful, all-seeing, and everywhere. You can't get any greater than that. And he's the Lord you serve. Neat, huh?

Pray:

Praise Jesus for his power.

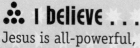

∴ I believe . . .

Jesus is all-powerful,
all-seeing, and
everywhere.

March 27

What's easier to do: build or destroy? Not sure? Try this experiment. Find a box of blocks. Maybe you have one left over from when you were a baby. Now build the best tower, wall, or house you can imagine. Done? All right. Go look for your little brother, little sister, or dog—it doesn't matter which. Put one of them in the same room with your block structure. What happens?

Things get destroyed, right?

So what's easier—to build or to destroy? Destroying is easy. Anybody can do it. You don't even have to think about it, because it comes naturally. Building, on the other hand, takes creativity, effort, discipline, and a plan. You have to know what you're doing and take the right steps to create something special. And that's exactly what God did for you.

Check out Romans 3:22-25 in the *Young Believer Bible:*

These verses say being made right with God only comes through believing in Jesus Christ, because everybody has sinned. God gave Jesus as a sacrifice so you could be forgiven and saved.

●●●

Which would've been easier for God?

a. To wipe out the whole earth—all the sinful people—and start over
b. To send his only Son to suffer and die so people could be forgiven

That's a no-brainer. The easiest thing for God would've been to destroy everything and start fresh. It only took God a few days to create the universe the first time. Why not do it again and see if humans get it right the second time? Maybe the new Adam and Eve would make the correct choice and follow God's commands instead of disobeying him.

Choice *b* is much more difficult. It takes sacrifice, planning, and the thirty-three years of Jesus' lifetime on earth. That's a lot longer than six days. Plus there's all the suffering. It's just too hard and too painful.

But as you know, God chose the second option. His Son suffered and died so we could be forgiven. And his sacrifice makes it possible for you and God to build a relationship together.

Building is always harder than destroying—but it's worth it.

Pray:
Thank God that he chose to do things the hard way.

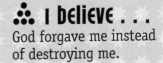

⁘ I believe . . .
God forgave me instead
of destroying me.

Who do you follow?

Some kids follow a popular athlete. They buy shoes because that athlete wears them in games. They drink the same sports beverage that he guzzles. They get their hair cut to match his.

Others follow a famous singer. They dress like she does and practice dancing like her. They watch all of her videos and even know the words to her songs.

Still other kids follow a favorite teacher. They like that subject best because she teaches it. Sometimes they stay after class to help.

Maybe you know kids who follow a cartoon character. They bring a lunch box to school with that character's picture on it and wear pajamas featuring that character's face.

A lot of kids follow their friends. They'll do things just because their friends do them. Sometimes they'll even form a club.

Do any of these kids sound like you?

Check out John 13:14-15 in the *Young Believer Bible:*

In these verses Jesus says he is the disciples' Lord and Teacher. He also says they should follow his example.

●●●

What's the first word you think of when you think of Jesus?

a. Friend. He's certainly that.
b. Perfect. He lived a sinless life.
c. Savior. You couldn't go to heaven without him.
d. Lord. He is ruler over all things.

You probably don't think of the word *teacher*. It's easy to admit that Jesus saved you from your sins. But it's hard to follow his teachings, because it can seem like there are so many. Don't let that stop you. He is your perfect example. Just follow him. And as you learn more about what he wants you to do, let him use you to accomplish his goals. You won't earn a grade from this Teacher—no, his rewards will actually be much greater.

Pray:

Tell Jesus you're going to follow his teachings.

∴ I believe . . .

Jesus is my teacher.

How do you communicate with your relatives most of the time?

a. Telephone
b. Letter
c. E-mail
d. Carrier pigeon
e. Smoke signals

You probably answered *a, b* or *c*. You have a lot of choices when it comes to communicating these days. But that wasn't always the case. Paper wasn't invented until a little over seventy years after Jesus died. Before that time people had to write on leather scrolls or parchment made out of plants. Pencils didn't come about until 1795, and the ballpoint pen was invented nearly 100 years later—12 years *after* the telephone made its debut. The phone was invented by Alexander Graham Bell in 1876, but the cell phone didn't hit the market until 1979. Letter writing has been popular for hundreds of years. But in the 1800s, people used the telegraph to get messages to their relatives quickly. Now nobody really uses the telegraph.

E-mail is a rather recent invention and might be the most popular way to communicate for a lot of people. It's quick, it's easy, and it can be free. But a big downside is that you don't get to hear the other person's voice.

Check out Psalm 116:1 in the *Young Believer Bible:*
In this verse David writes that he loves God because God hears and answers his prayers. God listens when you call out to him.

●●●

All of these high-speed, long-distance ways to communicate can't compare to the power and simplicity of talking to God through prayer. God's been receiving messages across the universe since he created it—that's thousands and thousands of years before e-mail was invented. You communicate with God the exact same way Christians have done it for centuries: by praying to him. You don't need a laptop with a portable modem or a fax machine. When it comes to getting your message across to God, you just say it and it's done.

There's a lot I want to tell God. Here's something I'm thinking about now:

_____

_____

_____

Just talk to him. Your message will always get through.

Pray:
Praise God that you can always talk to him.

I believe . . .
I can communicate with God through prayer.

My family owns a grocery store. One night a friend and I were helping my dad round up the carts in the parking lot. It was dark, and we were sort of bored, so we decided to give each other rides. My friend pushed me in a cart first.

But when I pushed him, we got out of control and ended up hitting the curb really hard. Fortunately, my friend and I were okay. But one of the cart's wheels fell off. We ended up putting the cart with the other ones and didn't tell my dad what happened. I don't think this is lying, but I still feel bad about not letting him know. Help!
Dangerous Dan
Wildsville, Louisiana

Dear Dangerous Dan,
Wow, what an adventure! If somebody had videotaped you guys, you could've won $10,000 on one of those funniest video shows. But that's not the point.

First, it's good you're both okay. Stunts like that can cause really bad injuries, so it's obvious that God protected you.

Second, the real issue here is you and your friend hiding the truth from your dad. That bad feeling you're experiencing is the Holy Spirit nudging you to do the right thing. You may have to face some consequences for wrecking the cart, but it would probably be worse if you didn't tell and your dad found out later—then you'd lose his trust. Fessing up is the right thing to do, and you'll feel better.

Check out Leviticus 19:11 in the *Young Believer Bible:*
This verse speaks for itself. It says clearly, "Do not lie."

● ● ●

If you look up the word *deceive* in the dictionary, you'll find it means to mislead or let someone believe something that isn't true. Deceiving someone is a sin. Hiding the truth is never a good idea. You've probably heard it said over and over again that lying is bad. But deceiving somebody can be equally harmful, because once the truth comes out—and it almost always does—then you'll have a lot of explaining to do.

Pray:
Tell God you're going to follow his rule in Leviticus 19:11 and not lie or deceive.

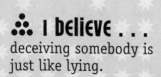

⁂ I believe . . .
deceiving somebody is just like lying.

March 31

Kelsey wanted to share God with people at school, but it seemed like no one wanted to listen. How was she supposed to give them the "Good News" if the only news they cared about was who made the basketball team?

When Kelsey did talk about her faith, people made fun of her. She felt so *different*. She wasn't allowed to watch the movies her friends talked about or listen to the music they played. Kelsey wanted to be a light for God, but no one seemed to understand.

Maybe you've faced the same frustration Kelsey has. You feel like there's a gap the size of the Grand Canyon between you and those who don't know Christ. How can you make a difference in their lives and show them the truth? Christians shouldn't be surprised when they feel this way. The Bible explains the reason for this great gap.

Check out 2 Corinthians 4:4 in the Young Believer Bible:

Satan has made the world blind to the truth of the Good News that Jesus saves us from our sins. Jesus reminds you that it should not be surprising that unbelievers don't understand the things of God.

●●●

Sometimes sharing your faith can be really hard. You want to, but it seems like no one wants to hear it. God gives us lots of opportunities to witness to others. And even when it seems your friends aren't listening, they're probably taking notice of your life. They may make fun of you because they don't know what to say. If you face teasing, don't react harshly. Instead, gently explain what you believe.

Nonbelievers often won't understand your beliefs. Only the Holy Spirit can change their hearts. What you can do is pray for those who don't know Christ and make the most of every opportunity to shine Jesus' light into a dark world!

Because I want to tell unbelievers the good news of Jesus' salvation, I'm going to write what I believe about God in 50 words or less so I'll know what to say to them:

_____

_____

_____

_____

Pray:
Ask God to open the eyes of the people you're telling about him.

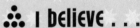

∴ I believe . . .
Satan has blinded the eyes of those who don't believe.

April 1

Quick! Look behind you. Is that a spider on the wall?

Ha, ha. Made you look. April fools.

Today is the perfect day for playing fun jokes on people. (Just make sure everybody laughs at the end, even the person you play the joke on.) After all, it's April Fools' Day.

Did you know that a law passed that says all children could eat ice cream for breakfast today?

Ha, ha. Got you again. April fools.

Want to know how this silly holiday started? Good. Because here it goes:

For thousands of years the world began the new year on April 1 instead of January 1. Weird, huh? But in the late 1500s, Pope Gregory XIII—the pope back then—introduced a new calendar for the Christian world that moved New Year's Day to January 1.

Some people didn't hear about the change (they didn't have cell phones, e-mail, or television) or didn't believe it, so they just kept celebrating New Year's Day on April 1.

Other folks who knew the truth played tricks on the unbelieving people and called them "April fools." Pretty soon everybody got the idea that New Year's Day came in January, but April Fools' Day stuck around too.

Check out Proverbs 26:11 in the *Young Believer Bible:*

This verse is kind of gross—but you'll have to read that part for yourself. The main point is that fools keep making the same mistakes over and over.

●●●

It's okay to pretend to be foolish one day a year, but the Bible has tons of verses about how bad it is to be a fool. Fools repeat mistakes, they don't listen to good advice, they refuse to learn the truth, they harm other people, and they get angry all the time. Do you think these are good character qualities?

Here are some good character traits I'd like to have:

1. _____

2. _____

3. _____

A fool writes something down and forgets about it. But a wise person sets a goal and accomplishes it. Will you work hard to become the person God wants you to be? It'll make him happy. No foolin'!

Pray:
Ask God to help make you wise—not foolish.

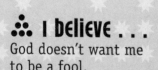

⁙ I believe . . .
God doesn't want me to be a fool.

Want to hear some jokes? Here they come.

Question: What do you give a sick bird?
Answer: Tweet-ment

Question: What should you do when it's raining cats and dogs?
Answer: Be careful not to step in any poodles.

Question: How do hens leave a chicken coop?
Answer: Through the eggs-its

Question: Why did the sheriff arrest the chicken?
Answer: It used "fowl" language.

Question: What is a dentist's favorite hymn?
Answer: "Crown Him with Many Crowns"

Knock, knock.
Who's there?
Canoe.
Canoe who?
Canoe let me in? I'm freezing!

Question: What do you call a duck that shakes?
Answer: An earthquack

Question: What do you call a pig in a pine tree?
Answer: A porky-pine

Check out Matthew 7:9-10 in the *Young Believer Bible:*

In these verses Jesus shows his sense of humor by asking the people a silly question. He asks parents if their children ask for bread, would they give them a stone? Or if the kids ask for a fish, would parents give them a snake? Now that's funny!

● ● ●

Ever wonder why you laugh at a silly joke? The reason is simple: God laughs too. You were created in his image, which means you have some things in common with God. Jesus sometimes used humor to get his point across. Think about it. If your friend asked for a sandwich and you handed him a rock, that would make you both laugh.

Sometimes it's hard to think about Jesus smiling and laughing, because he came to earth to do something very serious—he came to die for our sins. But Jesus didn't walk from city to city with a frown on his face. Jesus' kindness showed on his face. He probably smiled and laughed a lot—and he wants you to do the same.

Pray:

Thank God that he created us to laugh and have fun.

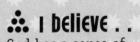

∴ I believe . . .
God has a sense of humor.

King of the beasts. The lion. Just its roar can send shivers down the spines of humans and other animals.

Did you know lions have 30 shiny, meat-chewing teeth? And when you add that to the fact that lions can weigh as much as 600 pounds, grow up to 12 feet long, and run as fast as 50 miles per hour, it's no wonder these predators are feared by all.

But lions don't just look imposing. Their muscled bodies can pounce into action at a moment's notice to catch food. And lions eat a lot. A male lion can consume more than 94 pounds of meat in a single day! Female lions can eat 55 pounds of food in 24 hours. (No wonder your family has never invited over a lion for dinner—it would cost a fortune to feed it!)

Of course, you'd be crazy to get anywhere near this fearsome animal. No, these creatures aren't cuddly. An animal like this has to be respected and even feared.

Check out Revelation 5:5 in the *Young Believer Bible:*
This verse calls Jesus "the Lion of the tribe of Judah."

● ● ●

Just like a lion, Jesus should be respected and feared for his power. He is the Lord of lords and the King of kings. He is all-powerful. And Jesus wants to be King of your life. He wants the old you to disappear and a new you—one that reflects him—to grow in its place.

It can be a little scary to let Jesus control your life, but if you let him, you'll find he is gentle and loving.

Pray:
Tell God you want him to consume your life.

⋮ I believe . . .
I should let Jesus, the Lion of the tribe of Judah, control my life.

April 4

Did you know it's easier to smile than to frown? Some days it may not feel that way. Every once in a while, you're probably just in a frowning mood. But scientifically speaking, smiling takes much less work than frowning.

A smile uses just 17 facial muscles, while frowning takes 43 muscles. No wonder people look miserable when they frown—they're working too hard! Smiling, on the other hand, takes no work at all.

Smiling is not only easy, it's natural. Babies are born with the ability to smile. You've probably noticed that if you smile at a baby he usually smiles back. Babies also smile a lot when they sleep. (Wonder what they're dreaming about?)

Here's more good news: Smiling is not only easy and natural, it's also good for you. Some experts believe smiling can make you feel better when you're in a bad mood. Imagine that! So now if you're grumpy, all you have to do is smile. You'll probably perk up, plus you'll make the people around you feel better too.

Smiles are contagious. Try it. Smile at people and see what happens. If everybody did the easy, natural, healthy thing and smiled more, the world might be a happier place.

Check out Ecclesiastes 3:12 in the Young Believer Bible:

King Solomon is considered the wisest man who ever lived. Here he writes that there is nothing better than to be happy and enjoy ourselves while we're alive.

●●●

Studies have shown that there are 18 kinds of smiles that show different levels or types of good feelings. Here's a family activity. Get everyone together in front of a mirror. See how many different types of smiles you can come up with. (You may start laughing!)

Now practice those smiles in everyday life. By following this simple piece of advice, you'll accomplish exactly what King Solomon said: You'll be happy and you'll enjoy yourself. First, you'll be happy because smiling makes you happy. Second, you'll be doing good and enjoying yourself because you'll be spreading joy.

Bet you never thought of smiling as a way of following God's Word!

Pray:

Ask God to help you be happy and look to him for joy.

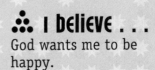

∴ I believe . . .
God wants me to be happy.

Don't you love hard work? Okay, maybe *love* is too strong a word. But don't you feel good after you've worked hard at something challenging? Sure, you're tired, beat, exhausted, spent. But you have a feeling of satisfaction for a job well done. Maybe you've helped your dad move rocks in a wheelbarrow from the front yard to the back. Perhaps you've helped your mom bake a billion cookies for a church bake sale. You may have worked really hard in soccer practice and run extra hard to score a goal. Or maybe you studied for hours and aced a math test. There's something nice about the tired feeling you have after you've overcome an obstacle.

But the same thing can't be said if you take the easy way out. Looking at a friend's paper for math-test answers or asking your older brother to move the rocks instead of doing it yourself doesn't provide the same satisfied feeling. It's like you're cheating yourself (or in the case of the math test—just cheating). Someone once said, "Hard work is its own reward." That was one wise person.

Check out Isaiah 41:10 in the *Young Believer Bible:*
In this verse Isaiah tells the people of Israel not to fear the threats of other countries because God is with them. God will strengthen them and help them overcome the obstacle.

●●●

Have you noticed that many people who believe in Jesus ask him to take away their challenges and make their lives easier? And God does want to help. But sometimes removing your challenges isn't really helping—and God knows that. Many times God is trying to teach you something through the obstacles he allows in your life. He wants you to be more like him. And sometimes removing your challenges wouldn't make you more like him—it would just make you weaker.

Next time you're faced with a challenge, try not to ask God to take it away. Instead, ask him to help you work hard and become stronger because of it.

Pray:
Ask God to give you the strength to overcome the challenges you face.

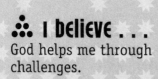

⁂ I believe . . .
God helps me through challenges.

I hope we don't have a quiz today, you think as you walk into social-studies class.

You find your desk and sit down. Just before the bell rings, a new kid walks into the room. He spots an open desk next to you and takes a seat.

Class begins, and your teacher makes an announcement. "Everybody pull out a blank piece of paper and a pencil. Pop quiz time."

Bummer. You reach into your backpack and pull out a sheet of paper and a pencil. Before the teacher can read a question, the new kid taps you on the shoulder.

"Can I borrow a pencil?" he asks.

No way! you think. *I don't know this kid.*

"Sorry, I don't have another pencil," you finally say.

"Sure, you do," the kid says. "You have a blue one, two yellow ones, and a camouflage one."

You look in your bag and realize the kid is 100 percent correct! You pull one out and hand it to him.

"Thanks," he says. "And how's your grandma?"

"She's out of the hospital and doing better now," you answer before you can think. Suddenly, it hits you: *How does he know about my grandma?*

You're getting a little freaked out and are about to ask how he knows so much about you when the teacher says, "Question one . . ."

Check out 1 John 3:20 in the *Young Believer Bible:*
This verse says God is greater than our hearts—he knows everything.

●●●

Something like the above story really happened. Read the beginning of John 4, where Jesus talks to a Samaritan woman. Their conversation is going along normally when— *bang!*—Jesus says something about her that a stranger would not know. She is so surprised that she goes back into town and tells everybody that she met a man who knows everything she ever did. The townspeople run out to meet Jesus.

Some kids might think it's scary that Jesus knows everything about them. But instead of being worried that God knows all about your mistakes and sins, you can be excited like the Samaritan woman. You can know that Jesus loves and accepts you just the way you are.

Pray:
Thank God for accepting you, mistakes and all.

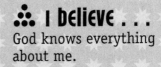

⁘ I believe . . .
God knows everything about me.

Every state has a nickname. Alaska is the "Last Frontier" because of all of its open space. Arizona is the "Grand Canyon State," which makes a lot of sense—that's where the Grand Canyon is. Washington calls itself the "Evergreen State." Guess it has a lot of trees. Delaware is known as the "First State" because it was the first state to join the United States.

One of the more interesting state nicknames is Missouri's—the "Show Me State." That means people from Missouri need a lot of proof before they believe something. They want to see it before they believe it. If somebody tells you something that you don't believe, you can say to him, "I'm from Missouri." And that means "Prove it to me. I want to see some evidence."

Maybe you have some friends who have a "show me" attitude when you talk about your relationship with Jesus. They want proof. They want Jesus to appear in front of them before they believe. Those feelings are understandable, and Jesus has a special message for those kids.

Check out John 20:29 in the *Young Believer Bible:*

This story in the Bible comes after Jesus has risen from the dead. Thomas, one of the disciples, says he won't believe Jesus is alive unless he sees the wounds in Jesus' hands and side. Jesus appears and Thomas believes. Then Jesus says, "Blessed are those who haven't seen me and believe anyway."

●●●

Some of your friends or family members probably don't believe in Jesus. Some folks can see the truth of God's Word right away, but others are like Missouri's "Show me" nickname. They don't believe in what they can't see. Don't give up on your friends. Pray for the Holy Spirit to soften their hearts to hear God's truth. Ask God to show himself to them through other people and through the beauty of God's creation. Then keep being their friend, and be like Florida's nickname—the "Sunshine State." Stay happy and positive that they'll eventually accept Christ.

Pray:

Remember the people you know who don't believe in Jesus.

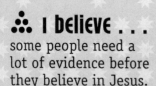

⁙ I believe . . .
some people need a lot of evidence before they believe in Jesus.

April 8

For years adventurers have searched for things described in the Bible. They've climbed high mountains looking for Noah's ark and dug through layers of sand to discover ancient cities.

Bob Cornuke, the founder of the Bible Archaeology Search and Exploration Institute (BASE) in Monument, Colorado, loves to look for things from the Bible. But Bob does it in an interesting way—he uses the Bible as his guide.

"The Bible is a compass that points us in the right direction toward finding these ancient locations," Bob says.

By following clues he's found in the pages of God's Word, Bob has identified what he (and some other experts) believe is the real Mt. Sinai, where God gave Moses the Ten Commandments. According to Bob's findings, the real Mt. Sinai is in Saudi Arabia—not in the Sinai Peninsula, as a lot of Bible maps show.

He's also uncovered what may be the anchors from Paul's ship that sank (see Acts 27).

But to Bob the Bible is more than a road map to cool discoveries. "It points us to how we should live our lives today," he says. "I think the Bible has more wisdom in it than all the libraries in the world. It's the most powerful text in the universe. And it's not just a book—it's God's Word. And when people recognize the power behind that, they'll have a change in their lives."

Check out Psalm 119:105 in the *Young Believer Bible:*
This verse says the Bible is a lamp to your feet and a light to your path. It helps you discover God's truths.

●●●

God's Word was written to direct you and show you how to live. Just as Bob follows the Bible to make amazing discoveries, you can follow the Scriptures to make some awesome discoveries of your own.

A lot of people like to give advice. Maybe you have some friends who like to tell you what to do or help you make decisions. And getting ideas from people is a good thing. However, if your friends' opinions go against God's Word, you have to make the decision to follow the Bible. As Bob says, "Man will oftentimes be wrong. Scripture will always be right."

Pray:
Tell God you're going to use the Bible as a compass for your life.

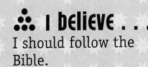

∴ I believe . . .
I should follow the Bible.

April 9

Long ago there lived a young prince who faced some big troubles. He was concerned because many of his Father's people spent too much time being afraid of the evil Black Marauder. The prince's Father was a good king—the best the land had ever seen. People were well provided for and protected. But some time ago, the Black Marauder had entered the land and terrorized the people.

The prince decided to do something about the problem. He knew the Black Marauder would never storm the castle, because the king was too strong. So the prince put on peasant clothes, slipped through the castle gates, and went out into the countryside. He became a regular person. The prince felt what it was like to be hungry. He was nearly run over by a horse cart when he didn't look before crossing the road. He slept under a tree because he didn't have enough money to stay at the inn. And whenever he talked with the people, he saw how afraid they were of the Black Marauder and how powerless they felt against him.

I guess it's up to me to stop the Black Marauder, the prince decided. *And with my Father's power, I can do it.*

Check out Hebrews 2:14-15 in the Young Believer Bible:

These verses talk about Jesus. Since we are made of flesh and blood, Jesus came to live as a human too. He died so he could defeat the one who holds the power of death—the devil. And because Jesus conquered the devil, we don't need to fear death.

● ● ●

You've probably figured out that the young prince in the story is like Jesus. And just as the prince left the castle to discover what it was like to live as a normal person, Jesus descended from heaven and lived as a human. Plus he came with a purpose. Jesus became a man to overcome the devil and rise from the dead. God's Son showed his awesome power by defeating the power that death had over humans. Because of this fact, you have no need to fear death.

Pray:

Tell God that through his power you're not going to be afraid of the devil or of death.

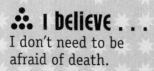

⁛ I believe . . .
I don't need to be afraid of death.

Think of the cutest, softest, fluffiest animal you can image. Most of you are probably picturing a puppy, kitten, or baby chick. What about a lamb? Nobody could argue that lambs are soft and cuddly.

In Old Testament days many of God's people raised sheep for food and wool, and they also needed sheep to sacrifice to God for the forgiveness of their sins. God's law in those days demanded the shedding of blood for forgiveness of sins. And perfect lambs were a popular animal to kill and offer to God.

Jesus talks a lot about sheep and shepherds in the New Testament. He says he's the Good Shepherd. He also says his sheep know his voice and follow him. Sheep, especially lambs, need a shepherd to take care of them. They need protection from enemies such as wolves. And they need to be led to fresh pastures to eat. You are one of God's lambs.

Do you want to hear something interesting? Jesus Christ was also called the Lamb of God.

Check out John 1:29 in the *Young Believer Bible:*

John the Baptist led the way for Jesus by telling people about the Messiah and baptizing them. In this verse, John the Baptist sees Jesus coming and calls him the Lamb of God—the One who takes away the sin of the world.

● ● ●

Thousands, maybe millions, of lambs were killed in Old Testament days by people seeking God's forgiveness. When Jesus came to earth he fulfilled the law. Instead of thousands of innocent little lambs dying, Jesus gave himself, perfect and unblemished, as an all-time, final sacrifice.

Jesus isn't called the Lamb of God because he follows God (which *is* why you are called a lamb). No, Jesus is God. He's called the Lamb of God because his death—his blood—paid the price for everybody's sins: past, present, and future. And he would have died just for you if you were the only one who needed his forgiveness.

Pray:

Thank Jesus for being God's Lamb.

∴ I believe . . .

Jesus is the Lamb of God.

Did you ever have one of those days when you kept running into the same friend no matter where you went? It's sort of fun, because it always ends in laughter.

You go to the shoe store—she's there.

You grab some lunch at Pizza Hut—she's there.

You head to the grocery store—she's there.

You walk into church—she's there.

You pick up a movie at the video store—and oh yes—she's there.

You can't help but laugh when things like that happen, because it's just so funny to keep seeing the same person everywhere you go. It's like déjà vu all over again. And maybe it feels like she's reading your mind.

But what if you saw the same person everywhere you went every day? Would that still be funny? Probably not. That would be weird. It would be like you couldn't get away from her. But wouldn't it be sort of cool if you saw God everywhere?

Check out Proverbs 15:3 in the *Young Believer Bible:*

This says God is everywhere. He keeps a watch on good people and bad people.

●●●

Here's a fun fact: God is everywhere. You can't go anywhere where he can't see you. And if you look for him, you'll find him wherever you go. That's kind of comforting. But it can also be kind of challenging. Because God is everywhere, he sees everything you do and always has his eye on you. He knows when you act correctly and when you mess up.

I know that God is always with me. Here's how that makes me feel:

_____

_____

_____

Pray:

Thank God that he always has his eye on you.

∴ I believe . . .

God is everywhere.

One day a sporting-goods store owner was having breakfast with his two sons.

"Hey, Ben," Dad said, as his oldest son shoveled a forkful of waffle into his mouth. "Can you come down to the store today and help me unload the new skateboards? It's a pretty big job, and I need a hand."

"No way," Ben said. "It's a beautiful day. I'm heading to the beach."

Ben loved to surf. And his bleached-out hair, long shorts, and tan arms proved he spent a lot of time doing his favorite sport.

"Well, how about you, Mark?" Dad asked his younger son. "Will you help me in the store?"

Mark looked like the perfect son, wearing a suit and tie even at breakfast.

"Of course, Father," the younger son said. "Nothing would make me happier than to help you."

Later that day, Ben strolled through the sporting-goods store's doors.

"Dad," he said. "My conscience was bothering me, and I couldn't enjoy the waves. If you need my help, I'm here for you."

"Great," his dad said, "get started in the back."

"All right," Ben replied. "But where's Mark?"

"I don't know," Dad said. "He never showed up."

Which son do you think was more helpful to his dad?

Check out Matthew 21:28-31 in the *Young Believer Bible:*

In these verses Jesus tells a story about two sons. The first son refuses to work with his father but then shows up and helps out. The other says he'll work but never does. Jesus uses this story to show that a person's actions are more important than words.

●●●

Actions speak louder than words. You've probably heard that before. And Jesus' story proves that point perfectly. It doesn't really matter what a person says. Anyone can talk like the perfect Christian and say all the right things about reading the Bible, memorizing verses, and helping others. But unless a person does all those things, his or her words mean nothing. God looks at your actions and the attitudes of your heart. It's important to walk the walk, not just talk the talk.

Pray:

Tell God you're going to let your actions do the talking today.

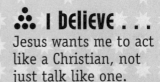

∴ I believe . . .

Jesus wants me to act like a Christian, not just talk like one.

Do your parents ever talk to you about saving money? You know, a penny saved is a penny earned? But saving can be hard. It's a lot easier to spend your money on candy and toys. *Mmmmm.* Candy.

A lot of parents have a rule that their kids have to put 10 percent of their money into a savings account before they can spend anything. That can seem unfair . . . until the time comes when those kids want to buy a new bike or video game. Then *voila!* They've got the money in the bank to buy it. Plus any money in the bank grows larger and larger. That's called interest. Let's say you put $100 in the bank and don't take it out for a while. When you go to pick it up, you might have $105, $110, or even more. You don't have to do anything to earn it! And the more money you have in the bank, the faster and bigger it grows.

Hmmmm. Maybe your parents are right about saving money. But there's something even more important that you should do with your money. Keep reading to find out what it is.

Check out Leviticus 27:30 in the Young Believer Bible:

This verse says you should give a part of everything you earn to God. Your money actually belongs to the Lord.

●●●

You've probably heard a pastor, youth leader, or parent talk about giving your "tithe." It's a silly-sounding word that rhymes with *blithe, writhe.* . . . (That's not helping, is it?) Tithe is just a fancy way of saying one-tenth, or one dime out of every dollar. Sometimes a tithe can feel like a lot of money. But when you realize that everything you have comes from God, including your money, it makes sense that it all belongs to him anyway. He's generous enough to let you spend most of it and asks for just a part back as a thank you.

Pray:

Ask God to help you understand that all your money belongs to him.

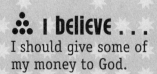

∴ I believe . . .
I should give some of my money to God.

Imagine traveling to another country with a close friend. You leave home knowing that you'll never return to your own country. When you get to the new country, people speak a different language. They do many strange things. And they believe in a different god and have an entirely different religion.

How would you feel if that really happened? Lost? Alone? Afraid?

Ruth experienced this when she left her country of Moab with her mother-in-law, Naomi. Ruth's love for Naomi made her give up her homeland and leave her own family and people. But God blessed Ruth's loyalty. She met a godly man named Boaz who married her and took care of Ruth and Naomi for the rest of their lives. And Ruth had a son named Obed. Obed became King David's grandfather and is part of the line of Christ. You can read all about it in the book of Ruth.

Check out Ruth 1:16-17 in the *Young Believer Bible:*

Ruth had a strong sense of loyalty to Naomi. She was willing to leave her country and her people, and even trust a new God—the one true God. She was so firm in her belief that she made a promise to Naomi and God that only death would separate her and her mother-in-law.

●●●

Another word for loyalty is faithfulness. A faithful person is consistently trustworthy and keeps his promises. Loyalty means being devoted to others. Everyone loves a loyal friend. A loyal pal won't disappear when the going gets rough.

Maybe you'll never be called upon to show the kind of loyalty that Ruth showed. You'll probably never have to leave everything you know and go to another country. But you have opportunities every day to show loyalty to your family and friends. Stand up for your family members and be a trustworthy friend. And most importantly keep your promises. God loves loyalty and so do others!

Because I want to follow Ruth's example, I'll think of some ways I can show loyalty to my friends and family:

1. _____

2. _____

3. _____

Pray:
Ask God to help you to be a loyal person.

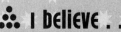

∴ I believe . . .
God wants me to show loyalty.

April 15

Jackie Change had everything a kid could want. She had a train big enough to sit on that traveled all over her house. She had a horse and a riding stable. She had a couple of ponies. Jackie didn't have a Nintendo GameBoy—she had two—and a big-screen TV. She had a Sno-Kone maker in her bedroom (the maid always kept it full of ice). Plus she had three identical dolls, four gigantic dollhouses, an indoor pool attached to her bedroom, a full video arcade, and a trampoline. And if there was anything Jackie didn't have, whenever she'd whine for it her dad would buy it for her.

But there was one thing Jackie didn't have: friends. She was so used to getting everything she wanted that she expected others to do whatever she wanted too. She only thought of her wants, her needs, her wishes. She never thought of anybody else. And this made Jackie a miserable person. Nobody could stand being around her. Most people (including her family) stayed as far away from her as possible.

Could it be that Jackie didn't have everything after all?

Check out 1 Timothy 6:10 in the *Young Believer Bible:*
This verse says that the love of money can make people do bad things. People who care too much about money and the stuff it buys may think of God less and wander away from him.

●●●

Money isn't a bad thing. In fact, it's nice to have because you can do a lot of fun things with it. But if you love money and think about it more than God, that's a bad thing. As great as money can be, it can't make you happy—but it can make you miserable, like Jackie. Some of the happiest and nicest people in the world have the smallest amount of money. That's because true happiness comes only from God. And when you're happy, you'll have more friends.

Pray:
Ask God to help you find your happiness in him.

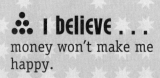

∴ I believe . . .
money won't make me happy.

April 16

A popular bumper sticker says, "He who dies with the most toys wins."

In other words, that whole idea of life is to get a whole lot of stuff. To people who believe that bumper sticker, life is a competition with the top prize going to the person who has the most cars, the biggest house, the best computers, and the coolest TVs. To them, doing well in life means getting a bunch of stuff that other people can see.

Shortly after the first bumper sticker came out, another one hit the market. It says, "He who dies with the most toys still dies."

The message of that sticker is that stuff doesn't matter. You can't take it with you, so collecting a bunch of things is worthless. If we think being greedy to own more stuff is what's most important, then we are missing out on what really matters.

Which bumper sticker do you think best describes Jesus' life?

Check out Isaiah 53:3-5 in the *Young Believer Bible:*
In these verses, the prophet writes about Jesus' life on earth hundreds of years before Jesus was born. It says Jesus would be rejected and despised by people. He would suffer for the bad things everybody does. And because he died to pay for our sins, we can receive his forgiveness, which we don't deserve.

● ● ●

You've probably heard a lot of people say you should follow Jesus. Maybe you've even read it in this book a time or two. But Jesus wasn't successful in a lot of people's opinions. He never owned a house and didn't have a lot of clothes. His best friends, the disciples, ran out on him when things got tough. The religious leaders hated him and had Jesus put to death.

Jesus' life, however, changed all the rules. Through his death, he made it possible for people to have a relationship with God—to be forgiven and made right in God's eyes. That was the purpose of Jesus' life and the plan God had for him all along. Unfortunately, a lot of people don't see that.

Pray:
Thank God for the ultimate purpose of Jesus' life—to bring forgiveness for your sins.

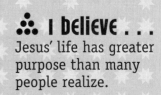

∴ I believe . . .
Jesus' life has greater purpose than many people realize.

"Did you hear about Renee?" Laura whispered.

"No, what about her?" Grace asked.

"Well, I heard she failed the math test."

"Oooh. That's not good."

"I know," Laura continued. "I think she may need a tutor, if you know what I mean."

The girls laughed.

"Uh, hi, Renee," Grace sputtered, glancing up.

Renee had walked up behind the girls in time to overhear the whole thing. Laura and Grace knew Renee from youth group. They hung out at church and even instant-messaged one another on their computers.

Renee just looked from Laura to Grace. Her eyes were cold.

"I thought you were my friends," she said. "Guess I was wrong."

Renee walked away, and Laura bit her lip. "I didn't know she'd take it so personally," she said softly. "I wish I hadn't opened my mouth."

Check out Ephesians 4:29 in the *Young Believer Bible:*
The things we say should help others, not tear them down. It's important to consider others' needs when we talk.

• • •

Our words have a powerful effect on others. They can cause pain or encourage. "Unwholesome talk," such as bad-mouthing, gossiping, and swearing, doesn't benefit others. Instead, God wants us to speak words full of kindness and compassion.

Think carefully before you speak. Will your words challenge, comfort, or encourage the person you're speaking to? Will they show that you're letting Jesus' love control you? Sometimes the wrong words just pop out. When that happens, apologize to the person hurt by your words and ask her to forgive you. Ask the Holy Spirit to help you speak only words that please God.

Here are a few statements that either help or hurt. I'll write next to each one how it might make someone feel to hear it:

1. "You're really good at writing." _____

2. "You're so annoying!" _____

3. "You have a pretty smile." _____

4. "Wrong again. You can't spell anything right." _____

5. "Thank you for helping me!" _____

Pray:
Ask God to help you avoid unkind talk.

∴ I believe . . .
the things I say should build up others.

Nancy had a problem. She'd been friends with Heather for a long time. Heather didn't know God, but she had a sweet personality and was a good friend. Nancy had told Heather about Jesus many times. She'd explained what a difference he'd made in her life. She'd even taken Heather to church.

Then it happened. One day Heather walked up to Nancy and said, "I think I want to ask Jesus into my heart."

At first Nancy was excited. But then she got scared. *What if I say the wrong thing?* she thought. *What if I explain something incorrectly?*

Nancy stopped, said a quick prayer to God, and asked for his courage to give her the right words to say.

"All right," Nancy finally said. "Heather, here's what you need to know about making the most important decision you're ever going to make."

Check out Matthew 28:19 in the *Young Believer Bible:*

In this verse Jesus says something very important before he returns to heaven. He tells his disciples to go to every nation, teach the people about him, and baptize them into God's family.

●●●

Here are some basics that everybody should know about what it means to be a Christian:

1. Everybody has done bad things that separate them from God (Romans 3:23).
2. God loves us and sent Jesus to earth to give us a way to heaven (John 3:16).
3. Jesus is the only way to heaven (John 14:6).
4. Jesus wants to have a personal relationship with us (John 1:12).

Nobody can earn his or her way into heaven. But your friends can accept Jesus by saying a prayer like this: "Dear God, I realize I am a sinner. I believe Jesus Christ died and rose from the dead so I could be forgiven of my sins and live forever with you. I accept your gift of forgiveness and eternal life. Thank you for always loving me and for allowing me to have a personal relationship with you. Amen."

Pray:

Ask God to give you opportunities to tell people about him.

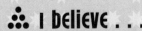 **I believe . . .**
God wants me to tell other people about him.

Have you ever seen a magician do his tricks or illusions? Maybe you were at a party, on vacation, or saw a performance on television.

Magicians pull off some pretty cool illusions. They can wave a stick over a big hat and pull out a rabbit. They'll ask somebody to come out of the audience, put that person in a box, and saw her in two . . . and then put her back together. They will put numerous swords through their assistant's body—without anybody getting hurt. They can even borrow a $20 bill from somebody in the crowd, light it on fire, stomp it out, and then pull the same bill out of their wallet—and it looks perfectly new.

A lot of times when you're watching a performance, you'll find yourself asking, "How did he do that?"

While a lot of these tricks seem impossible, there's always a simple explanation. The big hat might have a hidden panel where the rabbit hides until it's pulled out. The person's body actually fits in half the box, so it's never really sawed in half. The magician switches the $20 bill with a fake one before he burns it. The tricks may look cool, but they're still just tricks.

Check out Isaiah 25:8 in the *Young Believer Bible:*

This verse says the Lord will defeat death. He'll swallow it up and wipe away the tears from your face.

●●●

Jesus is no magician, although he did some things that would make any magician jealous. Jesus turned a little boy's lunch into enough food to feed more than five thousand people. Wouldn't you like to see a magician try to pull that off?

These are some of Jesus' miracles:

1. _____

2. _____

3. _____

When you think about it, Jesus did some awesome things. But the most amazing thing Jesus ever did was defeat death. Jesus was killed on the cross and buried in a tomb. But after three days, he rose from the dead. And it was no trick! Jesus conquered death so you could do the same. And unlike a magician, Jesus doesn't hide his secret. He tells you clearly how you can defeat death too.

He asks us to believe in him.

Pray:
Thank Jesus for conquering death.

∴ I believe . . .
Jesus destroys death.

Have you ever lain on your back on a beautiful spring day and stared into the air at the puffy, white clouds? If you haven't, you should try it sometime. It's fun to imagine what the clouds look like. Maybe you can spot one that looks like a bunny or a car or a plane or the Empire State Building. It's amazing how many different shapes you can imagine up there.

On the next cloudy day, try to spot these things:

a. a tree
b. a dog
c. a pizza

But what if you look up and see a bunch of white horses? Not clouds that *look* like white horses, but real horses. At first that might scare you. But then you realize that it's pretty cool. And it gets better.

The leader of this flying horse army is Jesus. He's riding at the front with crowns on his head. Behind him come thousands of people wearing white robes. And they're all coming to save the earth.

Believe it or not, someday that's exactly what will appear in the sky. The Bible is clear: Jesus will be back!

Check out Revelation 19:11-14 in the *Young Believer Bible:*

In this verse the disciple John writes about the future. He says he looked into heaven and saw Jesus riding on a white horse and leading God's army back to earth.

● ● ●

After Jesus died on the cross and rose from the dead, he hung out with the disciples for several weeks before he went back into heaven. Chapter 1 of the book of Acts tells us that Jesus traveled to heaven by floating into the sky right in front of the disciples. Then the disciple Luke writes that Jesus will come back to earth the same way he went to heaven—in the air (Acts 1:11).

But Jesus' second visit will be a lot different than his first. When Jesus was born in Bethlehem, he had come to earth to die so our sins could be forgiven. When he comes back the next time, he'll be a conquering warrior. And if you believe in him, then you'll be in his army.

Pray:

Ask God to help you remain faithful to him until he comes again.

∴ I believe . . .
Jesus is coming again.

April 21

There's a girl who wants to be my best friend. We're kind of friends, but now I don't think I want to be her friend anymore. Can you help?
Backing Off
Friend, Nebraska

Dear Backing Off,
Ending a friendship isn't easy. There are bound to be hurt feelings, especially when the other person wants to continue the relationship.

The first thing you should do is make sure you want to give up this friend-ship. What are your reasons for breaking it off? Do you want to ditch her because she's not cool and doesn't hang with the right crowd? If so, the problem may be yours—not hers. Does your friend drag you down or try to force you to make bad decisions? Pray and ask God to give you a peace and a clear direction to take with your friend. Be positive your decision isn't based on feelings that may change.

Once you're certain this is a relationship you shouldn't be in, you need to let your friend know. Avoiding or ignoring her without giving a reason isn't a good option. It will only hurt your friend's feelings even more. Get face-to-face and explain your decision. Be honest, but remember to speak the truth with kindness.

Check out Proverbs 16:13 in the *Young Believer Bible:*
This verse says kings like people who tell the truth.

●●●

Honesty can be a little tricky. Have you heard somebody say, "Sometimes the truth hurts"? Well, it's true. And when it comes to breaking things off with a friend, the truth will hurt—but it's still the best thing. Other times, such as when your sister gets a new haircut that you don't like, maybe being totally honest and saying, "Your hair looks terrible" isn't the best option.

As important as honesty is in your relationships on earth, it's even more impor-tant to be truthful with God. He already knows what you're thinking anyway. Just as kings value a person who tells the truth, so does Jesus—the King of kings.

Pray:
Ask God to help you be honest and loving at the same time.

⁂ I believe . . .
honesty is important
in relationships.

Things move fast. Do you ever feel that way? With microwave computers, high-speed Internet access and instant messaging, you hardly have time to slow down and talk with a friend. That's why a lot of people are turning to a new abbreviated language. Kids are using initials for words when they speak to one another and when they communicate electronically. It's a new, fun way to write. Do you know what these initials stand for? Write your guesses next to the initials.

a. AAMOF _____   b. WTG _____

c. NP _____   d. LMHO _____

e. SWIM _____   f. GMTA _____

g. BBL _____   h. B4N _____

Here are the answers: *a.* As a matter of fact; *b.* Way to go; *c.* No problem; *d.* Laughing my head off; *e.* See what I mean; *f.* Great minds think alike; *g.* Be back later; *h.* Bye for now.

How many did you get right? Speaking in code can be a lot of fun. But what if the person you were talking to didn't know the same code? It would be gibberish to her. Both of you would need to understand the code for you to communicate with each other.

Check out Proverbs 3:5-6 in the
Young Believer Bible:

These verses tell us to trust Jesus and not decide things based on our own understanding. If you trust God and follow him, he will show you the right decisions to make.

● ● ●

Sometimes people have a hard time understanding one another. Even if you speak the same language as your friend, there are going to be misunderstandings. And it doesn't take one of you speaking in code to mess things up. BION! (Believe it or not.)

That's why God says to follow him and not rely on your own understanding. God can make things clear to you. He'll lead you on the right path. He'll keep you going in the right direction. And he'll stop misunderstandings before they start.

If you start making decisions based on your own understanding, who knows where you'll end up. Understand? B4N.

Pray:

Tell God you want to understand things like he does so you'll stay on the right path.

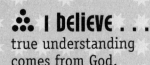

.:. I believe . . .
true understanding comes from God.

Have you ever heard stories about a 120-pound mom lifting a 3,000-pound car off her daughter who was trapped under the vehicle? Or maybe you've read about a kid who saved his little brother by moving a huge piece of broken playground equipment that had fallen on him. Well, if you have, the story is probably true.

Things like that happen all the time. Normal human beings accomplish amazing things during stressful and dangerous situations every day. The explanation for these amazing acts is actually quite simple: God created people to do awesome things under pressure. And he did it by enabling people to make something called adrenaline.

Adrenaline is a natural hormone that your body produces. When you get scared or hurt or excited, your brain pumps adrenaline into your blood to increase your heart rate, mental activity, and muscle ability. In other words, you're stronger, smarter, and ready for action.

Under normal circumstances, a tiny lady could never lift an automobile. But with adrenaline coursing through her veins, she might be able to do what she normally couldn't. God can do the impossible through you.

Check out 1 Corinthians 2:12 in the *Young Believer Bible:*

This verse says you have received a Spirit who is from God. The Spirit helps you understand what God has given to you.

●●●

God gave you the ability to make adrenaline to help you accomplish amazing things during intense situations. But when you became a Christian, God gave you something even more special: the Holy Spirit. Only the Holy Spirit knows God's thoughts. And he lives in you! The Holy Spirit has power that you can't even imagine—much more than it takes to lift a car off a baby.

So when you run into a serious problem and don't know what to do, don't just rely on adrenaline. Rely on the Holy Spirit. Ask him to give you wisdom and direction. Pray for his guidance. Ask for his strength. With the Holy Spirit in you, you can truly accomplish supernatural things.

Pray:

Tell the Holy Spirit that you want him to control your life.

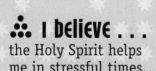

⁘ I believe . . .
the Holy Spirit helps
me in stressful times.

April 24

As a boy, Dave Dravecky dreamed of playing baseball in the major leagues. Dave worked hard and pitched his first no-hitter when he was eleven!

Dave's dream came true when as a young man he joined the San Diego Padres and helped them reach the World Series. After six seasons in San Diego, he moved up the California coast and became a starting pitcher for the San Francisco Giants.

Just when everything seemed to be perfect in Dave's life, doctors discovered a cancerous lump in his pitching arm. They had to remove it, along with most of Dave's shoulder muscle. They told him he'd never pitch again. But Dave knew a secret: "If God wants me to pitch, I'll be out there."

Nine months after his surgery, Dave pitched again for the Giants. The crowd went wild! But just five days after his comeback, Dave's arm broke, ending his baseball career. The cancer had returned. Doctors removed Dave's arm to save his life.

Dave could have been angry with God or given up hope. But instead he praised God. Dave knew God had a better plan for his life than he did. God had given Dave his first dream of playing baseball in the major leagues. Now he gave him an even greater dream—to tell others about Jesus Christ.

Check out Jeremiah 29:11 in the *Young Believer Bible:*

God has amazing plans for you. And he's working in your life to make them happen. God's plans for you are beyond what you could ever dream or imagine. He wants to give you hope and a wonderful future.

●●●

You may dream of being a professional athlete, a concert pianist, or a movie star. Dreams are good. God gives us dreams, and he often makes them come true. But God has bigger dreams for us than we have for ourselves. He has a marvelous plan for your life. He wants you to do great things for him!

Here are some of the dreams I have for my life:

1. _____

2. _____

3. _____

Ask God to show you the dreams he has for you. You can trust him to do what is best for you and help you through hard times.

Pray:

Ask God to help you trust his wonderful plan for your life.

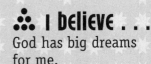

∴ I believe . . .
God has big dreams for me.

April 25

Look at this scene and see if you remember ever feeling like Nicholas. He's late for school and running all over the house looking for his backpack.

Nicholas (running into kitchen): Mom, where's my backpack?
Mom: I don't know. Where did you leave it last night?
Nicholas: I thought it was in my room, but now it's gone.
Mom: Did you look everywhere in your room?
Nicholas: Yes, even in my closet.
Mom: All right. Let's both go check it out. (They both walk into Nicholas's room, and he walks right past his backpack, which is sitting next to his dresser.)
Nicholas: See, it's not here!
Mom: Why don't you look to your feet.
Nicholas (looks down and sees it): Oh.
Mom (laughing): If it were a snake, it would've bitten you.

"If it were a snake, it would've bitten you." Now that's a funny saying. Why don't people say, "If it were a skunk, it would've sprayed you with a funky odor" or "If it were a porcupine, it would've stuck you"? Can you think of some of your own silly sayings?

1. _____

2. _____

3. _____

Check out Acts 17:24-27 in the *Young Believer Bible:*
This passage talks about how God designed things so people would seek after him. When you look for him you'll find him, because he's never very far away.

●●●

God wants us to look for him. He doesn't force us to believe in him, so it takes some effort on our part to find him. That's why everybody doesn't believe in God—they have to seek him.

But here's the cool part: When you start looking for God, he's right there. It's like you turn around and—*bang*—there's God. He's never far away from you. Just as Nicholas found his backpack, you'll find God when you look for him.

Pray:
Thank God that he's never far from you, and tell him that you're not going to wander away from him.

∴ I believe . . .
God is always close by.

Question: What do a puzzle, a combination lock, and a riddle have in common?
Answer: They all have only one correct answer.

Only one set of numbers entered in perfect combination will open a lock. If you're off by just a fraction, it's going to stay closed.

Puzzle pieces only fit together a certain way. You can try to smash the puzzle to get it together, but it won't look right in the end. The pieces are specially created to go together in just one way.

Riddles are designed to have just one solution. You can try to make up something, but a good riddle has only one right answer.

Can you think of some other things in life that have just one correct answer? What's the only right answer to each of the following questions?

1. 4 + 5 = _____

2. True or false: Elephants are usually purple. _____

3. How does a person get to heaven? _____

Check out 1 John 5:12 in the *Young Believer Bible:*
This verse is very straightforward in its message: If a person knows Jesus as her Savior, she's going to heaven. If she doesn't know him, she's not. It's that simple.

●●●

Look at the things you wrote down above. Did you say 4 + 5 = 20? Probably not. Did you agree that most elephants are purple? Again, most likely not! But did you write that the only way to heaven is through Jesus? Jesus said he is *the* way (John 14:6), and John said without Jesus there is no life. You have to know Jesus, have a relationship with him, and ask him to forgive your sins in order to spend forever with him in heaven.

Your friends, other religions, or television shows may say you just need to be a nice person or do more good things than bad to *earn* your way to heaven. But that's not true. First, going to heaven is a gift from a loving Father, so none of us can earn our way there. And second, just as a puzzle has only one solution, there's only one way to get to heaven: by accepting God's gift and inviting Jesus into your heart.

Pray:
Thank Jesus for making it possible for you to go to heaven.

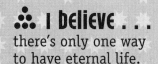

⁛ I believe . . .
there's only one way
to have eternal life.

Paul Patterson was never patient. When he had to wait in line for lunch, he pounded his foot. When he was waiting for his parents to drive him to soccer practice, he paced back and forth in the living room. When he was waiting for his little brother to get off the computer, he pouted and fumed. And when his friend Alex took too long lacing his skates, Paul pressured him to hurry up.

Paul had a problem. He had no patience. He couldn't pause and wait for things to happen. They had to happen now!

Do you ever feel like Paul? Are you ever impatient with others? Do you ever feel like you can't wait and have to have things your way, right away? Sometimes it's hard to show patience, but God says it's important. Patience proves you're putting others first.

Check out Ephesians 4:2 in the *Young Believer Bible:*
Being patient with other people is an act of love. Sometimes this requires putting up with others' mistakes and being kind even when they're not.

●●●

Maybe you've heard the saying "Patience is a virtue." A virtue is a good quality—a quality others admire. And according to God, patience is an important quality.

God is always patient with us, and he expects us to be patient with others. It's easy to start expecting people to do things our way, and if they don't, we often become impatient.

But we all like people to be patient with us. So why not return the favor?

"Making allowance for each other's faults" means slowing down, giving people time, and forgiving them instead of making selfish demands. Patience is a form of love and communicates that you care more about others than yourself. Will you practice patience today?

Pray:
Ask God to help you be patient.

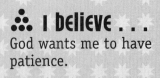

⁘ I believe . . .
God wants me to have patience.

Has your family ever planted a vegetable garden? You planted the seeds in the morning, added a little water, and by the next day you had huge, juicy vegetables.

Okay, you're right. That's not how it works (although it would be neat if it did).

Growing a garden actually takes a lot of time, work, and patience. First you have to break up the ground and make it soft before you plant the seeds. Then you have to water the seeds, make sure they get sunshine, pull up weeds that grow around them, and wait months for the plants to grow and for the vegetables to ripen.

If you work hard enough tending your garden, you're rewarded with a huge harvest. But you don't always see your efforts doing much. That's when you have to have faith that your hard work will pay off in the end.

Check out 2 Timothy 2:6 in the *Young Believer Bible:*

Jesus wasn't the only person who used examples from real life to teach truths about God's kingdom—Paul did it too. In this verse, Paul tells Timothy that hardworking farmers enjoy the "fruit of their labor." In other words, their hard work pays off.

●●●

Do you always get rewarded right away for doing the right thing? Probably not, which is why there's a lot to learn from a farmer. A farmer does the right thing every day, but it takes months for him to see and enjoy the results of his work.

The same thing can be true in your relationship with Jesus Christ. God doesn't always reward you right away for doing the right thing. Sometimes your godly actions are noticed and appreciated by people, and that feels great. But a lot of times your good decisions go unnoticed. That's when you need to trust God and know he's watching and that he's pleased with your actions . . . because he is.

Pray:

Ask God to give you faith—like a farmer—and to trust that he will reward your good actions in the future.

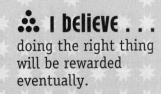

⁚⁚ I believe . . .
doing the right thing
will be rewarded
eventually.

One is the loneliest number. It doesn't have anybody to talk to. How sad. Not many people like being alone. Even the Lone Ranger had his buddy, Tonto, to travel with him. Tonto helped the Lone Ranger out of a lot of dangerous situations. He made the Lone Ranger more effective as a crime fighter.

When you think about it, two people work together a lot better than one. Check out these dynamic duos:

- Batman and Robin
- Shaquille O'Neil and Kobe Bryant
- Sam and Frodo

The list could go on. But did you ever wonder where the idea that two are better than one comes from? This idea and many other good ones originated in the Bible. After Jesus died and rose into heaven, the early church used the great idea of teamwork. Paul, who wrote most of the New Testament, always went from town to town with strong Christian friends. The ones mentioned in the book of Acts are Barnabas, Silas, Timothy, Priscilla, Aquila, Erastus, and Luke. (Luke, the author of Acts, never wrote his name but often wrote "we" when talking about his journeys with Paul.) Obviously, Paul agreed that two are better than one.

Check out Ecclesiastes 4:10 in the *Young Believer Bible:*

This verse says it's good to have friends because if you fall down, your friend can help you up. But it's sad when somebody falls down and there's nobody to help him up.

●●●

It's a good idea to have a friend who can watch your back, help you avoid getting into trouble, and encourage your relationship with Jesus. Sometimes it's difficult to stand for your beliefs when you feel that you're the only one who's a Christian.

Do you have friends who believe in the same things you do? You could get everybody in that group to commit to meeting once a week, even calling each other on the phone once in a while. Maybe you could form a Christian club that meets at school.

Because it's important for Christian friends to stick together, I'm going to write the names of some of my Christian friends. Then I'll call them to get together and figure out how we can best serve God as a group.

1. _____

2. _____

3. _____

4. _____

∴ I believe . . .

I should surround myself with good friends.

Pray:

Ask God to give you ideas of how you could serve him as a group.

It started as a chunk of wood the size of a loaf of bread. The wood-carver sawed off several oddly shaped pieces until the wood resembled a rectangle with four slender pegs. He whittled away at the rough shape, his eyes twinkling. He already saw what the awkward chunk would be. He whittled and shaved until the piece took shape.

Finally, he sanded and polished it. The wood-carver put away his tools and sighed with satisfaction. As he placed his creation on display in his shop's window, nearby customers gasped in delight. The horse made from mahogany wood seemed to gallop across the shelf, its mane and tail rippling in the wind.

"It's beautiful!" the admirers breathed.

Because the craftsman was working with wood, he was able to carve very fine, beautiful details into his creation.

Just as the wood-carver carefully fashioned his creation, God tenderly shapes his children. When you believe in him, he chips away and carves into your life until you're a beautiful reflection of him.

Check out Philippians 1:6 in the *Young Believer Bible:*

When you accepted Jesus Christ as your Savior, the Holy Spirit came into your life and began changing you. God is faithful, and he will continue to make you more like his Son. God began a good work in your life, and he will finish the job.

●●●

How does God shape you to be more like his Son? One way is through his Word. When you read the Bible, you learn how God wants you to act. You read about how Jesus, the greatest example, lived his life. And you learn of God's great plan for the world.

You may have some areas of your life that you haven't let God into. Maybe it's still hard for you to share your stuff with others. Or maybe you still get mad too easily at little things. In order to shape you, God has to be allowed into every part of your life.

Here's one area I need to allow God to change so I can be more like Jesus:

Pray:
Ask God to continue to make you more like Jesus.

∴ I believe . . .
God is shaping me to be more like Jesus.

May 1

Most believers would agree that people need to turn back to God. You may have been frightened to learn about school shootings, terrorist attacks, and other violence. That's enough to scare anyone. But God doesn't want you to be scared. You can take action. *How?* you wonder. Through prayer.

No matter how bad things look, God can change them. He can work miracles. The United States was founded on Christian principles, and God has made this country great. In 1775, the Continental Congress declared the first day of prayer for the country. In 1952, a law was passed that required the president to choose one day each year for a National Day of Prayer. In 1988, President Ronald Reagan went a step further when he officially made the National Day of Prayer the first Thursday in May. This week we'll celebrate that day.

All over the United States in churches, homes, schools, government buildings, and offices, people will bow their heads and ask God to bless, strengthen, and heal their country. The Bible says that God placed leaders in power. Although you're years away from being able to vote, now is a good time to start praying for your leaders.

Check out Romans 13:1 in the *Young Believer Bible:*
The message of this verse is clear: God is in control. He has put governments in place.

●●●

Who's in authority over you? As a kid, that can be a pretty long list. It includes your parents, teachers, principal, town mayor, president, governor, congressmen, senators, and policemen—just to name a few. Wow! But it's actually exciting that you have a long list, because that gives you lots of people to pray for on this National Day of Prayer. It's important to pray that your leaders will get to know Jesus as their personal Savior (if they don't already). You can play a big part in your world by asking God to work out his plan in your home, school, state, and country.

You may have heard this saying: "No prayer, no power. Little prayer, little power. Lots of prayer, lots of power." You can help make this National Day of Prayer the most powerful one yet!

Pray:
Ask God to bless your country.

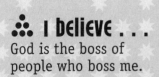

⁘ I believe . . .
God is the boss of
people who boss me.

I like dogs a lot, but my parents can't afford one. I know I shouldn't get upset about it, but I do. Any advice?
Puppy Lover
Dogpatch, Arkansas

Dear Puppy Lover,
By now you've figured out this fact: Getting upset doesn't help.
Have you noticed that anger can spread like a wildfire? You yell at your sister, your sister yells at your mom, and your mom yells at your dad (or something like that). Getting angry makes things worse, because it most likely upsets your parents. They'd probably love to get you a dog. But money is a problem for a lot of families. Parents have to make tough decisions. And they'd rather feed you than the dog. Putting yourself in their shoes may give you a better understanding of the situation and help you not become as angry.
Another thing that might help is to figure out other ways you can be around dogs. Maybe you could baby-sit your friends' dogs when they go on vacations. You could also set up a dog-walking business. If you know anybody who breeds dogs, you could volunteer to help when puppies are born. Then you could still care for and be around the animals you love!

Check out Psalm 37:8 in the *Young Believer Bible:*

King David sometimes had difficulty controlling his emotions. Here he says to do your best not to become angry, because it only leads to harm.

●●●

Anger is a strange feeling. But getting to the bottom of anger can help you deal with it. Next time you start feeling angry, ask yourself what's making you so mad. Are you frustrated or disappointed that things didn't go your way?

That's probably how Puppy Lover was feeling. She really wanted a dog but couldn't get one, which made her angry. Choosing to stay calm and talking to a parent can help. By figuring out what's making you angry, you can get over your anger sooner. And that's important, because as King David wrote: Anger only leads to harm.

Pray:

Ask God to help you figure out what's making you angry so you can deal with it the right way.

Do you ever feel small? Sure, you're growing older every day, and you know more about lots of things all the time. And you may be given more responsibilities the older you get. But do you ever feel that no matter how much good you do, it won't be enough to make a difference in the world? You might think only world leaders can create lasting change. The president makes decisions all the time that affect lots of people. The same thing is true in other countries. Leaders can make laws that take their country in a whole different direction, causing wars or bringing peace.

But powerful politicians aren't the only people who can make lasting change. If you've accepted Jesus into your life, you have the mightiest person who ever lived working through you. As a Christian, your actions matter. You can do awesome things no matter how big or small or young or old you are. So if you ever feel ordinary and powerless, just remember you have the King of kings and Lord of lords living in you.

Check out Judges 6:14-16 in the *Young Believer Bible:*

In these verses the Lord tells Gideon that he is going to save his people. But Gideon thinks this is impossible because he isn't even powerful in his own family. But the Lord says, "I will be with you." Gideon would win with God's help.

●●●

God used Gideon and a few hundred soldiers to defeat a powerful army from Midian to prove a point. Gideon wasn't big. He wasn't a leader or a masterful general. But God used him to win a great battle so everybody would look and see what God had accomplished. Doing big things is no big deal to God. After all, he just spoke and created everything in the universe.

God's still doing great things today through his people. Jesus talked a lot about love, grace, and forgiveness. Treating people the way Jesus asked us to sounds kind of simple and ordinary. But the ordinary stuff of Jesus can change the world. He proved that through his own life, and he can do the same through yours.

Pray:

Ask God to use the "ordinary" things in your life to change the world around you.

∴ I believe . . .
Jesus can change
the world through
ordinary people.

. I believe . . .
ger can be harmful.

Jason tossed and turned in bed. The clock read 2 A.M., but he wasn't close to falling asleep. He thought back to that morning. It had started out like any other day. He hadn't studied enough for his science test because he had overslept. Not good. Science was his most difficult subject.

When Mr. Cameron had passed out the tests, Jason had sighed heavily. He hadn't planned to cheat, but when he got stuck, his eyes wandered to Kendall Smith's paper. She was good at science. *Really* good. And before Jason had been able to force his eyes away, he'd seen two answers and had marked them down quickly. Jason knew it was wrong, of course, and didn't look again.

Now his conscience was killing him. *Even cheating on two answers is wrong,* he thought. It would take a lot of courage, but Jason knew what he needed to do. *I need to tell Mr. Cameron I cheated.*

Check out 1 Corinthians 16:13 in the
Young Believer Bible:

As a Christian, you need to be on guard against temptation to do wrong. Having courage is a big part of standing firm and being strong in your faith. Courage is the conviction and bravery to do what's right.

●●●

The word *courage* may make you think of a knight in shining armor riding off to save a princess or a firefighter running into a burning building. But courage isn't only for the big things. We all need courage to do what's right every day. That may mean standing up for a classmate, telling someone the truth, or speaking out about your faith.

Think of something you need courage to do today. God will always help you to do the right thing. The Bible is full of stories of how God gave ordinary men like Moses, Joshua, and Gideon extraordinary courage to do amazing things. No matter what scary task you're facing, God will help you do it!

Here are three things I need God's courage to do:

1. _____

2. _____

3. _____

Pray:
Thank God for giving you the courage to do the right thing.

What's your favorite food?

Pizza is really popular. Mounds of gooey mozzarella cheese on top of a c crust with tomato sauce makes a good meal.

Hamburgers and french fries are sold by the millions—make that billions. check out the signs outside McDonald's.

Chicken is good too. Grilled chicken, baked chicken, barbecued chicken, chicken, chicken casserole, chicken kabob, chicken Parmesan. Getting hungry

And then there are breakfast foods. Pancakes, waffles, scrambled eggs, and hit the spot.

Your favorite food may depend on where you live. If you live near the oce may eat a lot of fish. If you live on a farm, steak could be your first choice. If you another country, rice and chicken may come in on top.

And what about desserts? Do you scream for ice cream? Does a warm brow mode have your name written all over it? Ever get chocolate cravings?

Some of your favorite foods may be pretty good for your body, while oth not be.

But do you know what God wants you to feast on? Keep reading to find

Check out Jeremiah 15:16 in the
Young Believer Bible:

This verse says God's Word sustains us. Normally we think of food as sustenan Bible will make your heart full and happy because you believe in God.

●●●

Just as eating healthy food makes a strong body, "digesting" God's Word every sults in an exciting and growing relationship with Jesus. God's Word teaches y to live, gives you wisdom, helps you be a better friend, and explains how to li full of God's joy. When it comes to spending time in God's Word, he wants you up to the plate and ask for seconds.

Pray:
Commit to God to feast on his Word.

⠿ I believe . . .
God will give me courage to do what's right.

⠿ I believ
God's Word fe
relationship w   a

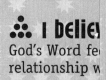

You receive tons of advice from your parents. Maybe they've even said one of the following things to you lately:

a. "Put a coat on before you catch a cold."
b. "Stop frowning or your face will freeze that way."
c. "No going outside until your homework is finished."
d. "Don't eat until we thank God for our food."

But do you know why they offer you those tidbits of truth?
They don't want you to have fun. Wrong.
They forgot what it's like to be a kid. Nope.
They want to protect you. Getting closer.
They love you, and it's their job to raise you. Correct!
The Bible says you're a gift from God to your parents. Then God trusts your parents to raise you the right way. That's a big responsibility, which may be why your folks seem stressed out sometimes.

It can also explain why your parents are always telling you to do something. They want you to be the best you can be. And if you think about it, why would you want to be less than your best anyway?

Check out Proverbs 22:6 in the *Young Believer Bible:*
This verse encourages parents to teach their children the right way to live. God understands the important responsibility parents have for their kids.

●●●

Isn't it nice to have people in your life who are willing to work hard to help you learn to live right? Hopefully you feel that way about your parents. Sure, sometimes a parent has to discipline you—but it's only because that parent wants the best for you.

Sometimes it's easy to take parents for granted. After all, it's their job to love you. And that's true. But it would make your parents feel extra special to hear that you love them too.

Here are three reasons I'm thankful for my parents:

1. _____

2. _____

3. _____

I'll make a point of sharing these things with my parents this week.

Pray:
Thank God for giving you your parents.

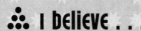

∴ I believe . . .
my parents want the
best for me.

What are your talents? What are you really good at? Write down some ideas:

_____

_____

Now ask yourself: "Is there any way I can use these things to serve God?"

Some kids make friends easily and are great at telling other people about Jesus. It's easy to look at them and see how they are serving God. The same is true with kids who sing well or play an instrument. They can perform in a church choir or band.

But sometimes it can be hard to figure out what you can do for God. Are you good at writing? Do you like to help people? Is reading your Bible fun? God can use all of those things. In fact, God can use any talent to draw people to him. And he's made everybody different. Who knows, maybe you're the person God wants to use to help the bratty girl at school get to know him. God has big dreams for you, and he's specially prepared you for those plans.

Check out 1 Corinthians 12:4-6 in the
Young Believer Bible:

These verses encourage anybody who wants to serve God. They say there are different kinds of gifts, service, and ways to work, but the same God is in charge of them all.

●●●

God is three persons in one: He's the Father, the Son, and the Holy Spirit. Each part of God has a special purpose in your life.

1. The Holy Spirit gives you gifts. There are lots of gifts, but only one Spirit in charge of them.

2. The Lord Jesus Christ is your example of what it means to be a servant. He served people by healing them, teaching them, and ultimately dying for them. There are lots of ways to serve, but only one Lord Jesus who set the perfect example about how to serve.

3. God the Father is over everything. He created the world, and it's by his power that it all works correctly. There are many ways to work but only one God who fits all of them together.

The Holy Spirit, Jesus, and God the Father all have special roles. And God has a special part for you to play in helping others come to know him. What part do you play in God's plan?

Pray:

Thank God that he gives you abilities to serve in his kingdom and then makes everything work together.

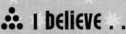

⁂ I believe . . .

God can use my gifts, service, and work in his kingdom.

What's your greatest wish? Do you dream of growing up to be a singer, artist, or professional athlete? Do you wish for your own room or daydream about getting the lead part in the school play? Maybe you long to have a pet more than anything.

God knows all your desires—the ones you talk about as well as the ones that you keep secret. And he wants to give you your desires. You may be thinking, *If that's true, then why don't I get everything I want?* That's a good question.

God doesn't give you *everything* you want. Sometimes he says no to our requests because he only wants to give his children good and perfect gifts, and he knows that just because we want something doesn't mean it's best for us. So how can you tell the difference between what's good and what's best in God's opinion? The secret is understanding how to be truly happy.

Check out Psalm 37:4 in the *Young Believer Bible*:

God will give you the things you truly desire. He takes joy in making your heart happy. But the secret to wanting the things God wants to give you is to first find your true happiness in your relationship with him. When you find joy in serving God, you will desire the things he wants to give you.

●●●

What do people in the world desire? Money? Brand-name clothes? Bigger and better toys? When you accepted Jesus as your Savior, he gave you new desires: the desire to get to know him better, the desire to serve him with your whole life, and the desire to tell others about him.

God wants your greatest desire to be to know him better. When you find joy in your relationship with him, he will give you godly desires. He may help you to serve him in special ways or give you a longing for something that he wishes to give you. And when you let go of what you want and choose what God desires for you, you'll experience greater joy than you can imagine. If you want what God wants, he will give you the things you long for!

These are some desires God has given me:

1. _____

2. _____

3. _____

Pray:

Thank God for loving you enough to give you the things you desire.

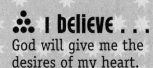

∴ I believe . . .
God will give me the
desires of my heart.

Mephibosheth trembled when the king's servant delivered the message: King David wanted to see him immediately.

I've been summoned before the king, he thought. *There could only be one reason he wants to see me.*

The young man had been in hiding since the day his father, Jonathan, died. He knew well that many times when a king died, the new king always killed the remaining family members so no one could take his crown. Mephibosheth looked down at his worthless feet. He had been five years old when they had fled the palace. His nurse had dropped him as she ran, crippling both his feet. Running from King David now was not an option for him.

Hours later Mephibosheth bowed before the king. He fought the horror welling up inside. But King David's words shocked and amazed him.

"Don't be afraid!" the king said. "I've asked you to come so that I can be kind to you because of my vow to your father, Jonathan."

The king went on to say he was giving Mephibosheth the land that had belonged to his grandfather Saul and was assigning servants to work the land. On top of that, the king invited him to eat at his table like one of his own sons. (See 2 Samuel 4:4; 9:1-13; and 19:24-30 in the *Young Believer Bible.*)

Check out 2 Samuel 22:51 in the *Young Believer Bible:*

In this song of David, he's praising God. He says God has given him great victories and shown him unfailing kindness. David showed his thankfulness for God's kindness by acting kindly toward others.

●●●

Kindness is acting in love. A kind person sees the needs of others and looks for ways to help them. How can you show others kindness?

One way you can show kindness is through your words. The Bible says an encouraging word cheers up others (see Proverbs 12:25). Another way you can show kindness is by your actions, by treating others the way you'd like to be treated. When you look for ways to show kindness to others, God will help you to do it.

These are three kind things I can do for someone today:

1. _____

2. _____

3. _____

Pray:
Ask God to make you kind and compassionate.

∴ I believe . . .
God's kindness helps me to be kind to others.

Do you still love playing in the mud? It's okay to admit it. People of all ages enjoy slopping around in the cool goo. You've probably even seen adults diving around playing mud football or volleyball. Or maybe you've seen mud racing on television.

What was your favorite thing to make out of mud? Mud pies? Mud angels? Mud mountains?

The great thing about mud is that it's so easy to make. It just takes a little water, a little dirt, and—*presto!*—you have mud.

Have you ever made a mud slide? It's great. All you need is a slight incline that leads into some water, like a stream or a lake. You jump in the water and start splashing it onto the ground. Then you hop out of the water, sit down at the top of the hill, and slide right in! If you use enough water and go down enough times, you can make a superfast slide. Oh, mud is great.

Check out Genesis 2:7 in the *Young Believer Bible:*

This verse talks about how God made people. God formed humans from the dust on the ground and breathed life into us.

• • •

As amazing as any human building project can be, it doesn't compare to what God can accomplish with mud. Although the Bible doesn't say that God used water to make people out of the dust, it's a good guess that he might have. Dust doesn't hold together very well. Mud does. Perhaps God used a little water to make humans in his image. It's kind of neat to picture God making us out of mud. Of course, since God can do anything, he could've done it without water too.

But in the New Testament, Jesus definitely uses mud to heal a blind man. The book of John says Jesus spit on some dirt, rubbed it in a blind man's eyes, and when the man washed it off he could see.

Pray:

Praise God that he can use ordinary things like mud to do miracles.

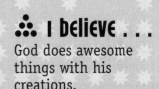

I believe . . .
God does awesome things with his creations.

Love can make you feel funny. Songs have been written about love. Poets have spent entire lifetimes putting words on paper about it. But it's hard to explain love.

You certainly love your parents. You love your pets, your brothers or sisters, and even your favorite food. But have you ever thought about what loving somebody means? Take some time to think about it now and write down some ideas.

1. I know I love somebody when: _____

2. I know I love somebody when: _____

3. I know I love somebody when: _____

4. I know I love somebody when: _____

Maybe you said you love somebody when you want to spend a lot of time with that person or you smile when you look at him or her or you want to do nice things for him or her. And all of those are good answers. Now think about how you can show God that you love him.

Check out Deuteronomy 6:4-5 in the *Young Believer Bible:*

These verses talk about how God's people—the Israelites—needed to look at God. God always has been and always will be the only true God. And they needed to love God with all their their heart, soul, and strength.

●●●

God's people, the Israelites, made a lot of mistakes, and a lot of times they didn't show God they loved him. They complained a lot. They forgot about the awesome miracles he performed (like parting the Red Sea). And they worshiped other things (such as the golden calf) instead of God.

The above verses tell you the basics of what God wants from his people—and that includes you! He wants you to know that he is the *only* God. And he wants you to love him with your actions, your thoughts, and your feelings.

Pray:

Commit to God that you're going to love him for the rest of your life.

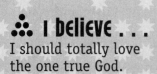

∴ I believe . . .
I should totally love
the one true God.

You've probably heard a lot about guardian angels. Stores sell dozens of angel figurines and pins. E-mails spread lots of stories about them. And angels are even the main characters of popular TV shows. With all the hype, what's the truth about guardian angels?

Which of the following do you think is true? Angels are

a. beings who have a glowing light on their heads at all times
b. beings God has assigned to protect me
c. humans who have died and are "earning their wings" by protecting me
d. people I know who have died and now watch over me

Angels are beings God has assigned to protect you. Before he created humans, God created angels. They act as his servants in heaven and on earth. Humans can never be angels, because they are different creations.

Check out Matthew 18:10 in the *Young Believer Bible:*
The angels of children have special access to God's throne. Kids are so important to God that their angels have first priority with him.

●●●

A lot of people focus on angels because it's neat to think that angels are protecting them. But angels are just servants of the true Protector: God. Guardian angels are evidence of God's love and care. Isn't it comforting to know that angels are looking out for you at all times?

Even though angels are amazing, they are only created beings. They're not gods. God created them, and he's the one who truly deserves your worship and adoration. So why not skip the guardian-angel pin and instead put your trust in your loving heavenly Father? He says he'll never leave you. The power of his protection is all you need.

Pray:
Thank God for his care and for his angels who protect you.

∴ I believe . . .
angels are God's servants who protect humans.

Studies have shown that the horse is one of the smartest animals. But do you think a horse knows that it's creating a huge field of crops when it's pulling a plow?

Let's see here . . .

Farmer: *Boy, it's hot out here plowing this field. But all of this hard work is worth it. Once the ground is tilled and the seed planted, this field will produce a good crop. That food will feed my family. And I can sell it to provide for our other needs.*

Horse pulling the plow: *Boy, it's hot. I wish the farmer would stop flicking me with that leather strap. At least it's keeping the flies off me. Some hay would be nice right now. Why do we keep going back and forth? I'm getting bored. I wish I had some hay. It seems like I'm always pulling this dumb thing. At least I get hay. I love hay. Mmmm, hay.*

The horse isn't thinking all that, but the point is that the horse only works for the farmer and has no idea about the farmer's plan. The farmer's best friend, on the other hand, would know what the farmer is thinking. That friend might even help the farmer when the crops are ready to be harvested.

Check out John 15:15 in the *Young Believer Bible:*

Jesus is talking to the disciples and tells them that he doesn't call them servants anymore. Instead he calls them friends. A servant doesn't know what the master is thinking. But just like you know and understand stuff about your friends, you can know and understand Jesus too.

●●●

Being Jesus' friend makes me want to serve him. Here are some ways I can do that:

1. Tell my friends about Jesus.

2. _____

3. _____

4. _____

5. _____

6. _____

When you're working for God, you're not like his horse—you're his friend. A horse, or servant, knows it's working but doesn't know why. Jesus said he tells you *everything* he knows about God. You know God's plans. You can read them in the Bible or receive guidance from the Holy Spirit because you're Jesus' friend.

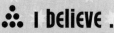

∴ I believe . . .
Jesus tells me all about his Father.

Pray:
Thank God that you're close enough to him to know his plans.

May 14

Question One: What do you do when your mom or dad calls you?

1. I pretend not to hear.
2. I call out to ask, "What do you want?"
3. I run the other way.
4. I say, "I'm not a dog, stop calling me."

If you're not looking to get punished, you probably answered number 2. Answering when somebody calls is the natural and right thing to do.

Question Two: What would your mom or dad like you to do when you're called?

1. Run up to them and ask, "What can I do for you?"
2. Start barking like a dog.
3. Hide under your bed.
4. Ignore the call.

Again, the answer is obvious. The best response is the first one—you run to your parent.

Acting politely means answering someone's call, which means movement. When you hear somebody calling, you move, right? Standing still isn't an option—that would mean ignoring the call. And if your parents are like most parents, they don't like to be ignored. Not paying attention to their call could mean big trouble.

How much more important is it, then, to answer God's calls with action?

Check out 1 Thessalonians 4:7 in the Young Believer Bible:

This verse explains that God does not call us to continue to do bad things. He calls us to change us. God wants you to live a holy life.

● ● ●

If you've prayed and asked Jesus into your life, then you've answered God's call. Now he wants you to follow him. But no one can follow Jesus while standing still. God wants his children to grow and be changed. Staying the same person and stuck in one place isn't an option. Holiness isn't natural. It means your life will change and move. It takes effort, commitment, and hard work. And most of all it takes God's help. But following God's call is always worth the effort.

Pray:

Tell God you're ready to move for him.

⁂ I believe . . .
when God calls, I
must move.

Young people have made some pretty amazing discoveries. Maybe one of the best happened more than 50 years ago in a desert in the Middle East.

A young goat herder was taking his goats to some water near the Dead Sea when he realized that one of his animals was missing. While he was climbing around on the cliffs to find his lost goat, he discovered some caves and threw rocks into the openings. When he threw a stone into one of the caves he heard a crashing sound.

He and a friend searched the cave and found some large clay jars that held some very old leather scrolls wrapped in linen cloth.

There are other versions to this story, but one thing is certain: the Dead Sea Scrolls (which is what this discovery is called) provide a lot of proof that the Bible is accurate. These scrolls date back to 150 years before Jesus was born and contain an entire copy of and some fragments from the book of Isaiah as well as writings from almost every book in the Old Testament.

Check out Proverbs 30:5 in the *Young Believer Bible:*

This verse says that every word of God is true. The Bible doesn't have any flaws.

●●●

Some people believe the Bible just because it's God's Word. God says it—and that's enough. Others need more evidence to believe. And that's okay too. God knows people are different. And for those people who need more proof, God has protected many ancient copies of his Word that prove it's accurate. In fact, more ancient pieces of the Bible exist than any other book! The Dead Sea Scrolls show the truth of the Old Testament, and there are even more original copies of the New Testament.

You can know that the Bible you read today is nearly exactly what people read thousands of years ago. And the God who guided people to write and copy down his Word is the same God who guides and loves you today.

Pray:

Tell God that you believe his Word is perfect.

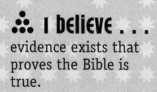

⁙ I believe . . .
evidence exists that
proves the Bible is
true.

Hudson Taylor tried to pray, but the words stuck in his mouth. Nineteen-year-old Hudson had come to pray for a sick woman and her starving children. As he tried to pray, the words wouldn't come because he knew he had to do something kind and unselfish. But the decision was so hard. Finally, Hudson reached into his pocket and gave the family his last silver coin, even though he had only one bowl of porridge left at home. As he ate his last meal, he remembered the Scripture that says, "If you help the poor, you are lending to the Lord—and he will repay you!" (Proverbs 19:17).

The very next day he received a package. In it was a gold coin worth ten times what the silver coin was worth. Taylor cried out triumphantly, "That's good interest! Invest in God's bank for twelve hours and it brings me this? That's the bank for me!"

Hudson learned that he could trust God in every area of his life. And he had many opportunities to trust God when he later went to China as a missionary. Civil war, fires, famine, and poor conditions gave the young missionary lots of reasons to pray. But through Hudson, many Chinese people accepted Jesus as their Savior.

Check out Romans 15:13 in the *Young Believer Bible:*

Because of the Holy Spirit in your life, you can choose to trust the Lord. When you trust in God, he fills you with joy, peace, and overflowing hope.

●●●

Do you trust God when things go wrong in your life? It may seem easier to try to solve problems on your own. But choosing not to depend on God's loving care means missing out on the blessings of seeing him provide.

Do you have something you need to trust God for today? Maybe your dad is out of a job. Maybe someone you're close to is sick. Or perhaps you don't know how you're going to pass a test at school. Whatever problem you're facing, let go and let God take care of it. When you do, joy and peace are sure to follow.

Pray:

Ask God to help you trust him.

I believe . . .
I can trust God with every area of my life.

Want to become a physics whiz? Here's a fun experiment you can do almost anywhere.

Step 1: Put on a pair of roller skates or in-line skates.

Step 2: Grab a football, basketball, or anything else that's fun to throw.

Step 3: Get a friend, some tape, a tape measure, and go outside to a flat surface.

Step 4: Use the tape to mark the ground at the front of your skates.

Step 5: Throw the ball to your friend. Be careful: you'll end up moving backward yourself. Let yourself roll naturally backward as far as you can. Mark where you end up.

Step 6: Have your friend go farther away, move to your original spot, and throw the ball again. Mark your new spot. Is it closer or farther away than your first throw?

Step 7: Continue to have your friend move closer and farther away and see how it affects how far you roll.

What did you learn?

_____

_____

_____

This experiment proves Isaac Newton's third law of motion, which says, "Every action has an equal and opposite reaction." The farther away your friend moved, the more force it took for you to throw the ball, which made you move farther backward.

Check out Isaiah 38:17-18 in the *Young Believer Bible:*
King Hezekiah loved God. He wrote to God after recovering from an illness that almost killed him. Hezekiah says it was good that he suffered because God's love kept him from destruction and God forgave all his sins.

● ● ●

Just as in physics where every action has a reaction, if your actions are good, you generally get positive reactions. If you study for a test, you'll have a better chance at getting a good grade. But the opposite is true too. Sinful actions cause negative reactions. If someone steals, he may get caught and have to pay a penalty. God sometimes allows us to feel the consequences of our sin.

The good news is that God is always ready to forgive you when you ask him—no matter what you did. Because Jesus paid the penalty for our sin, God forgives us and chooses to see us as if we had never sinned.

Pray:
Thank God that his forgiveness doesn't have limits.

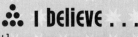 **I believe . . .**
there are consequences for sin, but God also offers forgiveness.

Rachel opened the box and looked inside. They were perfect! These were the roller blades she'd wanted for three months. She touched the hot pink laces and silver glitter stripes and sighed. Even though it felt like she'd been saving forever, Rachel still didn't have enough to buy the skates. And she probably wouldn't until her birthday—four months away!

Rachel already had skates, and they were in good condition. *But they're not cool like Phoebe's,* she thought. *These are just like Phoebe's.*

Rachel grabbed the box and found her mom in the cleaning supplies aisle.

"Mom, can you *please* buy these?" she whined. *"Please?"*

"Not today, sweetie," Mom answered. "I've told you before. You have to save your own money if you want those skates."

"But, Mom . . ."

"The answer is no."

Rachel stomped back to the sporting goods section and slammed the box on the shelf. "I never get *anything*," she grumbled. "I wish I had Phoebe's mom."

Check out Exodus 20:17 in the *Young Believer Bible:*

This is one of God's Ten Commandments. To covet something means to be jealous of and want something someone else has. This rule shows that it's important to be content with what God gives us.

● ● ●

Toys. Clothes. Video games. TV is full of commercials advertising all the latest stuff. Sometimes it may seem that you just can't live without those things. Plus if you see friends and kids at school who seem to have more than you do, it seems natural to become jealous.

It's easy to grow discontent and feel like you always need more. But God has given you everything you need: his presence, food, shelter, and clothes. Thinking about everything God has given you is a helpful way to chase those discontentment blues away.

I know God has given me a lot to be thankful for. When I think about these things, it's easier to be content. Here are some of my favorite gifts from God. Thank you Lord for

1. _____

2. _____

3. _____

Pray:

Ask God to help you to be content with what you have.

∴ I believe . . .
God wants me to be content with what I have.

Who's your biggest fan? Who's the person who supports you the most, the one who encourages you to do your best? Mom or Dad may be at the top of the list. They may come to your sports events, piano recitals, and school activities. Plus maybe they seem to think you can do anything.

Or maybe your best friend comes to mind. Your buddy is always there for you, cheering you on. Maybe you think of a teacher who believes in your abilities and encourages you to do your best. If you were ever accused of something bad, you could count on these people to come to your defense and believe in you. You'd probably want them there to tell others what a good person you are.

Parents, friends, and teachers may give you big-time support, but you have an even bigger fan. Jesus Christ is your number-one supporter. He believes in you 100 percent. In fact, he's the One who stands before God in your defense. Amazed? Keep reading.

Check out 1 John 2:1 in the *Young Believer Bible:*

If you know Jesus as your Savior, he gives you the power to say no to sin. But there will be times when you still choose to disobey God. When that happens, Jesus stands before the Father and reminds him that you are righteous because of Jesus' sacrifice. Jesus is the only one who can do this because he paid the price.

●●●

An advocate is a person who defends someone before a judge. That's what Jesus does for you. Even though you sin like everyone else, if you believe in Jesus as your Savior, he stands before God and defends you. And he's the best defender you could ask for, because he's the only one who can say, "I took the punishment for this person."

Earthly friends may support and even defend you, but only Jesus has the power to make you righteous before God. His blood was enough to cover your sin and give you back your relationship with God. When you're tempted to sin, remember your biggest supporter and make him proud by choosing the right action.

Pray:

Thank God for Jesus, who stands in your defense.

∴ I believe . . .
Jesus is my advocate.

May 20

How do NBA players get ready for the play-offs? They play a whole season, practice all the time, and develop into a strong team.

But what do you think would happen if the pregame prep went like this?

Mike: I think I'll play a game today. Hmm. What would I be good at? What about basketball? Yeah, I'll play basketball.

Joe: Me, too! And we're in luck. There's an NBA play-off game today; let's go join the team! I think we'll win!

Mike: Yeah, this will be great!

If an NBA team were put together this way, their games would be a joke. With no preparation, the players wouldn't stand a chance against the other teams. Instead, athletes put in hours and hours of training and practice before they ever compete. And when they're not on the court running drills and practicing free throws, they're in the gym building their muscles for strength and endurance. To be as good as Tracy McGrady, you have to train. And the Christian life isn't much different. Check it out!

Check out 1 Timothy 4:8 in the *Young Believer Bible:*

The apostle Paul reminds Timothy that, while physical training is good for some things, godliness is more important. A godly person will succeed in the areas that really matter—those areas that will last for eternity.

• • •

What's your favorite sport? Basketball? Hockey? Soccer? The New Testament often compares the Christian life to athletics. The apostle Paul was a bit like a personal trainer because he talked a lot about winning and preparing for competition.

Just as training for an athletic event is important, godliness takes practice too. How can you train to be godly? Reading God's Word each day is a good start. It's the ultimate playbook. Also, look for ways to practice doing the right thing, like obeying your parents and teachers and treating others with kindness. And when you see opportunities to be like Christ, take them! Make the goal! Take the shot! Score the touchdown! When you're exercising your spiritual muscles, you're guaranteed to win!

Pray:

Ask God to help you to train for godliness.

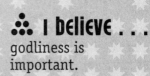

I believe . . .
godliness is
important.

May 21

Walk into a mall. Step into a bookstore. Flip on the television. Pop in a movie. Pick up a magazine. Listen to a CD. Go to a movie.

If you do any of the above activities, you can't help being bombarded by messages from the world. Do any of these beliefs sound familiar?

a. You have to hang with the right people.
b. You have to wear the right clothes.
c. Happiness comes from buying the newest products.
d. You need to grow up fast.
e. Your parents are out of touch.
f. There's no reason to listen to adults.

All right. Maybe these messages aren't blasted through the loudspeakers everywhere you go. But the world's messages are probably getting through to you in less obvious ways.

Maybe you like what you hear from popular music and movies. They certainly portray a cool image. The way the people look and the beat of the music can seem appealing. Some of what you hear may even sound okay.

But much of what the world says are lies that go against God's truth and his instructions. It's good to be careful about what you see and hear.

Check out Colossians 2:8 in the *Young Believer Bible:*

This verse says to watch out for ideas or images that pull you away from your relationship with Jesus Christ. Ideas based on human tradition and values of the world are often wrong. It's important to stick with what the Bible says is right.

●●●

We live in a faulty world. You've probably heard that sin entered the world when Adam and Eve gave in to temptation and ate the wrong fruit in the Garden of Eden. People's bad choices show up in wars, terrorist attacks, child abuse and neglect, and violence in the streets. But sin can also show up in the lyrics of a song or the images in a movie. God wants you as a believer to guard your mind. If you follow Jesus and his plans for your life, you won't get stuck in the world's wrong ideas.

Pray:
Ask God to show you when you're being pulled in the wrong way by the world's ideas—then get back to following him.

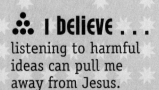

∴ I believe . . .
listening to harmful ideas can pull me away from Jesus.

May 22

My little brother is always bothering me. My parents want me to be nice to him, but it's so hard. What should I do?
Troubled Sister
Sister Bay, Wisconsin

Dear Troubled Sister,
Brothers can be wild creatures. They grunt. They burp. They make funny noises under their armpits. But somewhere deep down inside, you have to admit that you love 'em.

In the case of your problem, the solution is obvious. Your parents are right . . . again. (Doesn't that bug you?) Being nice to your brother is not an option. God asks you to get along.

Now have you ever thought about why your brother bothers you? Maybe, deep down inside, he loves you too. This information doesn't solve your problem—but it might help you understand the little guy. The good thing about understanding is that you can put your knowledge to work. Try spending some time with your brother. Find out the stuff he likes to do. If your brother feels like he's not left out of your life, he may stop bugging you.

Check out 1 John 4:21 in the *Young Believer Bible:*

This verse states very clearly that if we love God, we also must love our brothers and sisters. But it's not just talking about our families (which we *do* have to love). We're also commanded to love other people—our brothers and sisters in Christ.

●●●

Have you ever noticed that some people are hard to love? That bully on the playground—could anybody love him? Or how about the girl who's always making up stuff about other people and spreading rumors? Definitely unlovable? Well, here's the thing . . . God loves them, and he wants you to love them too.

Sometimes I get really annoyed when people bug me. I can think of a million reasons for being frustrated. But instead I'm going to write down some of the good qualities of one of the people who annoys me most:

1. _____

2. _____

3. _____

Next time I see this person, I'll remember to mention something about him or her that I like.

Pray:

Ask God to help you love the brothers and sisters in your family and in God's family.

I believe . . .
can help me love
ple.

Being president of the United States (or any country for that matter) would be cool. You could go to bed whenever you wanted. You'd have lots of people keeping you up-to-date on world events. You'd be a very powerful person! (Now don't go getting all power hungry!)

What are some things you'd do as president?

_____

_____

_____

The president has lots of great "toys." All right, so they're not toys, but they are powerful. If you were president, you'd have a private airplane to fly you all over the world. You'd have a helicopter to take you back and forth from the airport. You'd even have lots of bodyguards to protect you. But one of the best things you'd have is a phone that linked you to all the other world leaders.

Anytime you had an important question, you could pick up the phone and immediately be connected to the other most powerful people in the world. You wouldn't even have to dial. You'd just grab the receiver and talk. How much fun would that be?

Check out Ephesians 2:18 in the
Young Believer Bible:
This verse means that you have direct contact with God through the Holy Spirit.

●●●

Even though you're not president of a country (although someday you could be), you still have an awesome way to communicate. It's even better than the president's special phone.

Because you believe in Jesus, you have the Holy Spirit in your life. And the Holy Spirit talks to God the Father for you. The Holy Spirit can always give you guidance on any problem. The Spirit's a 24-hour-a-day, 7-day-a-week connection to the most powerful being in the universe! What do you think of that, Mr. President?

And you don't have to wait for an emergency to be connected to God. The Holy Spirit wants you to constantly depend on him. No obstacle is too big and no problem is too small for the Holy Spirit to handle.

Pray:
Praise God for sending his Spirit so you can always be connected to him.

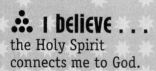

∴ I believe . . .
the Holy Spirit
connects me to God.

Question: When an actor is preparing to play a part in a movie or a play, what is the first thing he does?
Answer: He memorizes his lines.

If that actor went out on stage without knowing his lines, he would end up looking pretty silly. Learning his lines gives him a foundation for playing his role. Without them he would have no idea what to say, so he carefully studies his part in order to do his best playing his character. The more he thinks about his lines, the more accurately he plays the character. In the end, if he does his job, his audience will also understand the character.

Your life isn't a play or a movie, but God has given you a script: the Bible. It tells you who you are and how to live. And when you live by the script, others will see the character of Christ in you. But you won't be able to play your part if you don't know the lines. God's Word is the script that shows how to live life God's way, and Joshua recognized the importance of knowing it well.

Check out Joshua 1:8 in the *Young Believer Bible:*

God told Joshua to think about Scripture and "meditate on it," which means to study it. That way he would know how to live for God. Plus memorizing Scripture brings a reward: success!

• • •

There are many good reasons to memorize Scripture. First of all, when you memorize God's Word, you're "hiding it in your heart," so you don't have to have a Bible with you to remember what God says. Also, when people ask you about what you believe, you're prepared to answer them. Plus when you memorize Scripture, you can think about it throughout your day, which helps you understand it better.

Because I want to have God's Word handy when I need it, I'm going to memorize some verses. I'll start by memorizing the verses below. Then I'll find some of my own favorites to hide in my heart. I'll learn the script so I can play the part God has prepared for me!

Romans 3:23

John 14:6

1 Corinthians 15:3-4

Hebrews 3:14

Proverbs 3:5-6

Pray:
Ask God to help you hide his Word in your heart.

 **I believe . . .**
I should memorize Scripture and think about it often.

May 25

Some people are different.

No, this isn't about your weird cousin Louie who likes to mix milk and ketchup and drink it . . . although that *is* pretty different.

This is about special kids who are born with extra challenges to overcome. Everybody's born with obstacles in their lives. All babies are helpless at birth. But some babies are born without the ability to see. Others can't hear or are missing a finger or an arm. Still other kids will always be behind mentally.

It's sad that kids who are different tend to get picked on by other children. Maybe you've heard other kids use terms like *retard* and *mental*. Teasing people for things they can't change is cruel. And it's a shame that some kids can be so unkind.

Maybe you'd like to change the people around you. When other kids say those names or tease people, you can stand up for the kids being teased. You may not be able to stop the name-calling, because we can't change other people's bad behavior. But standing up for what is right is always the correct decision.

Check out 1 Timothy 4:4 in the *Young Believer Bible:*

This verse says everything—yes, *everything*—God created is good. Nothing he created should be rejected.

• • •

If you've ever gotten to know special-needs kids, then you've already figured out they can be some of the most loving and fun kids to be around. Unfortunately, many people judge them or are afraid of them without getting to know them.

If more kids knew the joy, friendship, and love you can experience in a relationship with a special-needs child, then there would be a lot less name-calling. Everybody was created in God's image. Special-needs kids have a lot to offer. But sometimes people need to find that out for themselves.

Pray:

Thank God for creating all the different people he made. Then do your best to get to know them.

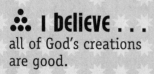

I believe . . .
all of God's creations
are good.

A lot of people say they believe in God. Of course, it's easy to say something and not mean it. Like when you tell your Aunt Bessie that you enjoy her lemon coconut bars with the graham-cracker-and-tuna-fish crust. (Well, most people probably wouldn't like those. Though eating one *is* more enjoyable than getting your teeth drilled by the dentist.)

Because it's so simple to say something without meaning it, what's the best way to tell if somebody means what she says? Often actions prove what someone says.

A magazine recently did a survey on the Internet and asked people if they believed in God. Almost nine out of ten people answered that they believed in God, which sounds great. Sometimes it can seem like you're not surrounded by a lot of Christians. But listen to this: the same survey showed that only a little more than three out of ten people attended church.

What happened to the other 60 percent of people who said they believed in God? Don't they want to go to God's house, worship him, and grow in their relationship with him? Guess not. Their actions don't back up their words.

Check out Hebrews 10:25 in the *Young Believer Bible:*

This verse says to not stop meeting with other people who believe in Jesus. When Christians get together, they can encourage each other.

●●●

Saying you believe in God is easy—you just need to move your lips. Going to church can be difficult—you have to wake up early, get ready, hop in the car, and drive across town. But the Bible is clear: We shouldn't give up gathering together with other believers.

Going to church not only allows people to see that you're a Christian (although it doesn't make you a Christian—only a relationship with Jesus does that), it also helps you grow in your faith.

Here are some of my favorite things about church:

_____

_____

_____

Next time you're dragging yourself out of bed on a Sunday morning, remember that you can encourage other kids at church to be better followers of Jesus as they encourage you.

Pray:

Tell God you're going to continue gathering with other Christians.

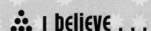

⁘ I believe . . .
I should get together with other Christians at church.

May 27

You're late for baseball practice. As you jump out of your mom's minivan and slam the door behind you, you catch your finger. *Ouch!*

Nothing hurts like slamming your finger in a door. Your finger may seem like a small part of your body, but when it's hurt, your whole body knows it! And think of all the things you can't do because one finger is out of commission: throw a baseball, draw a picture, play the piano.

Yep. That finger is pretty important. It may seem like your eyes or your heart is more important, but even though those are valuable body parts, some tasks require fingers!

In the Bible, the church is compared to a human body. Believers work together just like the parts of the body, and God makes it clear that every part is important. Each part needs the others to function.

Check out 1 Corinthians 12:12-14 in the *Young Believer Bible:*

The apostle Paul explains that the body is one unit, but it has many different parts. Each part has its own special purpose, and when all the parts work together, the body performs perfectly. It's the same way with believers in Christ. Each one has an important job. And every person is needed for the body of Christ to function properly.

●●●

If you were playing a video game, would you hold the controller with your feet? Not if you want to win! Feet aren't good for making small, controlled movements. At the same time, you wouldn't run a marathon on your hands. Each part of the body has a different function.

Although Jesus doesn't live on the earth anymore, his Spirit bonds Christians together. But each member of Christ's body has a different job. Some are good at teaching God's Word. Other believers are skilled at helping people. Still others are able to spend many hours in prayer.

What are you good at? Think of ways you can use your talents to serve God and other believers.

Pray:

Ask God to help you serve in the body of Christ.

 **I believe . . .**

I have a special job as part of the body of Christ.

Lenny was a liar. He loved to make up stories. He told Sarah that his dad was an astronaut. He whispered to Monica that his mom invented juice boxes. Lenny told Michael that he had a pet boa constrictor that was eighteen feet long and ate rabbits!

When the teacher asked Lenny to turn in his homework, he said his cat ate it and then his boa constrictor accidentally ate his cat. When he was late to school one day, he said the family's car broke down so he had to ride in their helicopter and parachute in. After the teacher sent him to the principal, Lenny told her his great-grandpa was a paratrooper in World War II and taught him how to sky dive.

Poor Lenny. He told so many lies that he forgot how to speak the truth. He even forgot to remember what he said. He told Rick he'd play basketball with him after school, and he promised Ryan that he'd join the after-school chess team. But he didn't do either. He just walked home after school every day and watched cartoons.

If Lenny told you something, would you believe him? Probably not, because Lenny's words are meaningless.

Check out Numbers 23:19 in the Young Believer Bible:

This verse says God is not like people. He doesn't lie; he doesn't change his mind. He always comes through on his promises.

●●●

You've lived long enough to realize people will let you down. Friends don't always keep their promises. Parents change their minds. Coaches don't always do what they say. And that can hurt sometimes.

God, on the other hand, isn't human. He doesn't lie. If you read something about him in the Bible, you can know it's true and trust that God will come through on his promises. And he promises you a lot of things in the Bible.

These are some of God's great promises:

1. _____
2. _____
3. _____

As I learn new things about God, I'll keep adding them to my list. I know he'll always come through for me.

Pray:

Thank God that you can always count on his promises.

∴ I believe . . .
God is totally believable and trustworthy.

Have you ever heard the phrase "There is strength in numbers"? It means that the more people are working together, the better chance there is for success.

Do you know a single military general who would go into battle alone? No way! That would be foolish. He would definitely be defeated. But if he goes into battle with a whole unit of soldiers, he has a much greater chance of victory.

Have you ever seen a single basketball player face an entire team? Probably not. That guy wouldn't stand a chance. What about a firefighter fighting a huge blaze by himself? No, it takes many firefighters to put out a major fire. One man alone couldn't do it.

Many areas in life require more than one person for success. It's the same with your spiritual life. One Christian alone is too weak to do the things God asks. But a believer who looks for the support of other believers can do many great things!

Check out Proverbs 27:17 in the Young Believer Bible:

A good Christian friend or two can help you become a stronger believer in Jesus Christ. When iron is rubbed together, it gets smoother and sharper. And the same thing will be true of you when you hang out with good Christian friends.

●●●

Do you have a tendency to say "I can do it myself"? That may seem like a brave attitude, but it's also a bit foolish. God designed people to work together and take care of one another.

Spending time with other believers is called *fellowship*. Think about Christian fellowship as a fire. When you spend time with other believers you're feeding the fire. As you see Christ in others, you become more excited about the things of God, and the flame grows bright and warm.

Now imagine if you were removed from that fire. It'd be easy to grow cold. To be all that God wants you to be, you must have the support of other believers. You'd be smart to think of ways to spend time around other Christians. With their help, you can do great things for God!

Pray:

Thank God for providing fellow Christians to help you live for him.

⸫ I believe . . .

I will be a stronger Christian if I spend time with other believers.

May 30

Do you ever get in trouble with your parents? Ridiculous question, right? Every kid messes up at times and causes his parents to become upset.

Maybe you forgot to take out the trash. Perhaps you went outside to play before cleaning your room. Or did you ever play baseball close to the house (even though your mom said not to) and hit a home run right into the living-room window? Oh wait, maybe that wasn't you.

The point is, it's impossible to go through life without getting in trouble with your parents every now and then. And what happens when you get in trouble? Parents can be very creative: forbidding TV for a week, grounding you for a couple of days, giving you extra chores. The options are endless.

But while you're being disciplined, do you think your parents ever stop loving you? Be honest. Your parents may be disappointed by your actions, but their love doesn't stop.

Check out Romans 8:38-39 in the *Young Believer Bible:*

This passage is one of the best at explaining how much God loves you. It says that nothing—not death, demons, nor deep depths—can separate you from the love of God that is in Jesus Christ.

●●●

It's impossible to cause God's love to change. All of us do things that disappoint God at times. God, like your parents, disciplines his children. His discipline is always good for you, although it may not feel like it. You may even feel as if God is far away from you and doesn't care. At those times it's especially important to remember God's love is dependable and true. Nothing can separate you from him.

Pray:

Thank God for his never failing love.

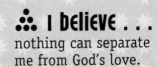

∴ I believe . . .
nothing can separate
me from God's love.

May 31

"Do you smell what The Rock is cookin'?"

If you've ever seen World Wrestling Entertainment, you may know what that means. The Rock is one of the most popular professional wrestlers on television. His athletic body and strong personality have made him not only a world-famous wrestler, but a rich movie star too.

He's really a pretty good actor on the screen and on the wrestling mat. Professional wrestlers practice their moves and plan the matches beforehand. Still, even though it's planned out ahead of time, for some reason professional wrestling is very popular—and dangerous.

Its athletes get injured all the time, sometimes seriously. And kids have died imitating the things they see on TV. That's pretty scary.

But did you know The Rock copied his name from a much stronger, much more powerful person who had the name thousands of years ago? It's true. Just pick up the Bible and see how many times God is called the Rock.

Check out 1 Samuel 2:2 in the *Young Believer Bible:*

This is from a prayer that Hannah, Samuel's mom, said to God. The verse says that nobody is holy like God. God is the true Rock.

●●●

There are many qualities of a rock that help me understand why people would see God as the Rock. Here are some of those qualities:

1. _____

2. _____

3. _____

Hannah said there is no rock like God—and the wrestler named The Rock doesn't even come close. God could sneeze and blow The Rock all the way to Pluto. (Not that he would, because he loves everybody. But God *could*.)

Rocks are strong. They last forever. You can build a powerful house using rocks. Rocks are a great place to find shelter during a storm. You probably thought of a lot of other things too. God will always support you and never let you down. He's your Rock.

Pray:

Tell God you're going to count all of his rocklike qualities.

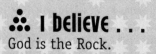

∴ I believe . . .
God is the Rock.

"You can't teach an old dog new tricks."

Ever heard that saying? Do you think it's true for all dogs? What if you had a superintelligent dog? Let's say your dog could answer questions, such as "What's on top of a house?" *Roof!* or "What does sandpaper feel like?" *Ruff!* or "Who calls penalties during a football game?" *Ref!*

That would be a really smart dog. That dog probably could be taught new tricks no matter how old it was. You could teach it to sit up, lie down, shake hands, give a high five, and spin around on its hind legs. How cool!

A lot of old dogs probably have the ability to learn new tricks. But because of that saying, people just don't try to teach them. That's too bad. The world may be missing out on a lot of undiscovered skills in those dogs. If they were taught new tricks, they could probably start a whole old-dog circus.

Or maybe that saying is true. Perhaps old dogs are afraid to try new things. Maybe they figure that if they learned something new they'd be too tired to try it out.

Check out Hosea 10:12 in the *Young Believer Bible:*

In this verse the writer encourages God's people to "plow up the hard ground of your hearts, for now is the time to seek the Lord." And if they do that, Hosea promises that God will shower his righteousness on them.

●●●

What kind of dog are you? Are you stuck doing the same things for God, or are you willing to try new things? God wants you to tap into all of your potential. That means he wants you to keep learning and doing new things for him. If there are things in your life that are not positive (like spending too much time playing video games or watching movies, or treating your friends and family badly), he wants you to "plow up the hard ground" and hand those things over to him. It's hard to break out of a bad habit. Obeying God and trying new things for him isn't always easy. But the results are worth the effort.

Here are some areas of "hard ground" (bad habits) in my life that I want to give to God:

1. _____

2. _____

3. _____

Pray:

Ask God to help you keep the "ground" soft in your heart so you're ready to follow new directions from him.

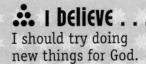

⁘ I believe . . .
I should try doing
new things for God.

Here's a weird question: Who's your favorite prophet from the Bible? Prophets prepared the way for Jesus, the Messiah. Here are a few you may know about:

Elijah was pretty cool. He was a guy who had a contest against the prophets of the false god Baal. When they couldn't make wood catch on fire by praying to Baal, Elijah dumped a bunch of water on the wood, prayed to God, and God consumed the whole thing with fire. Elijah also ran faster than King Ahab's chariot.

Elisha also did some amazing things. He raised a boy from the dead and helped a poor woman by miraculously making a few drops of oil last a long time.

And who can forget **Daniel**? It was awesome enough when God brought him out of the lions' den alive, but God also gave Daniel the ability to tell the meaning of King Nebuchadnezzar's dream even when the king couldn't remember it.

Jonah tried to run from God and got swallowed by a big fish. He had to learn his lesson the hard way. He made mistakes—don't we all?—but he's definitely memorable.

Isaiah was also an impressive guy. He wrote a big book in the Bible, and many of the things he predicted came true in his lifetime.

Now who do you think Jesus said was the greatest prophet?

Check out Matthew 11:11 in the *Young Believer Bible:*

Jesus says that there has never been anyone born who was greater than John the Baptist.

●●●

Sometimes it's hard to think about John the Baptist being great. He ate bugs, wore animal skins, and spent a lot of time baptizing people in a mucky river. But Jesus said nobody is greater than John. John's father, Zechariah, might have the answer as to why his son is so important. In Luke 1:76, Zechariah says John will prepare the way for the Lord. He will tell people how to be saved through Jesus' forgiveness of their sins.

While it might be hard for you to be swallowed and spit up by a fish (like Jonah) or run faster than a chariot (like Elijah), you can do exactly what John the Baptist did. You can help prepare the way for Jesus' return by telling others about the salvation he offers.

Pray:

Tell God you want to be like John the Baptist and tell others about God.

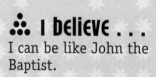

∴ I believe . . .

I can be like John the Baptist.

I recently had a really bumpy airplane ride where I thought we were going to crash. Now I'm afraid to ride in airplanes. My family has tickets for another trip next month. Can you help me get over my fear?
Scared
Tremblestown, Ireland

Dear Scared,
Being trapped in an uncomfortable situation is frightening. Whether it's being caught on a bumpy plane ride, stuck in an elevator, or enclosed in a car during a bad storm, it's scary to feel helpless.

But God doesn't want you to stay scared. He wants the best for his children. He knows you won't be able to overcome your fear with a snap of your fingers. But he does want you to rely on his promises of protection (they're all through the Bible) and the people he's put in your life (your parents, youth pastor, and friends) to help you beat your fears.

Talk to a parent about how airplanes scare you. They may have some good advice. Then pray to God and ask for courage and protection before you get on the plane next month. With prayer and trust in God's promises, and by talking through your fears with your parents, you'll see there's no reason to remain afraid.

Check out Isaiah 43:1 in the *Young Believer Bible:*

This verse says God has ransomed you. A ransom is a price paid to set a prisoner free. Fear can be a prison, just like sin is a prison that keeps us from God's peace. But if you are God's child, there's no reason to be afraid.

●●●

Do you know what's the all-time scariest thing? It's being separated from God forever. That's what happens to people who never ask Jesus to forgive their sins—they go to hell. So if you've prayed and asked Jesus into your life, there's really no reason to be scared of anything. He's ransomed you, and he tells you not to be afraid.

Sure, things may frighten you. God doesn't expect you to pretend to be brave when you're trembling on the inside. That's when he wants you to talk with a parent and ask him to help you overcome your fears.

Pray:

Thank God for taking away the greatest fear, and ask him to help you not be afraid in other situations.

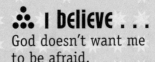

∴ I believe . . .
God doesn't want me
to be afraid.

June 4

Picture yourself sitting on your bike and staring down a hill at a nine-foot ramp. Twenty feet separate that jump and a six-foot landing ramp. You check your protective gear, say a quick prayer, and yank your bike into action. You pedal as fast as you can and hit 25 mph as you launch off the ramp. The specially designed cycle seems weightless below your floating body as you lift off the seat, kick out your legs, spin around the bike, and end up back in the saddle to execute a perfect landing.

Chad Herrington doesn't have to imagine this scene. As a top freestyle BMX rider, he's experienced it. He's also experienced his share of painful injuries.

"There was one crash when I was doing a back flip and 360-degree spin at the same time, and I ended up breaking nine bones and shattering two fingers," he says.

But Chad says that emotional injuries hurt as much, or more, than physical pain.

"In the past, I'd put my faith in friends or family and got nothing in return but sorrow," Chad explains. "But when I put my faith in my personal Savior, he has never let me down."

Check out Proverbs 18:24 in the Young Believer Bible:

This verse says that not all friends are good friends. It's best to develop a really close friendship with one or two people who stick by you, especially if one of those friends is your best buddy of all: Jesus Christ.

●●●

Having a lot of friends can seem like a great idea. But it can be hard to be a good friend to everybody. You'd have to be the Energizer Bunny to meet all your friends' needs and spend lots of time with all of them. And eventually your batteries would run down. Plus friends sometimes let you down. Have you ever had a friend say she'd meet you at the mall, then not show up?

God always shows up. And when he makes a promise, you can count on him to come through for you. He wants to be your best friend. Will you choose him?

Pray:

Tell God that you want to remain close to him.

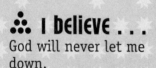

∴ I believe . . .
God will never let me down.

Have you ever seen a science-fair volcano? To make one, you first build a papier-maché mountain. Then you fill the inside with vinegar and baking soda, and the mixture begins to fizz and bubble. It rises and rises until finally it overflows and runs everywhere—similar to a real volcanic explosion.

Anger can be the same as the lava in a volcano. It may start with a small feeling of annoyance, but if you let it bubble and fizz inside, it grows and grows until—*BOOM!*—an explosion.

When you think about it, the lava bubbling inside a volcano isn't dangerous. It's not until it flows over that it causes problems. It's the same way with anger. Feeling angry is a natural emotion. But if you let your anger build up and explode, that's when it can cause harm to others and to you as well.

Check out Psalm 4:4 in the *Young Believer Bible:*

David had lots of reasons to be angry: his best friend's dad was trying to kill him, he was being forced to leave the palace, his son turned against him later in life. But David had some good advice about being angry: He said don't sin when you're angry. It's a good idea to deal with anger each day before going to bed.

●●●

How can you control anger? Writing down how you're feeling or counting to ten before you speak may help you avoid an angry outburst. You also have a choice to walk away from a situation that is making you angry.

Most importantly, don't let anger grow inside. When you're angry about something, take steps to deal with whatever's making you mad. Talk to a parent and ask God to help you have a right attitude.

Think about some things that make you angry. Perhaps you get mad when Mom asks you to do your chores or someone at school calls you a name or a younger sibling ruins your stuff. Make your own list. Write down what makes you angry and why. Then ask God to help you control your anger in each area.

I'm angry about . . . because . . .

Pray:

Ask God to help you control your anger.

⁝ I believe . . .
God wants me to
control my anger.

Have you ever noticed that kids eat a bag of M&M's differently? Some kids gobble them down a handful at a time. They act like there's an unlimited supply. It's as if they're not even tasting the candy as it's sliding down their throats. And before they know it, the bag is empty.

Other kids start eating their M&M's really fast, like the first group. But as they near the end of the bag, they start eating one at a time—so they last a little longer.

Still other kids dump the whole bag in front of them and sort the candies by color. These are the kids who like to save their favorite color for last. They might even give away their least favorite color to a friend.

The last group of kids eats their M&M's slowly, very s-l-o-w-l-y. They put one candy in their mouths at a time and let it rest and melt on their tongue. They savor each flavor. They'll even tell you each color has a specific taste. These kids get the most enjoyment and benefit from each M&M.

How do you eat your M&M's?

Check out Psalm 90:12 in the *Young Believer Bible:*
In this verse the psalmist asks God to help him be wise with how he spends his time.

●●●

Today's devo isn't about eating candy (although you may be craving a little chocolate). It's about making the most of the time God has given you. Do you live your life like the first group of M&M eaters—acting as if your days on earth will never be gone? Or are you like the last group, getting the most out of each day?

God's Word is clear: Every day should be treated like a gift from God. Enjoy each moment. Be careful with each day. Think about your daily actions. Do your best to make sure your choices please him.

Pray:
Ask God to help you live each day to its fullest.

⋰ I believe . . .
God wants me to make the most of my time on earth.

Technology can be great. CDs play perfect sounding music. DVDs show theater-quality movies. But your parents can probably remember a time when CDs and DVDs didn't exist. Your great-grandma was most likely born before televisions were invented. That's weird to think about, huh?

It's amazing when you realize that many common things in your home were created not that long ago. In fact, just a little more than 25 years ago, the first videocassette recorder (VCR) hit stores on this day—June 7, 1975. The Sony Betamax recorded and played tapes that were smaller than today's VCR tapes. And people were amazed that they could record and play shows from their televisions. (It's surprising how easily some people are entertained.) The first VCR cost $995, but now you can buy a machine for around $60.

Today people take VCRs for granted. They don't think it's so great to record shows from television—not when you can burn CDs and DVDs on computers. VCRs are old news. Old technology. Everybody wants the newest, the latest, the best. The old stuff bores them.

Check out Lamentations 3:22-23 in the Young Believer Bible:

These verses say the Lord's love never ends. He protects you. It's like God's love and compassion are new for you every day, because his faithfulness is great.

●●●

If you've been a Christian for a while, it may be easy for you to think that God is boring (like a VCR). He may seem like old news. Been there, done that. But when God looks at you and thinks about his relationship with you, he's never bored. He's always excited when you pray and think of him. His compassion for you is new every morning. Does knowing that the Creator of the universe is that excited about you make you equally excited about your relationship with him?

Pray:

Ask God to help you stay excited about your relationship with him. Tell him you don't want the excitement to wear off.

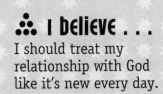

⁛ I believe . . .
I should treat my relationship with God like it's new every day.

June 8

Four people were flying in a twin-engine plane over Alaska: a pilot, a wealthy business-man, a father, and his son—who was a Boy Scout.

Well, everything was going great until one of the plane's engines started to sputter and stopped working.

"Uh, oh," the pilot said. "But as long as we have one engine, we'll be okay."

A few minutes later, the other engine quit.

"I'm sorry, guys," the pilot said, turning around. "Both engines are gone, and that's not the worst of it. The bad news is we only have three parachutes, and I'm using one of them."

With that, he grabbed a parachute and jumped out of the plane.

The businessman turned to the father and son and said, "I'm the best businessman on earth. Thousands of people rely on me. In fact, I'm one of the greatest men on the planet, so I need one of those parachutes."

He quickly grabbed one and jumped out of the plane.

The father turned to his son and said, "Son, I've lived a good life. I'm so proud of you. I want you—"

"Don't worry, Dad," the son interrupted. "It's okay. The so-called greatest man in the world just jumped out of the airplane with my backpack."

Check out Matthew 20:26-28 in the Young Believer Bible:

In these verses Jesus says whoever wants to be great must follow his example of serving others. Jesus came to serve and give his life to pay for everybody's sins.

● ● ●

Can you think of anyone who seems to think that being great means having a lot of money or becoming famous or having a lot of power? Jesus said being great only comes from being a servant. That's a hard concept to understand, but Jesus proved it with his life. God's Son was the greatest person to ever walk the planet, yet he served others and was never rich.

Here are some ways I could serve other people:

1. Person: _____   Service: _____

2. Person: _____   Service: _____

3. Person: _____   Service: _____

Now I'll commit to following through with my ideas.

Pray:
Tell God you want to follow Jesus' ultimate example of greatness by being a servant to others.

∴ I believe . . .
serving makes me great.

More than 11.5 million kids move with their families every year, which takes a lot of packing, unpacking, and cardboard boxes. Maybe your family moved recently or is about to move. How does that make you feel?

A lot of kids are sad when they move. They have to leave behind friends and familiar places. Other kids get scared about moving. They don't like change and want everything to stay the same.

Change isn't easy, but it can be exciting. God can use change to help you grow stronger in your relationship with him. He can teach you to depend on him more. It's good to focus on the positives in times of change. Here are a few good things about moving:

a. You have the opportunity to meet new people and visit new places.
b. You can still stay in touch with old friends through letters, e-mail, and phone calls.
c. God will be with you at your new home.

So while change may make you sad or fearful, remember what's most important and what will never change: God's love for you.

Check out Deuteronomy 31:6 in the Young Believer Bible:

This verse comes at a point of big change for God's people. Moses tells them that he's not taking them into the Promised Land; instead, Joshua will lead them. This may have scared some people, but Moses quickly takes away their fears by telling them not to be afraid because God is going with them and he will never leave them.

●●●

A few things in life remain the same: your parents' love for you, the sun rising in the east, flowers blooming in the spring, puppies being cute, ice cream tasting cold, rocks sinking in water.

These are some other things that never change:

1. _____
2. _____
3. _____

Did you write down "God's presence in my life"? That's one of the best things that never changes. Once you pray and ask Jesus into your life, he'll never leave you. And he'll always be there to help you through times of change.

Pray:

Thank God for being somebody you can always trust to be there for you.

∴ I believe . . .
God is with me in times of change.

June 10

Have you ever been to a family reunion? Your grandparents are there. You play games with cousins. Aunts tell you how much you've grown. And that wacky uncle pulls out quarters from behind your ears. Family reunions can be a lot of fun. You get to spend time with the people who are closest to you—your family.

Can you imagine if there were millions of people in your family—and they lived in every country in the world? What if all those people got together? That would be one big family reunion!

In the Bible, God describes those who believe in him as a family. And someday there's going to be an enormous family reunion in heaven. At that time you'll meet brothers and sisters in God's family whom you never even knew you had. They'll be from throughout history and from every country. What an exciting day!

Check out John 1:12-13 in the *Young Believer Bible:*

Everyone who believes in Jesus Christ as the perfect sacrifice for sin becomes a child of God. But becoming a member of God's family is not a result of physical birth. When you believe in Jesus as your Savior, you are born a second time. It is your spiritual birth.

●●●

Being part of God's family means you're totally accepted. You're also loved and protected. And you have many brothers and sisters. Even though some of them live in other countries and you'll never meet them on earth, someday you'll worship God together in heaven.

The Bible also says that Jesus is the firstborn among many brothers and sisters (Romans 8:29). That means that Jesus is your brother—if you've accepted him, you share the same Father and you'll be in heaven with him someday. What could be more wonderful than being a member of God's family?

Here's a list of the people I know who aren't part of God's family yet. Because I want them to know Jesus, I'll think of ways to tell them about the hugest family in the world!

1. _____

2. _____

3. _____

Pray:

Thank God for making you part of his family.

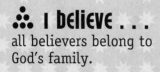

⁘ I believe . . .

all believers belong to God's family.

Who do you know better than anybody else in the whole world? Write down his or her name:

_____

Maybe you wrote down one of your parents, a best friend, a grandparent, or a sibling. Think of all the great times you've had with that person. Relaxing vacations, talking under the stars, playing games, sharing secrets—all of these things can create special memories.

But does the person you know best ever say something that totally surprises you? Of course! No matter how well you know somebody, there's still so much more that you don't know. Maybe you haven't even scratched the surface. You might know your special person's favorite color, where he or she grew up, parents' names, eye color, and ticklish spot. But do you know his or her dreams in life, what he or she hopes to accomplish for God, what he or she likes to eat?

Every time you talk to the person you know best you can learn something new. People are complex. They're not always easy to figure out. It takes time and effort to keep learning about someone.

Check out Psalm 19:7 in the *Young Believer Bible:*
In this verse David writes about God's law, the Bible. He says the Lord's law is perfect and revives your soul. You can trust what you read in the Bible.

● ● ●

Just like a special person in your life, the Bible can surprise you sometimes. Some adults have read the Bible again and again. But if you talk to them, they'll tell you that they still learn something every time they open God's Word.

You might know the Bible pretty well yourself. But as soon as you think you've figured out what's in there, something new will jump out at you. If you're not reading your Bible yet, now is a great time to start. God's Word will make you wise. And when you go back years from now and read verses that you read today, you'll still be surprised by the things you discover.

Pray:
Thank God that his Word is always new.

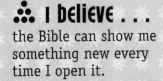
∴ I believe . . .
the Bible can show me
something new every
time I open it.

You probably have a whole drawerful of T-shirts. And T-shirts are great. You can find a color or a shirt with a saying that fits any mood you're in.

Do you have a favorite T-shirt? Maybe it's one with your favorite team's logo. Perhaps you like your pink "Princess" tee. A lot of T-shirts have words or silly sayings on them—some of which aren't very nice. Others have product or company names written across the front. It's sort of like you're a walking billboard for Old Navy, Coke, Tommy Hillfiger, or Disney. Maybe those companies should pay you to wear their shirts. After all, it's free advertising.

Christian companies make a lot of T-shirts too. Some fun choices feature VeggieTales. Have you seen the shirt that says, "His Pain Is Your Gain" with a drawing of Jesus on the back? There are lots of other shirts that have a message for people about God. Some kids are embarrassed to wear them. But what you wear can say a lot about what kind of person you are.

Check out 2 Corinthians 5:20 in the Young Believer Bible:

This verse says you're an ambassador for God—and that's a pretty cool thing. An ambassador is an important representative or messenger. That means God gives you the responsibility to represent him to your friends and tell people about Jesus.

●●●

When you wear a Christian T-shirt, you're telling the world that you believe in Jesus Christ. You're a walking advertisement for God.

Jesus doesn't physically walk the earth anymore, but he is present on this planet in the people who have given their lives to him. You're the closest some folks will ever get to seeing God. And you *should* spread the life-changing message of Jesus.

Putting on a "Jesus Lives" shirt may remind you who you're serving and how he wants you to treat people. Plus it will let the people around you know that you're a Christian, which might give you the chance to talk about your relationship with Jesus Christ.

Pray:

Ask God to give you opportunities to tell others about him.

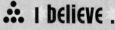

∴ I believe . . .

I need to let other people know I'm a Christian.

People spend huge amounts of time collecting things. Maybe you know somebody who likes collecting bugs or baseball hats or trading cards or dolls or aluminum cans. It seems like anything is collectible.

Heinz Schmidt-Bachem holds one of the strangest collections. According to Guinness Records, this German man has collected more than 150,000 plastic and paper bags. He has grocery bags, tote bags, tiny bags, and huge bags. And you're probably asking yourself, *Why would Heinz spend nearly 20 years of his life picking up bags?*

Good question. Here are some possibilities:

a. He's planning to open his own grocery store and wants to save money.
b. He's going to fill all the bags with helium and launch himself into space.
c. He had an extra room and needed something to fill it with.
d. He's trying to hoard all the bags in the world so everyone else has to carry everything by hand.

There's probably no good answer. People just like to hold on to stuff.

Check out 1 Thessalonians 5:21 in the Young Believer Bible:

The apostle Paul is very clear in this verse. His advice is to test everything we do and have in our lives. Keep only the good stuff.

●●●

Think of all the stuff you have in your room and all the things you do. You're probably surrounded by a lot of junk. Sure, you might not have 150,000 plastic and paper bags lying around your house. But your life may be cluttered with things that crowd out God. Maybe you have too many books that you spend time reading instead of making time to read the Bible. Or maybe you love sports so much that all your equipment fills your room and takes the place of God in your heart.

These are some things that clutter my life:

_____

_____

_____

Other things are worth holding on to, such as your relationships with family members and close friends, your Bible, your relationship with God . . . and your GameBoy (well, maybe not your GameBoy).

Pray:

Tell God you're going to look at the things in your life, throw away the bad, and keep the good.

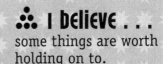

∴ I believe . . . some things are worth holding on to.

June 14

My dad works a lot, and I really miss him. What can I do to get him to spend more time with me?
Sad
Pápa, Hungary

Dear Sad,
A good first step to fixing this problem is communication. You need to let your dad know how you're feeling. You don't want to pester him or bug him all the time—dads tend to have a lot of pressures at work. But you should talk to him about your feelings so he understands that you need more time with him.

You may want to tell your dad that you don't expect spending time with him to be like a day at Disneyland. He doesn't need to take you places or buy you things. You can start by helping him out around the house. By lending a hand in the yard or with the car, you can "create" some extra time with your dad. Another idea is to begin a hobby together. Do you both like the outdoors? Then fishing and camping could be something you do with each other.

Whatever you do, don't lose hope. Sometimes dads get busy and need reminders of what's most important. With a little creativity and some conversation, you can have the relationship that you're looking for with your father.

Check out Psalm 127:3 in the *Young Believer Bible:*
This verse says you are a reward from God to your parents.

●●●

Some music, movies, and television shows make it seem like parents are the enemies of children. But that couldn't be further from the truth. Your parents, even if you don't live with both of them, are some of your biggest fans.

Sure, you might not always see eye to eye. You may fight, disagree, and get punished. During those times it's important to remember that God gave you your parents for a reason. You're his gift to them! It helps to make an effort to see their point of view. If you try really hard, you'll probably discover that they do the things they do because they love you and want the best for you.

Pray:
Ask God to help you develop a close bond with your parents—and then stay close to them in the years to come.

⁘ I believe . . .
God wants me to have a good relationship with my parents.

Lindsay couldn't wait to visit her grandparents for the summer in the country of SmileyLand (it's a make-believe place, okay?). Her grandpa had set up a job for her at the SmileyLand swimming pool. All she had to do was pick up towels and collect tickets, and she'd get paid $100 a day! Lindsay thought that was a lot of money.

When Lindsay's plane landed in SmileyLand, her grandpa picked her up and told her about a law in his country: "A person can take out of this country only what she brings in," Grandpa said. "You can't leave with any more money or stuff than what you have when you arrive."

But there was another rule: A person could send money home and have it deposited in her account.

Grandpa gave Lindsay a choice. "You can work hard, send money home, and benefit from your work when you go back," he said. "Or you can play all day and go home with what you have right now."

What would you do if you were in Lindsay's place?

Check out Matthew 6:19-20 in the *Young Believer Bible:*

In these verses, Jesus tells the people to store up their treasures in heaven—and not on earth. Treasures sent to heaven will last forever.

●●●

If you were in Lindsay's place, you'd probably work really hard, send a ton of money home, and then throw a big party when you returned.

Well, believe it or not, you *are* in the same situation as Lindsay. Heaven is your true home, and the stuff you get on earth can't be brought into God's kingdom. You leave this world with exactly what you brought: nothing! However, you can make deposits in your heavenly "bank account." Every time you treat a person with kindness, every time you tell somebody about Jesus, every time you put others' needs before your own, you're sending "treasures" to heaven.

Pray:

Tell God you want to work for heavenly rewards—not things on earth.

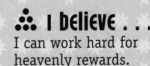

∴ I believe . . .
I can work hard for heavenly rewards.

Buying things wasn't always as easy as it is now. Today's huge malls and superstores put most everything at your fingertips. All you need is a little money. But if you wanted to buy something hundreds of years ago, the exchange would have sounded something like this.

You: Hey, that shirt and coat look really nice. What do you want for them?

Person with the items you want: What are you offering?

You: I have some rice and a goat. But if I give you the goat, I'll want those shoes too.

Person with the items you want: All right, that sounds like a fair deal.

Until there was paper money, people had to trade, or barter, for the things they wanted. If someone had grain and wanted some candy, he needed to find a person or store willing to swap with him. And sometimes those trades weren't fair.

European governments didn't start printing official paper money until the 1700s. France was the first country to do so. Because the paper money had value, it was easier to set prices and keep things fair for everybody. Now governments all over the world print their own money.

Check out Hebrews 13:5 in the *Young Believer Bible:*

This verse tells us to be happy with what we have. We need to keep from being greedy for money.

●●●

Today a lot of people talk about money. It seems like everybody wants it, and if they already have lots of it they still want a little more. Money can make people greedy.

God, on the other hand, doesn't care about money. He's still into trading. And do you know what? Jesus makes bad trades for our benefit all the time. In fact, he makes them every day to give you what you need. He takes your sin and gives you holiness. He takes your loneliness and gives you everlasting love. He takes your small hopes and gives you huge dreams.

Sure, God will take care of your physical needs—things you can buy with money. But he's much more interested in taking care of your spiritual and eternal needs (like joy and peace and salvation).

Pray:

Thank God for all he provides, and tell him you're going to be satisfied with what he gives you.

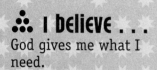

∴ I believe . . .
God gives me what I need.

Do you like riding in boats? Some kids get seasick. That's not fun at all, although it can be an interesting way to feed the fish your lunch. Yuck! Other kids love being on the water: the wind, the waves, the birds, the fresh air.

And there are all kinds of boats. Small sailboats, huge cruise ships, canoes, motorboats, yachts, dinghies. You can ride right next to the water in a small boat, such as a rowboat, or you can float way above the waves on an aircraft carrier, which is like its own city. One of the most important things on the bigger boats is a good anchor. Anchors keep boats in place during rough storms. They also hold boats in place when people go ashore. Without an anchor, even the strongest boats could be destroyed on land or lost at sea.

So next time you're heading out on the water, be sure to ask the ship's captain, "What kind of anchor are you using?"

Check out Hebrews 6:19 in the *Young Believer Bible:*

This verse talks about anchors. It says your hope in Jesus Christ is like an anchor. You can trust in Jesus' love and promises. He'll always be there. He'll never move. Your hope in him is secure.

●●●

Jesus spent a lot of time on the water. He knew a lot about boats. He calmed the sea during a terrible storm just by speaking a word. He walked on the water. Several of Jesus' disciples were fishermen, which means they knew a lot about boats too. So when you read that your hope in Jesus Christ is firm and secure like an anchor, you can be sure the writer knew what he was talking about. He understood anchors. Without a good anchor, you can lose your boat. Having a trustworthy anchor is important. And no anchor is stronger than Jesus. You can put your hope in him.

Pray:

Tell God you're going to trust him to anchor your life.

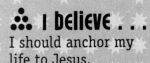

∴ I believe . . .
I should anchor my life to Jesus.

Petting zoos can be a lot of fun. No matter how old you are, it's fun to get up close to animals. What's your favorite animal at the petting zoo?

Chickens can be a little wild. They always seem to have a lot of attitude, clucking and strutting around.

Some petting zoos have deer. They're beautiful to watch.

And who doesn't like the rabbits. They're great to try to catch and pick up.

Baby cows are cute and easy to love. You might catch their big brown eyes winking at you. The sheep are nice too. They're messy but fun to pet.

Maybe it's too hard to figure out your favorite animal at a petting zoo. It's probably easier to pick out your least favorite. If you're like a lot of kids, your answer is goats.

Goats can get aggressive. If one has ever jumped up on you in the past, you probably don't want a repeat of that adventure! Their small heads and strangely shaped eyes seem weird. And their horns can be dangerous.

Thank goodness it's easy to tell goats from the other animals. If you want to stay away from them, you can avoid them and stick with the sheep.

Check out John 10:14 in the *Young Believer Bible:*
Jesus is talking in this verse. He says that he is the Good Shepherd. He knows his sheep, and his sheep know him.

●●●

There's a lot of talk in the Bible about sheep and shepherds. Usually humans are called sheep. That's okay. Although sheep aren't the smartest animals, they tend to be loyal. They stick close to their shepherd and follow him.

What's amazing about Jesus is that he knows which sheep are his just by looking at them. If you've seen many sheep, you know they look a lot alike. Sheep farmers even put tags in the animals' ears to tell them apart from other farmers' sheep. Jesus doesn't need tags. He knows you're his with just a glance. And although real sheep are dumb, you're smart enough to know to follow the Good Shepherd.

Pray:
Thank God that he leads you and protects you like a good shepherd.

⁜ I believe . . .
Jesus is the Good Shepherd.

Since you've asked Jesus into your heart, everything's gone perfectly—right? Every day is sunny. The birds always sing. Your grades are straight A's. You never have to study. You never get in trouble. You never hurt yourself or anyone else, and nothing goes wrong. It's like paradise.

That's not what happened to me, you say. *Things are still sometimes hard.*

And you're absolutely correct. Jesus didn't promise everything would go perfectly for you on earth once you accepted him as your Savior. His promise says you'll be in a perfect place where everything is wonderful once you *leave* earth.

Difficulties still exist in your everyday life. In some ways, it's hard to tell the difference between what happens to a Christian and someone who doesn't believe in Jesus. Both suffer pain. Both have accidents. Both get sick. Both are victims of natural disasters. Both have to overcome problems and challenges.

But there is one big difference in the lives of a Christian and a non-Christian here on earth: As a believer in Jesus, you know God uses your suffering for a greater purpose. A non-Christian doesn't have that hope.

Check out 1 Peter 1:6-7 in the *Young Believer Bible:*
As strange as it sounds, this verse says you should be glad when things go wrong in your life. When you suffer or experience trials, your faith in Jesus grows stronger and will encourage others.

●●●

Your circumstances might not change on this planet just because you believe in Jesus. But when you know your heavenly Father is watching over you, you'll be better able to handle tough things that come your way. As hard as it sounds, God wants you to rejoice when things don't go well.

Can you be happy that you have to study harder than the class genius in order to do well on a test, because you're developing endurance? Can you smile when your bike gets stolen, because you'll be able to comfort other kids when they lose something important to them?

When you accept your suffering with a heavenly attitude, other people will notice that you handle things differently because Jesus is in your life. Who knows? That might make them curious to know him too.

Pray:
Ask God for others to be able to see him in you when you're going through hard times.

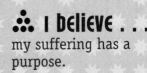

⁞ I believe . . .
my suffering has a purpose.

June 20

Marcus had the coolest bicycle. Polished chrome, 21 gears, state-of-the-art shocks, knobby wheels, gold-plated shifters—nobody had a better set of wheels. Marcus rode his bike everywhere. He loved to see the look on people's faces when he cruised by: It was pure envy. Marcus knew everybody wanted his bike, and he liked that fact. Sometimes he even heard people talking.

"Boy, Marcus has the best bike. I wish I had a bike like that."

Everybody knew Marcus because of his bike. His bike made him feel important. When he pedaled by, they'd say, "There goes Marcus." Even if Marcus was wearing his helmet and sunglasses so nobody could recognize him, he heard the same comment: "There goes Marcus."

As long as Marcus had his bike, he was happy. He even locked it up in the garage every night and checked to make sure the garage was locked too. He never wanted anything bad to happen to his bicycle. He couldn't image what his life would be like without that beautiful bike.

Check out Matthew 6:24 in the *Young Believer Bible:*

Jesus uses this verse to tell his followers that they can't serve God and things they own on earth. They need to have just one master and serve him.

●●●

Marcus was known for his bike. What are you known for? Maybe you're a great soccer or violin player. You might be the class brain. But the most important thing in life is to be known as Jesus' disciple, someone who follows him, learns from him, and loves him more than anything else.

These are some characteristics a follower of Jesus should have:

_____

_____

_____

Do you see those same traits in your life? Yes. Good. No. That's okay. You have time to grow and become more like Jesus. He'll give you the strength.

Pray:

Tell God that he's the most important thing in your life. Ask him to help you mean it more and more every day.

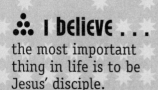

⁘ I believe . . .
the most important
thing in life is to be
Jesus' disciple.

Have you ever built a tree house? What did it look like? Did you have a big platform to sit on, railings to keep you from falling, and a secret door with a rope ladder? Climbing trees and building a tree house can be a great way to spend summer afternoons.

But chances are you've never seen a tree house like the ones in southern Oregon at the Out 'n' About Treesort. That's right: treesort. It's like a resort in the trees. For a little money, your whole family can spend the night up in the air. There are nearly 15 different tree houses, platforms, and forts. One even looks like a pirate's ship.

One of the tree houses is large with a bathroom, a small kitchen, and a sitting area. Another is one of the most popular rentals because it includes two tree houses connected by a swinging bridge. Another one, called The Treezebo, is built 37 feet off the ground—higher than any of the others. And the tree lovers at this treesort will even teach you how to build your ultimate tree house.

Check out Psalm 1:2-3 in the *Young Believer Bible:*

These verses explain that if you enjoy God's Word and work at learning more about him, then you're like a tree planted by a stream. Your life will show lots of growth, you'll be strong, and God will prosper and bless you.

●●●

Folks at the Out 'n' About Treesort will tell you one of the most important things in building a good tree house is picking the right tree. You want a strong, dependable tree—one that's not going to fall down or break. Before you put effort into building something in a tree, you want to make sure it's going to last.

God thinks the same way. He wants strong trees. Trees with deep roots that hold on to him. Trees that bear fruit. Trees that won't fall over. When you read your Bible and grow closer to him, you become like a strong tree. And God will build his own character in you that will last forever.

Pray:

Thank God for choosing you to be a tree for him.

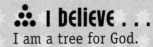

∴ I believe . . .
I am a tree for God.

Matt loved to in-line skate. Give him sunny weather and a sack lunch, and he'd spend the entire day at the skate park. He'd been skating for a while, so he'd mastered a lot of moves. His favorite thing was to grind the rails. Acid grind, soul grind, X-grind—he could do them all. He worked a little on his jumps and grabs, but he was the best grinder at the park and liked to stick to himself. Younger skaters looked up to Matt, which he thought was cool.

One afternoon a new skater showed up at the park. After fiddling with his skates for a few minutes, he skated over to the half-pipe and waited his turn to drop in. And once he did . . . watch out! He started by just hitting some big air. Then he mixed in some grabs and ended by nailing an awesome McTwist.

"Dude, you're hard-core," Matt said to the new kid as he skated up to him. "You've got to teach me some of your stuff, 'cause you're totally my new hero."

Check out Revelation 15:3 in the Young Believer Bible:

In this verse some of the people in heaven are singing a song to God, saying he does great and marvelous things. He is the King forever, and everything he does is just.

●●●

Sometimes it's easy to get caught up in everything the world says is good. A lot of stuff gets in the way of God. It's easy to start thinking that a cool skater or a famous new singer has it all. Then it's tempting to put them in a place that only God deserves.

Only Jesus deserves the number-one-hero spot in our hearts. He's the King forever. And even though he's never pulled a miller flip or a genie grab on in-line skates, he's the one who gave someone the idea to create in-line skates and who provides the creativity to people to invent awesome tricks.

Sure it's okay to have other role models and people you want to be like. But it's also important to make sure that Jesus stays at the top in your life, because his amazing deeds make everything else look pretty weak.

Pray:

Praise God for his greatness.

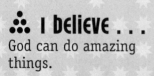

∴ I believe . . .

God can do amazing things.

June 23

Have you ever seen a commercial like this one?

"New from ToyCo, it's the amazing Friend in a Box!

"Feeling lonely? Need somebody to talk to? Friend in a Box could be the perfect companion for you.

"Just run to your local toy store and purchase your new best friend. Turn on Friend in a Box—give it a name like George, Katie, Billy-Bob, or Sue—set the control switch to how you're feeling, and get ready for Friend in a Box to make you feel better.

"If you're *mad*, you may hear, 'Don't be angry. You're so nice.'

"If you're *lonely*, Friend in a Box might say, 'People are missing out! You're a great person.'

"If you're *sad*, you can listen to Friend in a Box encourage, 'Don't worry; it will be fine.'

"It's the perfect friend from ToyCo! And best of all, Friend in a Box doesn't care how you treat it. Ignore it. Throw it in a toy chest. Keep it under your bed. Smash it with a bat. Friend in a Box will be there for you.

"Note: Some assembly required. Batteries not included."

Check out 1 Corinthians 1:9 in the
Young Believer Bible:

This verse says God has invited you into a friendship with his Son, Jesus Christ. Friendship with Jesus means you have a constant companion who's interested in you.

●●●

Some people think Jesus is like a Friend in a Box. When they want something from him, they pop open the lid and get what they need.

But God wants to have a much better and deeper relationship with you. He wants you to tell him what you're thinking and feeling all the time. He wants you to spend time learning more about him. He wants to be the last person you talk to at night and the first one you talk to in the morning.

Sure, having a relationship with Jesus takes more effort than owning a Friend in a Box. But the benefits are a lot greater too. Plus God has no batteries to replace!

Pray:

Tell Jesus you want him to be your best friend.

⁂ I believe . . .
God wants a
relationship with me
all the time.

A lot of adults make fun of lawyers.

Lawyers have a bad reputation because it seems that many of them care more about making money than about helping people. But the fact is lawyers play an important role in the justice system. They study the law. They know the rules. And most try to make sure the right thing gets done. Think about what it'd be like if someone got in trouble and didn't have a lawyer. That person would probably feel pretty confused in court. Maybe she'd say the wrong thing. And she probably wouldn't know how to defend herself in court. That would cost her big time.

It'd be kind of scary to try to plead a case before a judge if you didn't know what you were doing. Lawyers protect people and make sure their rights aren't violated.

Check out Romans 8:34 in the Young Believer Bible:

This verse paints a neat picture of heaven. It says that no one can put you down in God's eyes, because Christ Jesus is at the right hand of God, defending you to him.

●●●

Have you ever watched a court show on TV? The defense lawyer is on the side of the person on trial. The lawyer for the other side is called the prosecutor, and he tries to convince the judge that the person is guilty. The defense lawyer works between the judge and prosecutor to come up with a good result for his client.

Jesus is your defense lawyer in heaven. He fights for you. Satan tells God about all the bad stuff you've done and says, "There's no way you should let [fill in your name] into heaven. That kid has messed up a thousand times. You can't have all that sin up here." But Jesus leans over to God and says, "Yeah, it's true that [fill in your name] has made mistakes. But I died for that person. That person is blameless."

Pray:

Thank Jesus for always standing up for you.

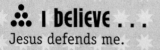

⁙ I believe . . .
Jesus defends me.

Deborah had an important job. Long before, God had chosen her to lead the people of Israel. But the wicked Canaanites oppressed the Israelites day and night. Things got so bad that they cried out to God. God told Deborah that he would deliver the people through a general named Barak. Deborah sent for Barak and gave him the message. She told Barak that God would help him defeat the Canaanite general, Sisera.

But instead of being willing to be used by God, Barak refused. He said, "I will go, but only if you go with me!"

It wasn't Deborah's job to go into battle. She could have said, "No. God gave *you* this job!" But instead she said, "I will go with you. But since you have made this choice, you will receive no honor. For the Lord's victory over Sisera will be at the hands of a woman."

Deborah went with Barak, and Israel defeated the Canaanites. Barak missed out on the honor of being used by God. But because Deborah was willing, God used her to free her people. (You can read the whole story in Judges 4:1-16.)

Check out 1 Peter 5:2 in the *Young Believer Bible:*

God asks his followers to serve him and others willingly. Your eagerness and willing attitude to do whatever God asks of you, including helping others, pleases him.

●●●

Are you willing to do *anything* God asks you to do? Sometimes that may require doing something scary or uncomfortable. But when you willingly serve God, he will bless you and help you succeed.

What is God asking you to do today? Maybe he wants you to talk to someone who's down. Or perhaps he's asking you to give up doing something you know is wrong. Maybe he's telling you to share your faith with someone who needs to hear his Good News. Whatever God's speaking to your heart, you can be sure you'll receive the greatest blessing when you willingly obey.

Pray:

Ask God to help you be willing to do what he asks of you.

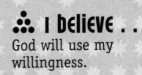

∴ I believe . . .
God will use my willingness.

Do you have a parent who has to travel for business? A lot of kids do. When your mom or dad is gone, things can feel weird around the house. There's an empty chair at the dinner table. Less noise and excitement are in the air. Fewer hugs and kisses are exchanged. Not as many things get accomplished, and you might feel lonely. Fortunately, most business travel takes only a few days. Then your parent is back, and things return to normal.

But what would it be like if your parent had to be gone for a week, a month, a year, or even longer? Kids with parents in the military often have to say good-bye for months at a time. That's really hard. At the same time, those children know that their parents have an important job to do. Sure they miss them. But it's easier to have them leave knowing their folks are on an important mission. And when they come back—it's time to party!

Check out 2 Thessalonians 1:7 in the Young Believer Bible:

This verse says God will provide rest. Rest feels comforting, especially during tough and tiring times. Even though life can be hard, God's ultimate comfort will come when Jesus Christ returns to earth with his powerful angels.

●●●

When Jesus died and rose from the dead three days later, the disciples felt like you do when your parent returns from a business trip . . . probably even better! They were so happy to see Jesus again and to be able to talk with him. And Jesus spent more than a month with the disciples before going back to heaven. But before he left, he told the disciples that he'd return again.

Jesus is coming back. And this time he won't be a tiny baby. He'll come as a mighty warrior surrounded by powerful angels. When Jesus returns, it'll be like a parent coming back from serving in the military. You'll feel ultimate comfort. All of your worries will be gone. You'll be totally safe. Plus you'll be part of the biggest party ever.

Pray:

Thank God for the comfort he gives you now, but even more for the comfort he'll bring when he comes back.

∴ I believe . . .
Jesus is coming back.

How do you knock on your best buddy's door?

A single rap on the door.

Knock.

Maybe you prefer to play a little tune.

Knock-knock-knock-knock-knock. Knock. Knock.

Ringing the doorbell is a good technique. It usually gets quick results.

It'd be pretty silly not to knock at all—someone who just stands at the door and waits for somebody to open it may have to wait a long time.

So how about this idea? Next time you go to your best friend's house, step up to the door and just start knocking.

Knock, knock, knock, knock, knock, knock . . .

And don't stop knocking until somebody answers the door.

Knock, knock, knock, knock, knock . . .

All right, so maybe this isn't a great idea. It would be kind of annoying. Actually, it would be *really* annoying. But believe it or not, that's exactly how God wants you to knock on his door.

Check out Matthew 7:7 in the *Young Believer Bible:*

In this verse, Jesus gives you some good advice. He says to ask him for something, and it will be given to you. Look for something, and you'll find it. Knock, and the door will be opened for you.

●●●

When Jesus said, "Keep on knocking, and the door will be opened," he meant knock and don't stop knocking! He doesn't mind you rapping on his door all the time. He won't get annoyed; in fact, he wants you to knock and to refuse to quit.

Knock, knock, knock, knock . . .

Don't forget this fact about Jesus. He never gets tired of your prayers and requests. And he always wants to hear from you and be close to you.

Pray:

Tell God you're going to keep knocking on his door and trusting him to answer.

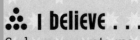

⁝ I believe . . .

God never wants me to stop knocking on his door.

LaRonda's mom dropped her and her friend Emma off for an afternoon at the new mall.

"See you at five," Mom said as she pulled away.

LaRonda and Emma scrambled inside and went right to the food court.

"Hey, there's Wendi and Autumn," Emma said. "Let's see what they're doing." Emma and LaRonda ran over to their friends.

"Great mall, huh?" Wendi said.

"We haven't seen much of it yet," LaRonda admitted. "What are you up to?"

"We're going to catch a movie after we go outside for a smoke," Autumn answered.

"I didn't know you smoked," LaRonda said.

"Sure, I just don't do it at school and make sure my parents don't know about it," Autumn said. "You want to try?"

I've seen a lot of people smoke on TV and in the movies, LaRonda thought. *They make it look fun. And my mom will never find out.*

"No, thanks," Emma piped up, interrupting LaRonda's thoughts. "We haven't seen any stores yet. Let's go, LaRonda."

The friends turned and left.

"Thanks," LaRonda said to her friend once they were out of earshot of the other girls. "I almost made a dumb choice."

Check out 1 Corinthians 10:13 in the Young Believer Bible:

This verse shows that kids have faced the same temptations for years. God is faithful to never allow you to be tempted beyond what you can handle. Besides, God will always— that's right, always—provide a way out.

●●●

LaRonda received help from her friend to resist the temptation of smoking. But God can use a number of things to help you avoid giving in to temptation. Maybe the Holy Spirit will prompt you to make the right choice. Perhaps you'll just have a gut feeling about doing the right thing. Whatever it is, remember that God always wants to help you when you're tempted.

These are some things that I've been tempted to do:

_____

_____

_____

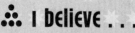

∴ I believe . . .

when I'm tempted, God provides a way out.

Be on the lookout when temptation comes . . . and it will come. And know that there's always a way out.

Pray:

Praise God for always giving you a way to steer clear of temptation.

Have you ever been part of a club? Maybe you've joined a club where all the members wear the same things and know a secret handshake.

It's great to belong to something that's bigger than yourself. When club members work together, they can accomplish awesome things.

What would you do if you belonged to the world's greatest club—a club that everybody wanted to join? A lot of kids might walk around and brag that they were part of the best group of people.

"I'm better than you," they might say, "because I'm part of the Aces, and nobody's better than us."

But how would you feel if a member of the Aces was always bragging that he was part of the club and you weren't? Would you want to tell him to be quiet, punch him, or run away? Probably. It's kind of annoying when someone brags that he is better than you.

Check out 1 Corinthians 1:30-31 in the *Young Believer Bible:*

These verses say that Jesus Christ is the One who makes believers acceptable to God. So we shouldn't brag that it's something we did.

●●●

Sometimes kids who know Jesus act like they're in a special club for members only. They only hang out with other Christians and act as though people who don't know Jesus aren't as good as they are.

But that's exactly the *opposite* of how God hopes we'll act when we know him. It's only because of God's forgiveness and the gift of his Son that we can have a relationship with him. No one can do anything to earn membership in God's "club." God wants everybody to know him and join in. And he wants us to do all we can to bring others into that club.

And one of the best ways to do that is to tell them about your awesome club president: God.

Pray:

Tell God that you're not going to brag about yourself, but instead you'll brag about him.

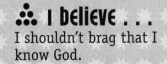

⁂ I believe . . .
I shouldn't brag that I know God.

Did you ever hear this story when you were younger? Reggie Rabbit loved to explore the forest. He thought everybody was his friend. He never hurt anyone and expected other animals to treat him the same way. He just wanted to wander in the woods and have fun.

The Fox family, however, weren't fans of Reggie. The Foxes thought Reggie would make a better meal than a friend. Ferdinand and Freda Fox decided to go out, catch Reggie, and bring him home for supper. They hid next to a stream bordered by trees and waited. At noon, Reggie needed a drink and hopped down to the stream. Just as he dipped his head into the water, Freda and Ferdinand jumped out of the bushes.

"Yikes!" Reggie cried as he darted away from the foxes.

The foxes ran after Reggie. Reggie dipped and dashed around trees and over hills until he was almost too tired to go on. The foxes stayed right on his tail. When Reggie was about to give up, he spotted his friend Harvey Horse. Reggie scampered to his friend and hopped on his back.

Harvey turned and faced the Foxes.

"Do you have a problem with Reggie?" Harvey asked.

"No problem," Ferdinand said.

"We were just playing," Freda added as they slunk back home.

Check out Proverbs 2:8 in the *Young Believer Bible:*
This verse says God guards your path as you walk through life. Because of your faith in him, he protects you.

● ● ●

Do you think the Foxes were more afraid of Reggie or Harvey? Obvious answer, right? Nobody's scared of a bunny. But a fox wouldn't feel too good if it was kicked or stepped on by a horse.

Now think about your own life. Even if you treat everybody as you should, there are bound to be kids who may want to harm you. Whether they're known as bullies, thugs, or troublemakers, unfortunately they're out there. And when they're bothering you, you need to run to God. The Lord is your protection. Unless you're six feet two inches tall and weigh 215 pounds, bullies probably won't be afraid of you. But they should be afraid of the One who protects you.

Pray:
Thank God for his protection.

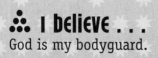

∴ I believe . . .
God is my bodyguard.

A few years back almost four thousand kids who attended church youth groups were given a survey. It asked them 193 questions about all areas of their lives—especially about their relationship with Jesus Christ.

One finding stood out. It said only one out of five kids reads the Bible every day. Fewer than one out of three read the Bible once a week.

This same group of kids weren't asked how much television they watched, but if they are like most kids in our country, almost all of them would've said they watch TV every day. And a lot would've answered that they watch 20, 30, or even 40 hours a week. (Sound like anybody you know?)

There hasn't been a study, but it's safe to say that reading the Bible has more value then plopping down in front of the television.

Check out 2 Timothy 3:16-17 in the *Young Believer Bible:*

These verses say that every word in the Bible comes from God. The Bible helps Christians get ready for every good work, because it straightens us out, teaches us, and prepares us to live right.

●●●

If you're not reading your Bible and praying to God daily, now is a great time to start. Learning about Jesus Christ will help you grow closer to him. And there's no better way to learn about God than by reading his Word.

You don't have to read all of Genesis in one night. Just get yourself in the habit of opening your Bible and reading for one minute a day. Then pray for another minute. Pretty soon you may want to increase your time. You might be surprised by how much you will learn.

Because I want to make Bible reading a habit in my life, I'm going to commit to reading it every day for a month:

(My name) _____ will read the Bible every day this month.

Pray:

Tell God you want to change your habits to learn more about him.

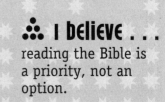

⁙ I believe . . .
reading the Bible is a priority, not an option.

Maggie thought she was great at archery. If anybody asked her, Maggie would say, "I only shoot bull's-eyes. I never miss."

Nobody could argue with Maggie, because she'd never shot an arrow in front of anyone. All the townspeople ever saw was Maggie walking into the forest carrying a bow, a quiver full of arrows, and a can of paint. Then she'd return hours later with a big smile on her face. "All bull's-eyes again," she'd gloat.

The townspeople believed Maggie, but they were starting to get annoyed by her boasting. One time she bragged, "I'm so good that I can close my eyes, spin around three times, and still shoot a perfect bull's-eye."

That was too much.

"Prove it," the townspeople said.

The mayor walked to a tree 70 feet away and hung a target on it. Maggie closed her eyes and spun around three times. She drew back an arrow on her string and let it fly. *Twang!*

The air soared straight and true, and hit directly in the middle of . . . the front door to the mayor's house.

But was Maggie embarrassed by her poor shot? No way! She grabbed her can of paint, walked up to the door, and drew a target around her arrow so that it was perfectly in the center.

"Bull's-eye!" she screamed.

Check out 2 Corinthians 13:7 in the
Young Believer Bible:

In one of the last verses in this book, Paul tells his brothers and sisters in Christ not to do anything wrong. God wants us to aim for perfection with our lives.

●●●

Maggie probably isn't as good an archer as she thinks she is. It's easy to hit the target if you shoot first and draw the target later. But God's target doesn't move when it comes to how he wants his followers to live. He made certain rules that he wants us to live by. We can't go grab a can of paint and draw a new bull's-eye for him.

If you want to hit God's target with your life, it'll be necessary to learn to "shoot straight." That means getting to know what God expects of you, thinking about your decisions, and praying for wisdom. Then aim carefully and hit the bull's-eye.

Pray:

Ask God to help guide your life to hit his mark.

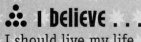

I believe . . .

I should live my life aiming to hit God's target.

A lot of kids like messing around with cards. A fast game of Go Fish or Crazy Eights can really get the competitive juices flowing. But have you ever tried to build a house out of cards? All it takes is a good breeze or an off-balance card to bring the whole structure crashing down.

So would you believe that a college student in Ames, Iowa, built a house of cards that was 24 feet 4 inches high? That's about four times taller than your dad.

Check out these facts listed in *Guinness World Records:*

- The structure took 13 days to build.
- It was 127 stories high.
- It took more than 60,000 cards to create.
- No glue or other adhesives were used to hold the cards together.
- The house did eventually fall to the ground.

I guess nobody should be surprised by the last fact (which didn't appear in *Guinness*). After all, it's not like there are many uses for a card house.

Check out Matthew 7:24-27 in the Young Believer Bible:

Jesus loved to tell stories, called parables, that proved a point. This parable talks about two builders: one who built a house on sand and one who built on rock. When the storms came, the house built on rock (or God's Word) stood firm, while the one on sand crashed down.

●●●

Choosing where to build your life is an important decision. You can choose to live your life without following God's instructions. Or you can build your life using the strong foundation of God's Word. The better choice is obvious. God never changes; he never moves. He's like a rock. But what's popular—the rules other people live by—can change all the time. Building on that is like constructing a house of cards—it's only a matter of time before it falls. Are you building your life on God's foundation?

Pray:

Commit to God that you'll build your life on what he says.

∴ I believe . . .
I should build my life
on God's foundation.

Watching fireworks is great. The explosions. The colors. The sounds. The ooohs and aaahs. And everybody has a favorite kind.

Some like the huge round ones that seem to fill the whole sky in dazzling colors. Other kids enjoy the really loud ones. You know the kind . . . they just go up and *BOOM!* There's a big blast of white light. And how in the world do they make the smiley face and heart-shaped fireworks? And then there are the ones that fizz and make noise.

There's just one problem with fireworks—they're over too soon. They zoom into the air, explode in vivid, bright colors, and then they're gone. Over and over again it's zoom, boom, disappear.

Wouldn't it be cool if somebody could invent a firework that would light up the sky for five or ten minutes? Someone could launch a couple of those into the air and entertain everyone around for a long time. But until someone invents a long-lasting firework, workers will have to keep shooting them into the sky one after another, because once the fireworks go off, they vanish so quickly.

Check out 2 Corinthians 4:6 in the *Young Believer Bible:*

This verse uses the word "light" two times. God is the One who first commanded light to shine in the darkness, and he allows his light to shine in your heart and gives you the light of Jesus.

●●●

God's light is a forever kind of light. It's kind of like a star, but even better. A firework, on the other hand, makes a flash in the night and disappears. Fireworks can be exciting, but they're gone too quickly.

When it comes to your belief in Jesus Christ, think about being a star instead of a firework. Stars shine steadily and consistently. Even if you don't always feel on fire for God like a firework, try to remember that being like a star that lasts is more important than being a firework that burns out.

Pray:

Ask God to help you stay consistent and true to him.

∴ I believe . . .

I should let my light shine like a star that lasts, not a firework that disappears.

Wally Wheeler couldn't wait for the Ultimate Challenge Mountain Bike Race. He'd watched it on television the year before and knew he could win. The course covered 150 miles, went over two mountains, and reached an altitude of 13,150 feet.

His coach, Craig Crankshaft, thought Wally had the ability to win because he was strong, athletic, and tall. Craig had won the Ultimate Challenge years before and gave Wally tips to be a champion.

- "Ride 50 miles a day in the mountains," Craig said. But instead of riding outside, Wally rode his exercise bike for an hour while watching television.
- "Eat healthy foods," Craig said. But instead of eating chicken and vegetables, Wally ate doughnuts.
- "Get lots of rest," Craig said. But instead of sleeping, Wally stayed up late playing video games.

On the day of the race, Wally looked great wearing his helmet and riding gear. His bike sparkled. When the race started, he took off like a flash. He zoomed down the first hill and pedaled hard up the first mountain. He led for the first 100 miles, but then something happened.

Wally's leg muscles cramped up and wouldn't move, his lungs burned, his eyes drooped . . . and he failed to finish the race.

Check out Luke 6:40 in the *Young Believer Bible:*

Jesus says students are not greater than their teachers. However, if a student works hard and fully trains himself, he can be like his teacher.

●●●

Wally thought having a good coach, a desire to win, and lots of natural ability would help him win the race. Just one problem: he didn't put the effort into training. Because he didn't work hard, his body didn't have the strength to finish the race.

The same is true in your relationship with Jesus. Without going to church, reading your Bible, and praying, you won't have the spiritual muscle to complete the "race" God has mapped out for you. You have the best coach who ever lived: Jesus Christ. With the right training, you'll be able to reach the mountaintops of life with him.

Pray:

Ask God to give you the strength and determination to train hard to follow him.

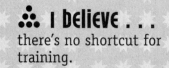

I believe . . . there's no shortcut for training.

July 6

Have you ever felt trapped between two friends? If you have, this conversation may seem familiar:

Jan: Andrea really bothers me. She didn't pick me for her science partner.
You: Maybe she thought you wanted to be with somebody else.
Jan: She knew I wanted to be her partner. She just thinks I'm dumb at science, so she picked Jenny. But don't tell her I said that.

(Later that day you see Andrea.)
You: I heard Jan's mad at you.
Andrea: She is?
You: She said you think she's not good at science.
Andrea: I never said that. Jan's a liar. She always talks with Jason in class, so I thought she wanted to be his science partner.
You: She said you picked Jenny first.
Andrea: And you believed her. You tell her we're not friends anymore!
You: But it sounded like—
Andrea: You think she's right, don't you? (She storms off.)

⁙

It's not good to be caught between friends. Even if you're trying to help, it's easy to say the wrong thing and find yourself feeling beat up.

Check out Proverbs 11:13 in the *Young Believer Bible:*
This verse says a gossip tells other people's secrets, but someone who's trustworthy can keep a secret.

● ● ●

Which would you rather be known as: a gossip or a trustworthy person? Easy question, right?

Gossips don't keep many friends. Once they've broken a friend's trust, it's difficult to earn it back. Nobody likes to have her secrets spread around.

Keeping a secret, on the other hand, earns a friend's trust. And trust helps strengthen a friendship and binds people closer together.

Just one warning: Keeping a secret is great, but if your friend could get hurt or is doing something illegal, then it's good to tell a parent, teacher, or trusted adult who can help. Watching out for your friends—even when it means breaking a promise— makes you a trustworthy person.

Pray:
Ask God to give you the wisdom to know when to keep a secret and when it's best not to.

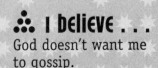

⁙ I believe . . .
God doesn't want me to gossip.

"C'mon, let's go this way," Jeremy said.

"I don't know," Kyle answered. "Shouldn't we wait for the guide? The nature walk starts in 10 minutes."

"Nah, let's take this trail. It looks more fun."

The boys started down the trail. They chatted excitedly about the fun they'd been having on their camping trip. Jeremy pointed out a chipmunk, and Kyle identified plants and flowers along the way. But pretty soon the narrow path ahead of them didn't look like a trail anymore. The boys looked behind them. They saw only leaves and brush. The trail had disappeared!

"I think this was a bad idea," Kyle said.

"Me, too," Jeremy whispered. "Let's wait here for the guide to find us."

The boys waited for hours until the guide located them and directed them back to camp. Later that night when the campers were heading off to bed, Jeremy said, "That's the last time I make my own trail."

"You can say that again," Kyle agreed. "Next time I'm waiting for the guide."

Check out Romans 8:14 in the *Young Believer Bible:*

Paul is writing a lot about the Holy Spirit in this whole chapter. He says that those who are led by God's Spirit are children of God.

●●●

There are many different beliefs in this world. And many of them are not the truth. Sometimes it's hard to know which ones are true and which ones aren't. God gives us the truth in his Word, but he knows that we need help finding our way through all the world's choices.

Instead of leaving you alone to try to figure it out, he gave you the Holy Spirit— your own personal God guide. The Spirit helps lead you to what is true. And when you're doing something wrong, he gives you that feeling that there's a better choice.

When you come across a belief that you don't think is true, look at what God says about it in his Word. Then ask the Holy Spirit to help you know the truth. With the Holy Spirit as your guide, you'll never get lost.

I want to follow God's way, so I'll find out what he says about his truth in these verses: Psalm 32:8; John 14:6; John 16:13; John 17:9, 14, 17; Romans 1:25.

Pray:

Thank God for giving you the Holy Spirit as a guide.

I believe . . .
the Spirit of God leads me.

This kid on my soccer team thinks he's awesome and I'm terrible. He also makes fun of me because I believe in Jesus. Can you help me?
Picked On
Ball, Louisiana

Dear Picked On,
Soccer can be great: playing outside, making friends, learning new skills, and competing against other teams. Of course, that's not always what happens. Sometimes teammates don't get along. Sometimes certain players think they're better than everybody else. Maybe your coach needs to remind this person what it means to play a team sport. Teammates should cheer one another on, help one another out, and want the best for one another.

As the saying goes, "There's no 'I' in team." That means it's important to take care of one another. If a team is just a bunch of individuals without the common goal of team success, then it won't be a very strong team. The best teams don't have a lot of star players. They have athletes who want the best for the team—not for themselves. So don't worry about what this kid thinks. If he's out for himself and you're out for the team, you'll be a more important member of the team in the long run.

But you have another problem here too. You're being teased because you believe in Jesus. In cases like this, it's best to get some advice from the Bible.

Check out 1 Peter 4:16 in the *Young Believer Bible:*
This verse says if people make fun of you because you believe in Jesus, don't be ashamed. Instead you have a reason to praise God, because they're seeing Jesus in you.

●●●

If Christians throughout history let the ridicule of other people get them down, think what wouldn't have been accomplished for God's kingdom. Jesus said, "Since they persecuted me, naturally they will persecute you" (John 15:20). And being like Jesus is a Christian's goal, so congratulations! That should be encouraging to you. If someone has noticed that you have a relationship with Jesus Christ, then your light is shining for God. Keep letting your light shine, even if people make fun of you.

Pray:
Ask God to give you the strength to handle it when people make fun of you because of your faith.

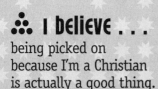

❖ I believe . . .
being picked on
because I'm a Christian
is actually a good thing.

What are some of your favorite things to do in the summer? Is going to a water park one of them?

Millions of kids every year visit water parks. With slides, tunnels, tubes, giant buckets, wave pools, and rafts, it's a great way to spend the day and stay cool.

The slides can be thrilling. Some are incredibly steep so you feel like you're free-falling until you end up landing smoothly in a pool of water. Other slides have so much speed and so much water pumped through them that you can actually go uphill! And you may have been on slides that spin you around until you come out at the bottom feeling dizzy.

Water slides are much different from regular slides you find at a playground. With playground slides, you often can stop yourself before you get to the bottom and climb back up. But once you step on a water slide—*zoom!*—you're on a wild ride that can't be stopped.

Check out Joel 2:12-13 in the *Young Believer Bible:*

Joel writes this after God's people have turned their backs on the Lord. Even though the Israelites had treated God very badly, God says they can still return to him. God doesn't get angry very easily, and he doesn't want to have to punish people.

● ● ●

Have you ever heard the term *backslider*? That's what some people call Christians who start making bad decisions that pull them away from the Lord. It's not that God goes anywhere. It's that people let themselves slide away from him.

Now here's a tough question: When people slide away from God, do you think it's more like a water slide or a playground slide? Because of God's mercy, the answer is a playground slide.

If you mess up and fall away from God, you can at any time decide to stop yourself and go back to him, just like you can stop on a playground slide. God's ready to forgive you no matter what you do—just like he's been doing for his people for thousands of years.

Pray:

Thank God that he's patient and always ready to forgive.

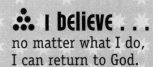

⁂ I believe . . .
no matter what I do,
I can return to God.

Do you like your name? Some kids have really cool names like Dax or Celine. Other kids have sort of normal names, such as John or Stephanie. But what if your name was Ima Hogg? That would be the worst. Certainly no parent would be silly enough to name his child Ima Hogg.

Well, the truth is, more than 120 years ago a parent was that silly. Before James Stephen Hogg became the governor of Texas, he had a daughter whom he named Ima. (Maybe if he had another little girl, he would've named her Ura.)

Kids at school probably teased Ima Hogg. It would be easy to make fun of her name. But Ima must not have let the other kids' taunts bother her. She became a strong and famous person. Ima learned a lot about art and became a collector. She started the Bayou Bend Collection of the Museum of Fine Arts. She also started the Houston Symphony. Not bad for a person with a silly name.

Check out 2 Thessalonians 1:11-12 in the Young Believer Bible:

In these verses Paul writes that he's praying for the church in Thessalonica. He prays that they would honor the name of the Lord Jesus, because Jesus' name has power.

● ● ●

Ima Hogg probably wasn't too thrilled with her name. Maybe you don't like your name either. Some kids aren't too excited with the name their parents picked out for them; however, there's not a lot they can do about it.

But Jesus wants to give you a special name—it's the name *Christian*. It means "Christ one," or one who believes in the teachings of Jesus Christ. It says you're his, and you're guaranteed to live with him forever in heaven. Once you pray to accept Jesus into your life, he gives you that name. And because that name comes from the Son of God, you can be proud of it.

Pray:

Thank God that you can be called a Christian, and tell him you're going to try hard to live up to that name.

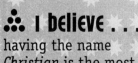

∴ I believe . . .

having the name *Christian* is the most important thing.

Have you ever been fishing at a lake? You cast out your line and wait to see the bobber go under. When it does, you jerk your pole back to hook the fish. Then you reel in your catch!

It's a long process, but anyone who loves fishing will tell you it's worth it. Of course, there are many different kinds of fishing—fly-fishing, ocean fishing, and commercial fishing to make money. And each kind of fishing requires different equipment and skills. But every type shares the same goal: catching fish!

Peter and Andrew were two Jewish fisherman. Each day they would row their boat out on the Sea of Galilee and drop their nets. On a good day, their nets would overflow with fish. One day a man they had never met came by, and he had a very strange message about fishing.

Check out Matthew 4:19 in the *Young Believer Bible:*
Jesus said if Peter and Andrew followed him, he would show them how to fish for people. He had a plan for them to net people into the kingdom of God.

●●●

Fishing is an exciting sport. It's thrilling to hook a big fish and reel it in. Sometimes it puts up a fight. Other times you can land it easily in the boat. It takes work. It's important when you're fishing for people to rely on God to do the work. He gives you the opportunities to tell others about him, but he's right there, working in people's hearts and helping them understand that they need his forgiveness from their sins.

How can you be God's kind of fisherman? First of all, you have to know some kids who don't know Jesus as their Savior. Be on the lookout for people who don't know Christ: neighbors, kids at school, members of your soccer team. Be a friend to those people, and then tell them about Jesus. With God's help, you'll have many great "fish" stories to tell!

Pray:
Ask God to grow your ability to reel other people into his family.

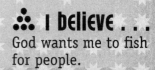

⁂ I believe . . .
God wants me to fish for people.

July 12

Craig had climbed the toughest mountains in the United States. He loved working his way up a solid rock wall. But one day when he was climbing in a remote part of the Rocky Mountains, his favorite sport almost got him killed.

Craig and his climbing partner miscommunicated directions to each other, which resulted in Craig falling 60 mph 100 feet to the ground. He landed on a pile of rocks, but amazingly he didn't die. His climbing buddy rushed to his side, tried to stop his bleeding, and called 911 on a cell phone. Within 40 minutes a paramedic found the pair.

When another paramedic arrived, they stabilized Craig, put him on a stretcher, and carried him to a place where a helicopter could land—it took six hours! By the time the helicopter arrived at the hospital, doctors didn't think Craig would live. Well, he did. Not only that, he beat the odds by walking again just five weeks after the accident! And Craig gives all the credit to God.

Craig's story is true. Every day in the newspaper and on television you can see and read about similar modern-day miracles. Someone has a cancerous tumor, but the next week it's gone and doctors are amazed. A baby is born way too early with no chance to live and survives. God is doing miracles all around you.

Check out Job 9:10 in the *Young Believer Bible:*

Job trusted in God's power. In this verse Job says God does marvelous things that we can't understand. The Lord does more miracles than anyone can count.

●●●

Every day God does miracles, most of which never make the newspaper or TV headlines. Just the fact that we can travel safely is a miracle. The tilt of Earth and its distance from the Sun—miracles, because if they were just a bit different people could not survive on our planet. The way that plants grow and rain falls—also a miracle.

God is in the miracle business. Nothing is impossible for him. Sometimes he's just waiting for you to ask him and believe with all your heart that he can work. It's important not to limit God. Ask for the impossible, then hope and wait to see what he does.

Pray:

Praise God that he still does miracles.

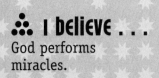

⁛ I believe . . .

God performs miracles.

Have you ever thought about how sin came into the world?

Before time began, God existed. And he's always been holy, which means he has never sinned. Then he created the world. Along with the oceans, mountains, and animals, God made humans—Adam and Eve.

He placed them in a beautiful garden where they walked with him each evening. Can you imagine walking with God, just like a friend? He gave them only one rule: "You may freely eat any fruit in the garden except fruit from the tree of the knowledge of good and evil. If you eat of its fruit, you will surely die."

Well, you probably already know what Adam and Eve did. Yep, they ate from the tree. And through their disobedience, sin came into the world.

Check out Romans 5:12 in the *Young Believer Bible:*

Because of Adam's disobedience, sin and death entered the world. And because of his sin, all people sin, and all people will someday die.

●●●

Adam and Eve made a choice to disobey God. Their sin could have been the end of God's wonderful plan for humans, but God didn't let people's sin stop him. Instead, he sent Jesus to save, or buy back for God, all those who believe in him so that their relationship with him could be restored.

Because of that gift, we can be okay with God even though we sometimes do wrong. God hates sin because sinful acts always go against his perfection and holiness. But he knows we will sometimes make wrong choices, and through his grace, he can still use us. When we disobey, we can ask for God's forgiveness and continue serving him.

Maybe you've been afraid God can't use you because of your sin. First John 1:9 says when you tell God about your sin, he forgives you and makes you clean.

Because I want to have a close friendship with God, I'll write to him about my sin and thank him for his forgiveness.

Pray:

Thank God for the gift of his Son, who brought forgiveness for sin.

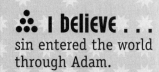

∴ I believe . . .
sin entered the world through Adam.

Adventure video games can be a lot of fun. You wander through a fantasyland trying to rescue a princess, find a treasure, or solve a mystery. You might be a person, a monkey, a dragon, a hedgehog, or some other creature.

It's exciting to defeat danger and overcome obstacles at every turn. Maybe you walk a thin bridge over a deep gorge. Perhaps you have to sneak past fierce warriors. Or maybe there's a huge creature guarding a clue that you have to figure out.

But don't worry, it's just a video game. If your character doesn't make it, you have a couple more chances. Most video games give you three to five lives to get things right. If you know a special code, you might even earn endless lives. Then you just keep coming back over and over again.

Having endless lives would certainly make things easier and less stressful. You wouldn't have to worry if you mess up—you could just keep trying. And sooner or later, if you played long enough, you could defeat the game . . . no matter how many lives it took.

Check out Romans 2:7 in the *Young Believer Bible:*
This verse urges you to constantly seek to do good and be honorable with your life.

●●●

As great as video games can be, they're not real life. In real life you can't swim underwater for ten minutes without taking a breath or jump twenty feet into the air. And once your life is over, that's it—you don't get more lives to come back to do it better. In video games you can take big chances and risks. In real life you have to think carefully *before* you do something.

It's good to keep this fact in mind as you live your life: You have only one life with which to please God. The choices you make matter now and in the future. The things you do have consequences. So why not live smart, honor God, and have fun?

Pray:
Tell God you're going to live to please him, because you only get one chance at life.

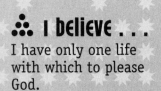

⁙ I believe . . .
I have only one life with which to please God.

Have you ever played a soccer team that had a really tough reputation? Even before the game started, you knew they'd be good, because you'd heard about them from other people. You had heard they were fast, strong, could pass perfectly, and could kick the ball as hard as mules. Sometimes a team's reputation is so good that you might feel that you have no chance to win even before you step on the field.

Of course, sometimes a reputation isn't all that it's cracked up to be. Maybe you've faced a team with a great reputation, but you won the game easily. Reputations come from hearing stories from other people. Stories can get blown out of proportion and exaggerated. We can't always believe all the stories we hear, especially when it comes to someone's reputation.

Sometimes the information is correct; other times it's not true.

Check out Habakkuk 3:2 in the *Young Believer Bible:*

This verse comes from Habakkuk's prayer. The prophet says that he knows about the amazing things God has done. He's in awe of the Lord's deeds and wants them to be more well-known.

●●●

These are some words I think of when I think about God:

1. _____

2. _____

3. _____

4. _____

While reputations can't always be trusted, you can always trust what you hear about God when you read the Bible. In the Old Testament, God had an awesome reputation. He brought plagues on Egypt. He brought down Jericho's wall. He defeated other gods. He helped his people win wars against impossible odds.

And not only does God live up to his reputation, he goes beyond it. No matter what you read in the Bible or hear from other people, God is greater than any story about him. Words can't even describe God's greatness.

Pray:

Pray and ask that God's deeds become better known to everybody in the world.

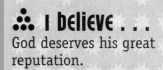

∴ I believe . . .
God deserves his great reputation.

Queen Esther brushed her dark, shiny hair. She shivered thinking about what she had to do. It seemed like just yesterday King Xerxes had chosen her as his new queen. Now the very future of her people—the Jews—depended on her. Three days ago her cousin Mordecai had told her that the king had approved a law to kill all the Jews. Going before the king without being summoned by him was punishable by death, but Mordecai convinced Esther that God had placed her in the palace for the purpose of saving her people.

After praying and fasting, Esther went before the king. He was so happy to see her that he spared her life. Through a clever plan, Esther revealed an evil plot and convinced the king to save the Jews. Because of Queen Esther's courageous actions, a whole nation was saved. You can read all about this brave woman in the book of Esther.

Check out Esther 4:14 in the *Young Believer Bible:*

Mordecai recognized that God could use anyone to save the Jews. He saw that God had allowed Esther to become the queen for this specific reason. And if she was willing, God would use her to deliver her people.

● ● ●

Have you ever moved? There are lots of difficult things about moving: leaving your friends, going to a new school, and getting used to a new church. You may question why God allowed it. But he has a specific purpose for you in each place he puts you.

Are you willing to let God use you for his work in any situation? Look at each new circumstance as an opportunity to serve God. Look at the people around you. Is there someone who needs a friend? Maybe God has placed you in a position where you can speak up for him and people will listen. Even the school you attend provides many opportunities to serve God. You can choose to be like Esther by keeping your eyes open and being ready to act with courage when God presents you with a task.

Pray:

Tell God you're willing to be used by him in every circumstance.

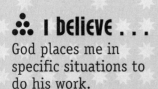

∴ I believe . . .

God places me in specific situations to do his work.

Tommy Toymaker hired Gilbert Gadget to construct an assembly line with robots to work at it. Gilbert could build anything. And in no time, he had created a group of robots that could build whatever Tommy wanted.

At first things went great and Tommy became the most popular toy maker in the world. But one day the robots stopped working. Tommy tried to fix them, but he couldn't. Tommy's workers tried to fix them, but they failed. Finally, Tommy called Gilbert to come back to the toy-making plant.

Gilbert walked into the factory, looked under a few panels, flipped a few switches, fiddled with some levers, and messed around with some wires. Suddenly, the robots sprang to life and started creating toys again.

"Just send me a bill," Tommy said to Gilbert as Gilbert left the factory.

Two days later Tommy got a bill for $10,000. He couldn't believe it. He wrote back to Gilbert, saying, "Are you crazy, $10,000!?! All you did is flip a few switches and fiddle around with some stuff. Send me a new bill that shows what I should really pay you."

Several days later a new bill came. Tommy opened it up, and it was still for $10,000! But under the bill it read, "Flipping switches and fiddling around: $100. Knowing what switches to flip and how to fiddle around: $9,900."

Check out Colossians 1:16 in the
Young Believer Bible:

Paul uses this verse to say that God created everything—things we can see and things that are invisible to us. All things were created by him and are used for him.

● ● ●

Just as Gilbert was the only one who knew exactly how the robots worked, God is the only one who knows exactly how you're wired. As your Creator, he understands you and loves you like no one else could. But not only did God design you and build you, he also "bought" you by giving his Son's life to save you from your sins. Because God designed you and his Son died for you on the cross, you can totally trust him with your life. You couldn't be in better hands.

Pray:

Tell God that you trust him with your life and that you want to be used by him.

∴ I believe . . .
I can trust God
because he made me.

Gymnasts do things that look impossible. They spring head over heels, turn back flips, and land perfectly on a tiny beam. They run at top speed, do three handsprings, and land a triple-twisting triple-flip on the floor exercise. And they make it all look easy. But as amazing as they are, you rarely see one of them earn a perfect 10.

Did you know that nobody scored a perfect 10 in Olympic gymnastics until Nadia Comaneci did it in the 1976 Summer Games in Montreal? She was just 14 years old when she stepped out to perform on the uneven bars. At the end of her routine, her score came up 1.00. Her coach was furious. How could they give his athlete only 1 out of 10? Certainly she had earned better than that.

Then the announcer told everybody that they had just witnessed the first 10 awarded in Olympic history. Perfect 10s were so unheard of that scoreboards weren't designed to post a double-digit number, which is why her total read 1.00.

In that Olympics Nadia scored seven perfect 10s—four on the uneven bars and three on the balance beam—and won three gold medals. It was incredible.

Check out Deuteronomy 32:4 in the *Young Believer Bible:*

This verse comes from the song of Moses that he wrote for the people of Israel. It says God's works are perfect. He does no wrong, and all of his ways are just and fair.

●●●

God can do no wrong. That's right, never. It's not in his makeup. He doesn't know anything but perfection. He can't mess up. Can't stumble. Can't make a mistake.

Do you think you can live up to God's standards by yourself? Of course not. No one can. We all wobble on the balance beam of life all the time. But with Jesus in your life and through his forgiveness, God doesn't see your imperfections. He only sees his perfect Son in you. And because of that, he always scores you a perfect 10.

Pray:

Praise God that he never makes mistakes and is always perfect.

∴ I believe . . .
God is perfect.

What kind of music is your favorite? There are tons of styles to choose from: pop, country, alternative, rap, jazz, gospel, classical. With all of these options, there's certain to be a sound to fit your tastes.

If you break down music to its most basic element, it is just notes on a page. And those notes have one purpose: to be arranged to create a sound. Only the listener can decide if he likes how those notes turn out.

Following Jesus is a lot like being a songwriter. But instead of musical notes, you must organize the basics of Christianity—Bible reading, prayer, worshiping God, talking with other Christians, telling people about Jesus, studying about God. Some kids really like to pray. Others can memorize tons of Bible verses. Still others love to sing about God. The more practice you give to each basic, the more comfortable you'll be doing each one. The more you pray, the more enjoyable it becomes. When you read your Bible every day, you begin to crave it more and more.

And as you write your life's "song" to God, don't forget to use all the basics of following him, because you can't create a beautiful song without using all the notes.

Check out Psalm 108:1 in the *Young Believer Bible:*
In this verse, David says he's confident in God, which gives him reason to sing God's praises. David used his whole soul to make music that honors God.

●●●

Have you noticed that all Christians aren't the same? Just as music comes in many forms, so believers in Jesus Christ are different. If you follow David's advice and tie your heart tightly to God's, then together you can make a beautiful song that will draw others to him.

But God also wants your life to honor him. God has given everybody who believes in him unique gifts. Not everybody can speak like Billy Graham or sing like Jaci Velasquez. But if you use your gifts for him and put your whole self and your whole soul into serving him, then your life's song will also be a sweet sound in God's ears.

Pray:
Ask God to give you the strength to make a special song for him.

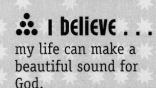

⁂ I believe . . .
my life can make a beautiful sound for God.

You probably don't like to wait in line at the movie theater or wait for your food to come at a restaurant when you're hungry. It's not fun to wait.

Fast-food restaurants have figured out that kids and parents don't like to wait—they want to eat. Drive down any road and you'll find all kinds of places to pick up fast food. But which one do you choose? Chicken? Hamburgers? French fries? Tacos? Sandwiches? The competition is fierce and there are so many choices. Businesses spend more than $13 billion—yes, billion—a year advertising fast food.

Do you want to hear an amazing fact? Studies show that more kids recognize McDonald's golden arches than know what the cross of Jesus is. Wild, huh? Actually it's pretty sad.

Fast-food restaurants want us to eat—now! And that's what we're doing. More than $110 billion was spent at fast-food restaurants in the United States in 2000, proving that nobody likes to wait.

Of course, by not waiting, people are probably eating a lot of stuff that isn't all that healthy, like extra fat, salt, and chemicals. Sometimes waiting for a good meal at home would be a better idea.

Check out Micah 7:7 in the *Young Believer Bible:*

Things aren't going too well for God's people in this passage. They're making a lot of bad choices. But the prophet Micah says he's going to watch in hope for the Lord. He's going to wait for God, because Micah knows the Lord will hear him.

●●●

Nobody likes to wait, but sometimes waiting is the best thing. Waiting to eat good food instead of fast food can be healthier. And waiting to hear from God before acting can make you wiser.

God always hears your prayers, but he doesn't always answer right away. Sometimes he wants you to wait. Waiting isn't easy. Taking action and doing something seems better, more productive. But having the same attitude as Micah can help you as you wait. Keep praying to God, trust him, try to learn what he wants to teach you, and expect that he will answer.

Pray:

Tell God you're going to trust him and wait for him when he doesn't immediately answer you.

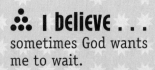

⦂ I believe . . .
sometimes God wants me to wait.

Do you like juggling? Once you're good at it, you can keep three, four, five, six, maybe even seven balls in the air at one time. Of course, the more balls you have in the air, the harder it is to keep things from falling apart.

Imagine for a moment that you're juggling. Even if you're a terrible juggler, you can pretend that you're great at keeping the balls moving. You have a golden ball that stands for your relationship with God. There's a red ball for your family, blue for sports, green for hobbies, orange for friends, and so on. You can try to keep all the balls in the air at once, but if you try that, your relationship with God is up in the air an awful lot! It's hard to hold on to him when you're so busy with everything else in life. But you have another option. You can always keep the golden ball in one hand. This way you might have to cut back on some of the other activities so you won't be juggling as many balls, but you'll always have the most important ball close to you. It'll never be lost up in the air.

Which way do you think is the best way to juggle?

Check out Psalm 46:10 in the *Young Believer Bible:*

This verse reminds you to take the time to be quiet and think about God. He will be shown honor by all the nations throughout the world.

• • •

In order to live right, believers in Jesus need to always hold on to the golden ball. *But then I won't be able to juggle as many balls,* you think. *I'll have to give something up.* Well, that might be true. But if you drop the golden ball, the others will fall as well. When we're too busy, it's hard to think straight and keep right attitudes and thoughts.

There are a lot of things keeping me busy these days. Here are some of the things I do:

1. _____
2. _____
3. _____

Does God have a bigger place in your life than your other activities? Is there anything you need to let go of? By keeping the golden ball in your hand, you'll be less distracted and better able to honor and please God in everything you do—even if that means doing fewer things.

Pray:

Tell God you want to slow down and praise him.

I believe . . .
being quiet to think about God draws me closer to him.

I have two little sisters—but it feels like I have seven of them. They bug me all the time, and we don't even share a room! What can I do?
Bugged
Sistersville, West Virginia

Dear Bugged,
Isn't it a pain that you're so interesting? Because that's why your sisters are always around. They bug you because they love you and are interested in what you're doing. In fact, you're probably one of their role models. Little kids just naturally look up to their parents and older siblings. So before you try to toss your little sisters out of your life, keep their feelings in mind. You can have an awesome impact on them and help them grow up into great people—and that's pretty cool.

But you also need to have some time alone. Playing with your friends or doing homework can go better without your sisters around. It would be good to talk to your parents about setting up rules for the girls to follow about giving you space and time to yourself. Then sit down and explain to your sisters that you love them but can't be with them all the time.

It wouldn't be good to completely shut out your sisters. Someday you'll discover they might make great friends.

Check out 1 Timothy 5:8 in the *Young Believer Bible:*

This verse says if a person doesn't care for people in her own house, then she's worse than somebody who doesn't believe in God.

●●●

God thinks family is really important. The Bible says you're one of his children and part of his family. And he wants you to treat your family on earth well too. After all, he put you in that family.

When Paul writes to Timothy that providing for family is part of being a believer in Jesus, he's probably talking about more than giving them money. He's talking about love and friendship and encouragement. Sure, not every minute of family life is a party. But God thinks that making an effort to care for family is a good idea.

Pray:

Thank God for your family, and tell him you're going to try to treat them right.

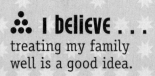

⁂ I believe . . .
treating my family
well is a good idea.

Imagine yourself riding your bike down the street. Suddenly you hit a rock, veer into the curb, and fly into the air. Fortunately you land in some grass and aren't hurt—but your front bike tire is totally bent. You walk your bike home, go into the garage, and find a hammer. *Whack. whack, whack.* You smash your bike's rim with the hammer trying to get it straight. (Not a smart plan.)

As you're beating your bike, one of your dad's friends drives by in his car. "Need any help with that?" he shouts.

"No, I'm fine," you reply.

Your dad's friend drives away shaking his head. A couple of days later you're back on your bike, wobbling down the street. (You never did get that tire totally straight.) Out of nowhere a cat runs in front of you, forcing you to turn quickly and hit a tree. Again, you're not hurt, but your bike has a bent frame. You decide to jump on it to straighten it out (again, not a good idea).

This time your dad drives by. "Need some help?" he asks.

"No, I'm fine," you answer, hopping up and down on your poor bike.

Check out Psalm 121:2 in the *Young Believer Bible:*
In this verse the psalm writer is very clear who helps him. His help comes from the Lord, who made the heavens and the earth.

●●●

Isn't it funny how people sometimes need help, but they don't ask for it? They're willing to smash something or jump up and down trying to fix it on their own, when they should just ask for help. Jesus wants us to ask him for help. He's waiting, but a lot of times we say, "No thanks, I'm fine."

The truth is that sometimes we're not fine. We've all sinned, which separates us from God. Only Jesus can forgive our sins and offer us a personal relationship with God.

If you haven't asked Jesus to help you know God, why not pray to him today? Jesus won't stop helping you. He'll always be there when you need him.

Pray:
Thank Jesus for being your ultimate helper.

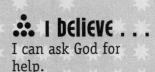
∴ I believe . . .
I can ask God for help.

July 24

It's summer . . . time to enjoy a family vacation. Once the plans are made, it's fun to get excited about where you're going. Is it the beach, the mountains, a lake, a national park, a relative's house? The time before you leave on a trip can seem to drag along. And as the moment to leave gets closer, you just have one thing left to do: pack.

Packing is the key to a good vacation. You don't want to forget your shorts, socks, shoes, underwear, toothbrush, sunglasses, pajamas, shirts, swimsuit, or other important items. Packing can take a lot of time and planning.

If you don't pack something before you leave, it won't be in your suitcase when you arrive. But you don't discover if you did a good job packing until you start unpacking. Unpacking can be very interesting. Maybe you find something in your suitcase that you hadn't planned to bring, but you realize later that you totally needed it.

Check out Proverbs 29:18 in the
Young Believer Bible:

This verse says when people don't accept God's guidance, they run wild. But you'll be happy if you obey God.

• • •

You may be asking yourself what packing for vacation has to do with the Bible. Good question. And here's your answer: Just as it's important to unpack your suitcase to see what's inside when you're on vacation, it's even more crucial to unpack what's hidden in God's Word to discover all the wonderful things he has in store for you.

God has packed all kinds of wisdom into the Bible. He planned everything in his Word, and it's perfect. God did an awesome packing job. Every time you read the Bible, you can unpack something new. If you keep studying God's Word, you'll understand more about God and more about what he wants you to do. And once you understand God's commands, it's easier to follow them, which leads to blessing. Now how about a great summer?

Pray:

Ask God to help you unpack his Word, understand it . . . and follow it.

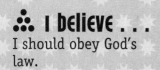
∴ I believe . . .
I should obey God's law.

If you've ever had your mouth washed out with soap, then you know what an awful experience that is. That tactic to encourage nice language has been around for years. Can you imagine (or remember) what that tastes like? Not good! Just suds, bubbles, and a disgusting flavor.

Parents sometimes wash their children's mouths out if they say bad words, such as cuss words. The punishment is pretty bad—so most kids quickly learn to stay away from those words. And some words should be avoided. Perhaps some of them just popped into your mind.

But did you think of the words *gosh* or *gee*? Those two words might not seem so bad, but if you look them up in a dictionary, you'll find that they are substitutes for the name *God*. And you certainly wouldn't use his name lightly, because God doesn't appreciate his name being used without the respect it deserves.

Check out Exodus 20:7 in the *Young Believer Bible:*
This verse says that God won't let anyone go unpunished who misuses his name.

● ● ●

The Bible is serious when it talks about how to use God's name. We should only use the name of God in reverence, like when we're praying to him, praising him, crying out to him, or worshiping him in some other way. God's name deserves respect.

Many kids probably don't think twice when they say *gosh* or *gee* or even *God*. Maybe if they knew how much that hurts God, they would be more careful about how they talk.

Does your speech show that you follow Jesus? Even a little disrespectful word isn't a good thing. There are plenty of other fun expressions to use, such as: *Man, Wow, Cool, Awesome, Sweet, No Way,* or *Stoked*. Or you can make up a fun expression of your own.

Pray:
Tell God you want to respect his name with your words and actions.

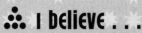

⁘ I believe . . .
God's name is special and should be treated that way.

July 26

Jordan and Scott had been playing video games for hours.

"This Rad Racer IV is awesome," Jordan said. "I wish I had this game."

"Boys," Scott's mom called down to them in the basement, "come up for a snack."

Scott ran to help his mom and asked Jordan to clean up the video games. In a couple of minutes, Jordan joined Scott at the table for some food.

"I think that's enough video-game playing," Mom said. "Why don't you boys go outside."

Scott and Jordan spent the rest of the day throwing around a football and playing with Scott's remote-control car.

Jordan went home when it started to get dark, so Scott went back downstairs to play some more Rad Racer IV. But when he looked at the game console, he couldn't find the cartridge.

I bet Jordan stole my game! Scott thought. *He said he wished he had it.*

Scott ran upstairs to the phone as his face turned red with anger.

"Hey, you thief!" Scott shouted into the phone. "Where's my video game?"

When Jordan denied taking it and hung up, Scott went back downstairs. He reached for a different game and noticed something behind the console . . . Rad Racer IV.

Check out James 1:19 in the *Young Believer Bible:*

Jesus' brother James probably wrote this verse. And James wants readers to notice what he says, because he writes, "Take note" (NIV). That's like saying "Listen up." He has a few good words for us about listening well, thinking before speaking, and avoiding getting angry quickly.

●●●

Here's how I think Scott should have handled the situation differently:

_____

_____

_____

If we lose our temper and falsely accuse a friend, we put our friendship in jeopardy, which means we run the risk of losing that friendship. By taking James's advice to be a good listener and be slow to get angry, Scott could have avoided making Jordan feel bad and himself look foolish.

God gave us emotions for a reason. And it wasn't so we could get mad and scream at our friends. Our emotions allow us to feel love, compassion, and forgiveness—all qualities that come from God.

:: I believe . . .

I shouldn't let my emotions get the best of me.

Pray:

Thank God for your emotions, and ask him to help you keep them under control.

When you get a new puppy or kitten, who falls in love first: you or the animal?

The answer is probably you. Sure the puppy may wag its tail or the kitten may purr when you pet it, but it doesn't know you in the beginning. All it knows at first is that it had been living with its mom, brothers, and sisters, and now it's in a strange place. At first, it may even be scared.

You, on the other hand, know your pet. You picked it out. You gave it a name and started taking care of it from day one. You even make sacrifices for your pet, such as staying up late when it whines, feeding it, washing it, and cleaning up after it. You show your pet you love it in a lot of ways.

Eventually, your pet figures things out and starts to love you. It sees your face every day. It enjoys playing with you. And it notices how much you take care of it. That's when the two of you grow close.

Check out Romans 5:8 in the *Young Believer Bible:*

This verse talks about how God loves us. God showed his love by sending his Son, Jesus, to die for us, even when we were being disobedient and didn't know him.

●●●

Just as you love your pet before it loves you, God loved you first. Sure, you're not God's pet—you're his child—but the idea's the same.

God loved you before you loved him and *before* you were even worthy of being loved. Even though he knew people would do all kinds of things to show God they didn't love him, he sent Jesus to die for them.

That's love. That's sacrifice. And it's certainly a lot harder than waking up in the middle of the night to let your pet outside. Once you understand God's love, it's easier to love him. It's a very natural love, just the way your pet loves you.

Pray:

Thank God for loving you first and showing you how to love.

I believe . . .
God loved me first.

What if the president came to you with a very important job? Imagine that he told you that you were the only one who could do it, and if you failed many lives would be lost.

Whoa! That's a lot of pressure, you may be thinking. *I don't know if I'd accept the mission.*

Now what if the president told you that there was no chance you would fail? What if he said that he'd prepared Special Forces to go out with you and give you full protection? And what if he promised his own help to complete the task, no matter what the cost?

You'd probably feel a lot better about going on the mission with the president's word that he would help you and that you would definitely succeed. You might even get excited about being entrusted with such an important job.

"Bring it on!" you'd say. "I'm ready to serve."

Check out 1 Thessalonians 5:24 in the *Young Believer Bible:*

God has called you to do specific tasks for his glory. And this verse tells you that he is faithful and will accomplish what he has told you to do. What a wonderful guarantee!

●●●

Serving God can seem like a big job. Sometimes the things he asks you to do seem difficult or even impossible. But the great news is that the all-powerful God has promised to always be with you and help you with everything he calls you to do.

What are some things that God may be asking you to do? Love an unlovable person? Be kind to a brother or sister? Tell a friend about Jesus? Do these jobs seem too hard to do on your own? Ask God for help. The One who gave you the assignment will help you complete it. And you get the joy of being part of God's plan!

These are three things I believe God is asking me to do:

1. _____

2. _____

3. _____

Pray:
Thank God for promising to help you do his work.

⁂ I believe . . .
God will help me do his work.

Martha had been working hard all day. She had been up at the crack of dawn, preparing the bread for the evening meal. Martha's younger sister, Mary, offered to help, but she wasn't much good because she was so distracted.

"I can't wait until Jesus comes!" she said, her eyes dancing.

She won't be so happy if Jesus comes and the meal is uncooked, Martha thought.

Soon Jesus arrived. Martha wanted to make sure everything was just perfect, so she continued working. She noticed Mary had planted herself at Jesus' feet without even a thought of helping. The harder Martha worked, the more irritated she became with her sister. *She should be helping me!*

Finally, Martha could stand it no longer. She interrupted the conversation, saying, "Lord, don't you care that my sister has left me to do the work by myself? Tell her to help me!"

Jesus' answer surprised Martha. "You're worried and upset about so many things," he said, "but only one thing is important. Mary has chosen to spend time with me, and that time will not be taken away from her." (You can read the actual story in Luke 10:38-42.)

Check out Mark 12:33 in the *Young Believer Bible:*

Loving God and those around you is more important to him than sacrifices or service. God expects obedience, but what he desires most is your love.

●●●

Do you ever get busy *doing* things for God? You memorize a bazillion verses for Bible club. You spend time serving others. You go to church every chance you get. When you think about it, there's *a lot* you can *do* for God.

But sometimes the best way to show God you love him is just to spend time with him. You can't physically sit at his feet like Mary did, but you can read the Bible, talk to him in prayer, and sing praise songs to him. Special time with the Lord will help you in your service to him.

If you're a worker bee and want to do things for him, God loves you and is pleased when you serve him. But it's even more important to spend some quiet time with him each day.

Pray:

Ask God to help you make time for him every day.

⁂ I believe . . .

I show God my love by spending time with him.

Doesn't it bug you when somebody does something wrong and gets away with it? Maybe you've seen students cheat on an assignment without the teacher finding out. Or perhaps you've had friends who stole something from a store and didn't get caught. Maybe your big brother scooted his green beans into the trash when your mom wasn't looking, so he didn't have to eat them.

At times like that, a couple of thoughts probably ran through your head:

a. *Boy, if they're getting away with that, maybe I should try it too.*
b. *I wish they'd get caught. Maybe God could send a lightning bolt from heaven to zap them.*

The first thought, of course, isn't a healthy one. As your parents have probably said to you before, "If all of your friends jumped off a cliff, would you do it too?" Of course not. Just because somebody makes a dumb decision doesn't mean you have to follow.

The second idea has a ring of truth to it. Although God doesn't send lightning bolts and you might never see it, he does guarantee that people guilty of sin will be punished.

Check out Nahum 1:3 in the *Young Believer Bible:*
In this verse Nahum writes that God takes his time before getting angry. At the same time, God has great power and never lets the guilty get away without being punished.

●●●

People like quick justice. Somebody commits a crime, the police track him down, and—wham-o—he's in jail. Maybe you always want to see other kids get what they deserve when they do something wrong.

But God doesn't work that way. He often gives all of us what we *don't* deserve: mercy, love, compassion, and a second chance. God is slow to get angry.

However, just because you don't see somebody get punished doesn't mean that person escapes trouble forever. God just has a different time frame. And he promises that the guilty will always be punished . . . in his time.

Pray:
Thank God that he's a just God.

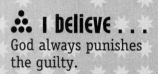

⁂ I believe . . .
God always punishes the guilty.

A good friend can be hard to find. What if there were a "friend" store where you could go and pick out friends? Which kind of friend would you most likely choose?

a. a funny friend who could make me laugh
b. a smart friend who could tell me interesting facts
c. a caring friend who could make me feel better when I'm upset
d. a quiet friend who would listen to me
e. an athletic friend who would play sports with me

Friends come in all shapes, sizes, and personalities. And that's the great thing about them. Each one is special and has something different to offer. But how can you be sure your friends will stick with you and encourage you to grow closer to God? Finding friends *isn't* as easy as going to a store and picking them out. Sometimes friends end up being selfish or mean. The book of Proverbs has some good advice about this topic.

Check out Proverbs 13:20 in the Young Believer Bible:
This verse shows that it's important to spend time with people who are wise. Wise people know the right thing to do and do it. Hanging out with foolish friends can actually hurt you.

●●●

Picking your pals is an important task and one to take seriously. You spend a lot of time with friends, so they *will* influence you—for good or for bad. If you're always spending your time with kids who cuss, chances are you'll catch yourself cussing too. Or if you hang with friends who gossip, you'll most likely begin spreading rumors as well.

A good start to surrounding yourself with wise people is to make sure your closest friends know the Lord. Christian friends will encourage your faith and help you grow strong. Some other qualities to look for are honesty, wisdom, and loyalty. Sound too good to be true? One way to begin is by trying to be a good friend yourself. Then the right kind of people will be attracted to you. A good friend is a treasure; look for yours carefully!

Pray:
Ask God to help you choose friends wisely.

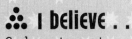

∴ I believe . . .
God wants me to choose my friends wisely.

August 1

What's old?

Spoiled milk is old—old enough that it doesn't taste good anymore.

Parents are old. Well, at least they're older than you. They have to be, after all, because they're your parents.

Teachers are old. Some of them might look like they've been at your school forever.

Antiques are old. Just the name "antique" makes you think of something old and fragile . . . and possibly valuable.

Great-grandparents are old. They can probably remember a time when TVs, radios, and home computers didn't exist.

Buildings are old. Well, some of them are. Certain castles in Europe have stood for thousands of years.

Methuselah was old. He's the person in the Bible who lived for 969 years—that's seriously old.

Rocks are old. Now you're talking. Rocks have been around since God created the earth.

In some ways, all of the things in the above list are old. Age is kind of funny to think about. Compared to a baby, you're old. But if you compare a baby to a fruit fly, the baby's old because she's been alive since she was inside her mother.

But one thing's for sure: God is older than everything and everyone.

Check out Isaiah 40:28 in the *Young Believer Bible:*

This verse tells you some of God's characteristics. He's everlasting. He'll never grow tired. He understands everything.

•••

God lived before he formed the earth. God was around before time started—because he started time. If you compare God to the universe, the universe would be a baby. No, even younger than that. God is infinite, which means he has no beginning and no end. God is everlasting. Do you know what that means? It means he'll last forever.

But unlike a lot of things that get old and fall apart, God stays the same. He never gets tired. He never grows weary. He's the same awesome, powerful, mighty God who made everything at the beginning of time. And he'll continue being that same awesome God forever and ever and ever and ever. . . .

Pray:

Praise God that he never grows tired and lives forever.

∴ I believe . . .

God exists forever.

August 2

What's your favorite ride at the amusement park? Bumper cars? Ferris wheel? Log ride?

All of those are great. But a lot of kids like the thrill of a roller coaster. Classic wooden roller coasters shake and rattle with excitement. Steel roller coasters spin and twist upside down. Some roller coasters let your feet dangle as you ride, while others give you the thrill of flying.

If you're looking for the ultimate roller-coaster ride, there's just one place to go. Cedar Point in Sandusky, Ohio, features some of the wildest coasters in the world, including Top Thrill Dragster. This steel scream machine is the fastest and tallest roller coaster in the world. Check out these stats:

- Riders go down a 420-foot tall drop at a 90-degree angle. If you're not into geometry, 90 degrees is straight down!
- You'd better be buckled in tight, because you'll reach speeds of 120 mph! You'll probably never drive that fast in a car . . . unless you're on the German Autobahn.
- Six 16-passenger trains will allow about 1,500 riders to experience the thrill of their lives every hour.

Check out Joshua 1:7 in the *Young Believer Bible:*

This verse says to be strong and courageous when it comes to following God's commands. Learning what's in God's Word will make your life thrilling and successful in God's eyes.

●●●

People are willing to pay a lot of money and take big risks to squeeze some excitement out of life. Amusement parks make millions of dollars every year (and spend millions—Top Thrill Dragster cost $25 million to build) giving people thrills and chills. And folks keep coming up with bigger, better, faster, and scarier rides.

But God has a secret: If you want an abundant, exciting life, all you have to do is follow him. He wants you to have fun and be amazed at life. When you know God's Word and follow his plan for your life, every day can be like a day spent at an amusement park. Well . . . without the cotton candy.

Pray:

Tell God you're going to live an exciting life for him.

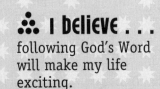

∴ I believe . . .
following God's Word will make my life exciting.

A friend's dad just died. Now when I see my friend, I get nervous I'll say the wrong thing. I'm starting to avoid him, but I know that's the wrong thing to do. I still want to be friends, so could you give me some ideas on how to help him through this hard time?
Concerned
Death Valley, California

Dear Concerned,
There's nothing worse than losing somebody you love. Your friend probably feels lost and sad and alone. Just continuing to be his friend is one of the best things you can do. Don't pretend that nothing happened and that everything's all right. Listen if he needs to talk about his feelings. Be honest about your own feelings. Let him know that you'll be his friend no matter what and that he can count on you to be there for him. Help him with homework if he's falling behind at school. Invite him to sleep over. Don't worry about saying the wrong thing. Showing you're a faithful, trustworthy friend says more than words ever could.

And don't forget to pray. Only God can heal your friend and give him the strength to make it through this difficult time. Ask God to surround your friend with his love and draw him close.

Check out 2 Corinthians 1:3 in the Young Believer Bible:

In this verse the apostle Paul writes that we can praise God because he's the source of all of our comfort.

● ● ●

Jesus is there for you in every situation. He's been around since before time began, so he's seen everything and knows what to do all the time. Nothing happens without him knowing about it.

But sometimes things happen that don't make any sense: a loved one dies, a pet runs away, parents decide they don't want to live together anymore. When situations like that happen in your life or in your friends' life, turn to God and ask him to show you what to do. He can give you the right things to say and heal your sad heart.

Pray:

Thank God that he can comfort you in all situations.

∴ I believe . . .
Jesus comforts people who mourn.

August 4

Eric Liddell loved to run. As a young man, he ran 100-meter races in his homeland of Scotland. Soon he became the British champion. Eric had great determination. Once he finished first in a race after being knocked off the track by another runner. Running was important to Eric, but something else was more important: God.

Eric continued to succeed as a runner and earned a spot on the 1924 summer Olympic team. His country had high hopes for the blond-haired, blue-eyed young man. But when Eric learned that his qualifying race was on a Sunday, he refused to compete. Eric believed Sunday was a day for worship, and he didn't want to put running ahead of God. God blessed Eric's devotion and allowed him to race in two other events—the 200-meter and 400-meter. Eric ran his best for God. He took bronze in the first race and won gold in the second.

Eric continued to put God first in his life by going to China as a missionary. Many Chinese people accepted Christ because of his godly example and genuine love. Eric was just an ordinary man, but God helped him to do extraordinary things because Eric always put him first.

Check out Exodus 20:3 in the *Young Believer Bible:*

God wants to be the most important thing in a believer's life. Putting other things first is the same as making those things gods.

●●●

What are the things that are most important to you? How much time do you spend on those things? How does the amount of time you spend getting to know God better compare to the time you spend on other things?

Here's what I spend my time doing:

1. Activity: _____ Time Spent: _____

2. Activity: _____ Time Spent: _____

3. Activity: _____ Time Spent: _____

4. Activity: _____ Time Spent: _____

You can put God first by spending time with him each day and by obeying him. Sometimes you may have to make hard choices, as Eric did. But with God's help you can choose to put him first. When you do, God will bless you and help you do great things for him.

Pray:

Ask God to help you put him first.

∴ I believe . . .
God wants me to put him first in my life.

August 5

What if you had a friend who never let you down? He was always there for you and never went back on his promises. On top of that, he always put you first. He wanted to play whatever you did and had fun doing it. And most amazingly, what if he never did anything wrong? He would be the perfect friend. Anyone would want a friend like that. But a pal as unselfish as that would be hard to come by. In fact, could anyone live up to that glowing description?

One person could, and he did. You probably can guess that it was Jesus. But can you picture Jesus as one of your friends—just a not-so-regular boy your age? You hear a lot about Jesus as a baby and a lot about him as a grown man. But you may forget that he was also a kid like you.

Check out Luke 2:52 in the *Young Believer Bible:*

The Bible doesn't talk a lot about Jesus' childhood, but this verse says that Jesus grew just like any other child. He grew physically, but he also grew in knowledge and in wisdom. As he grew, his relationships with God and other people developed too.

●●●

Jesus knows what it's like to grow up. It's hard! He experienced growing pains, rejection from friends, annoying brothers and sisters, and parents asking him to do chores—all the stuff a regular kid deals with. The only difference was that Jesus never sinned. He faced all that hard stuff, and he still pleased God in everything he did.

That can give you hope. It's not impossible to be a kid and please God. It's hard sometimes, but with God's help you can say no to sin and grow into a godly young person. When you're tackling something difficult, remember that you have a best friend who understands exactly how you feel. And with him by your side, you can meet any challenge.

Pray:

Ask God to help you grow into the person he wants you to be.

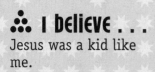

❖ I believe . . .

Jesus was a kid like me.

August 6

The Venus's-flytrap is a meat-eating plant with a special technique for catching the flies it feasts on. Its leaves look like mouths lined with little hairs like teeth, and the plant's sweet nectar attracts bugs. When a bug buzzes its way to the edge of the leaf, the hairs are disturbed, and the mouth snaps shut! That means a fly may stop by for a tasty snack only to become the main course.

Sin is the same way. The Bible says that the tricks of the devil are a trap. Sin may look attractive, but choosing to sin can turn out horribly. Fortunately, the Bible tells you how to avoid the tricky trap of sin.

Check out 1 Timothy 6:11 in the *Young Believer Bible:*

Believers can avoid the trap of sin. With God's help, many Christians do say no to sin. This verse tells us to flee from wrong desires. When we run after righteousness, godliness, faith, and love, we won't get eaten up by sin.

●●●

So how can you steer clear of sin? First, identify the things that tempt you to do wrong. Those things are like the sweet nectar of the Venus's- flytrap. It may seem okay to disobey your mom and go to a friend's house or to make fun of your younger brother. And what about cheating on a test? Getting a good grade without studying may look very good.

But it's important to see sin for what it is: a deadly trap. The Bible says that giving in to sin can destroy your life (see Ezekiel 18:30). The good news is that Jesus won the victory over sin and can help you escape its destruction.

Because I want to be ready to make the right choices when I'm tempted to sin, here's how I'll respond if I face these situations:

1. When my brother or sister is bugging me I'll respond by _____ .

2. When I want to watch something on TV that I'm not supposed to I'll choose to _____ .

3. When my friends want to do something I know is wrong I'll say _____ .

Pray:
Ask God to help you avoid the trap of sin.

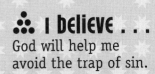

⁛ I believe . . .
God will help me avoid the trap of sin.

What makes you happy? Check any of the following that apply:

- ❏ Spending time with friends
- ❏ Eating ice cream
- ❏ Riding my bike
- ❏ Playing with my dog

- ❏ Going on vacation
- ❏ Playing video games
- ❏ Watching a movie
- ❏ Other: _____

You can probably make a long list of the things that make you happy. But what happens when things don't go your way? Your bike gets a flat tire. Your older brother eats the last bowl of ice cream. Your vacation is canceled because Dad has to work. Can you still be happy?

King David in the Bible talked about a deeper happiness than people and things can give. It's called joy. Joy allows you to be happy no matter what the circumstances. So where can you get this joy? Read what David says to find out.

Check out Psalm 16:11 in the *Young Believer Bible:*

David had learned the secret of true joy, which made him love praising God. Not only does God give you life when you believe in him, but as you spend time with him, he fills you with joy. Just being with God brings joy.

●●●

Can you really be glad when things are going badly? Sure you can. That's because joy is based on how close you are to God and how much you realize all the things he has done for you. And although your life may change, God never does. If you believe in him and have asked him to be your Savior, then he has given you eternal life. And when you look forward to the joy of heaven, you will have joy now too.

Think about all the things God has done for you. He loves you more than anyone else can. He has saved you from being punished for your sins. He promises to never leave you. He guides you and protects you. Those are some great reasons to be filled with joy.

These are more things about God that bring me joy:

1. _____

2. _____

3. _____

Pray:
Thank God for giving you joy that will never go away.

⁘ I believe . . .
God fills me with joy.

August 8

Picture yourself wearing your favorite outfit. What does it look like? Describe it here:

_____

_____

You may have written down a favorite T-shirt or described a great pair of shoes. The fact is, most kids have a favorite outfit that they wear a lot. You know, clothes that go from the laundry room to their bodies in an instant and eventually end up with holes from being worn out.

But does your favorite outfit change a lot? Do you dress to fit the latest trends? Society will tell you that you need the latest fashions to look and feel cool. Television commercials and magazine ads try to show you what your favorite outfit should look like.

It's easy to spend too much time making sure you look a certain way. While it's good to try to look your best, there are a lot more important things to think about. Instead of having to wear what's plastered on a billboard, it's better to focus on what's attractive to God, such as trusting him and showing love toward others.

Check out Matthew 6:25 in the *Young Believer Bible:*

In this verse Jesus tells us not to worry about what we eat or what we wear. Life is more important than food. And our bodies are more important than what we put on them. God will take care of you.

●●●

God doesn't care what we wear. And he doesn't want us to care too much either. Sure, we should shower, keep our hair clean and brushed, and dress nicely. But we don't need to spend a whole lot of time and energy on our "style."

Jesus says there are more important things for me to think about than my outfit. Here are a few:

1. _____

2. _____

3. _____

Following Jesus' advice will never go out of style.

Pray:

Thank God for providing your basic needs of food and clothing so you can concentrate on more important things.

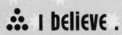
∴ I believe . . .
I shouldn't worry about what I'm wearing.

Rebekah hated sharing a room with her younger sister. *If I had my own room then Erica wouldn't always get into my stuff,* she thought. The more she thought about it, the more she felt like it wasn't fair that she had to share.

When she told her dad what she was thinking, he shrugged his shoulders and answered, "Well, Rebekah, sharing is a natural part of life. Unless you live by yourself in a cave, you're going to have to share. And sharing a room is pretty common. Lots of kids have to bunk with a brother or sister."

Guess what! God loves it when we share. Sharing a room is like a spiritual boot camp—like in the military. Boot camp is training time to shape men and women into good soldiers. It is usually hard work, but those who go through it are stronger because of it.

Giving up some privacy and having to share space with a sibling may be hard sometimes, but you can bet that God is using it to shape you into an unselfish person. And sharing a room is just the beginning of all you can share with others.

Check out 1 Timothy 6:18 in the *Young Believer Bible:*

Part of doing good is being generous and willing to share. It pleases God when you share what you have with others. Generosity is the opposite of selfishness.

● ● ●

If you have to share a room, you can look for ways to make sharing more pleasant. Everyone needs privacy sometimes, so try to find a place you can go when you want to be alone. And maybe you could set up fun "roommate" traditions, such as playing games, reading a book out loud, or listening to tapes before you go to bed.

If you don't share a room, maybe you have to share something else, such as the computer, the television, or the basketball. Sharing doesn't mean you have to hand over your stuff whenever the other person wants it. But it does mean looking for opportunities to give generously to others.

It may help to remember who your stuff actually belongs to. Everything belongs to God. He's just allowing you to take care of it for him.

Here are three things I sometimes have a tough time sharing:

1. _____

2. _____

3. _____

Pray:

Ask God to help you share what you have.

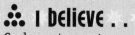

∴ I believe . . .

God wants me to
share with others.

Have you ever felt the need for God's help? Maybe your home was wrecked by a natural disaster or perhaps you were surrounded by bullies—and only God could save you.

What did you do?

God's people in the Old Testament often found themselves trapped in a corner. There was nothing they could do to save themselves, so they turned to God.

One time the powerful kingdom of Assyria surrounded Jerusalem and threatened to attack. The Assyrians had been destroying cities all over. But King Hezekiah knew God and trusted him to deliver the city. And do you know what? God did exactly that. You can find out how God saved Jerusalem by reading 2 Kings 18–19.

Check out 2 Kings 19:15 in the *Young Believer Bible:*

This verse records the beginning of a great prayer by King Hezekiah, who had gone up to the temple to pray. He said that God is the God of Israel and God over all the kingdoms of the earth.

●●●

Some great prayers are recorded in the Bible. The Lord's Prayer that Jesus prayed is probably the best known, but King Hezekiah's prayer is also an excellent one to use as a pattern for your own prayers.

Hezekiah starts off by praising God, and God deserves our praise too. But most people spend more time asking God for stuff than praising him—which is the opposite of how it should be.

Hezekiah's prayer is a good reminder that God alone is God over all the kingdoms of the earth. He made the heaven and the earth, and he is our God.

Here's my prayer of praise to God:

_____

_____

Pray:

Tell God that he deserves your praise and that you're going to give it to him.

∴ **I believe . . .**
only God is over all
the earth.

If someone asked you to prove you are a Christian, what evidence would you provide? Maybe you would offer some of the following proof:

a. I go to church.
b. I read my Bible.
c. Everyone in my family is a Christian.
d. I pray every day.
e. I'm a good person.

All of those things may be true, but those facts alone don't prove you're a Christian. You could wake up, put on cleats and shin guards, grab a soccer ball and go to a field, but that wouldn't make you a professional soccer player. Belief in Jesus Christ and his sacrifice on the cross is the basis of true faith. But there is another test of genuine faith mentioned in God's Word: hanging on to faith even if you're being persecuted for it. The first believers in Jesus suffered a lot of persecution; however, in the midst of their hard times, their faith grew and grew.

Check out 2 Thessalonians 1:3-4 in the *Young Believer Bible:*

Real faith lasts. It survives and is even made stronger through difficult times. When you trust God through the trials in your life, your perseverance proves that your faith is genuine.

●●●

How strong is your faith? When things are going well, it's easy to take God for granted. You may go through all the actions: attending church, reading your Bible, and being a good person. But is your relationship with God real? Trusting God through hard times shows true faith. God uses those times to shape your faith. Sticking close to God during painful situations can help you fully understand how faithful God is.

Maybe you haven't had many trials. How can you make sure your faith is real? First, expect that you will face trials in your life and be prepared. How will you react? Will you trust that God is in control and doing what's best for you?

Second, build a relationship with God. Read his Word often and talk to him in prayer. Then when hard times come, your faith will be strong because you'll have a close friend right by your side.

Pray:
Thank God for trials that strengthen your faith.

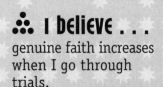

⁂ I believe . . .
genuine faith increases when I go through trials.

I have a friend who's always fighting with me. When I try to tell her to stop, she plugs her ears and walks away. Later she just pretends like we didn't fight, but it bothers me. What can I do?
Bummed Out
Battle Creek, Michigan

Dear Bummed Out,
Bickering buddies can really bring you down. It's just not fun spending time with somebody who always wants to do combat. But here's something to think about: It usually takes two people to fight. Think about recent arguments you've had with your friend. Is there anything you could have done to keep things from getting ugly?

When arguments do happen—and in most relationships they're unavoidable—you can't force your friend to work things out right away. But you can pray for her. Ask God to change her heart and make her more willing to deal with the problem. And when she pretends that the fight never occurred, you need to say how much that hurts your feelings. If she won't listen to you and the fights continue, you may want to think about finding a new friend.

Check out Proverbs 15:1 in the *Young Believer Bible:*
This verse says that by speaking gently, you can calm someone's anger and maybe even stop arguments before they start.

●●●

It's great to have friends. But anytime two people spend a lot of time together, eventually something's going to happen to hurt somebody's feelings. That's just human nature. People are emotional beings who make mistakes.

As followers of Jesus Christ, all of our words and actions are supposed to reflect our Savior. That's not easy to do, but it should be our goal. We all need to make sure we're not doing anything to start fights.

By staying calm and being thoughtful, you'll be better able to live at peace with your friends . . . and with your enemies.

Pray:
Ask God to help you be a more gentle person who reflects his gentleness.

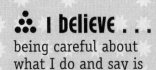
∴ I believe . . .
being careful about what I do and say is important.

Plants are amazing. It seems like anywhere a seed lands, a plant can grow. Have you ever seen a tree growing out of the side of a mountain? Almost impossibly, it hangs on with its roots going into the rock. Plants grow out of the cracks in a sidewalk . . . or even in the desert.

Desert plants are some of the most impressive and beautiful. They survive on just a few rainstorms each year. The creosote bush is one of the most common plants found in North America's hottest deserts. This bush grows only about four feet high and sometimes has pretty yellow flowers. But the coolest part of the creosote is hidden. Under the soil, its roots may go down hundreds of feet. Nobody knows for sure which plant grows the deepest roots, but the creosote might be a good guess. Miners once found roots from a creosote bush several hundred feet under the ground.

Not only can the creosote bush live a long time without water, it can just plain live a long time—up to two hundred years in some of the world's hottest, driest places. Now that's amazing.

Check out Colossians 2:6-7 in the *Young Believer Bible:*

These verses say we should do more than just receive Jesus into our lives. We need to take root and grow in him.

●●●

We can learn a lot from the creosote bush when it comes to our relationship with Jesus Christ. When we ask Jesus into our heart, we're like little plants with short roots. But as we grow in our relationship with him, our roots go deeper.

Can you imagine how hard it'd be to pull a creosote bush out of the ground? It'd be impossible even for a truck to move it. And that's how we need to be with Jesus.

When those dry times come and you're not all that excited about your faith, remember those deep roots. Hang on to Jesus. Wait for the refreshing rains. He'll never let your roots go dry.

Pray:

Ask God to help you grow deep roots in him.

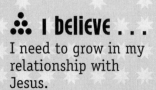

∴ I believe . . .

I need to grow in my relationship with Jesus.

Hiking through the woods with somebody who knows about plants can be a lot of fun. Your guide can show you what poison ivy looks like *before* you walk through it. He can point out which tree bark is edible and help you pick berries and mushrooms to eat.

When you're with someone who knows a lot about the forest, you're more likely to feel safe—like you could survive out in the wild.

The same thing can't be said of hiking with somebody who's clueless but acts like he knows everything. That can be sort of scary . . . even life-threatening. He might say, "I know what poison ivy looks like. It has rough leaves that grow in clumps of five." But the truth is poison ivy has smooth, shiny leaves that grow in threes.

And not all mushrooms and berries that you find in the forest are safe. One mistake could land you in the hospital—or worse.

No, it's a lot safer to stick with someone who knows what he's doing in the forest.

Check out Micah 6:8 in the *Young Believer Bible:*
This verse says the Lord has shown us what is good. And he wants us to do what's right, to love mercy, and to walk humbly with him.

●●●

Picking the right guide for a hike is important. And you couldn't have a better guide through the forest of life than God. He knows every twist and turn. He'll always keep you on the right path.

God shows you what is good. He steers you away from harm. He never leads you through a poison-ivy patch. You can know his commands and plans are good for you. And all he asks in return is for you to walk humbly with him, to show mercy to others, and to choose right actions.

By doing those things you'll experience life in a whole new way. Plus, you'll feel safer and have a more exciting time.

Pray:
Tell God you want to hike through life with him.

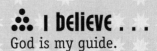
I believe . . .
God is my guide.

August 15

Think about the best reward you ever received. Maybe it was a trophy for an outstanding athletic accomplishment. Maybe it was an award for doing well in school. Or maybe your parents gave you a gift for doing your chores faithfully or going a whole month without talking back to them.

Let's face it. No matter what form they take, rewards are great. It's exciting to receive something in exchange for your hard work. Rewards give you extra motivation to do things well.

Did you know that God created you to love rewards? *But isn't it selfish to want a reward?* you may be thinking. No. It's only selfish if we let the reward become our only motivation for serving God. But it's actually healthy to think about rewards. They make all the hard work worth it and give you incentive to keep doing your best.

Check out Matthew 25:14-29 in the Young Believer Bible:

Jesus tells the story of a man giving money to his servants to invest when he goes on a journey. By the time the man comes back, two of the servants have doubled the money. But the last servant has buried his portion. Naturally, the master gets upset that the third man didn't do all he could with what he was given.

● ● ●

The Bible says that eternal life is a free gift from God. There's nothing we can do to earn salvation. But if we know Jesus as Savior, we'll one day receive rewards for the things we do for God on earth.

Since rewards shouldn't be our only motivation, maybe you can look at it this way. If God gives you a talent, you should use it. Then out of his love, God rewards you for doing your best for him.

Are you serving God each day? God wants to reward his children. Some of those rewards will come in the form of blessings on earth. But many others will be awarded when we get to heaven. That's exciting news!

Pray:

Thank God that you can use the things he gives you for him.

∴ I believe . . .

God rewards me when I put the things he gives me to good use.

August 16

Your best friend has a problem. A new basketball is missing from her garage. Your friend remembers putting it away the night before, but now it's gone. And that's not all. The neighbor two doors down is dribbling a new ball.

"That's all right," your friend says. "My ball probably rolled out of the garage and down the street. That kid doesn't know it's mine. Or maybe it's not mine anyway."

What's your response?

a. Sprint down the street, grab the ball away from the kid playing basketball, and put your feet in high gear back to your friend's house.
b. Walk over to the kid dribbling the ball and scream, "You're a thief! Give my friend's ball back."
c. Trust that your friend has the situation under control.
d. Call your friend a wimp and go home.

The best answer is *c*. Rather than get involved in your friend's problems and possibly make matters worse, it's good to let your friend handle the situation. Your friend's parents may also be able to help. It's your job to be supportive and let your friend do what's best.

Check out Proverbs 26:17 in the Young Believer Bible:

This verse says that getting involved in a quarrel you're not part of is like yanking a dog's ears. When Solomon wrote this long ago, dogs weren't pets. They were wild, which meant they would bite anyone who tried to grab their ears. Likewise, you could also suffer pain if you put yourself in the middle of a friend's fight.

● ● ●

When your friend has a problem, it's natural to want to come in and solve everything. But it's important not to get in the way of God and his plan for your friend's life.

God gives people grace—or extra calm, patience, and understanding—when they're in difficult situations. Maybe that's why people can seem calm in the midst of big problems. It's easy to jump to a wrong conclusion or do something that messes everything up. Trust God to work in your friend's life, and pray that he'll provide all the grace and wisdom needed.

Pray:

Ask God to help your friends and make you wise
enough to stay out of their problems.

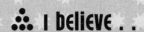
I believe . . .
I shouldn't take on
my friends' problems
as my own.

What do you like to eat? Pizza, right? That's what most kids say. Hamburgers, hot dogs, and chicken nuggets would probably be pretty high on the list too. And don't forget cake, cookies, and ice cream.

If you lived near the Amazon River in Brazil, your favorite food might be fish. The Amazon is one of the longest rivers in the world—running about 4,075 miles. It has more kinds of fish than any other river anywhere. More than 2,400 species of fish have been found in the Amazon! That's more kinds of fish than can be found in the entire Atlantic Ocean (which measures more than 33 million square miles!). One time a scientist pulled a 700-pound catfish out of the Amazon, which would be enough food to feed a small village for a week. And every year new species of fish are found in the river. So . . . how do you want your fish served? Fried, boiled, broiled, stuffed, grilled, pickled, raw, sautéed—there are almost as many ways to eat fish as there are fish to eat.

Check out Genesis 1:28 in the *Young Believer Bible:*

In this verse God tells Adam and Eve to fill the earth with people. God also says that they should rule over fish, birds, and animals.

●●●

You won't find God flipping burgers at a fast-food restaurant, but try not to forget that all the food you eat comes from him. He created all the animals and put humans in charge of them, giving his okay to eat them.

Of course, if you choose not to eat animals, that's okay. He allows you to make your own choices. And some people choose not to eat meat. But God made lots of other things to dine on, such as grains, nuts, vegetables, and fruits. And the best part is that God designed food supplies so that they'll never run out. As long as plants keep growing and animals keep multiplying, there will always be food.

Pray:

Thank God for his great design in giving you food.

❖ I believe . . .

God provides food for me.

August 18

Armadillos are funny-looking, armor-plated animals. Just like humans, they're mammals, which means they have hair and their babies are born alive. But did you know the nine-banded armadillo is always born four at a time, either all boys or all girls? When one baby is born, it automatically has three siblings with the same birth date.

Can you imagine having three brothers or sisters the same age as you? If you all liked tennis, you could probably play a mean game of doubles!

How many brothers and sisters *do* you have? One? Two? Seven? Maybe you have a twin. Siblings can be fun . . . and frustrating. Sometimes you may wish there weren't so many kids in your family, while other kids may hope to have a baby brother or sister. But either way, you can't do anything about the family you grow up in.

Instead of thinking it would be so much better some other way, why not try to show your family that you're thankful to be part of it? And try extra hard to tell that little brother of yours how special he is to you.

Hey, it could be worse. You could be a nine-banded armadillo.

Check out John 8:35 in the *Young Believer Bible:*
In this verse Jesus says a slave doesn't really belong to a family; however, a son is part of a family forever.

●●●

Anytime a few people get together and live under the same roof, trouble is sure to follow. In other words, your family won't always get along perfectly. You'll have fights. Your parents will discipline you. You'll wish you had a little more space to yourself.

But the fact is you're part of your family forever. You may not always like your other family members; however, *liking* is different from *loving,* and God asks us to love others.

Because I want to show my family that I love them, I'll write down some ideas about how I can do that:

1. Mom: _____

2. Dad: _____

3. Brother/Sister: _____

4. Brother/Sister: _____

5. Brother/Sister: _____

Now I'll turn my words into actions and truly show my family members how much they mean to me.

Pray:
Thank God for your family.

∴ I believe . . .
my family is forever.

For ages and ages, people have searched for ways to live forever. And the quest for eternal life keeps getting stranger and stranger.

Spanish explorer Juan Ponce de León spent much of his life looking for the Fountain of Youth (the water from the fountain was supposed to make people young forever). He was the first explorer from Europe to search Puerto Rico and Florida in the early 1500s. But he died after natives in Florida shot him with a poison arrow.

A few companies make lots of money every year by freezing people after they die. These people ask to be frozen, because they hope they'll be able to be defrosted in the future and brought back to life. But the fact is . . . they're still dead.

And today there's a guy with a Web site who says he can help humans live forever by wearing magnetic rings and foot braces. What do you think the chances are that *that* will work?!

As a believer in Jesus Christ, you have the ultimate solution to death. Only Jesus can give you eternal life, because he died for everybody.

Check out 2 Corinthians 5:14-15 in the *Young Believer Bible:*

These verses say that because Jesus Christ has died for everybody, believers in him have died to their old ways of sin. Believers don't live for themselves; they live for Jesus.

●●●

When you pray and ask Jesus to come into your life, it's like you're taking part in his death. The sin you had is gone. He died for the bad stuff we all do, taking our punishment so we don't have to pay the price.

If you're a believer, then you're dead to your old life and you're a new person living for Jesus. Do you feel new?

I know God wants to change me to be more like him. Here's what's new about me since I became a believer in Jesus.

_____

_____

_____

It's neat to think about all the ways God is changing you. And if you live for Jesus, you live forever.

Pray:

Ask God to help you live for him and continue to change you to be more like him.

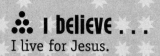

⁂ I believe . . .
I live for Jesus.

Discipline. Does that word bring a smile to your face? Probably not. Instead it may create an image in your mind of a not-so-happy Mom or Dad entering your room and dishing out punishment. Even if you deserve it, discipline is not a happy event. Sometimes you may even wish you could go through life without it.

Imagine what your life would be without discipline. No long lectures, privileges taken away, or unpleasant jobs. You could do anything you wanted and never get punished. You'd grow up never having any consequences for poor choices. That may sound like the good life, but what would happen in the long run?

You'd continue living in a selfish way and eventually *would* have to pay the price for your actions. You're human, which means you'd most likely make many costly mistakes before you learned to live wisely. And in the end, your life without discipline would actually hurt you. Discipline teaches you things now that you need to know later.

Check out Proverbs 3:11-12 in the *Young Believer Bible:*

We should see the Lord's discipline as a sign of love. God wants you to be happy, and sometimes discipline is the only way he can steer you in the right direction.

●●●

People learn from their mistakes. And loving discipline helps you to learn and grow so you don't make a mistake that ruins your life.

God may discipline you when you sin to keep you from making bigger mistakes down the road. Have you ever done something you know is wrong that brought a terrible result? That may have been God's discipline. He knows that sin always leads to destruction, and he wants to protect you.

Instead of being upset when God disciplines you, remember that he loves you very much and uses discipline to shape you into a godly young person. When you respond in repentance and obedience to God's correction, you will learn and grow. Have you received the Lord's discipline recently? If you have, be thankful that he cares enough to teach you how to live for him.

Pray:

Thank God for his loving discipline.

∴ I believe . . .
God disciplines me
because he loves me.

BANG! Peter sat straight up in bed.

What was that? he thought. His heart raced and his palms got sweaty. The house creaked and groaned from the wind. *It was probably just the garage door slamming shut.* Peter tiptoed over to his window, which looked out over the garage. The side door was shut tightly. Nobody was in sight. Then he saw movement! A couple of raccoons slipped back into the trees.

Peter sighed. *Silly raccoons,* he thought.

This was the third time he'd woken up scared in the past week. He looked across the room at his brother, Ben, sleeping peacefully. Peter didn't like the dark, and his imagination always got carried away.

Why can't I be more brave? he thought.

Check out Psalm 27:1 in the *Young Believer Bible:*

Even though David faced many scary situations, he remembered that God would save him. He realized he had nothing to fear because God was with him. He trusted in God's great strength.

●●●

What are some things you're afraid of? Fear is a natural part of being human. Many Bible heroes such as Abraham, Moses, and Joshua were afraid at one time or another. Sometimes you face scary situations: a sick grandparent, a move to a new city, or a bully at school. But if Jesus is your Savior, you don't have to be afraid of anything. In the Bible, God reassures people over and over not to be afraid.

God is always with you, and he's much more powerful than anything that could hurt you. He has saved you, and he will give you strength during hard times. Most importantly, no matter what happens in this life, Jesus will take you to live with him when your life is over. So you have nothing to fear.

Here are three things I'm afraid of:

1. _____

2. _____

3. _____

Now ask God to help you trust him and not be afraid. When you give your fears to him, he'll give you peace.

Pray:
Thank God for saving you and being with you at all times.

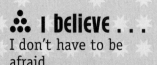

⁝ I believe . . .
I don't have to be afraid.

Amanda loves playing the piano. She plays at her family's restaurant in Colorado, at competitions around the country, and at her school. But when she played at her school's talent show, she ran into a problem. The school's piano was so old and out of tune that it didn't sound right. That's when Amanda got an idea: She'd save the tips she made playing at the restaurant and buy the school a good quality piano.

After one year, she'd saved about one thousand dollars—only about one-quarter of what she needed. But then one night a newspaper reporter noticed the sign on Amanda's tip jar that said all of the money would be used to buy her school a piano. The reporter did a story about Amanda's goal, and money poured in. Six months after the story appeared, she had nearly four thousand dollars! She took the money and picked out a brand-new, shiny piano. Now because of Amanda's generosity, everybody at her school knows what it's like to play on a good instrument.

Check out Deuteronomy 22:4 in the Young Believer Bible:

This verse says that if we see someone who needs help, we should do something about it.

● ● ●

You don't often find a lot of oxen or donkeys tipped over in the road these days, so this verse is probably meaningless to you. Right? Wrong.

The point of this verse is simple: If you see a need, try to meet it. If your Sunday school needs new markers, instead of complaining about the old ones, buy a new set. If your sister needs help with her math, help out. If your dad needs a little assistance with the yard work, do it before he asks you.

All I have to do is look around to see lots of places where I can help. Here are some ways I can help at home, in my neighborhood, at school, or at church:

_____

_____

Each opportunity to help is an chance to do something great.

Pray:

Ask God to show you ways that you can help out.

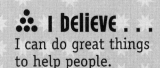

∴ I believe . . .
I can do great things to help people.

Walk into any health-food or grocery store and you can't miss all the sports drinks that promise huge results. There's Gatorade, PowerAde, Get-Big-Muscles-If-You-Drink-This-Ade, Superhuman Strength-Ade. (All right, some of those are made up.) But sports and muscle-building drinks bring in the big bucks.

Wouldn't it be cool if there was something called "Christian Power-Ade"? The commercial might sound something like this:

Man wearing superhero costume with gold cross on the front: Hey, kids! Want to have the faith of Daniel, the strength of Samson, the joy of David, and the power of Elijah? Then grab a bottle and guzzle down 12 ounces of Powerful Christian-Ade. That's all it takes to be the Christian that God wants you to be. Powerful Christian-Ade has been scientifically formulated to increase your faith and knowledge of God's Word. And that's not all. It tastes great too! Available in apple, grape, berry-berry-good berry, and forbidden fruit, it's the drink that boosts your spiritual power. Don't hesitate. Buy yours today!

Check out 1 Samuel 10:5-7 in the
Young Believer Bible:

In these verses the prophet Samuel tells Saul to go to a place where he'll meet some other prophets. At that time, the Spirit of the Lord will come down and Saul will be changed into a different person . . . because God will be with him.

●●●

It's funny to think about special drinks that could make your relationship with Jesus better. But as you know there's no Christian Power-Ade available in stores. However, God gives you a way to tap into his power: the Holy Spirit.

Saul followed Samuel's advice, received God's Spirit, and became a new person. If you want to receive the Holy Spirit, all you have to do is pray to receive Jesus' salvation and ask God to come into your life. God will put his Holy Spirit inside you to help you all the time.

The Holy Spirit is better than any sports drink, and he'll actually give you the power to serve God and understand him better.

Pray:
Thank God for sending his Spirit to help you become a better follower of Jesus Christ.

⁘ I believe . . .
the Holy Spirit gives
me power to serve God.

Summer storms can be awesome. Weather has immense power. The United States has the most intense tornadoes on the planet.

On average the U.S. has 100,000 thunderstorms a year—about 1,000 of which cause tornadoes. Tornadoes are hard to predict but can pack quite a punch. Winds in an F5 tornado (the most powerful) can reach nearly 300 mph, and some smaller twisters have 72 mph winds. Tornadoes' sizes and how long they last also vary a lot. Some can last more than an hour and spread out for over a mile, while other twisters last just a few minutes.

Late summer is also prime time for typhoons and hurricanes. Hurricanes cause about $5 billion in damage in the United States every year. In 1980, Hurricane Allen had winds of almost 190 mph. But the problem with hurricanes isn't just the winds. Huge waves (as high as 42 feet) and lots of rain (the record is 6 feet in one day) can cause flooding.

There's no doubt that nature is powerful . . . but Jesus is even more powerful than that.

Check out Luke 8:24 in the *Young Believer Bible:*

You might have heard this story in Sunday school. The disciples are caught in a huge storm. The boat is bobbing around and filling with water. Jesus, however, is peacefully sleeping. "We're going to drown!" the disciples scream to wake up their Master. Jesus stands up, tells the wind and waves to quiet down, and everything becomes calm.

●●●

As awesome and destructive as tornadoes, hurricanes, and typhoons can be, one word from Jesus calms any storm. God created the earth and designed weather systems for a purpose, and he can control exactly what happens.

If you're ever caught in a terrible storm, remember that Jesus rules the weather. Pray and ask for his protection and calm. His power is limitless. And his words can quiet a raging storm.

Pray:

Praise God that he can control all things on Earth.

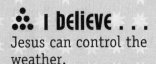

∴ I believe . . .
Jesus can control the weather.

A lot of things can pull you away from God. Television shows sometimes make it seem like believing in God isn't cool. Every once in a while you might hear a teacher say something that isn't true according to the Bible. Popular songs talk about things that totally go against what God says is right.

And as you get older, more and more things will try to tempt you down the wrong path. A 1997 study by the Partnership for a Drug-Free America found that one out of every four kids between the ages of nine and twelve had been offered illegal drugs. That's kind of scary. And that doesn't even count the number of times children were offered cigarettes or alcohol. Drugs, alcohol, and cigarettes hurt the body and mind. Some can even kill a person—instantly. Have you ever been offered any of those things? You might want to practice saying no beforehand. How about this answer? "No way. No how. And just plain NO!"

Making the right choice when it comes to drugs and alcohol could save your life.

Check out James 4:7 in the *Young Believer Bible:*
This verse tells you to humble yourself before God (which means to put yourself under God's control) and to fight against the devil's temptations. If you resist the devil, he'll run away from you.

●●●

God has a great plan for your life—and drugs and alcohol *aren't* part of it. Satan tries to tempt kids away from God with all sorts of things. But drugs and alcohol are two of his top temptations because they make it impossible to think clearly and make good decisions.

The best thing you can do is never even try drugs and alcohol. Ever. Do your best to avoid the devil's traps. Stay close to God, his rules, and his promises. Then the devil will run from you.

Pray:
Ask God for the power to stay away from the devil's temptations.

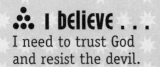

∴ I believe . . .
I need to trust God
and resist the devil.

What do you think of when you hear the word *church*? Write down some of your thoughts:

_____

_____

_____

_____

You might picture a building when you think about church. Some amazing churches have been constructed throughout the ages. The great cathedrals in Europe are incredibly impressive. Churches have been made of glass, rock, bricks, wood, even bamboo. Some churches meet in schools, and some even meet in tents.

A lot of churches have stained-glass windows, and many of them have a cross in the sanctuary. Meeting rooms and classrooms for Bible studies and other programs are common, and some even have gymnasiums where people get together for potlucks and just to have fun.

As you can see churches come in all shapes and sizes.

But do you know what Jesus meant when he said the word *church*? Keep reading to find out.

Check out Colossians 1:18 in the Young Believer Bible:

This verse says Jesus is the head of the body of Christ. The body is another name for the church.

•••

The word *church* isn't used in the Bible until the New Testament. That's when Jesus tells the disciple Peter that he's going to build his church on him.

If Peter had thought the church was a building, don't you think he would've been pretty scared? *Oh no, Jesus wants to put me in a wall with bricks and mortar. Yikes!* Peter might have thought.

But Peter knew exactly what Jesus meant. When Jesus said "church," he meant people who follow him. If you know Jesus personally, then you're part of his church. A church is alive and growing and always changing. You don't even have to meet in a building to have a church. Churches can gather anywhere: a jungle, a beach, a mountain, a park. Whenever Christians get together, they're having a church meeting.

Pray:

Thank God that you're part of his church and that he's the leader over all.

∴ I believe . . .
the church is everyone who believes in Jesus as Savior.

August 27

See how you rate on this "work out" quiz.

Question 1: When Mom asks me to help out by vacuuming the house, I say:
1. "All right, that sounds great!"
2. "I'll do it in a little bit, because I'm playing with my little brother now, and you always ask me to play with him."
3. "I can't, because the dog ate the cord."

Question 2: When your youth group decides to clean up around the church by picking up trash, you:
1. put on some gloves, roll up your sleeves, and grab a garbage bag.
2. spend the first hour looking for a pointy stick to use to spear the trash, so you don't have to bend over.
3. bring along your dog, hoping it'll eat the trash.

Question 3: While baby-sitting for your neighbors, you take your eye off little Timmy and he gets into the refrigerator and dumps out a gallon of milk. You:
1. put Timmy in his playpen and grab a mop.
2. leave the milk there . . . after all you're the baby-sitter, not the maid.
3. bring over your dog to lick the floor clean.

If you said all 1s, you've got the top answers. Otherwise you might need a little help with your work ethic.

Check out Colossians 3:23 in the
Young Believer Bible:
This verse says to work hard at everything, like you're doing it for God, not people.

●●●

Work can be hard. That's why it's called work. It's not always a lot of fun. But a change of attitude does amazing things to help make the work more pleasant. When we think about who we're *really* working for, we're more challenged to do our best cheerfully. The Bible says no matter what we do we should do it for God.

You may please your parents, impress your friends, or make your teachers happy when you do a good job. But ultimately, pleasing God is the best goal. And that's motivation to do an excellent job.

Pray:
Tell God you're going to work hard for him.

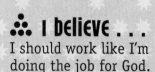
∴ I believe . . .
I should work like I'm
doing the job for God.

Have you ever heard the phrase "Nobody's perfect"? Well, it's true. No one lives a perfect life.

But maybe you know people at school who act like they're perfect. They pretend they never do anything wrong. Doesn't that bug you?

The truth is, nobody alive is any more perfect than you. One sin, fifty sins, a thousand sins—it doesn't matter to God. Everyone has the same title: sinner. Just one wrong thought or bad action is enough to keep a person out of God's kingdom. He is totally holy and can't stand unrighteousness near him.

Sounds pretty desperate, huh?

And it would be a hopeless situation if it weren't for Jesus. Through his perfect love, sacrifice, and forgiveness, we can be perfect in God's eyes.

So next time some kid is acting like Mr. or Miss Perfect, don't let it bother you. Instead, concentrate on your own actions. Are you acting like Jesus would? If you worry more about your own actions, you'll be less bothered by everything else.

Check out Hebrews 10:14 in the *Young Believer Bible:*

Jesus Christ left heaven, came to earth, and lived a perfect life so he could die for all of us. This verse says his sacrifice on the cross makes his believers perfect forever.

●●●

If we're honest, we probably all have to admit to acting like we're perfect at times. Admitting our mistakes is hard. But whenever we mess up, the best thing to do is pray and ask God for forgiveness right away. Don't wait. Pray and try to do better.

Maybe you've never prayed to God to ask him to forgive your sins. If you haven't, you can pray this prayer:

"Dear God, please forgive me. I know I've made a lot of mistakes, because nobody can live a perfect life. But I believe Jesus was perfect, that he died and rose from the dead so I could be forgiven of my sins and live forever with you. Thank you for that gift. Amen."

If you just prayed that prayer, congratulations! You're a believer, which means you're on God's path to perfection. Although you're not perfect now, someday—with Christ's help—you will be.

Pray:

Thank God for sending his perfect Son to die for you.

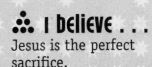

⁘ I believe . . .
Jesus is the perfect sacrifice.

Philippe Petit became world famous in 1974 by stringing a wire between the World Trade Center towers in New York City and walking across it eight times in one hour. That's right: he stood one-quarter of a mile above the ground balanced on a three-quarter-inch wire. Only a 27-foot pole, buffalo-skin slippers, and tremendous balance kept him from falling to his death. You see, Philippe never uses a net.

This French-born high-wire walker has performed many other amazing stunts since then. He's escaped death walking wires at Notre-Dame Cathedral in France and at Sydney Harbour Bridge in Australia. And one time during a youth retreat at a cathedral in New York City, he asked for a volunteer to cross a tightwire with him. A young girl raised her hand. The two climbed high in the air, and the girl clung to Philippe's back as the pair made it safely from one side to the other. After her adventure, she said that she had to trust Philippe totally with her life. She would've died if she had tried to walk the wire on her own.

Check out Isaiah 12:2 in the *Young Believer Bible:*

This verse says God is your salvation. Only he can save you. Trust in God and don't be afraid.

●●●

Think of what it would've been like to be that girl clinging to the tightrope walker's back. She knew she couldn't walk across the gap on her own—she had to totally trust him.

What a great picture of God in your life. Without God you could never get across the gap created by the sin in your life. All you could do is die trying to do everything to be good enough. But God sent his Son, Jesus Christ, to pick you up, put you on his back, and bring you into heaven. You have to totally trust in Jesus, because like everyone else, you can't do it on your own. You have to rely on his strength.

Pray:

Commit to God that you're going to trust him with your life. And admit that you can't make it on your own.

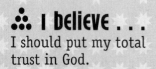

⁂ I believe . . .

I should put my total trust in God.

NASCAR driver Bobby Labonte has always been geared to drive. He's been racing since he was five years old. And at age six, he won the national quarter-midget racing championship.

Now on most weekends throughout the year, Bobby takes his life into his hands behind the wheel of a race car. Top-speed turns in tightly packed groups could lead to a fiery crash at any moment. When you're inches apart from two other cars in a high-banked curve going 170 mph, you don't have time to think about fear. Drivers rely on their instincts, nerves of steel, vice-grip concentration, and trust in each other.

"It's pretty neat to be going that fast and have confidence in the guy racing beside you," Bobby says. "Guys aren't going out there to be crazy and stupid."

But there's an even bigger reason this Winston Cup champion isn't afraid when he's cruising at speeds of more than 195 mph—it's his faith in Jesus Christ. Bobby's been through some difficult times and has seen God help him.

"I've had to rely on Somebody who has a lot more power than I do," Bobby says. "And God always steps in."

Check out John 6:40 in the *Young Believer Bible:*
In this verse Jesus says it's God's desire that everyone who believes in his Son will have eternal life. Jesus will raise up everyone who trusts in him.

●●●

Bobby Labonte isn't afraid of risking his life on a racetrack, because he knows if he dies his soul will immediately be in heaven with Jesus Christ. And when you know Jesus as your personal Savior, you can be equally confident about your future.

Jesus himself said if you believe in him you'll have eternal life. You can't earn your way to heaven. There's nothing you can do to erase your sins—whether you've lied, cheated, or been jealous and coveted other kids' things. Everybody has sinned. God knows all about your sins, but he's also ready to forgive you through Jesus Christ.

Pray:
Thank God for his guarantee that, if you trust in him, you will live with him in heaven.

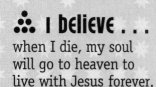

∴ I believe . . .
when I die, my soul will go to heaven to live with Jesus forever.

What's your favorite school subject? No fair saying recess—it doesn't count. Most kids have a certain subject they enjoy, but maybe you're not sure what that subject is yet. Quick! What's 2 + 2? If you said 5, math probably isn't your best bet. Do you know how many states are in the U.S.? If you guessed 50, you may be a geography whiz. What do humans breathe? If you answered oxygen (air is also a correct response), then maybe a career in science is in your future. Can you recite the entire book of Leviticus? Come on, it's only 27 chapters long! What's that you say? You don't memorize the Bible in school. Unless you're in a Christian school or are homeschooled, that's probably true.

But if you went to school with Jesus when he was a child, you would be able to quote all of Leviticus. One of the most important school subjects in Jesus' day was Scripture memorization. Boys memorized every word of Genesis, Exodus, Leviticus, and Numbers. Girls memorized some of those books, but they also studied Psalms.

Who do you think had a harder school day: Jesus and his friends or you and your pals?

Check out Psalm 119:97-98 in the *Young Believer Bible:*
These verses say it's important to know God's Word because it helps you follow his commands and do what he wants you to.

●●●

What information do you have memorized? You probably know your parents' names, your birth date, your best friend's phone number, and lots of other information. That's all good stuff. But how many Bible verses do you have rattling around your brain? You might have memorized John 3:16. If not, that's a good place to start. Then you could move on to Romans 3:23, 1 John 1:9, and Psalm 119:11 as well. Try to memorize three verses this week. (Here's a hint: if you need an easy one, John 11:35 is the shortest verse in the Bible.)

I'm going to hide God's Word in my heart by memorizing three verses this week. They are:

1. _____

2. _____

3. _____

Pray:
Tell God you're going to try very hard to learn more of his Word.

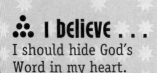

⋰ I believe . . .
I should hide God's
Word in my heart.

Darcy had never pictured herself sitting here—in a cold and stuffy funeral hall. Darcy had never been to a funeral. Up front, lying in a casket, was her grandmother. Darcy felt strange seeing her grandmother wearing a lot of makeup and such a dressy outfit.

Grandma never wore that much makeup, Darcy thought. *I don't think she'd like this at all.*

Grandma liked being outside, working in the garden, planting flowers, baking cookies, singing at church, and playing games. *And Grandma liked being with family,* Darcy thought as she looked around at her relatives. *She would've loved seeing everyone.*

Darcy pictured her grandmother taking out her camera, snapping photos of her grandkids and great-grandkids. Darcy smiled as she choked back tears. She missed her grandma.

Darcy knew Grandma had lived a good life. And she knew the older woman had suffered from a lot of health problems the last few years.

"This is a time of celebration and remembrance," the pastor said when he stood up. "Florence knew Jesus Christ as her personal Savior, and she's with him right now."

Picturing her grandma in heaven helped Darcy feel better. Darcy knew she had gone to a better place. But it was still hard.

Check out Matthew 5:4 in the *Young Believer Bible:*

This verse is from one of Jesus' most famous talks, called the Sermon on the Mount. Jesus says people who are sad will feel better—they will be comforted.

●●●

Sometimes things happen that are hard to understand. A pet runs away. A family member or a close friend dies. Somebody gets badly hurt. But in the middle of these difficult situations, God wants you to turn to him. He's waiting to comfort you.

He understands your feelings; he knows it's okay to feel sad when somebody dies. Maybe you don't know how to feel. God has given you parents who love you and want the best for you. If you talk to them, they might be able to help you deal with your sadness. Be honest with them. Talk about your feelings. Cry on their shoulders. Ask them any questions that you may have. Tell them if you're afraid. Remember the happy times. With God's and your parents' help, you'll make it through.

Pray:

Thank God for the comfort he gives you.

I believe . . .
God is my comforter.

How do you get ready for school? You probably start by opening your eyes—a good beginning for anybody. But then one of two things will happen depending on your makeup.

If you're a morning person, you leap out of bed, full of energy and ready to start the day. A smile spreads across your face as you head down the hall to breakfast. You're usually in a good mood as you munch on oranges and Apple Jacks, and you're happy to see your family. After breakfast you sprint upstairs to take a shower and get dressed. A quick brush of the teeth and a glance in the mirror, and it's out the door.

If you're a night owl, you roll out of bed and try to feel your way to the door without opening your eyes. You stumble downstairs, pick up a box of cereal and a carton of milk, and pour them directly into your mouth. A grunt is the only sound you make to greet your family. Then it's upstairs to take a shower (maybe), brush your teeth, get dressed, look in the mirror, and slouch out the door.

As you can see, morning routines may differ, but most people finish getting ready by looking in the mirror to make sure they look okay.

Check out James 1:23-24 in the *Young Believer Bible:*

In these verses James compares looking in a mirror to reading God's Word. He says if you hear God's Word but don't do what it says, then you're like a guy who looks at himself in the mirror, steps away, and forgets what he looks like—not very smart.

●●●

What would you do if you looked in the mirror and noticed you had a huge chunk of cereal stuck to your face? You'd probably wipe it off right away. Now what would you do if you read something in the Bible that you knew you should be doing, but weren't? It's easier to ignore that, right? But God's Word should act like a mirror in your life. If you read something in the Bible that you don't see in your life, God wants to help you change for the better. Then your reflection will look more like Jesus.

Pray:

Ask God to help you make your actions reflect Jesus.

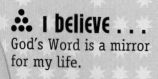

∴ I believe . . .

God's Word is a mirror
for my life.

Being punished isn't fun. If you think about the whole process, it can be kind of rough.

First, you mess up and do something that you shouldn't. Next, you feel bad about it. Then your parents find out. And then comes your punishment. But even when that is over, sometimes you still feel bad.

Do you ever find it hard to talk to your mom or dad after you've been punished? You know, you still feel guilty or bad—especially if you really messed up. Sometimes you might hang your head, look at the ground, mumble when you talk, or try to avoid them altogether. Even if you know your parents forgive you, it's still possible to feel shy or embarrassed because you know you let them down.

Check out Ephesians 3:12 in the *Young Believer Bible:*

This verse says through your faith in Jesus Christ, you can approach God without fear, knowing that he'll welcome you.

●●●

Believers never have to feel guilty around God. He doesn't want his children to feel bad when we come to him. His forgiveness is complete.

Of course, when we mess up, we still need to ask for his forgiveness. And we have to mean it. God knows our hearts. He knows if we're just pretending to feel bad.

Once you ask for forgiveness, your sin is removed, forgotten, and you're perfect again in God's sight. How does that make you feel?

Here's how I feel about being forgiven and perfect in God's eyes:

_____

_____

Jesus' sacrifice makes it possible for you to confidently come before God without wondering whether he'll accept you. Your faith in him allows you to know God personally.

So next time you really mess up, ask your parents to forgive you, ask God to forgive you, accept your punishment, and then keep your head up and know your relationships are still strong.

Pray:

Praise God that you can come directly to him with your needs and that you never have to feel guilty about your past sins.

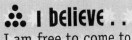

⁘ I believe . . .
I am free to come to God with confidence.

Do you know two of the most dangerous words in the English language?

Wild armadillo? No.

Rock-slide area? Nope.

Piano lesson? Wrong again. But good guess.

Cafeteria food? Getting closer.

Two of the most dangerous words are *if only.*

They may not look scary at first, but if you use them a lot, you'll end up getting badly hurt. Just take a look.

If only I was more athletic.

If only I could play the trumpet like Tommy.

If only my nose was smaller.

If only my eyes were a different color.

If only my brain wouldn't mix up the letters so I could read better.

If only I didn't have to sit in this wheelchair all the time.

Using the words *if only* can cause lots of trouble because they lead you to compare yourself to other people. When you begin to compare, you lead yourself into despair and feeling bad about yourself. It's easy to start comparing yourself to your classmates, siblings, and friends, but God wants you to be satisfied with exactly who you are—even if things aren't perfect.

Check out Romans 8:28 in the *Young Believer Bible:*

Paul writes something in this verse that should take the words *if only* totally out of your vocabulary. He says God takes everything—any situation, any physical trait, any circumstance—and uses it for your good.

● ● ●

Bad things happen—it's a fact of life. Maybe your parents have told you, "Life isn't fair." (It's not. God blesses us far more than we deserve.) But God has plans for your ultimate good. He can take any bad situation in your life and turn it into something good. All you have to do is let him. So instead of saying, "If only," say, "Bring some good from this, God."

Pray:

Tell God you're going to trust him to turn *everything* in your life into something good.

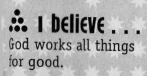

⁝ I believe . . .
God works all things for good.

September 5

So you want to be popular? Who doesn't? We all want to have friends. Being popular certainly sounds better than playing a one-person game of four-square. (Wow, that'd be a lot of exercise.) Of course, there would be some advantages to not having friends—you'd never lose a one-on-nobody basketball game. And even if you managed to get beat, you wouldn't have to tell.

But if you still want a lot of friends, try one of these strategies.

No. 1: Act cool. Buy the coolest clothes. Watch the coolest television shows. Say the coolest words. Hang out with the coolest kids. This may cause you to lose some of your current friends, but it will be worth it, right? (Maybe not.)

No. 2: Become a sports star. This option will require total dedication. You'll need to practice all the time. Lift weights. Eat right. Sleep nine hours a night. And think only about winning. You probably won't be able to hang out with your friends anymore, but once you score that game-winning shot—you'll be the CPAS (Coolest Person at School).

No. 3: Be yourself. While this strategy might not make you the most popular kid in school, it may help you grow stronger friendships that last. Being content with the way God created you will also make you a better friend.

Which do you think is the best choice?

Check out 1 Corinthians 15:33 in the Young Believer Bible:

In this verse, Paul says that "bad company corrupts good character." That means hanging out with the wrong people can mess you up. If you want to follow Christ and live in a way that pleases him, it's probably better to find friends who have good values and are good people.

●●●

Being popular may look fun, but if you have to change the way you act to get a lot of friends, it's not worth it. Following what the "group" does isn't always the best thing, just the easiest.

God made you unique and gave you special abilities. If you like music, play with the band. If you have a talent for acting, try out for a play. God wants you to use your talent. It's best to please God, not other people. He loves and respects you more than any friend could.

I want to please Jesus and have a close relationship with him. Here are some things I'll do to show him that I care more about what he thinks of me than about what people think of me:

_____

_____

Pray:

Thank God for the way he created you, and ask him to help you to enjoy being yourself.

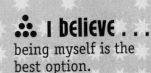

I believe . . . being myself is the best option.

What do you want to be when you grow up? Adults have probably asked you that question a lot. You do have a lot of choices.

You can be a butcher, a baker, or a candlestick maker. Just kidding. How about a professional soccer, baseball, football, or hockey player? That would be cool.

Then again, maybe you want to be a famous musician or a movie star. A lot of people work in banks or with computers. You could be a computer programmer, engineer, or technician.

Did you ever think about working with animals? You could work as a trainer, veterinarian, or zookeeper.

Most people own cars, so car salesmen will always have jobs.

There are also a lot of Christian ministries. You could work for one of them or be a missionary spreading the Word of God.

God knows what you're going to do. But what you do for a job isn't as important to him as who you are as a person.

Check out Proverbs 22:4 in the *Young Believer Bible:*

This verse says that being humble and fearing and respecting God lead to riches, honor, and a long life.

● ● ●

What you choose to do with your life may make a big difference to the world. Policemen and firemen have the ability to save lives. Doctors can rescue people from death. Lawyers can make sure that justice is done and that bad people go to jail. Nobody could argue that all of these are good jobs.

But your character—becoming a godly person—can do even more good on earth. Making godly decisions and following God's Word can change the lives of people around you forever. If other kids decide to follow Jesus because of you, their life will be changed, and so will the life of their family members and all of their future generations—that's possibly millions of people. So next time somebody asks you what you want to be when you grow up, you can say, "I want to be a godly person."

Pray:

Tell Jesus you want to develop godly character.

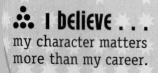

∴ I believe . . .
my character matters
more than my career.

Here's an exciting true story.

After the terrorist attacks on September 11, 2001, a seven-year-old boy in Virginia was riding in the car with his mother when a person on the radio said he was taking bids (a bid is like an offer) on tickets to a big country-music concert to raise money for families affected by the tragedy. The little boy really wanted to go to the concert, so his mom let him call the station and bid $60, which was everything he had in his savings account.

But when the disc jockey heard the bid, he said, "Sorry, we already have a higher offer."

"That's okay," this little boy replied. "I want you to keep my money to give to those families anyway."

The disc jockey was so surprised by the young boy's generosity that he played their conversation on the radio. Pretty soon the phone rang at the radio station again. "I want that little boy to be able to go to the concert," a woman said. "I'm going to add $100 to his bid." Again the phone rang: "I want to add $1,000 to his bid."

The phone rang and rang. By the end of the day, more than $115,000 was raised for the victims of September 11, because one little boy said, "You can keep my money."

Check out 1 Timothy 4:12 in the *Young Believer Bible:*

This verse is a great one for you to memorize. It says you shouldn't let people look down on you because you're young. Instead, you can be an example for other believers in Christ with your speech, love, faith, life, and purity.

● ● ●

The little boy in Virginia was probably younger than you when his generosity caused all kinds of adults to support a good cause. His example resulted in thousands of dollars of giving. And one of the neatest parts of this story is that when the musicians heard about what had happened, they let him come up on stage during the concert. Later President George W. Bush sent this young boy a letter to say what a great example he was to everybody.

Pray:

Thank God that you can do great things for him, even though you're young.

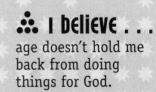

∴ **I believe . . .**
age doesn't hold me
back from doing
things for God.

September 12

Who makes all the important decisions for a football team during a game?

Not sure? All right, let's make it easier. It's multiple choice. You choose:

a. the water boy
b. the cheerleaders
c. the head coach
d. the punter

What's your answer? Even if you've never watched a minute of football, you probably knew the head coach makes all the important decisions. It's his responsibility to know the players and put them in the best positions. He calls the plays. He decides who's in the game. And if things go wrong, he's the one a lot of people blame.

But the coach doesn't work alone. He gets lots of help and input from his assistant coaches and coordinators, who work directly with the players.

There are running-back coaches, offensive-line coaches, defensive coordinators, and lots of other people involved in making the football team work correctly. They're the ones who work with the athletes every day and make them better players. It's their effort that ultimately leads the team to victory.

Check out John 15:26 in the *Young Believer Bible:*

In this verse Jesus says he's going to send you a Counselor. The Counselor comes from God the Father and knows Jesus personally. He will give you truth about God and Jesus. That Counselor is the Holy Spirit.

●●●

Ready for another question? If heaven had a football team, who would be the head coach? God, of course. So if God's the Head Coach, who's his coordinator who works with his players every day? If you said the Holy Spirit, then you're correct.

The Holy Spirit is your personal Coordinator. He knows what the Head Coach is thinking and can pass that information on to you. But you have to be willing to hear and obey.

The Bible doesn't use the word *Coordinator* for the Holy Spirit. Instead it calls him your Counselor—which is the same thing. And if you're wise, you'll listen to the Holy Spirit's good counsel.

Pray:

Thank God for sending his Spirit of truth to help you every day.

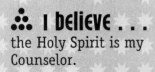

∴ I believe . . .

the Holy Spirit is my Counselor.

Have you ever heard someone say "When life hands you lemons, make lemonade"?

As goofy as it sounds, this saying holds a lot of truth. First, it says that life *will* hand you lemons. It doesn't say *if*, and it doesn't say life *might* hand you lemons. It says *when*.

Lemons are the bad things that happen in life. Maybe a pet dies. Maybe your best friend decides not to be your friend anymore. Perhaps you're not treated fairly by a teacher. Whatever it is, you'll have to face your share of lemons in life.

The second part of that saying is the hardest to follow—"make lemonade." In other words, take the bad things that happen and make the best of them. Look for the positives. Find the good part.

Sometimes finding the good part is really difficult. When a friend turns her back on you, it hurts. Sure, you can make other friends. But it hurts right now. Making lemonade is probably the last thing you want to do. That's why it may be a good idea to add another sentence to that saying: "When life hands you lemons, make lemonade. And God is the ultimate lemonade maker."

Check out Psalm 141:8 in the *Young Believer Bible:*
King David faced a lot of difficult situations. In this verse he writes that no matter what, he will look to God for help. He will hide in God when circumstances get rough.

●●●

God can take the worst situations in your life and make something good from them. At first, you may find it hard to see the good, but over time you'll look back and see how God turned bad things to positive experiences in your life. And here's the best part: while you're waiting for God to make things better, you can hide in him. Use that time to get to know him better. Take comfort that God loves you, cares for you, and can use bad things to make you stronger and more like him. When things get tough, look to God and take comfort in his strength.

Pray:
Thank God that you can always find shelter in his love.

∴ I believe . . .
when things get tough, I can hide in God.

Christy bowed her head. The sixth grader stood at her school's flagpole to pray. A number of students and teachers stood beside her. It was 30 minutes before the bell rang, so Christy closed her eyes and prayed for God to take over her campus. A boy started singing a song. Slowly, everybody joined in.

This is the best See You at the Pole ever, Christy thought. *I'm glad I came.*

Christy is one of the millions of elementary, middle school, and high school students who will join together to ask God to make a difference at their schools at the annual "See You at the Pole" event, which was launched in 1990.

Do you ever feel like you're one of the few Christians at your school? In a few days, you may not feel that way anymore. That's because the third Wednesday of September has been designated as a prayer day for students. You can pray around your school's flagpole while millions of kids in the United States, Canada, Guam, South Korea, Turkey, Japan, Australia, and the Ivory Coast (just to name a few of the countries) are praying at their own schools.

Check out Matthew 18:19-20 in the *Young Believer Bible:*

In these verses, Jesus says that if two Christians agree on something and ask God for it, then God will do it. Jesus adds that when Christians get together as a group, he is right there with them.

●●●

Think of how great it would be to meet with God. You'd probably have lots of questions about the weather, what heaven is like, or why bad things happen. But you'd most likely have some things to ask him for: that your best friend would become a Christian, that you'd do well on your test, that the country would stay safe from war.

Want to hear something even better?

Every time you pray with other believers in Jesus Christ, God *is* right there with you. So when you're praying for your school in a few days, remember who's with you around the flagpole.

To be ready to pray at my school's flagpole, I'll write down some of my prayer requests:

1. _____

2. _____

3. _____

Pray:

Thank God for being close to you. Ask him to help a lot of kids show up for See You at the Pole.

∴ I believe . . .
God shows up when Christians get together.

Did you ever wish you had a fairy godmother? You could ask her to turn your cat into a motorized scooter. A rock could become a new football. A washcloth could be transformed into a beautiful dress. (You probably wouldn't want to put all those things together at the same time—unless you want to be a dress-wearing, football-carrying, scooter rider.)

As you know, fairy godmothers don't exist in the real world. But before you get discouraged, here's some good news. You have heavenly beings watching over you who are much more powerful than the imaginary fairy godmothers mentioned in books. God's angels are always close by. They take care of you in ways you can't even see and keep you safe from harm. And they're there to help you in times of trouble.

Check out Daniel 6:22 in the *Young Believer Bible:*

This is one of the more well-known stories of an angel protecting one of God's children. Daniel has just spent the night in the lions' den and come out unharmed. He tells the king that God had sent an angel to shut the lions' mouths.

●●●

Who needs fairy godmothers when you have guardian angels? Angels surround you with God's protection. An angel is a special being created by God to help do his work. They don't sleep, they don't eat, and they never get tired.

Angels are talked about a lot in the Bible. And they're still doing a lot for God today. When you're in trouble or need help, don't forget to call out to God to send his angels. Angels may not change a pumpkin into a carriage, but they can shut a lion's mouth and do much more than you can imagine.

Pray:

Thank God for his guardian angels who protect you.

.∴. I believe . . .
angels watch over me.

Do you sometimes wish that you could teach your class? It might look something like this. Your teacher would walk into the room and announce:

"Okay, class, today our lesson will be taught by [fill in your name here]. I've always been amazed at [your name]'s understanding of this history lesson about the Middle Ages. So [your name], please come to the front of the room and share with everybody your great knowledge of this subject."

Then you'd step forward and say:

"Thanks, Ms. Fuzzyhead. I'm glad my hours studying this subject will come in handy. I know so much about it, and I appreciate the chance to share with you. And I look forward to teaching you, because after all, everybody loves learning about the Middle Ages."

All right. That's probably *not* how it would go. It would probably look more like this: "Ahhh. Uhhhh. Yeah. So the Middle Ages happened a long time ago, and a bunch of people caught the plague and died and stuff. It was bad. And uhhhhh, I think I hear my mom calling. Bye."

Check out Matthew 10:24 in the Young Believer Bible:

In this verse Jesus says a student isn't greater than his teacher. And he adds that a servant is not greater than his master.

●●●

School isn't always fun. (It's okay to admit that, right?) Learning can be hard. Figuring out difficult homework may get frustrating. Sometimes you might feel like messing around, especially if you see other kids doing it. And some kids just enjoy giving the teacher a hard time. They disrupt class, treat the teacher disrespectfully, and act like they don't care about school—as if they're above the teacher.

The Bible says students aren't above their teachers. Teachers are there to help everybody learn. You can help by working hard and by trying to be a good example. Encourage your teachers in school and out, because you have a lot of other teachers: parents, Sunday school teachers, coaches. By respecting your teachers, you'll probably learn a lot more and have more fun too.

Pray:

Tell God you're going to respect your teachers.

∴ I believe . . .
I need to respect my teachers.

Ever have one of those days when nothing goes right? Your cat throws up in your shoes. The dog eats your homework. Your basketball team loses. Your hair won't lie right. The teacher calls you to the board to solve the only problem that you don't know how to answer. Your hamster dies. Somebody steals your bike.

You know that kind of day.

But wait! It gets worse. You break your glasses. You have to go to the dentist to get a cavity filled. Your skateboard splits in two. The lunchroom's serving mystery meat—again. You lose your retainer. It rains while you're at recess, then clears up when you go back inside the school. You get a pop quiz in history class. Your best friend tells you she's moving. McDonald's is out of fries. All the high scores get erased off your favorite computer game.

Are you getting the picture? This is not a good day.

The trash bag breaks as you're carrying it to the garbage. Your mom runs over your trumpet with her car. The movie you want to see is sold out.

Isn't it good to know that God is there to help you even on your most horrible, terrible, very awful, superbad day?

Check out Psalm 130:5 in the *Young Believer Bible:*

This verse encourages Christians to count on the Lord for help. In tough times, God's Word can guide you, encourage you, and give you hope.

●●●

Where do you go when your life gets rough? To your parents? A friend? The barn to hang out with the horses? You can find comfort in all of these places. But God also wants you to wait on him to pull you out of your bad day.

God knows what bothers you. He can see your struggles. He understands when you feel that circumstances are impossible. At those times it's important to remember God and pray for him to help you through your situation.

Pray:

Thank God for the hard times and that he's always there to help.

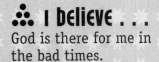

∴ I believe . . .
God is there for me in the bad times.

September 18

In 1975, a young boy named Oliofa lived in Papua New Guinea, an island in the Pacific Ocean. No one in Oliofa's village believed in God because no one had ever told them about him. Instead they worshiped evil spirits and followed a witch doctor.

Oliofa looked at the beautiful mountains and rivers and knew in his heart there was a God. So he began to pray that God would send someone to tell Oliofa about him. Every day for three years he prayed that someone would come. One day a missionary from Australia came to Oliofa's village. The missionary explained that God loved everyone and sent his Son to save all people. Because Oliofa had been talking to God for three years, he eagerly prayed to accept Jesus as his Savior. Oliofa learned all he could about the Bible and eventually taught others in his country about the one true God. God had answered his prayer!

Check out Psalm 55:16-17 in the *Young Believer Bible:*
This is a promise for anyone who calls on the Lord. When you cry out to God, he will save you. And no matter what time of the day you pray, he hears your prayers.

●●●

If you know Jesus as your Savior, his Spirit lives in you. He wants you to call on him whenever you need him. You can talk to him anytime—first thing in the morning, during lunch at school, even in the middle of the night. And he will always hear you.

Will God always answer the way you expect? No, but God is wise and good, and you can trust him to do what's best.

What do you need from God today? You can ask him to help you know him better as Oliofa did. You can also pray that your friends who don't know Christ will choose Jesus as their Savior. You can ask God to heal people you know who are sick or help people who have other needs. No request is too small. God cares about every detail of your life. Talk to him today!

Pray:
Thank God for listening to your prayers.

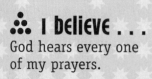

∴ I believe . . .
God hears every one
of my prayers.

September 19

It's science time.

What's at the center of our solar system?

a. A big orange lightbulb
b. A pile of space dust
c. A massive burning ball of gases called the Sun
d. Disney's newest theme park: Disneyworld Outer Space

Of course the answer is *c*. Everything in our solar system revolves around the Sun. And it's the Sun that keeps all of the planets in their orbits.

Check out these other hot Sun facts:

• The Sun is gigantic. If the Sun were a basketball, Earth would be the size of a dot on a piece of paper.
• The center of the Sun is at least 10 million degrees. That's hot enough to fry an egg in an instant (and melt the pan it's in).
• The Sun has a ton of gravitational force. If you weigh 75 pounds on Earth, you'd weigh more than 2,000 pounds on the Sun.
• The Sun is a long way away. If you drove 60 mph in a car, it would take 176 years to get to the Sun if you cruised $^{24}/_7$.

As you can see, the Sun is a super star!

Check out Revelation 7:17 in the Young Believer Bible:

This verse gives us a glimpse into heaven. The Lamb—Jesus Christ—is at the center. He leads those who believe in him to living water and wipes away their tears.

• • •

Just as objects in the solar system revolve around the Sun, your life should revolve around God's Son. The Sun and Jesus Christ have many similarities and differences. One of the obvious differences is the Sun is far away, while Jesus is always close to you. A similarity is that the Sun keeps Earth warm and helps things grow. Jesus does the same thing—he helps you grow to be more like him and keeps you warm with his protection.

Here are more similarities and differences between God's Son and the Sun:

1. _____

2. _____

3. _____

Pray:

Tell Jesus you want him to be the center of your life, just as the Sun is the center of the solar system.

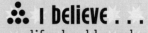

∴ I believe . . .
my life should revolve around Jesus Christ.

September 20

Do you know any bullies? Many schools and neighborhoods have them. These kids don't smile much and can be really mean. Maybe you've had a bully pick on you before. How did it make you feel? Were you scared? angry? Bullies can be frightening. They like to use threats and violence to make other kids feel weak. Their goal is to feel big, so they try to make others feel small. And a lot of times bullies are pretty big kids.

But did you know that deep inside, most bullies feel small? They use their size and strong words to hide the fact that they feel pretty awful about themselves. Bullies are really just sad kids on the inside.

So next time you see a bully, try not to shrink back in fear. Think of how the bully may be feeling, and try to treat him like you would anybody else.

Check out Matthew 5:39-44 in the Young Believer Bible:

Jesus says some pretty radical things in these verses. He says if someone hits you on the cheek, then you should turn your other cheek toward him as well. Then the Lord says if somebody forces you to carry his stuff for one mile, walk with him two miles. And you should let people borrow things from you. Jesus ends this section by saying that you should love your enemies and pray for people who treat you badly.

●●●

Jesus says and does some things in the Bible that may seem pretty strange. He makes friends with people nobody else likes. And he tells his followers to be nice to people who hurt them. What Jesus says in the above verses can help you a lot when a bully crosses your path. Instead of being afraid, you can quickly think of ways to show God's love to a bully. Give him a pencil, share a snack at lunch, pay him a compliment, be his friend at recess, pray for him. By following Jesus' advice, you may end up being friends with someone you once thought of as an enemy.

Pray:

Ask God to give you the strength and courage to treat mean people nicely.

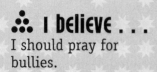

∴ I believe . . .
I should pray for bullies.

Scene One: You're at the store with your mom. As you wander down the toy aisle, you spot Safari Jack. He's the only action figure you're missing from your Out of Africa collection. He's been sold out for months—but there he is. Your collection could be complete for only $8.99 plus tax.

Just one problem. You're out of cash. You'll get your allowance this weekend, but it will take three weeks' worth of allowance to buy Safari Jack. You turn and see your mom walking toward you. She's smiling. What do you do?

Scene Two: You're in line for lunch at school. Just the smell of pizza and tater tots has your stomach rumbling in anticipation. You reach into your pocket for your lunch money and . . . nothing. It's gone! You remember your dad giving it to you, but now you can't find it.

Fortunately, you spot your best friend across the cafeteria. *I bet I know how I can get some lunch money,* you think. What do you do next?

If your answer to the above two scenes is "borrow some money," you're not alone.

Check out Romans 13:8 in the *Young Believer Bible:*
This verse says we shouldn't let our debts pile up. The only thing we should owe somebody is our love.

•••

A lot of kids borrow things from their friends and parents. Clothes, toys, games, money—the list could go on and on. And sometimes borrowing something is necessary, like asking a friend for some lunch money. But getting into the habit of borrowing probably isn't a good idea.

Did you know most households in the United States owe more than $16,000? (That's not counting money owed on a house.) It's just bank loans, cars, and credit cards. Borrowing things—especially money—can get you into trouble. That's why the Bible says to owe nothing, except for your love.

I'll write down anything I owe to somebody:

_____

_____

Now I'll make sure I pay it back sooner rather than later.

Pray:
Tell God you're going to follow his advice in the Bible about debt.

∴ I believe . . .
if I borrow something, I should pay it back right away.

September 22

What do you think of when you hear the name Frodo Baggins? If you're a fan of *The Lord of the Rings*, then you know he's a hairy little hobbit who saves the Middle-earth. And guess what? Today is Hobbit Day. It's the birthdays of Frodo, his uncle Bilbo, and their creator, J. R. R. Tolkien.

But why celebrate Hobbit Day?

There are lots of reasons to celebrate this day, because you can learn a lot from a hobbit. *The Lord of the Rings* movies and books tell the story of these folks. Frodo was the smallest in a group of adventurers who set off to destroy an evil ring and defeat the enemy. But what Frodo lacked in size and strength, he made up for in determination. The ring would have destroyed the men, elves, dwarves, and others in Frodo's group. But the ring didn't ruin Frodo's kind heart. He knew that destroying the ring was his responsibility, and he wasn't going to back down—no matter what the odds. Frodo never gave up. He never asked to be a hero, but at the end of the story he was the hero.

Check out 1 Samuel 17:4-7, 33, 48-51 in the *Young Believer Bible:*

These verses tell the story of David and Goliath—the ultimate tale of God using a small person to accomplish an impossible-looking task. David was just a boy, but God helped him defeat a nine-foot giant, because he trusted in God.

●●●

Do you ever feel overwhelmed by a task? Do your responsibilities in school, sports, music lessons, and family chores make your head spin? Is a bully pushing around your friends and making life miserable?

If you're facing any of these troubles or any other problems, you may want to look at David—or even Frodo—as an example. Neither one was big or strong. They didn't scare their foes. In fact, their enemies probably thought they were weak because of their size. Even though they were small, they both triumphed over impossible problems. And you can too. Trust God. Aim high. Don't give up. Then watch God use you.

Pray:

Thank God that he uses people of all shapes and sizes to accomplish great things.

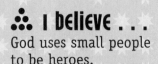

∴ I believe . . .
God uses small people to be heroes.

In Kurt Warner's first three seasons as an NFL quarterback, he won the league's Most Valuable Player Award twice! And in that same amount of time, he threw for more than 12,500 yards and completed nearly 100 touchdowns. Not bad for a guy who never wanted to play quarterback.

When Kurt was your age, he loved playing wide receiver. "I was pretty fast and pretty quick back then," Kurt says.

He didn't start playing quarterback until his freshman year of high school, when the coach picked him to play the position.

"If I could have talked him out of it, I would have tried," Kurt says. "But I had no choice at the time."

Actually, Kurt had two choices:

No. 1 Quit the team.

No. 2 Learn his new position.

He chose option 2.

After that he went from all-state high school player to sitting on the bench through most of college. He was cut from his first NFL tryout with the Green Bay Packers and took a job stocking shelves at a grocery store. He finally returned to playing football, first as an Arena League quarterback, then as an NFL Europe player and ending up as a Super Bowl MVP. He didn't follow an easy road.

"I can say that a lot of the lessons I've learned and a lot of the character that I've developed came from those times when things didn't play out exactly how I wanted them to," Kurt says. "That's when God showed me his plan or the things that I needed to work on."

Check out Romans 5:3-4 in the *Young Believer Bible:*

In these verses Paul describes a chain reaction of events. He says that problems and trials produce endurance, endurance produces character, and character builds hope.

●●●

Your life probably isn't a string of one success leading to another. Just like Kurt Warner, you will face bumps in the road . . . sometimes major ones. It's at those times that you decide what kind of person you want to be.

You can give up, or you can continue trying. And you know what God wants you to do. When you persevere and overcome an obstacle you build character and become more like him.

Pray:

Thank God that he's in control, then press on and put your hope in him.

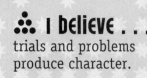

I believe . . .
trials and problems
produce character.

I'm really shy. Because of this, I have trouble making friends. I'd like to have more friends. How can I overcome my shyness?
Shy Guy
Lone Rock, Saskatchewan, Canada

Dear Shy Guy,
Some people are naturally outgoing and make friends easily. They tend to be the most popular kids. Other people are uncomfortable in large crowds. They like to stick to themselves. Some kids fall between these two types of people. So it's important to remember that God created everybody unique and special. Being shy is okay, just as long as it doesn't keep you from being around other people too much.

One of the best ways to come out of your shell and gain new friends is simply to be friendly toward others. A smile, a kind word, or a helpful action can show people you're a person worth getting to know—and you are! When people talk to you, look them in the eyes instead of staring at the floor. Speak clearly and confidently. And when you walk down the school hall, smile at those around you. God knew what he was doing when he created you. You just need to let other kids know that too.

Check out 1 Thessalonians 5:15 in the Young Believer Bible:

This verse has some great friend-making advice. It basically says don't be mean when people are mean to you; instead, be kind to everybody.

● ● ●

One of your main jobs as a Christian is to tell your friends about your Savior, Jesus Christ. You don't always have to tell them with words—your actions say a lot. But if you don't have any friends to tell, it's hard to spread the truth about Jesus.

Showing kindness is one of the best things you can do to share God's love with others. Being nice will draw people to you. People will naturally want to know you because you're a nice person. Some silly guy on TV once said, "It's nice to be nice to the nice." That sounds funny, but it's true. When you're nice to others, they'll be nice to you, and before you know it you'll have friends.

Pray:

Ask God to help you be kind in all situations.

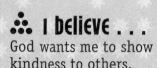

∴ I believe . . .

God wants me to show kindness to others.

Maggie walked out of the lunch line carrying her tray. It was piled high with the cook's special lasagna. The layers and layers of meat, sauce, and cheese smelled great. She also had a salad with French dressing, cherry pie, and a large orange drink.

She scanned the lunchroom looking for her best friend, Marti. She spotted her at a back table. Marti waved and pointed to an empty seat next to her. Maggie smiled and started walking. She got about halfway there when her shoes slipped on some spilled milk that covered the smooth floor.

Whoosh! Maggie's arms shot straight up . . . and so did her food. As she slipped to the ground, she looked up in horror. *Why did I wear my white sweater today?* she thought as her food piled down on top of her.

"Oh no!" she said.

But nobody heard her. They were too busy laughing and pointing at the girl splattered in red and orange sitting in the middle of the cafeteria floor. *How embarrassing!*

Have you ever had an embarrassing moment like Maggie's? Write about it now:

_____

_____

_____

_____

Check out Matthew 6:33 in the *Young Believer Bible:*

In this verse Jesus says the number-one thing you should do is seek God and be concerned most about living for him. If you do that, you won't have any worries about your life.

● ● ●

Why do you think you get embarrassed? Sure, it's no fun feeling foolish or being laughed at. But the worst part of embarrassment comes from wondering what others are thinking about you. Maybe they think you're clumsy, uncoordinated, or dumb.

Caring about what people think of you can be a good idea, but it's not the most important thing in life. What's most important is what God thinks of you. And if you have asked him into your heart and are seeking after him, you can know that God is proud of you no matter what. He loves you and thinks you're perfect—even in the midst of the most embarrassing moments.

Pray:

Ask God to help you focus on what he thinks—
not on what other people think.

∴ I believe . . .
I should seek God and
not worry what other
people think of me.

Watching sports on television can be fun. It's great when your favorite team wins. But have you ever been to a sporting event to see your favorite team in person? Fans go wild. Cheerleaders jump up and down, cheering for their team's players. Some spectators paint their faces—or even their entire bodies. Some people spend lots of money to buy a jersey of their favorite player to wear to the game. And other folks dress up in costumes. Many fans wear their favorite team's colors . . . except for those silly guys who take off their shirts in freezing weather and shout and yell. People eat hot dogs and nachos and have fun.

Maybe you've been at a game when the crowd stands up and starts doing the wave. Sometimes the noise can get so loud you have to cover your ears. Fans will stomp their feet, clap their hands, and scream at the top of their lungs. They go wild the whole time they're at the stadium.

It looks a lot like church, doesn't it? Well, probably not.

You're right. It doesn't look like church at all . . . but maybe it should.

Check out 1 John 4:4-5 in the *Young Believer Bible:*

These verses say there is only one way to ultimate victory. There is only one way to overcome evil in the world, and that's to believe that Jesus, the Son of God, is your Savior.

● ● ●

Going to church may not seem nearly as much fun as attending a professional sporting event. People get a lot more excited watching sports. Church can seem sort of boring at times. Maybe you've even seen somebody fall asleep at church. But fans don't fall asleep watching their favorite team. They're too busy cheering and having fun.

Guess what? No matter how good your favorite team is, God's team is better. God's team is the champion of the universe. The end of the Bible says that God's team wins. Satan loses. And God rules all. Now *that's* something to get excited about!

Pray:

Ask God to help you be more excited about being on his team.

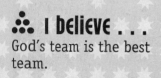

∴ I believe . . .

God's team is the best team.

September 27

The friendships you make now can last a lifetime. But how good a friend are you? Take this quiz to find out.

1. You hear that your best friend said something bad about you, so you decide to:
   a. go to your friend and find out if the rumor is true.
   b. immediately say something mean about your friend to get even.
   c. pretend that nothing happened even though your feelings are hurt.

2. When your friend comes over to your house, he always messes up your room. That makes you want to:
   a. tell your friend that he can't come over to your house unless he helps pick up before he leaves.
   b. sarcastically say, "Thanks for destroying my room, because I love picking up stuff. When I'm done here, I'll come over and clean your room too."
   c. only play outside with your friend—even when temperatures are 20 degrees below zero.

3. Your friend cheats when you play games or quits playing when she's losing, so you:
   a. say you can't play with her until she can play fairly—even when she's losing.
   b. dance around and sing, "I'm the best. You're the worst. You can never beat me."
   c. just live with it. After all, your friend's not going to change.

Check out 3 John 1:11 in the *Young Believer Bible:*

Jesus' disciple John tells his friend to follow only what is good, not what is evil. God's children do good.

• • •

Misunderstanding and conflicts are bound to arise between friends. That's why the best answer to the above questions is always *a*. If you talk with your friend about the problem, you're doing the right thing. Not only can this help your friend, but it may make your relationship stronger.

Striking back with mean words or actions isn't what God wants you to do. Avoiding a problem or pretending it's not there isn't a healthy choice either. As John said, follow only what is good—that's what God wants you to do.

Pray:

Tell God you're going to try to do what is good in your relationships . . . and in all areas of your life.

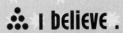

I believe . . .
I should do what is good in my relationships.

Cloning is pretty strange. It's wild to think that scientists can create an exact match of an animal from just a single cell. But that's exactly what they can do. In fact they've been able to do it for years.

One of the most famous cloning experiments was done in 1997 in Scotland. Scientists used a single cell from one sheep to create a genetically identical sheep. They named the new sheep Dolly.

Some people say scientists shouldn't mess around with cloning because they're playing God. They're creating things God never intended to make. Hopefully one day everybody will agree that human cloning is wrong.

But even if scientists could create a genetically identical version of you, would it be you? The new person might look like you and sound like you, but it wouldn't be you. You're unique. Nothing could change that.

People also try to clone or make their own "gods." Whether it's money, drugs, possessions, or other religions, people try to make new gods. But the fact is, there's only one true God—and he can't be duplicated.

Check out Malachi 2:10 in the *Young Believer Bible:*
In this verse the prophet Malachi encourages God's people who had strayed away from their faith. He reminds them that everybody has one Father—the one true God who created everybody.

●●●

A line from a popular Christian song says, "God is God and I am not." Seems kind of obvious. We can't control the seas. We don't know what's going to happen in the future. We didn't create everything. Yet some religions teach that we are minigods. Nothing could be further from the truth.

You are created in God's image. If you've accepted Jesus as your Savior and have asked him to come into your life, then God's Spirit lives and acts through you—but you aren't God. There's only one God: God the Father almighty. No one is greater. No one else deserves our worship and praise.

Pray:
Tell God that you believe that he is the one and only God.

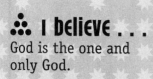

∴ I believe . . .
God is the one and
only God.

Think of a world without rules.

At first you might think that sounds cool: you could eat candy all day, go to bed whenever you want, drive a car when you're 12. You could skip school or decide not to do your math homework. That would free up a lot of time for television watching and video-game playing. *Hmmm.*

But if you think a little harder, you'll see that a world without rules would be a dangerous place. You'd have a constant stomachache and no teeth from eating all the candy. Cars would sit in heaps along the road from all the kid drivers who couldn't see over the steering wheels. And your mind would become a gray pile of mush from not having to think and learn in school.

Rules are actually good things. They help us make good choices and protect people. They make the world safer for all of us. Plus a lot of rules were made for our own good.

If you never went to school and never did math homework, it would be hard for you to get a job.

Of course, without a job you'd have more time for television watching and video-game playing. But then again, you wouldn't have any money to buy a TV or video games. *Hmmm.*

Check out 1 Peter 2:13-14 in the *Young Believer Bible:*

These verses talk about obeying authorities, such as the police, government leaders, judges, and the law. These verses say that people who do wrong will be punished. However, you may be rewarded for acting properly.

●●●

Life needs order. Teachers are in charge of students. Parents are in charge of kids. Law-enforcement officials guide parents. Governments rule societies. God is over the governments. In fact, God created the world in an orderly way. For things to work as God planned, there has to be law and order. Deuteronomy 32:4 says God does no wrong. He is upright and just. That means God is perfect, and he rewards people who do good deeds and punishes those who are guilty of wrongdoing. God is loving, but his perfection also requires his justice. Following the rules—society's and God's—is one thing you can do to honor him and give him the respect he deserves.

Pray:

Ask God to help you follow the rules.

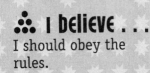

⁂ I believe . . .
I should obey the rules.

September 30

You've probably seen the commercial on television that shows a fortune teller who offers to tell you all about your future if you just call the number on the TV screen. What you might have missed is the small print at the bottom of the screen that says it will cost $3.95 a minute to talk to her.

Now you're probably thinking, *Nobody would really call. That would be dumb. It's all fake.*

And you'd be right. These people don't have truth. But folks do call. Advertisements like that bring in millions of dollars every year. People want to know the future. They want to hear the secret mysteries of life. And they'll trust anybody, even a silly-dressed person on TV who wants to charge them a lot of money.

The really sad part is, God wants to tell us some things about our futures at no charge. God knows looking into a glass ball or flipping some cards doesn't tell the future. Only he controls what's going to happen. He knows your future and your dreams. And all he wants is for people to believe in him.

Check out Daniel 2:27-28 in the *Young Believer Bible:*

In these verses Daniel tells King Nebuchadnezzar that God can do what no wise man or magician can. God can reveal secrets.

• • •

God showed his power through Daniel many times. At this point in the story, King Nebuchadnezzar wanted to know the meaning of a dream he had had. Just one problem: he wouldn't tell anybody his dream. All of the wise men, enchanters, and magicians failed to give the king the correct answer.

That's when Daniel stepped in and saved the day. God told Daniel King Nebuchadnezzar's dream and helped him interpret it. God revealed the secrets of the king's heart.

And God knows your dreams right now—not just the dreams you have at night—but your dreams for the future.

These are some of my dreams:

_____

_____

_____

_____

Now put your dreams in God's hands and watch him bring your future to life.

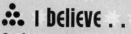 **I believe . . .**
God reveals special secrets to people who believe in him.

Pray:
Thank God for knowing and guiding your future. God reveals special secrets to people who believe in him.

Those competitions to see who's the strongest man can be a lot of fun to watch on television. Hulking, four-hundred-pound dudes show off their strength by throwing trees, stacking gigantic boulders on top of each other, pulling cars with their teeth, hurling large rocks over a fence, and other far-out tests of strength.

And when the contest concludes, almost always a giant-of-a-man from the mountains of Switzerland named Heinrich ends up as the champion. Now that's incredible.

But if you take a close look at this competition, it can seem kind of silly. Admit it. How often do you find yourself needing to throw a giant tree? Probably not every day. Maybe this contest should feature useful events such as unscrewing a stuck lid off a jar, carrying a packed laundry basket down a flight of stairs, or pulling weeds with really long roots out of the ground.

Or if that's too boring, perhaps events could be added that show *really* amazing feats of strength. Having the competitors move a mountain or part a river would be totally impressive.

Oh, wait. Only God can do that.

Check out Jeremiah 32:17 in the
Young Believer Bible:
This verse says God is so powerful that nothing is too hard for him.

• • •

Watching huge guys carry heavy stuff may be fun, but dreaming about God's greatness can be even better. Have you ever asked yourself if God could create a rock so big that he couldn't lift it? (Heinrich wouldn't have a chance with this stone.) That's a good question, and the answer is yes—and no. God can create anything, so he could easily make a rock so big that he couldn't pick it up.

But here comes the neat part: As soon as he had made this mammoth rock so big that he couldn't lift it, he'd turn around and pick it up in one hand. Nothing is too hard for God. Nothing is impossible for him because he's more powerful than anything he created.

Pray:
Praise God for his awesome power.

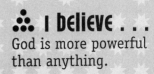

∴ I bELiEVE . . .
God is more powerful
than anything.

October 2

Here's a story you've probably never heard before:

Betty Bigbat was the best softball player in the world. Just the wind from one of her swings knocked over people in the stands. Thousands of people came out to watch her play.

At the softball world-championship game, the stands were crammed with people waiting to watch Betty. In the first inning, she hit a towering home run over the left-field fence. In the fourth inning, Betty bashed the ball out of the park to right field. By the last inning, Betty had belted three home runs, but her team still trailed by two runs.

With two outs and two runners on base, Betty needed to hit a home run for her team to win. The opposing team's pitcher threw a fastball. "Strike one!" shouted the umpire. The pitcher threw a tricky curveball, and Betty swung. *Whoosh!*

"Strike two!" the umpire yelled.

The pitcher threw another ball on the inside corner of the plate.

"Strike three. You're out!"

"Are you blind?" Betty screamed. "That was a ball. Everybody in the stands knows that pitch was inside!"

"That may be," the ump said. "But there's only one opinion that counts—that's mine. And you're out."

Check out Ephesians 5:15-17 in the *Young Believer Bible:*

These verses say it's very important to live as God wants you to. Seeking God's will and making good choices will help you make the best of your life. Foolish people don't try to live for God.

●●●

Like the umpire who called Betty Bigbat out on strikes, God's opinion is the *only* one that matters. But unlike the umpire in the game, God always makes the right call when it comes to your life. It doesn't matter what your friends think or what you read in a magazine, God's way is best. Sometimes God's opinion may not be popular, and you may miss being able to go along with the crowd. But if you're following what God says, you can be confident that you're doing the right thing.

Pray:

Tell God you want to live for him and follow what he wants in your life.

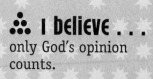

⁙ I believe . . .
only God's opinion
counts.

Computers keep getting faster, smaller, and sleeker looking. The Internet is everywhere. You can take pictures and send e-mail messages with a cell phone or surf the Web anywhere with a wireless modem.

Research shows that nearly 50 million children are on-line in the United States. That number skyrockets when you also count kids all over the world. Kids-only Web sites, chat rooms, and games can make the Internet a lot of fun.

But as you're having fun, don't forget to be safe. Just because a person says he's twelve doesn't mean that he is. Some people lie on the Internet to try to harm children. FBI agents surf the Web every day to try to find and catch these bad people. The agents pretend to be 12-year-olds and see if anybody asks them inappropriate questions—and it happens a lot. Here are some safety tips to follow:

- Stay away from chat rooms. That's where a lot of bad people hang out.
- *Never* arrange a meeting with a person you meet on-line.
- Don't post photos of yourself.
- Never give out your real name, school, address, phone number, or your parents' names.
- If you receive inappropriate messages, don't respond to them and tell your parents about them.

Check out Psalm 12:7 in the *Young Believer Bible:*

In this verse David says the Lord will keep you safe from people who try to lie and deceive you. He will protect you forever.

●●●

Unfortunately there are some evil people in the world. That's what sin can do. But instead of being scared and worried, you can choose to trust Jesus for your safety. He will protect you from deceitful people. And one of the ways he protects you is by giving you common sense and loving parents.

Follow their rules for using the computer and remember the guidelines above. God can help guide you through everything. If you ever feel uncomfortable chatting online, it could be the Holy Spirit telling you to log off. Be careful. And thank God for keeping you safe forever.

Pray:

Tell God you trust him to protect you.

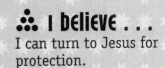

∴ I believe . . .
I can turn to Jesus for protection.

October 4

Today is a historic day. Do you know what happened?

a. Ice cream was invented.
b. Scientists realized the amazing intelligence of dolphins.
c. The first rocket that went around Earth was shot into space.
d. A man drove a car more than 700 mph.

The answer is an earth-shattering one—it's *c*.

On October 4, 1957, the Soviets launched *Sputnik I,* the first man-made object to orbit Earth. *Sputnik I* stayed in orbit for only three months before falling back down to Earth. Now that may not sound too impressive anymore, because these days the United States has joined with Russia and numerous other countries to create the International Space Station—a huge city in space that will never (hopefully) fall back to this planet. Spaceships are launched all the time carrying astronauts into Earth's orbit.

But it was *Sputnik* that proved that humans could send things into space. It also caused a huge interest in space exploration that eventually led the United States to land the first man on the Moon 12 years later.

Check out Genesis 1:16 in the *Young Believer Bible:*

This verse is one that describes part of God's creation. It says God made two great lights: one for the day (the Sun) and one for the night (the Moon). He also made the stars.

●●●

Space is fascinating. Movies have been made about it. Scientists research it. Astronauts explore it. And at night, it's kind of fun to look at it through a telescope. But only one person fully understands space—God. He created the universe and everything in it. Scientists with all of their advanced equipment and rockets can't explain space. They can only guess at all that's up there to discover. God's amazing power is shown in space. His creativity is shown in its size and detail.

The whole world was in awe when *Sputnik I* was launched into space. Just think how much more you can be in awe every time you look into space and realize that you know its Creator.

Pray:

Tell God you're going to think of him when you look into space.

∴ I believe . . .

God created space—
and everything in it.

If you had some really good news or knew a great joke, who would you tell? Your parents? Your grandparents? Your best friend?

What if the good news was for everyone? Would you put an article in the newspaper? Announce it over the intercom at school? Tell everyone you meet?

You have some good news. And it's not just good news; it's really, really good news. You've probably guessed by now what it is. The Good News is the gospel—the news that people can be saved from their sin if they believe Jesus Christ took their punishment for sin when he died on the cross and rose again. What news could be better?

So how do you get the word out? This is the kind of news you can't keep to yourself. It's like a good joke with the perfect punch line. Everyone needs to know! And that's no joke.

Check out Mark 16:15 in the *Young Believer Bible:*

Jesus doesn't want us to keep the news of his salvation to ourselves. He wants believers to go everywhere and share the Good News with everyone. Jesus wants all people to hear about him. No one is left out.

●●●

Sharing the gospel with others may seem like a tough thing to do. A lot of people don't seem to want to hear about Jesus. But God commands that we tell them. Jesus is the only way to God. If people don't know that, they'll miss having eternal life.

Think of someone you know who hasn't accepted Jesus yet. How can you tell him or her the Good News? Maybe you can invite that person to a special event at your church. Maybe you can just talk about the things God has done for you. Or maybe you can ask, "What do you believe about God and why?"

If you get a conversation started, the Holy Spirit will help you know what to say. It's important to know God's Word. The Bible says, "If you are asked about your Christian hope, always be ready to explain it" (1 Peter 3:15). Are you ready?

Pray:

Ask God to help you tell others about Jesus.

I believe . . .
God wants me to
share his Good News.

Got a milk mustache?

If you look at billboards and in magazines, you can find ads showing famous people with lines of white on their upper lips from drinking milk. You can see athletes, actresses, and models all wearing milk mustaches. But you never see those same people walking around with white upper lips in public. That's probably because with a quick swipe of the back of their hand, their milk mustache is gone.

If you want something with real staining power, you've got to drink Kool-Aid. A milk mustache just wipes right off. Kool-Aid lasts. It can take days for a Kool-Aid mustache to wear away.

Isn't it funny that something good for you, such as milk, wipes off so quickly. It's like you didn't even drink it. But something with a lot of sugar and dye that's not so great for your body sticks around awhile. People can always tell when you have had a drink of Kool-Aid.

Check out Hosea 14:2 in the *Young Believer Bible:*
In this verse God's prophet tells the people of Israel to return to the Lord. If you go to God and ask him to forgive your sins, he's gracious enough to do exactly that.

● ● ●

Which would you rather be known for: having a milk mustache or wearing a Kool-Aid face? You'd probably agree that milk is the healthier beverage (unless you're allergic to it), and you may prefer to be known as a milk drinker.

The Israelites in the Old Testament walked around much of the time as if they were stained with Kool-Aid mustaches. People could see that the Israelites made a lot of bad decisions. (Not that drinking Kool-Aid is evil.) They turned away from God, worshiped idols, and didn't follow his ways.

Everything you do leaves a residue, or a stain. Whether it's white from milk or blue from Berry Blue Kool-Aid, your actions show to others and are obvious to God. You can't hide anything from him. Be sure to always be honest with God . . . because the bad stuff tends to take a while to wear off.

Pray:
Ask God to help you quickly admit your sins to him and seek his forgiveness.

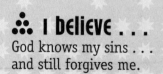

⁂ I believe . . .
God knows my sins . . .
and still forgives me.

Think about your friends. What makes them special? Why do you have fun together? You can probably think of a lot of ways to describe your friends. Choose one friend and write down some information.

Name: _____   **Age:** _____

Hair Color: _____   **Eye Color:** _____

Favorite Food: _____   **Name of Pet:** _____

Favorite Thing to Do Together: _____

Hidden Talent: _____

Thing You Most Like: _____

Best Subject in School: _____

Best Personality Trait: _____

If You Wrote a Book about Your Friend, You'd Call It: _____

Were you able to fill in all the blanks? If you didn't have all the info, you may want to call your friend and get the answers. It's fun to think about, learn about, and grow closer to your friends. Friends help shape you into the person you are. They're always there to help. And no two are alike.

Now think about God. How much do you know about him?

Check out Psalm 145:17-20 in the *Young Believer Bible:*

David describes God in these verses. He says the Lord is righteous and filled with kindness. God is near to anyone who calls on him. He saves people and hears their prayers. The Lord protects everybody who loves him, but he destroys wicked people.

●●●

You don't have to wonder what God is like, because all the information is in his book, the Bible. It's already been completed and printed. And it's the best-selling book on the planet. The Bible describes God from the beginning of Creation to coming to earth as baby Jesus to helping Christians every day as the Holy Spirit. You don't have to guess what God is thinking or what he's like, because the answers are all right there.

Every author of the Bible's 66 books can give you insights about God. So if you don't know something about him, you can read his Word. The truth about him is in those pages.

Pray:

Thank God that you can know his character because it's described in his Word.

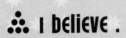

∴ I believe . . .
the Bible tells me
what God is like.

October 8

Do you ever make mistakes?

Hint: This isn't about a missing-a-question-on-your-math-test mistake. No, everybody does things like that accidently.

Do you ever make mistakes *on purpose?* You know, like the times you do things you *know* you shouldn't do. Here are some possibilities (not that anybody needs help messing up):

• fighting with your brother or sister
• sneaking a piece of candy when you were told to wait until after dinner
• peeking at a friend's paper at school
• not telling your parents the truth

The options are endless, and everyone's answer to the question should be "Yes!" Everybody messes up. Everybody makes bad decisions. Everybody breaks God's rules. It's called sin, and it's nothing to be proud about.

Sin is something to think about and try to overcome. Anyone who wants to figure out how to follow God's law better can look at Jesus' life and turn to him for his power and example. He knows what you're going through.

Check out Hebrews 4:15 in the *Young Believer Bible:*

This verse says Jesus understands all our weaknesses. He was tempted, just like we all are, when he lived on earth. But unlike the rest of us, he never sinned.

● ● ●

Jesus knows your weaknesses. He knows everything about you. And he especially understands how you're tempted. Jesus was a kid just like you. Well, sort of like you. He felt temptations just like you. But he was God's Son, so he never sinned.

Maybe he really wanted a second helping of dessert, but his mom said to only have one. The difference between Jesus and everybody else is that he never gave in to temptation. He always obeyed his parents. He didn't fight with his brothers and sisters. He always made the right choice and never sinned.

Jesus didn't avoid sinning to show off. He lived a sinless life so he could take on all of our sins and pay our punishment for the times that we mess up. Jesus *didn't* sin so we could be forgiven when we *do.*

Remembering that fact the next time you're about to do something wrong might help you make the right choice.

Pray:

Ask God for his strength to say no to temptation, and do your best to follow Jesus' example.

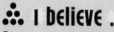

∴ I believe . . .

Jesus was tempted,
but he never sinned.

October 9

No one liked to be around Joe. It wasn't that he looked bad. It wasn't that he dressed bad. It wasn't even that he smelled bad. But Joe had a *bad* habit. Anytime he talked to people, he ended up telling them about how great he was.

According to Joe, he was the toughest hockey player, the smartest Bible quizzer, and the best skater around. If he wasn't talking about how great he was, he was bragging about the trips he'd taken or the things his parents had given him.

Other kids got tired of hearing Joe talk about himself and his successes, so everyone avoided him. Even Joe's best friend, Will, stayed away. Joe wondered why no one wanted to hang out with him. Joe needed to learn a thing or two about humility!

Check out James 4:10 in the *Young Believer Bible:*
God is the one who sees your heart, and he knows if you're giving him credit for the things you have and are able to do. If you truly depend on him, he will bless you.

●●●

What things can you do well? God gives each person a special set of abilities and gifts to be used to bring him glory. Sometimes it's easy to get caught looking at the things you've done, which can lead to becoming prideful. Pride is taking credit for your accomplishments. The opposite of pride is humility—recognizing that God is the One who helped you to succeed.

Jesus was the ultimate example of humility. Even though he was God, he washed his disciples' feet, he allowed men to spit on him, and he finally died on the cross even though he had never sinned. Jesus treated everyone with respect and always gave God the glory for everything he did.

When you show humility by always giving God the praise for the things you do, he will bless you.

These are some of the things I do well. I know that God deserves the credit for giving me talents and abilities, so I'm going to dedicate them to him:

_____

_____

Pray:
Ask God to help you be humble and give him glory.

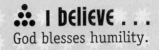
∴ I believe . . .
God blesses humility.

Nasty McGrudge was the meanest kid alive. His eyes were yellow. His teeth were black. Flies circled his filthy spiked hair. He hated everybody, and nobody cared for him much either.

The only thing that brought a smile to Nasty's grouchy face was making fun of other kids. When Jessie fell, Nasty yelled, "Have a nice fall? See you in the spring." When a basketball bounced off the rim and hit Ronnie on the noggin, Nasty shouted, "That's using your head!"

Nasty wanted every other kid to feel as rotten as he did, so he tried to fill everybody's head with bad thoughts. "You're dumb," he'd whisper in the halls. "You can't do anything right," he'd write on the bathroom walls. One time Nasty made a banner for school that read "Give up, now!"

Everywhere Nasty went, he spread gloom.

Check out John 8:44 in the *Young Believer Bible:*

Jesus is talking to people who don't believe in him. He says they love to do the evil things the devil does. And the devil has no truth in him; he's a liar and the father of lies.

● ● ●

As bad as Nasty sounds, he's not nearly as evil as the devil. Satan makes Nasty seem innocent. But Nasty and Satan do share something in common—they love to make people feel rotten.

Satan wants to make you believe all kinds of terrible lies, such as:

a. You're not smart enough.
b. You're not good enough.
c. You're too tall.
d. You're not tall enough.
e. You're not talented enough.
f. God can't use you.
g. You'll never amount to anything in God's eyes.

Here's the truth: God already holds you up like a trophy. And he's thrown Satan out of heaven like the trash. Don't believe Satan's lies. All Satan knows how to do is lie. Believe what God says: You're perfect to God because Jesus is perfect. After all, God can't lie. He always tells the truth. And in God's eyes you're his wonderful child.

Pray:

Ask God to help you listen to his truth and block out Satan's lies.

∴ I believe . . .

Satan is a liar.

You've probably seen the signs in your dentist's office: Only Brush the Teeth You Want to Keep.

That's good advice. Here's some more:

- Only wash the body parts that you want clean.
- Only wave at people you want to know.
- Only comb the hair you want to look good.
- Only water the plants you want to grow.
- Only practice the sports you want to be good at.
- Only put oil on the bike chain you want to work.
- Only pick up the toys you don't want broken.
- Only hang out with the friends you want to keep.
- Only feed the pets you want to live.

All right, so it wasn't all good advice. But do you see a theme?

Here's the deal. If you want something to succeed, you have to work at it. Anything worth doing takes effort.

If you don't care about having teeth and want to be forced to gum your food when you're older, don't brush them. It's that simple. And in several years you could have a beautiful toothless grin.

Check out Zephaniah 2:3 in the *Young Believer Bible:*

The Lord said these words to his prophet Zephaniah. He tells you to beg the Lord to save you and to do what is right.

•••

God's love for you is already at maximum levels. You can't do anything—or not do anything—to change the fact that God totally loves you.

But you can do something to change how much you love him. Just as you put effort into taking care of the things that matter to you (such as your teeth, toys, or pets), you also need to put energy into your relationship with Jesus Christ. And the good news is that God tells you exactly what to do:

a. Seek him.
b. Do what he commands.
c. Strive for righteousness.
d. Work to be humble.

It's the plan for success. All you have to do is follow it every day—just as you brush your teeth every day.

Pray:

Tell God honestly that you're going to work on your relationship with him.

∴ I believe . . .
my relationship with
Jesus takes effort.

October 12

If someone were chasing you, where would you run? Who would you run to? Maybe you'd run straight to your mom or dad. Maybe you'd find a teacher. Or perhaps you'd run to a police station.

Why would you search for those people? Probably because you believe they could protect you from danger. Either they've proven that they care about you, or their job is to protect people. A trusted grown-up does have the power to keep you safe in many situations.

Now imagine you could have a bodyguard always by your side. Wouldn't that be much better? And what if your bodyguard had an entire army with him to help you if you got into trouble? You'd never have to worry about bullies or dangerous people. And you wouldn't have to fear anyone. The Bible says that if you believe in Jesus, you have this kind of protection.

Check out Psalm 32:7 in the *Young Believer Bible:*

David was often in danger, and many times he had to run for his life. In this verse, he says that God is a hiding place. No matter how much danger or trouble you are in, God can protect you. Have you ever been comforted during a frightening time by a song? David says God surrounds you with songs of victory.

●●●

God can protect you better than anyone else can. He cares about you and sees when you're in trouble. He has an entire army of angels looking out for you. And he never sleeps, so he sees you day and night.

Maybe you're afraid of a bully at school and what he might do to you. Or maybe you're about to go on a trip but you fear flying. Maybe you're facing a scary situation. No matter what the circumstance, God will be your safe place.

Here is something I'm facing now that makes me fearful:

_____

_____

_____

Now pray about the thing you fear and ask God to deliver you. Next time you feel afraid, remember God's protection and talk to him. He's always with you.

Pray:
Thank God for his protection.

∴ I believe . . .
God protects me from harm.

October 13

Betsy was Malia's best friend. From the moment the two girls met on the first day of third grade, they'd been inseparable. Betsy was a perfect best friend. She had a bubbling laugh that made Malia start laughing, and when the girls were bored, she always had great ideas of things to do. Plus she knew when something was wrong, and she could make Malia smile.

But then Katherine showed up at school. In her friendly way, Betsy became Katherine's friend and introduced her to other kids in the class. Malia knew Betsy was just being nice, but she felt left out because of all the time Betsy spent with Katherine. The more Malia thought about it the worse she felt.

I can't believe I'm jealous of Katherine! she thought. *But that's how I feel.*

Have you ever felt jealousy creep into your life? You may be surprised, but the Bible says that God is jealous. God is also perfect. So read on to find out how these two characteristics can both be part of who God is.

Check out Deuteronomy 6:14-15 in the Young Believer Bible:

After they left Egypt, the Israelites encountered many other religions and false gods. God made it clear that they should worship only him because he was jealous of their attention.

●●●

Wait just a minute! you may be thinking. *Isn't jealousy a sin?*

Jealousy can be a sin. But the word *jealous* has more than one meaning. One definition is "carefully guarding a possession." Since you are God's child, he is jealous of your attention. He wants you to love and serve only him. But he is also holy, and his heart is good and just. Even people can have "good" jealousy. Surprised? Paul says: "I am jealous for you with the jealousy of God himself" (2 Corinthians 11:2).

Jealousy becomes a sin when we envy what others have. First Peter 2:1 says, "Get rid of all malicious behavior and deceit. Don't just pretend to be good! Be done with hypocrisy and jealousy and backstabbing." God never demonstrates this kind of jealousy, and neither should we.

Instead, focus your attention on him and serve him with your whole heart!

Pray:

Ask God to help you have only the right kind of jealousy.

I believe . . .
God is a jealous God.

October 14

Have you ever seen a cartoon where the main character has to make an important decision and two little images appear on his shoulders? Usually one is dressed as an angel, and the other one looks like the devil. Both of these little guys whisper in the main character's ears, trying to convince him which way to go. It sounds something like this.

Jim (main character): I really want a big bowl of ice cream, but Mom said I had to wait until after dinner.
Angel image: That's right, Jim. And Mom's always right.
Devil image: Just do it, kid. Ice cream has lots of calcium. It's good for you.
Angel image: Don't listen to him, Jim. He just wants you to get in trouble.
Devil image: Yeah, but he just wants you to be stuck eating spinach and green beans.
Jim: I can't decide!
Angel image: Do what you know is right. You can do it, Jim. Resist temptation.
Devil image: Do what feels right. You know you want it, kid.

Check out John 16:13-14 in the *Young Believer Bible:*
These verses talk about the Spirit of truth, which is another name for the Holy Spirit. Jesus says the Holy Spirit will guide you into truth and make you able to understand what he has heard from God.

●●●

While cartoons and other shows poke fun at what goes on when you're caught in a tempting situation, there's actually a lot of truth to them. Maybe you've felt like Jim. Perhaps you were about to make a bad decision when you heard a voice inside your head telling you to stop. Some people say it's your conscience talking to you, but if you know Jesus and have asked his Holy Spirit to come into your life, then you know it's his Spirit helping you do the right thing.

That's what's so great about the Holy Spirit. He tells you when you're doing something wrong. The other voice you hear is your sinful nature. Tuning in to the *right* voice will make a big difference in your life.

Pray:
Tell God you want to tune in to the right voice and follow his guidance through the Holy Spirit.

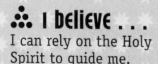

⁙ I believe . . .
I can rely on the Holy Spirit to guide me.

October 15

Gripe. Whine. Complain.

Admit it, you've done all of those things before . . . everybody has. It's easy to find yourself complaining when you don't get your way or whining when you don't get something you want. But do you gripe, whine, and complain a lot? Time to be honest.

If you find yourself doing those things all the time, today's your day. It's Grouch Day! Get up and celebrate.

Of course, because you're a grouch, you won't be in the mood to celebrate. Grouches aren't much fun to be around. They're always thinking of themselves instead of other people. Grouches would rather frown than smile, and they make other people miserable.

All right, so maybe you're not a grouch. Maybe you just slip up from time to time and find yourself griping about your circumstances—like doing your chores, cleaning your room, practicing the piano, or doing homework.

Being a grouch is something to avoid. All it takes is a few negative thoughts and words to start a habit of grouchiness. The grouch habit can be kicked, so why not boot it right out of your life?

Check out Psalm 68:3 in the *Young Believer Bible:*
This verse says God's children can rejoice and be filled with joy and gladness in God's presence.

●●●

Grouches come in all shapes, sizes, and ages. Maybe you have a parent—or a brother or sister—who's grouchy a lot.

If you find yourself being upset all the time, you may need an attitude adjustment. A grouch looks at what he doesn't have. God's children need to look at everything God has given them. A grouch feels like he never gets a break. As God's child, you need to realize that he's given you the biggest break of all by dying for you *and* forgiving your sins.

Because you have Jesus in your life, you can be filled with joy—not grouchiness—even when things don't go your way. Just remember what God has done for you, think about your future life in heaven, and live joyfully for him.

Pray:
Tell God you're going to work hard not to be grouchy.

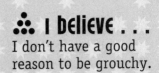
∴ I believe . . .
I don't have a good
reason to be grouchy.

Having friends is great. You know they'll be there for you. You can share stuff and have fun hanging out. But sometimes friends do things that you don't like. Maybe you have a friend or two who like to swear. Most kids start swearing because they want a cool image. But maybe they talk tough to hide feeling insecure.

If you have a friend who cusses, what should you do?

Being a good example with your language is a start. You could encourage your friend to watch what he says. It's easy to follow the crowd—and the sad fact is a lot of kids swear. Standing up for right language isn't so simple, but your friend needs your good example. So hang in there and don't give up on him.

At the same time, be careful that you don't begin swearing too. Picking up the bad habits of people you spend time with is easier to do than sticking with what's right. By not swearing, your actions will speak louder than your words ever could. And even if your friend acts like he doesn't notice, he will pick up on what you do and *don't* say.

Check out 1 Peter 3:10 in the *Young Believer Bible:*

This verse says if you love life and want to have happy days, then you need to "keep your tongue from speaking evil."

● ● ●

Your words say a lot about who you are. If you cut people down, make fun of them, or tell jokes about them, then others will think you're a mean person. But if your words encourage people, challenge them to make good decisions, and help them feel good, then your speech is honoring to Jesus and helpful to others. Cuss words shouldn't be part of a Christian's vocabulary. By watching what you say, you can be a bold witness to your friends. And if your friends don't know Jesus, then it's a good idea to pray that they'll start a relationship with the Lord. God can change their hearts and their speech.

Pray:

Tell God you want his help to make sure your words honor him.

∴ I believe . . .
I should watch what I say.

October 17

If a police officer stopped you in a store and asked you to come with him, would you do it? You probably would. Why? Because you recognize that a police officer has authority over you.

You could choose not to obey and:

a. run away, screaming, "I didn't do it! I didn't do it!";
b. duck behind a clothing rack and pretend to be a coat;
c. drop to your hands and knees and start crawling, hoping you can lose him in the sock department.

But you probably wouldn't do any of these things, because you know if you disobey a police officer, you'll have to face consequences. It's actually better for you to cooperate. But what if you disagreed with the officer's decision? Would you still obey? Read what God says about authority.

Check out Hebrews 13:17 in the *Young Believer Bible:*
God tells us to obey our spiritual leaders. Even when we don't agree with them, we should obey because they have to answer to God. And we should take it a step further by trying to make our leaders' jobs a joy. Their position is a heavy responsibility, and they need our support.

●●●

Authority is the power to influence or command another person's behavior. Who are your authorities? In addition to spiritual leaders, those in authority over you include parents, teachers, the government, and police officers like the one in today's story. Every person in authority over you was placed there by God, the ultimate authority.

Obeying God means obeying those in authority over you. Obeying with a good attitude is much better than obeying while complaining. Your good attitude will make your leaders' jobs a pleasure. Do you make your parents' job a pleasure? That may not always be easy. A good place to start is by telling your parents that you appreciate them. Obeying quickly without complaining is exactly how God wants you to respond to authority. When you obey authority, you obey God.

These are three ways I can support those in authority over me:

1. _____
2. _____
3. _____

Pray:
Ask God to help you obey authority.

∴ I believe . . .
God wants me to submit to authority.

Going to a beach by an ocean can be really fun. There's so much to do: fly a kite, play Frisbee, swim, build sand castles, body surf, and much more. Picking up shells can be cool too. A lot of kids have seashell collections.

Thousands of different kinds of seashells can be found all over the planet. They include lion's paw, alphabet cone, apple murex, angel wings, abalone, and conch. The best place to pick up shells is the Great Barrier Reef in Australia. Beaches in the Philippines rank second. And Sanibel Island in southwestern Florida comes in third.

Walking along Sanibel, you can reach down and scoop up hundreds of different kinds of shells. You can find smooth bright shells, round shells, shells in the shape of a cone, and shells of all colors.

But do you know what a shell is? It's a mollusk's home. Mollusks are slimy creatures that create shells to live in. When a shell washes up on a beach, it usually means the mollusk has died or has been eaten. If a mollusk didn't die, you could never take home a beautiful shell.

Check out Romans 4:25 in the *Young Believer Bible:*
This verse says Jesus died for everybody's sins, but then he was raised back to life so we could be made right with God.

●●●

Sometimes a death is necessary for you to end up with something beautiful. That's the case with seashells. But an even better example of that is Jesus Christ. If Jesus hadn't died and been raised back to life, you couldn't know him personally. He wouldn't be your best friend. And God couldn't see you as perfect and justified through his Son.

Jesus' death makes all of this possible . . . and more. Think about the beautiful things that have come into your life because of Jesus' death. You may have great friends at church who know Jesus too, or you might feel more joy and peace because you're a believer.

These are some beautiful things in my life that I want to thank him for right now:

_____

_____

_____

Pray:
Praise Jesus for all the reminders of how he makes your life beautiful.

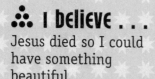

∴ I believe . . .
Jesus died so I could have something beautiful.

It was one of the most glorious moments in Israel's history. After marching around Jericho for seven days the people gave a great shout, and God caused the walls of Jericho to fall. Victory was theirs!

God commanded the people to burn the city and take nothing for themselves. Instead they were to offer all the gold and silver to him. But one of the men, Achan, disobeyed God's command and took a robe, some silver, and a wedge of gold and hid them under his tent.

A few days later, three thousand Israelites went out to conquer Ai, a small town that should have been easy to defeat. But something went wrong. Thirty-six Israelites died, and the rest retreated in fear. Joshua was distressed and asked the Lord what was wrong. God told Joshua that Israel had sinned, and he had removed his presence.

Joshua went through every tribe, clan, and family until the culprit was discovered: Achan. Achan and his family died for Achan's sin, but what he had done affected the whole nation. (You can read Achan's story in Joshua 7:1, 16-26.)

Check out Joshua 22:20 in the *Young Believer Bible:*

When Achan disobeyed God's command, many people died because of his wrong choice. All of Israel was punished for Achan's sin.

●●●

When we choose to disobey God, our sin *does* affect others. Sometimes our wrong actions have obvious consequences for others.

If you include another person in your wrongdoing (maybe by asking someone to lie for you), that person may suffer the same punishment you do.

But sometimes our sin affects others in a less obvious way. For example, if you have a habit of saying mean things about people, your younger brother or sister may think that kind of talk is okay and start the same bad habit. Their spiritual life may be damaged because of your example.

Even if it seems as if you're the only one affected by your sin, someone else is *always* affected. That's worth thinking about when you're tempted to make wrong choices. You probably don't want to suffer for someone else's sin, and someone else probably doesn't want to suffer for yours.

Pray:

Ask God to keep you from sin, because that will hurt others.

I believe . . .
my sin affects others.

Jana's party was the talk of the school. Jana's dad worked for the professional music industry, and her family had a big house outside of town. He'd arranged for a famous new artist to perform a special concert. There'd be all kinds of games, food, drinks, and fun.

"Isn't Jana's party going to be great?!" Katy said as she ran up to Chelsea. "I know exactly what I'm going to wear."

"Yeah, I guess," Chelsea mumbled as she looked at the ground.

Katy was shocked. She knew Chelsea from church. Chelsea was normally smiling and bubbly.

"What's the matter?" Katy asked. "You're going, right?"

"I'd like to," Chelsea answered, "but I didn't get an invitation."

"What? I thought the whole school was going," Katy said. "Something must've happened to your invitation."

"Nothing happened to it," Chelsea said as her eyes started to tear up. "I thought it might've gotten lost in the mail, but when I asked Jana she said she didn't want me at her party."

Chelsea pushed past Katy and ran toward the girls' bathroom. Katy caught up with her as Chelsea was blowing her nose.

"Well," Katy said, putting her hand on Chelsea's shoulder, "if Jana doesn't want you at her party, I'm not going either. Come over to my house and we'll have a party of our own."

Check out Hebrews 13:1 in the *Young Believer Bible:*

This verse says Christians should keep loving each other. Christians are part of God's family, and families stick together and help each other in all situations. And family members are there for one another especially in the bad times.

●●●

Katy could have ignored her friend and gone to the big party, but she put Chelsea's needs above her own. That was being a true friend. When you put your friends first, you're being like Jesus and showing God's love to other people.

The Bible says you're in God's family if you're a Christian. Christians should watch out for, care for, and help our family members.

God's family will always be there for you.

Pray:

Ask God to give you opportunities to help other believers.

∴ I believe . . .

I show God's love
when I care for other
believers.

What if someone told you that she could be everywhere at once, control whether it rains or snows, and know people's secret thoughts? Would you believe her? Probably not. Everyone knows it's impossible to do those things.

No person, no matter how smart or strong, could be everywhere. And no one can control the weather or read people's minds. Those things are impossible.

Many things in the world are outside your control. You may be able to think of lots of things that seem impossible. But guess what? You may have more power than you know. You may not be able to control time and space overnight. But you can do awesome things. Check it out!

Check out Philippians 4:13 in the Young Believer Bible:

The apostle Paul accomplished great things for God. Through his efforts, thousands of people came to know Jesus Christ. But Paul knew his strength came from God. Because God is all-powerful, nothing was impossible for Paul.

●●●

Some things may seem impossible: passing a test, making a three-point shot in basketball, or obeying your parents. You may get discouraged when a task seems too hard. But if you believe in Jesus, you have God's power in you. And nothing is impossible for him. He created the entire world out of nothing! He can be everywhere at one time. He knows everything, including the thoughts and heart of each person.

A God that powerful can do anything. And he can definitely help you when you face a difficult situation or have a hard job to do. So ask him to help you when you get into an impossible situation. And remember that when something seems impossible, it's very possible with him.

On a piece of paper, list some things in your life that seem impossible. Keep the list in a spot where you'll see it, and pray about them every day. God may not always do what you want, but keep track of the impossibilities he helps you accomplish! He may answer in ways you never imagined.

Pray:

Thank God that you can do everything with his strength.

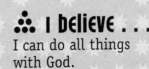

I believe . . .
I can do all things with God.

Have you noticed that life can be a lot of work?

First, you have homework. Practicing multiplication tables, calculating difficult equations, measuring circles, figuring out word problems—it's all a lot of work. And that's just math! Don't forget history, science, language arts, and all your other classes.

Second, there's housework. Unless your family has enough money to hire somebody to clean, you probably have your share of chores. After all, the dog can't walk and clean up after itself. In addition to taking care of pets, you might be responsible for cleaning your room, taking out the trash, and washing dishes.

Third, you probably have some activities that you enjoy. But you don't improve at playing the trumpet or shooting hoops without practice. And that means work.

Fourth, think about your relationships. Building strong friendships takes time and energy. And don't forget about the people you love most at home. Playing with brothers or sisters and doing nice stuff for your mom or dad takes effort.

Sure, you have to work at other things. But it's just too tiring to think about right now!

Check out Genesis 1:1 in the *Young Believer Bible:*
The first verse of the Bible is pretty interesting. It doesn't say God was sitting around bored, or that he was lonely and wanted something to do. It says God *created*. He was working and active.

●●●

The term "work ethic" describes the way someone views work—someone with a good work ethic is a hard worker. God provides you with a great example. His work ethic is amazing. He never sleeps, never plops down to zone out and watch TV, never goes on vacation.

Your first glimpse of God shows him working. He's creating and forming the heavens and the earth. That's quite a lot of work. God is still at work in your life (and in the lives of all people) every day.

No one could ever work as hard as God—not even in a big group working together. God shows us that working is good. But don't forget to follow his example and relax too—even he rested on the seventh day.

Pray:
Tell God you want to join him in working at the things he's doing in the world.

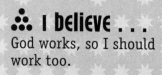

⁂ I believe . . .
God works, so I should work too.

One night a boy was in bed praying to God. He had a lot on his mind, so he had gone on for quite a while.

". . . And God, help me do well on the history test. Well, at least better than Joelle. She bugs me. Please help me remember the stuff I studied. And help my parakeet to get better. And God, I really do believe in you, but I'd really like to see you sometime. If you could just appear, that would be great because I have some questions to ask you. . . ."

All of the sudden, with a great flash of light, God appeared in the boy's bedroom.

"Wow! It's really you!" the boy said.

"Yes," God replied. "What are your questions?"

"Is it true that a thousand years are the same as a day to you?"

"That is true," God said. "I am beyond time."

"How about money?" the boy continued. "Is there money in heaven?"

"No," God said. "Money is meaningless to me."

"So one million dollars is like a penny to you, right?" the boy said.

"I guess so," God said.

"Then can I have a penny?" the boy asked.

"Give me a day to get it to you," God answered.

Check out Psalm 90:2-4 in the *Young Believer Bible:*

These verses talk about the permanence of God. He has existed forever. A thousand years are like just a few hours to him.

●●●

Time has amazing power. Over time, water and wind can change a beach or even a mountain. Every second that ticks away means you're another second older. Time never quits, so you never stop aging—and at your age, that's great!

But God doesn't think about time the same way we do. God is above time. He invented it. He never ages. He was around before he formed the mountains, so he's older than they are. A thousand years fly by in a blink of his eye. Yet he also understands time and wants you to make the most of the time he's given you.

Pray:

Commit your time to growing closer to God.

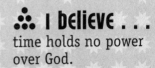

∴ I believe . . .
time holds no power over God.

Fiona always had to be first. Whenever her classmates lined up, Fiona forced her way to the front. When it was time to choose teams on the playground, she insisted on choosing first. And at home, she demanded to be the first to do everything.

One day Fiona's mother said to her three children, "I have a special surprise for you!"

"Oooh, I'm first! I'm first!" Fiona yelled.

"Okay," her mother said, "line up."

Fiona and her brothers lined up, Fiona in front. Mom came out with a plate of three cookies. Two were large and one was small. Fiona's eyes got big. She could almost taste the big cookie full of melted chips.

But to Fiona's dismay, her mom started at the back of the line, offering the plate to Fiona's little brother. He took a big cookie. Then Mom offered the plate to Fiona's other brother. By the time it got to her, only the small one was left.

"Here, Fiona," Mom said, offering her the last cookie.

"That's not fair!" Fiona yowled.

"What do you mean? I was only following the Bible's way of doing things."

"What?" Fiona asked.

"God's Word has a different order," Mom explained, pulling out a Bible. "Let me show you."

Check out Mark 9:35 in the *Young Believer Bible:*

Jesus told his disciples that if they wanted to be first in heaven, they had to put others first by being servants.

● ● ●

Do you ever have a hard time putting others first? Whether or not it's a problem for you, it's always good to be reminded to look for ways to practice being a servant. You could let your siblings do things first. At school, you could think of your classmates before you think of yourself. If you want to do something, they probably want to also.

When you serve others, not only do you shine the light of Christ, but you earn heavenly rewards. Putting yourself last on earth will make you first in God's eyes. And that's what really matters!

These are some ways I can practice being a servant by putting others first:

_____

_____

_____

Pray:
Ask God to help you put others first.

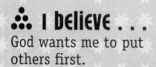

∴ I believe . . .
God wants me to put others first.

Taylor sat outside with her friends at the homeschool group activity gathering. Mrs. Grandy stood on a big rock in front of the group and called everyone to attention.

"All right, kids," Mrs. Grandy said. "Our next science project will require that you form into groups."

Great, Taylor thought, *it will be fun working together, because we can share what we know.*

Taylor ended up with Abby, Jacob, and Nick. Mrs. Grandy told them to find a spot in the big field they were sitting in and mark off a square yard of ground. The team had to describe all the plant and animal life they found in their area and draw a picture. Then a group member had to check the area every day to see if any animals had walked through or if anything new was growing.

Taylor's group ended up splitting the responsibilities so everybody could do what he or she was best at. Jacob loved to draw, so he did the illustration. Abby lived close to the field, so she checked it every day for new activity. Nick noticed a lot of details and kept great notes. And Taylor typed up the report on her new computer to make it look really professional.

Check out Acts 2:42 in the *Young Believer Bible:*

As the early church started to grow, believers in Jesus Christ committed themselves to getting together, talking together about important things, praying for one another, and learning more of God's teachings.

●●●

What's more fun: working on a project individually or as a group? Group assignments can be a lot more fun, and you may even learn more because you can hear what other people have to say about what they're learning.

Learning about Jesus is kind of like studying subjects in school. Doing things as a group can be good for a lot of reasons. That's what the early church discovered when they spent time together, and it's still true today. Early church members hung out together, talked about God, prayed to him, and studied Jesus' teachings. And God wants you to follow their example by going to church and Sunday school to be with other believers.

I can think of some good things that happen from studying the Bible as a group:

_____

_____

_____

Now commit yourself to gathering with Christians as you learn more about Jesus.

Pray:
Thank God that there are other Christians who can help you grow closer to him.

∴ I believe . . .
God wants me to make going to church a priority.

October 26

"Do you swear?"

Has anybody ever asked you that?

No, the question isn't whether you use cuss words. This is about whether you swear to do something, such as when you make a promise or join a club or pledge to keep a secret.

There are all kinds of swears. Maybe you've sworn about something with your friends or you've seen someone swear to do something on TV. A lot of kids pinkie swear; that's when they lock pinkies. There are spit swears too, when kids spit in their hands and shake. And there are swears even stranger than that.

If you've ever done a swear, how did it make you feel? Weird? Silly? Bad?

Sometimes you're not quite sure why something feels wrong, but it does. If that's the way you felt about swearing, you were right. There is something wrong with it. Swearing isn't something you should do lightly. Just ask Jesus.

Check out Matthew 5:34-37 in the *Young Believer Bible:*

In these verses Jesus tells us not to swear, also called taking an oath or a vow. God takes these very seriously. Jesus says to simply mean it when you say yes or no.

● ● ●

Jesus has a definite opinion about swearing. He says not to do it. Instead he encourages you to be a truthful person. If you are known for being truthful, then other people won't need you to prove it by swearing that you're being honest.

If you always keep your word, then people will know you're going to follow through with what you say even if you don't swear. And that's the kind of person God wants you to be—a young man or woman of God who says what you mean and means what you say.

So next time a friend asks, "Do you swear?" tell her that you're always honest and you don't need to swear, because you follow Jesus' example and keep your promises.

Pray:

Thank Jesus for being such a good example of keeping promises.

⁙ I believe . . .

I should keep my word—without swearing to it.

Cartoons, television shows, and movies show some great action. You can watch smash-'em-up, crash-'em-up chase scenes. You can also see high-flying adventures in space. And you might see warriors from the past searching for treasure and trying to save their land.

But as great as TV and movies can be, they don't compare to the action and excitement you can find in the Bible.

The Bible? you may be thinking. *It's just a bunch of words and rules.*

And you're right. The Bible does tell you about God and how to live. But it also contains historic battles, incredible feats of strength, daring rescues, amazing miracles, horrible natural disasters, and much, much more. The pages of the Bible come to life with awesome stories of people who followed God long ago.

Don't believe it? Just start reading your Bible and see what you find.

Check out Acts 16:31 in the *Young Believer Bible:*

This verse comes at the end of a really exciting story. Paul and Silas sit chained in prison, but they're not worried. Instead they're singing and praying to God. Suddenly an earthquake hits. The prison doors fly open and the prisoners' chains fall off. The jailer wakes up and is about to stab himself. (He would have been killed anyway for allowing the prisoners to escape.) But Paul tells him that all of the prisoners are still there. The guard is amazed and asks what he needs to do to be saved. That's when Paul and Silas tell him the simple truth: "Believe on the Lord Jesus and you will be saved."

●●●

The Bible makes God's truth clear. Of course, a lot of people don't understand the Bible's wisdom. They think they have to impress God to get into heaven. Or they think that he'll let everybody enter his kingdom. But that's not what the Bible says.

God's Word states that when you believe in the Lord Jesus, you will be saved. That's all it takes to guarantee that you'll spend forever with God: belief. Now that *is* exciting.

Pray:

Thank Jesus that because you believe in him, he gives you the gift of salvation.

⁑ I believe . . .
I am saved because I believe in Jesus.

October 28

Joshua propped up the rake against the side of the house. He had just finished raking the whole yard. He let out a sigh of satisfaction. The job had taken him most of the morning. He would take a lunch break and then put the leaves into bags. When he finished the job, he would receive a hard-earned five dollars. He ran into the house, washed his hands, and sat down to a peanut butter and jelly sandwich.

After lunch he grabbed some plastic bags and slipped out the back door. His eyes grew wide when he saw the yard.

"Oh no!" he yelled.

Leaves were spread out everywhere. His three-year-old twin brothers threw leaves gleefully into the air, while the family's German shepherd pranced through the mess.

Joshua sighed. *I just wasted my entire morning,* he thought.

Check out 1 Corinthians 15:58 in the Young Believer Bible:

Paul tells you to be enthusiastic about doing God's work because it's never a waste. What you do for God is eternal, while things you do on this earth only last for a short time.

●●●

Don't you wish that everything you do would matter? that everything you make would last forever? that nothing you do would be a waste? When you work for Christ, everything *does* matter. You help God accomplish his plan, you touch other people's lives, and you earn eternal rewards from God.

Nothing you do for God is unimportant or a waste of time. So there's no reason you shouldn't serve him with your whole life. The world may tell you that money and success are what's important, but ultimately those things *are* a waste. They won't matter in heaven.

If you look for ways to participate in the Lord's work, he'll surely show you what you can do to help. Nothing else will give you a greater sense of satisfaction than working for the King!

These are three ways I can serve God this week:

1. _____

2. _____

3. _____

Pray:

Ask God to help you serve him with your whole life.

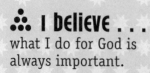

∴ I believe . . .

what I do for God is always important.

Have you ever had a friend who couldn't make up her mind?

One day you're her best friend, but the next she likes Mary more than you. She tells you that she doesn't want to join the after-school drama club, but the next week she's trying to become the club president. One week she says pizza is her favorite lunch, but then you overhear her saying she prefers meat loaf. She chooses Stacey as a partner in science, but then she asks if she can switch to be with you.

Friends like that can drive you crazy. You never know what they're thinking. It's like they have two minds, and they use each one on different days. One brain likes you, but the other one doesn't. One brain says she wants to run for student council, but the other one thinks chess club would be more fun.

The Bible calls that double-mindedness . . . and it's not a good thing. A double-minded person doesn't stand strong for anything.

Check out 1 Kings 18:21 in the *Young Believer Bible*:

The people of Israel kept switching back and forth between following the one true God and the false god Baal. The prophet Elijah finally confronts them and tells them to decide to follow one or the other. The people say nothing, because they don't know the truth anymore.

● ● ●

God doesn't want you to be wishy-washy. He wants you to make a commitment to him and stick to it.

God's people in the Old Testament seemed to change their minds as often as they changed clothes. One day they saw amazing miracles and believed in God. The next day they were hungry, forgot about God, and started worshiping idols. The Israelites wouldn't stand strong for God's truth; instead they combined ideas from the world with God's ideals. The two just didn't agree.

God's Word is clear: Worship God alone. If you truly believe Jesus is Lord, then it's important to act like it. He wants you to be sold out about your relationship with him. Stay close to God, and try not to waver as you strive to follow the truth.

Pray:

Ask God to help you seek after him and remain strong in your commitment to him.

⁂ I believe . . .
I should make up my mind to follow only God.

Brad didn't want anything to do with Christianity. He said he'd never go to church. He'd make fun of any kid he saw praying. And when the new Bible club started at school, he went around pulling flyers off the walls, crumpling them up, and throwing them away.

"I don't believe in anything I can't see," Brad said. "I can't see God, so I don't need him."

Jeri tried to get through to Brad. "Don't you know what Jesus did for you?" she asked. "If you read the Bible you might change your mind about him."

"I've read some of the Bible," Brad said. "It's boring. Leave me alone, you Jesus freak!"

Other kids tried to show Brad God's love, but he always got mad and yelled at them. He even pushed Marcus.

⁙

Do you think there's any chance God could use Brad, or do you think it's hopeless? The answer may surprise you, because God's been changing the hearts of people like Brad for thousands of years.

Check out Acts 9:13-15 in the *Young Believer Bible:*

In these verses the Lord is talking to Ananias from heaven. He tells Ananias to go into the city and find a man named Saul. Ananias doesn't want to do it, because he's heard how Saul arrests and harms Christians. But the Lord says, "Go and do what I say. For Saul is my chosen instrument." (v. 15)

●●●

God uses some pretty unlikely people to spread his Good News to the world. Maybe his strangest pick was Saul, whose name became Paul (maybe you've heard of him).

Saul would have been the last guy most people would have expected to become a follower of Christ. In fact, before he became a believer, his job was to stop Christians from telling others about Jesus. He arrested and hurt Christians. But God picked him for a very special job. And as always God knew what he was doing.

Paul's faith in Christ amazed people. He went on missionary journeys to tell others all over the world about Jesus. He planted churches and saw thousands of people come to know Jesus. Plus Paul wrote most of the New Testament. Not bad for a guy who was anti-Christian until he met Jesus.

Pray:

Thank God for Paul—an example of what God can do in someone's life.

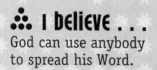

⁙ I believe . . .

God can use anybody
to spread his Word.

Are you afraid of the dark? A lot of kids are. But did you ever think why? Darkness itself isn't scary. God created the world so it would be light part of the time and dark the other part. Darkness just means there's a lack of light.

Of course, it's hard to see in the dark. Maybe that's why the dark is so frightening to some kids—they can't see. Our eyes need light to see.

In the dark at night it's usually tough to tell where noises are coming from, and that can be frightening. The imagination can run wild trying to figure out what's making those sounds.

Another reason kids get scared of the dark might be that their brains don't work as well at night. The body is designed to shut down and sleep then. And that makes it hard to think clearly.

In the morning, it's easy to realize that the things that seemed creepy in the dark were really nothing at all.

Check out 1 Thessalonians 5:5-6 in the Young Believer Bible:

These verses say you're a child of the light. You do not belong to darkness and night. Because you are God's child, you belong to the day. So be on your guard and stay alert.

• • •

God is light. There is no darkness in him. He is a perfect, beautiful, warm, glowing light. And if you're a believer, then you're his child. Just like the Moon reflects the light of the Sun, you reflect the light of God's Son—Jesus Christ. When people look at you, they should see the light of Jesus. Here are some good tips for living in Jesus' radiant light:

- Don't let yourself stray into the darkness.
- Stay away from evil thoughts, scary books, and bad influences.
- Keep in line with God.
- Be alert for things that could lead you away from him.
- Make sure your behavior reflects God's glory.
- Do what you know he would want you to do.
- Make healthy choices.
- Always pray that you will stay close to him.

Pray:

Tell God you want to stay near the warmth of his light.

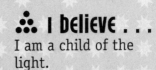

∴ I believe . . .
I am a child of the light.

Remember how much fun you had playing with Play-Doh when you were younger? Maybe you still have fun with that colorful clay. (It's okay to admit it.) You could roll it together and mix colors and create all sorts of fun things. Perhaps you even had one of those machines that squeezed Play-Doh to make cool shapes.

But here's a quiz. What kind of Play-Doh is more fun to play with: the kind that has been sitting out of its can for a few minutes or the kind that's been left out for a few months? (Okay, so that wasn't such a hard question.)

Play-Doh that's left out for months becomes hard and unmoldable. It might as well be thrown away. It breaks and chips and isn't good for anything, unless someone's trying to make a rock.

On the other hand, Play-Doh that is put back in its can remains useful. A kid can do almost anything with it. It is a lot more fun to play with this kind of Play-Doh.

Check out Isaiah 64:8 in the *Young Believer Bible:*

This verse says you are God's Play-Doh. He's the One who creates something amazing from your life.

● ● ●

When you think about it, people are a lot like Play-Doh. If we remain away from God for a few months by not reading the Bible or praying to him, we can get hard and unmoldable. It may be more difficult for God to use us, because we're stiff and unwilling to be shaped and changed by him.

But if you stay close to God and in his hands, you will remain soft and moldable. By praying to God and not straying away from him, you will know better how he wants you to act. Then when God wants to shape you to be more like him, you'll be ready and willing to be molded into his image.

Pray:

Ask God to help you stay soft and moldable for him.

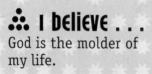

∴ I believe . . .

God is the molder of
my life.

November 2

The annual canned-food drive at church was right around the corner. The pastor made a plea the Sunday before the big day.

"Next week is the day we collect cans of food," he said. "There are many needy people in our community who could use our help. Please dig deep and bring whatever you can."

Jonah asked his mom if they could make a special trip to the grocery store to pick up some cans. Jonah's family had a lot of money, he lived in a big house, and he had a heart for helping others.

Susie also got her mom and dad involved. Both of her parents had to work hard to earn enough money to pay the bills, but she never went hungry. She went through the family's pantry to find some cans to donate.

Jamie knew what it was like to skip a meal. She did it all the time with her mom and little sister, because they hardly had any money. But she still knew she had more than many other kids. She took most of the change from her piggy bank and bought a can of food.

On Sunday, Jonah brought a few cases of food—about 50 cans in all. Susie dropped in 10 cans. And Jamie quietly slipped in her one can.

Who do you think made the biggest sacrifice to help others?

Check out Luke 21:1-4 in the *Young Believer Bible:*

These verses tell a story you may have heard before. Jesus is watching people put their gifts in the temple collection box when a poor widow drops in two pennies. Jesus says she has given more than anyone else.

●●●

Based on what Jesus said about the widow, he'd probably say Jamie gave the most. That's because God looks at our hearts and what motivates us to do something. He knows it was easy for Jonah to give, but Jamie had to sacrifice. By giving to somebody else, she had to go without something. God loves it when his children put others' needs above their own. And it makes him happy when you sacrifice to do the right thing.

Pray:

Ask God to give you the determination to make sacrifices to serve his kingdom.

∴ I believe . . .

God appreciates and understands my sacrifices.

November 3

Astronauts have really cool jobs. Soaring through space. Fixing satellites. Doing experiments in zero gravity. Building a space station. Looking down at Earth from miles above.

Did you know that by the time the space shuttle clears the launch tower it's already going 150 mph? When it gets into its rotation above Earth, it travels 17,500 mph. That's five miles a second!

If you want to be an astronaut, it's a good idea to study hard in math and science. And a lot of astronauts are pilots and flew in the air force or navy, so you may want to plan on doing that.

Do you know who the first space traveler was? (Or should that be *what* was the first space traveler?) The answer is a dog.

The Soviets put a female dog named Laika on *Sputnik II* and launched her into orbit on November 3, 1957. Laika was the first animal to get a bird's-eye view of Earth. Sensors measured Laika's heart, breathing, and movement to make sure she was okay. Her successful trip into space and back blazed a path for humans to take on the dangerous job of going into space.

Check out Psalm 33:6-8 in the *Young Believer Bible:*

These verses say when the Lord spoke, all of the heavens and stars were made. All the people on Earth should fear the Lord and be in awe of him.

● ● ●

Many astronauts have said once they went into space they could understand God's greatness better. Looking at Earth and gazing into the galaxy, they realized the awesomeness of God's creation.

When you think about it, Earth is pretty small. It's just one tiny planet near a medium-sized star (the Sun) in a small solar system that's part of one galaxy out of millions of galaxies in the universe. Yet God chose to send his Son to this planet to die for us, his creations. That's kind of mind-boggling, but it's true. And hopefully that fact will help you love and respect God more . . . even if you never make it into space.

Pray:

Praise God for showing his power in his creation.

⁘ I believe . . .
I should respect the size of God's creation.

Jeremy sighed from the backseat of the car. He'd done his chores all month to earn a trip to the science center. His friend Brock was supposed to come along, but at the last minute, Brock called and said he couldn't come because he was grounded.

Jeremy was really disappointed. But he went to the science center anyway, and after he'd checked out the germ exhibit with enlarged models of strange diseases and bacteria, he felt better. His younger sister, Candace, went with him, which ended up being pretty fun. And things got even better when Dad offered to take them all out for ice cream on the way home.

But when Jeremy walked into the ice-cream shop, he saw something that made his heart sink. There was Brock sitting with Leo and Chris. Brock spotted Jeremy and looked away with a guilty expression on his face. Jeremy was so upset that he couldn't even enjoy his scoop of chocolate chip, his favorite flavor.

Why did Brock lie to me? he thought. *I'll never trust him again!*

Have you ever been lied to? It hurts when someone doesn't tell you the truth, and it's hard to trust that person again. But there's Someone who will never lie to you.

Check out Hebrews 6:18 in the *Young Believer Bible:*

God never lies. Everything he says in his Word is true. You can believe everything he says and live with courage and confidence in God's love, because you know that God's promises are true.

●●●

It is impossible for God to lie, because he is truth (John 14:6). That's great news for us, because it means we can fully trust everything God says. Each story in the Bible really happened. He will keep every promise. And most importantly, Jesus' sacrifice on the cross really is enough to save us from sin.

But there's someone who doesn't want you to believe the truth. Satan will distract you from what is true and even lie to you to keep you from believing the wonderful promises of God.

Are you believing God's truth or Satan's lies? A good way to know the difference between the two is to read God's Word and arm yourself with the Truth!

Pray:

Thank God for being completely truthful.

.·. I believe . . .
God does not lie.

The archaeologist is an expert on fossils. The musicologist specializes in the field of music. The zoologist is an authority on animals. If you want to know about human beings and their history, the anthropologist is the person to talk to. The volcanologist—you guessed it—knows all about volcanoes and spewing lava. And don't forget the biologist, the cardiologist, and the ecologist. They're all experts in something too!

If someone was an expert on you, they would be called a(n) (write your name in the blank) _____ ologist.

Well, guess what. Someone is an expert on you. There's Someone who knows everything there is to know about you—even more than you know about yourself. Not only that, but he loves you more than anyone else can and cares about everything going on in your life.

Check out Matthew 10:30 in the
Young Believer Bible:

God knows everything about you, even how many hairs are on your head. If he knows such a little detail, think how much he must care about you.

● ● ●

How does it make you feel to know someone knows everything about you? If God knows every little detail about who you are, then he understands perfectly what you're going through. And there's nothing you can hide from him. As your own personal expert, God knows how you're feeling all the time, and he sees everything you do. So you can talk to him about anything.

What does that mean for you? Anytime you don't know what to do, you can ask God for help. Because he knows you inside and out, he'll help you make the right decision. And you can rest in the fact that since he knows the tiniest things about you, he also knows the big things, such as what hard things you'll go through, your future career, and where you'll live.

God cares about the big things, the small things, and everything in between. So when you need help, go to the expert!

Pray:

Thank God for caring about every detail of your life.

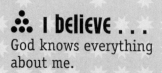

∴ I believe . . .
God knows everything
about me.

Imagine that you got an assignment last month to write a book report about a famous person from history. And imagine that the book you choose has to be at least 100 pages long.

Wow, you thought. *I have a lot of choices.*

You talked with your dad about ideas. He thought a report on baseball player Jackie Robinson would be cool. You asked your mom for suggestions. "I always thought it'd be neat to learn more about Mother Teresa," she said. "Or how about reading a book about Joan of Arc?"

Your sister thought Martha Washington would be good. And your best friend said you should read a book about the guy who invented the traffic light.

You talked and talked, searching for the perfect idea. You planned to type it out and put it in a special binder. *It's going to be my best report ever,* you thought.

Suddenly it's today, and you realize . . . the report's due tomorrow. You rush to the library, grab the first book you see, get home, crack open the cover, and start reading. Three hours later you're so tired and bored that you give up.

You end up writing the report anyway. But when you turn it in, you know it's not your best work.

Check out Proverbs 14:23 in the *Young Believer Bible:*

This verse says hard work will bring profit. But if you only talk about doing something, nothing will get done.

●●●

You've probably put off an assignment and rushed to do it at the last second. Everybody has. Maybe you got an A, but perhaps you didn't do as well as you had hoped.

A lot of kids like to sit around talking about what they're going to do. They talk and talk but never do anything. The Bible says that's not a good idea. Talking is fine. Planning is good. But if all you do is talk and plan, you'll never accomplish anything.

God rewards hard work. When you're older, working hard will help you make money. But for right now, putting effort into assignments will help you get good grades. And as far as book reports go . . . well, how about doing one about Jesus Christ?

Pray:

Ask God to help you be a hard worker.

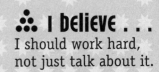

∴ I believe . . .
I should work hard,
not just talk about it.

Gideon was the little brother. No one paid much attention to him. There was nothing special about him. He even thought of himself as the least important person in his family. Gideon didn't expect to ever do anything amazing. On top of that, he was a wimp. His people, the Israelites, were constantly being attacked and plundered by the Midianites. And Gideon lived in constant fear.

One day, while Gideon was hiding from the Midianites, the angel of the Lord—perhaps God himself—appeared to Gideon. "Mighty hero, the Lord is with you!" he said.

Mighty hero? Gideon probably thought. *He must have the wrong guy.*

The Lord continued, "Go with the strength you have and rescue Israel from the Midianites."

Me? Gideon reminded the Lord of his lowly position. But that didn't matter. "I will be with you. And you will destroy the Midianites as if you were fighting against one man," the Lord assured Gideon. When Gideon finally believed God would use him to free Israel, he obeyed. God did as he promised and helped Gideon lead the Israelites to victory over Midian. (To read the whole story, take a look at Judges 6–7.)

Check out 2 Corinthians 12:10 in the Young Believer Bible:

God tells you that his power is actually greater when you are weak. When you can't do something and hit an obstacle that seems impossible, you are forced to rely on God. Paul even says he is glad about his weaknesses, because it means that God's power can work through him.

●●●

Weakness isn't something anyone likes to admit. Instead, people try to show others that they are strong and have everything under control. As a kid, you may feel pretty powerless. Maybe you even feel like Gideon—unimportant and insignificant. Perhaps you think you could never do something great for God. Think again!

The exciting thing about being a Christian is that the weaker you are, the more God can use you. He actually chooses those who are weak to show his power. When you allow God to use you in spite of your weakness, he gets all the glory.

Pray:

Thank God for using you when you are weak.

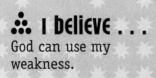

⁂ I believe . . .

God can use my weakness.

Go stand in front of the mirror. What do you see? Not bad, huh? God doesn't make mistakes. He created you exactly as he wanted. Everybody is made in his image. That means you look like God.

Do you believe everything God created is perfect? It's true. He could've made humans with three heads or five legs, but he didn't. He designed men and women. Every part of your body has a purpose—even hair. And those tiny hairs that you really can't see in your nose and ears are especially important.

If you think about it, nose hairs have a pretty crummy job. They filter out dust and dirt so your lungs get good clean air. Nose hairs sort of keep your lungs clog-free. It's a messy job, but somebody has to do it!

Ear hairs help you hear, and the hair on your body helps to keep you warm. Plus a great hairstyle makes you look cool.

No matter what part of the body you can think of, God created it for a purpose and it has a job to do.

Check out 1 Corinthians 12:27 in the Young Believer Bible:

This verse says you are part of the body of Christ, his church. Everyone who believes in Jesus has a special part in his work.

●●●

Sometimes it's easy to feel like a nose hair: unnoticed, unappreciated, and kind of sticky. But when you know Jesus Christ as your Savior, you can be confident that you're an important part of his body.

You might be a mouth—a kid who can bring people to Christ with your wise words. Or you might be his feet, traveling long distances to share God's Good News with other people in far-off lands.

Not everybody's part is easy to notice. Your job might be to encourage other people and make sure they get their jobs done. It may not sound like much. But every job in the body of Christ is necessary—just as even a nose hair is important.

Pray:

Tell God you're going to do your job in his body with joy—whatever it is.

∴ I believe . . .
I am a necessary part of the church.

Choices—the choices you make say a lot about who you are. They show other people what's important to you.

- A teacher makes a mistake and records an 87 in the grade book when you scored a 78. Do you take the better grade or tell her about the mistake?
- Your little sister runs into the kitchen, accidentally bumps into the table, and ruins your science project. Do you scream at her until she cries or forgive her and make her feel better?
- Your dog escapes from the backyard and makes a mess in your neighbor's lawn. Do you sneak your dog back to your house and hope your neighbor never finds out who did it or clean up your neighbor's yard?

As you read the above choices, you knew the correct answers, right? But maybe the other options didn't sound too bad either. Temptations like the wrong answers above happen all the time. God knows you'll be tested. Passing the tests comes down to making good choices.

Check out James 1:12-14 in the *Young Believer Bible:*
These verses say that God gives the crown of life to people who endure testing. God is never tempted to do wrong, and he doesn't tempt anyone either.

● ● ●

You will be tempted. Every day you have a lot of decisions to make. You can choose correctly or make bad choices. It's up to you. When you make good choices, you develop positive habits. You grow stronger in your faith and learn to stick with God. And when you continue to make the right choices day after day, you become a more mature Christian. You don't lack anything.

I become more like Jesus by imitating his actions and doing the right things. These are some qualities about Jesus that I want people to see in me:

_____

_____

_____

Next time you feel tempted to make a bad decision, think about Jesus and the characteristics he wants you to develop. Then make the right choice.

Pray:
Ask God to help you stick with him and become more like him.

∴ I believe . . .
when I overcome temptations, my faith grows stronger.

November 10

It's probably not too hard for you to go to church. Sure, it isn't easy to wake up early on Sunday and get all dressed up. But then it's a simple car ride, or maybe a walk, to arrive at your nice church building.

But in countries such as North Korea, Iran, and Cuba, Christians your age sneak to secret church services in the forest or in homes. They could get in big trouble if certain people find out about them. Others huddle together with their family and read a Bible that has to be hidden during the week.

Did you know that more Christians have died for their belief in Jesus Christ in the last 100 years than in the previous 1,900 years combined? More than 400 Christians will die today. These are scary facts, but true.

Here's information about a few countries where believers are under attack.

- China: More Christians are in prisons in China than in any other country.
- Pakistan: Under the law of Islam, those who worship Christ can be killed.
- Sudan: Christian families are often split up. Women and children are sold into slavery for as little as fifteen dollars each.

Check out Hebrews 13:3 in the *Young Believer Bible:*
This verse tells Christians to remember people in prison. We should also pray for believers who are mistreated, just as if we were suffering as they are.

●●●

You might be asking, "What can I do for these Christians in other countries?" The best thing you can do is pray.

Prayer is more powerful than any of us could ever realize. Only God can change hearts. And God does listen to his people.

Here's an idea: Take a 20-day prayer challenge. Starting this week and finishing at the end of November, choose a country to pray for. Pray that the Christians who live there will receive Bibles. Pray they'll grow closer to God and introduce their friends to Jesus. Pray that the leaders will find the truth of Jesus Christ.

You can make a difference.

For the next 20 days, I will pray for believers who are suffering in _____.

Pray:
Thank God for allowing you to live in a country where you can freely worship him.

∴ I believe . . .
God wants me to remember persecuted Christians.

November 11

Ready for a serious question? This is a deep, earth-shattering, teeth-rattling, bone-jarring question that's sure to rock your world, so you've got to be ready for it. Okay? Here it is:

What's your favorite color?

Just kidding—that wasn't the real question. Here's the real one:

Whose example do you follow in living your life?

Now don't automatically say Jesus Christ. That's obviously the correct answer. Try to be really truthful. Is there an athlete or a singer who you try to be like when you dress and talk? Perhaps you have an older brother or sister who you think is really cool. Your parents can also be excellent role models. Actually, you might turn out to be a lot like your parents, because they have a huge effect on you. Friends also make a difference in your decision making. Maybe you try to fit into a crowd and be accepted.

The challenge, of course, is to have your first answer be the real answer—because your first answer was probably Jesus. That's who you should try to pattern your life after. He's the One to follow in your day-to-day decisions.

Check out 1 Peter 2:20-21 in the Young Believer Bible:

These verses have a message most people don't want to hear. Basically they say believers are going to suffer. If we suffer for doing wrong things, we deserve it. However, if we suffer because of following Jesus Christ, God is pleased with us. Jesus suffered, and he's our example.

•••

Sometimes following Jesus feels easy. You give your little sister a hug instead of a punch in the arm. No problem. You help the new kid with his homework. Score two for the home team. But what if following Jesus meant you had to give the money you wanted to spend on a new video game to a needy family? Or what if standing up for God meant you would get a bad grade in a class at school? That wouldn't be so easy, huh?

Pray:

Promise God that you're going to follow him, even if it makes your life harder.

∴ I believe . . .

I should follow Jesus'
footsteps no matter
what.

You have a tape measure, a ruler, a scale, and a measuring cup. Which one of the above measuring devices would work best to figure out:

a. the length of a blade of grass?
b. how much an elephant weighs?
c. how far it is around a basketball?
d. the proper amount of flour to use in baking cookies?

The answers to these questions are probably obvious. They are: *a* = ruler; *b* = scale; *c* = tape measure; *d* = measuring cup.

But what could you use to measure God? Would anything work? A scale wouldn't do the trick, because we can never weigh his love. A tape measure wouldn't work, because he's bigger than we can imagine. A measuring cup wouldn't help, because his goodness is too much for any cup to hold. So what could we use to get a better understanding of God?

The best thing might be to ask God to measure himself. And in God's Word, we find the answer.

Check out Revelation 1:8 in the *Young Believer Bible:*

In this verse John quotes God from heaven. And God says, "I am the Alpha and the Omega—the beginning and the end . . . who is, who always was, and who is still to come."

●●●

God is so big that you can give yourself a headache wondering just how big he is. Some adults who have studied God for a long time say the more they learn about him, the more they realize how much more there is to learn. That's kind of cool.

Here are some questions I have about God:

1. _____
2. _____
3. _____

You can never fully understand everything about God—and that's a good thing. He's mightier, greater, and more powerful than anyone could ever dream. He's been around forever, is around right now, and will be around in the future.

Pray:
Thank God for his majesty and that he's always there.

∴ I believe . . .
God has always been and always will be.

What comes to mind when you think of the word *brother*? Do you picture an older guy teasing and wrestling around with you? Or do you see a younger kid who looks up to you and gets into your stuff? Brothers tend to be high-energy, fun-loving human beings.

Do you have an older brother? Sometimes older brothers can be hard to live with. If they're old enough to drive, they might be gone a lot. And they probably like to hang out with their friends. But great older brothers do a couple of things: (1) they teach you a lot; (2) they protect you.

You can learn a lot from older brothers. They know secrets about how to get high scores on video games. They can help you fix your bike. And they can give you tips on your homework. An older brother has done more things than you've done, and he can use that experience to help you as you grow.

Plus older brothers will make sure nothing happens to you. If somebody's bothering you at school, they can step in. They'll always watch your back to make sure you're all right.

Check out Hebrews 2:11 in the *Young Believer Bible:*
This verse says that Jesus and the people he makes holy are part of the same family. Because of that fact, Jesus isn't ashamed to be your brother.

● ● ●

There are a lot of benefits to being in God's family. Here are a few:

_____

_____

_____

_____

When you ask Jesus into your heart, you become part of his family.

One of the best parts is that Jesus calls himself your brother. And since Jesus has been around since the beginning of time, it's safe to say that you're Jesus' little brother or sister. That means you can look to Jesus to do the things an older brother should: teach you and protect you. And that's exactly what he promises and wants to do.

You couldn't have a better big brother than Jesus!

Pray:
Praise God that you're part of his family forever.

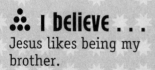

⁘ I believe . . .
Jesus likes being my
brother.

I always get A's on my tests, and my classmates are starting to tease me. What should I do? I'm tired of being smart.
Genius
Smartt, Tennessee

Dear Genius,
Sometimes it feels like being smart isn't cool. But in the long run, you'll go further because of your intelligence.

Don't feel bad about your grades, but also don't make a big deal about them. Nobody likes a person who brags. Make sure you're not bringing some of the teasing on yourself by showing off your latest A. When tests are handed out, quietly put yours in your folder without a lot of fanfare.

Whatever you do, don't try to do poorly on purpose. God has blessed you with some serious brainpower. He wants you to use your talents for him. Keep studying and trying to put your gift to good use.

And if classmates continue teasing you about your grades, think how you can change the subject and make them feel good about themselves. You may also want to help other kids by being a tutor to those who need help.

Check out 2 Timothy 2:15 in the *Young Believer Bible:*
This verse says to show God that you can work hard and know the truths in his Word.

●●●

How would you rate your knowledge of the Bible?

a. Bible Master—you know it all
b. Bible Student—you're still learning
c. Bible Baby—you haven't learned much of God's Word

How does your rating make you feel? Do you feel good about what you know of the Bible, or are you embarrassed? God doesn't expect you to know everything, but he does want you to put some effort into learning his Word.

The apostle Paul's advice to you is to do your best for God. Work at learning the Bible, so you'll be prepared to tell others what you know about God. The better you know the Bible, the better you'll be able to be used by him.

Pray:
Tell God you don't want to be ashamed about what you know, and you want to do your best to learn his Word.

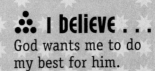
∴ I believe . . .
God wants me to do my best for him.

Around the holidays you probably hear a lot about helping the needy and those less fortunate. Take this quiz to see if you know who the needy are. Circle one of the following.

The needy are:

a. the poor

b. the homeless

c. widows and orphans

d. all of the above

If you chose *d*, you're getting pretty good at multiple-choice questions, because that's the right answer.

When Jesus Christ was on the earth, he made it clear that as his followers we need to help those who don't have as much as we do—especially those who are alone, such as widows and orphans.

The needy are all around you. And if you think honestly about it, you probably have more than you need. The Bible tells you why you should look for ways to help those who have less than you do.

Check out Matthew 25:34-36 in the Young Believer Bible:

Jesus explains that he will reward those who help people who are hungry, thirsty, needy, sick, or in prison. The King in the story stands for God. Taking care of hurting people is so important to him that when you care for the needy, you're giving directly to God.

●●●

You may wonder how you can help the poor and homeless. Maybe you could volunteer with your family to serve a meal at a shelter. Or you could collect toys for children who don't have any.

There are lots of ways you can help people less fortunate than yourself. Ask your mom or dad to help you get involved. Everybody is precious to Jesus, and he wants you to love them too.

Here's my list of some ways I can help those who are poor, homeless, or alone:

1. Get a list of widows in my church and find out if I can do any household jobs or yard work for them.

2. Call a shelter and find out when my family can help serve a meal.

3. _____

4. _____

5. _____

Pray:

Ask God to show you ways to help the needy.

⁂ I believe . . .
when I help those in need, I help Jesus.

The holidays are quickly approaching. You'll probably get your cheeks pinched a few times and hear "My, how you've grown!" over and over again from relatives you haven't seen in a while.

This holiday season show your family that you've done more than grow physically—demonstrate that your manners have grown as well by taking this short quiz.

1. Your Aunt Rhonda has flown across the country. When she walks into your house, you:
   a. wave at her and keep watching TV.
   b. smile, walk over to her, and give her a hug.

2. You sit down at the table, grab your napkin, and:
   a. quickly fold it into the shape of a turkey.
   b. unfold it halfway and place it in your lap.

3. While your dad says grace, your best response is:
   a. to steal your brother's fork while his eyes are closed.
   b. bow your head and listen.

4. Your mom asks for the salt, so you:
   a. help yourself to some salt, then pass it.
   b. pass her both the salt and pepper.

5. You meet Uncle Ralph for the first time, so you:
   a. look at the floor and weakly offer him your hand.
   b. look him in the eyes, smile, and firmly shake his hand.

Check out Philippians 1:27 in the Young Believer Bible:

In this verse Paul tells his Christian friends in the city of Philippi that they should live in a way that shows they belong to Christ—as citizens of heaven.

●●●

Hopefully, you answered *b* to all of the above questions. Good manners—known as etiquette—come down to acting respectfully and using common sense. Manners show that you are not only maturing as a person, but that you're becoming a more mature Christian as well.

People, especially adults, are impressed by good manners. Wouldn't it be cool if your good manners allowed you to share about Jesus with one of your family members who doesn't know him? It could easily happen. So remember at all times that you're representing Christ, and do your best to become an etiquette expert.

Pray:

Tell God you're going to try to have good manners to honor him.

∴ I believe . . .
my manners matter.

"Why me?"

It's an easy question to ask, and one you probably ask when things happen to you that don't seem fair.

Your family's car breaks down before the big hockey game. "Why me?"

Your mom cooks tuna casserole—your least favorite food. "Why me?"

You lose your favorite bracelet. "Why me?"

A kid at school teases you a lot because he doesn't like the way you look. "Why me?"

It's natural to think about yourself. After all, you're with yourself all the time. But God doesn't want you to be totally wrapped up in yourself. He wants you to think about other people—even people who are mean.

God cares for everybody, even those who don't follow him. He wants everybody to have the opportunity to know him. The real-life story of Jonah is a perfect example of that.

Check out Jonah 4:10-11 in the *Young Believer Bible:*

These are the last verses from the book of Jonah. He's already run from God, been swallowed by a great fish who later spits him back up on land, and seen Nineveh turn back to God. This is where God scolds Jonah for being more concerned about himself than he was for the Ninevites.

●●●

The Ninevites were horrible people. It would be hard to find more detestable folks in the whole Bible. They were evil, violent enemies of Israel.

They pretty much committed every sin you could imagine.

And here's the amazing part: God still had compassion on them. When he sent Jonah to them, God gave the Ninevites a chance to turn to him and stop their evil ways, which they did.

The weird thing is that Jonah didn't want them to be forgiven. He wanted God to judge all 120,000 Ninevites. He wanted their whole city to be destroyed. Jonah was more concerned about himself than he was for those people.

Next time you run into kids you're sure God couldn't love, remember Jonah and try to show them you care . . . because God does.

Pray:

Ask God to give you his attitude when you're dealing with people who seem unlovable.

∴ I believe . . .

God wants me to be concerned about other people.

Grace watched the tears slip down her friend Olivia's face. Olivia's grandmother had died two days ago. Grace knew that Olivia's grandma wasn't a Christian—she was a Buddhist. And Olivia wasn't a believer either. Grace had been telling Olivia about Jesus for many months, and now she saw another opportunity.

"I'm so sorry your grandma died," she said. "You really should accept Jesus so *you* can go to heaven."

Olivia looked up, eyes flashing. "How could you say that?" she sputtered. "Why would I want to go to heaven if my grandma's not going to be there?"

"I'm sorry," Grace said, looking down.

⁛

Grace had the right motive and meant to be nice. She wanted her friend to accept Jesus as her Savior. But did she use the right words? Probably not.

Check out Colossians 4:6 in the *Young Believer Bible:*

Paul reminds Christians that their words should be carefully chosen. Our speech should always show God's grace and never be bitter or tasteless. We should seek God's wisdom to gently answer everyone.

●●●

In the movie *Mary Poppins,* the whimsical nanny sings, "Just a spoonful of sugar makes the medicine go down." What she means is when something is hard to do or say, it can often be sweetened to make it easier to accomplish.

As a follower of Christ, you are called to speak the truth in a loving way. Sometimes people in the world won't want to hear what you have to say. But that doesn't make it any less important for you to share the truth.

So how can you make the gospel sweet to a world of hurting people? Ask God to give you wisdom as you share the truth about Jesus to others. Be sensitive to what people are ready to hear. When her friend was hurting, Grace could have just listened and reminded Olivia that God loved her.

I'll think of some things I can say to share God's truth in a way that sounds sweet to people:

Pray:

Ask God to help you choose words that are easy for others to swallow and still full of truth.

⁛ I believe . . .

I should choose words of truth and grace.

Which assignment would you rather complete: a book report or a speech?

Most kids would pick a book report. Reading a book, writing what you learned, and turning it in to the teacher isn't too scary. But the opposite often is true about a speech. Many kids—and adults—are intimidated by speaking in front of a group of people. Some experts say you can get over your nervousness by picturing the audience in its underwear. But that sounds kind of silly and would probably only make you laugh.

The funny thing is that it takes about the same amount of preparation to do a book report as to write a speech. To do a book report, you read a book and write something down. The same is true with a speech: You do research and put together your talk.

Now here's the million-dollar question: Which report helps you remember the most about your subject? If you're being honest, you probably said the speech. Because you have to practice what you're going to say and then tell your class about it, the information tends to stick in your brain better.

Check out Mark 5:19-20 in the *Young Believer Bible:*

After Jesus healed a man who was demon possessed, he instructs the man to tell all his friends what the Lord had done for him. The man understands all that Jesus has done for him, so he obeys, and many people are amazed by what he tells them. When you tell others about Jesus, you gain a better understanding of everything he's done for you.

●●●

How do you feel about telling other kids about Jesus? You probably think it's a good idea. Maybe you've even invited friends to church or told them something Jesus has done in your life. But just like giving a speech in school, sharing what you know about Jesus can be intimidating.

However, you don't need to let fear stop you. By talking about Jesus, you can gain a better understanding of him. When you have a conversation about Jesus, you may realize something about him that hadn't occurred to you before.

Pray:

Ask God to give you opportunities to tell other kids about him.

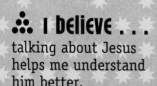

∴ I believe . . .
talking about Jesus
helps me understand
him better.

November 20

When Marcie received Janelle's birthday invitation in the mail, everything looked normal at first. The party was the following Saturday at the skating rink. Hot dogs, cake, and ice cream were going to be served. But that's when things got strange. In big, bold letters at the bottom of the card, it said, "DON'T BRING ANY PRESENTS!"

That's weird, Marcie thought. *You can't have a birthday party without presents.*

Marcie couldn't imagine a birthday party without loads of gifts. She loved opening all the things people gave her.

Then Marcie noticed something written under the big, bold letters that was even stranger. It said, "Instead, please consider bringing a few dollars to give to Enrique—a little boy in Ecuador."

Who's Enrique? Marcie thought.

Marcie couldn't stand it anymore. She picked up the phone and called Janelle.

"Why is Enrique getting all your birthday presents?" she asked as soon as Janelle answered.

"I really don't need anything," Janelle said calmly. "Plus Enrique hardly has anything. We sponsor him through a ministry in Ecuador, and he sends us pictures. He's just so nice that I want to do something nice for him."

Hmmm, Marcie thought. *That's not so strange after all.*

Check out 2 Corinthians 9:7 in the Young Believer Bible:

This verse says you don't *have* to give to others. God wants you to make up your own mind about what to give. He wants you to give from your heart, because he loves a cheerful giver.

●●●

If you ever get the chance to travel to another country, you'll probably find that the kids who live there own less than you do. But you'll most likely notice a couple of other things as well. First, you'll probably discover that they're generous. Even though they have less, they tend to be more willing to share their food and possessions. Second, you'll see that often the kids are happy. They realize they don't need a lot of things to be joyful.

Now think of everything God has given you. He's given you the ability to make choices and to think for yourself. But he's given you a lot more as well.

Here's a list of some things God has given me:

1. _____
2. _____
3. _____
4. _____
5. _____

Pray:
Ask God to help you give cheerfully to other people.

 **I bELiEVE . . .**
I should be giving because God has given me so much.

Snow is cool. No, make that cold. Duh, right? The coolest part of snow is all the fun you can have in it. You can go sledding, ride down a hill on an inner tube, build snow forts, make snow angels, create a snowman, or even have a snowball fight.

And if you live near mountains, you can also go skiing and snowboarding. The speed of skiing and jamming through moguls can't be beat. And when you think about snowboarding, you picture huge air. Watching professionals fly out of the half-pipe and pull three spins before landing is amazing. The combination of grabs, spins, and big air makes snowboarding look awesome. And riding through terrain parks, grinding on pipes, and flying off jumps can be a blast.

But there's another side to snow besides all the fun you can have in it. Snow is beautiful. If you peek outside right after a snowstorm, the land looks peaceful blanketed in a cover of fluffy white. Snow hides everything underneath it. Even if the grass is brown and the trees are bare, a dusting of snow makes everything appear perfect and white.

Check out Isaiah 1:18 in the *Young Believer Bible:*

In this verse the Lord tells you that no matter how red your sins are—no matter how much they stand out—the Lord can make you clean, like the whiteness of snow.

●●●

Just like snow covers up nasty-looking grass and craggy rocks and makes them appear smooth and perfect, God's forgiveness does the same thing to sin. Your sins jump out at God. Because he is perfect and holy, he requires holiness from everybody who wants to go to heaven. Sin makes you imperfect. It's like you have a big red *X* on your forehead.

But the Lord says he will make your red sins as white as snow. And he does more than cover up your sin and make you *appear* perfect. The Lord totally removes your sin and makes you *truly* perfect and white. There's no red left in you when the Lord finishes, so all God sees is perfection.

Pray:

Thank the Lord that through his forgiveness you become as white as snow.

⁘ I believe . . .

the Lord makes my sin
as white as snow.

Amy looked in the mirror. Tears streamed down her face. Even though she was only five years old, she had believed God would answer her prayer. Her mother had told Amy the Lord would answer if she prayed. Amy had brown eyes, but she wanted blue eyes more than anything. One night, she prayed that God would make her eyes blue. In the morning she jumped out of bed and ran to the mirror.

Soon after Amy started crying, her mom appeared at the bedroom door. When Amy told her mom what was wrong, her mom explained that no was an answer too. God had given Amy brown eyes for a reason, even though she may never know why.

Many years later, Amy went to India to be a missionary. When she arrived, she learned about the temple girls. These girls were sold as slaves to the temple and forced to do terrible things. She really wanted to help the girls. But since only Hindus were allowed in the temple, Amy couldn't figure out what was really going on. So one day, Amy stained her skin with coffee, dressed in traditional Indian clothes, and entered the temple. Now she understood why God had given her brown eyes. She never could have passed as an Indian with blue eyes!

Check out Psalm 40:5 in the *Young Believer Bible:*

God has wonderful plans for you. David, who wrote many praises to God, says that God has done more for us than we could ever tell.

●●●

God has wonderful plans for you. Maybe you've asked God for something, he said no, and you wondered, *Why does God sometimes answer no?* It is because he always answers your prayers in a way that follows his perfect plan. He always has a very good reason for whatever he does or allows.

You may never know the reason God allows something to happen or not to happen. But maybe someday, like Amy, you will understand why God answered the way he did. Even if you never understand, you can know he is working out his plan for your good. If God has said no to your prayers, remember he knows your future and is working everything out for the best.

Pray:

Praise God that's he's in control of your life.

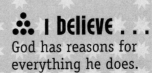

I believe . . .
God has reasons for everything he does.

Some days do you feel like your relationship with Jesus is going pretty well? Maybe you were doing a good job following him and his commands. If you've felt that way, maybe you've even said a prayer like this one:

Dear Lord,

I thank you for this day. I'm amazed at what you're doing in my life and the changes you've made in me. God, so far today I can't think of anything I've done wrong. I haven't fought with my brothers or sisters. I've done everything my parents have asked me to do with a good attitude. My thoughts have been focused on you. Thank you for creating me exactly how you did. I don't even think I've been jealous of my friend's new bike at all. I haven't lied, cheated, or stolen anything. I haven't sworn or been rude. I'm even praying to you right now. This is great!

But now, Lord, I'm going to get out of bed. I know it won't be as easy to think about you as it is now, and I'll probably mess up a lot. So please be with me and help me to continue to do what is right.

Amen.

Check out Hebrews 2:18 in the *Young Believer Bible:*
This verse says that because Jesus was tempted when he walked this planet, he is able to help us when we're being tempted to do the wrong thing.

●●●

It's easy not to sin when you're sleeping or lying in bed first thing in the morning. Those are times when you can relax and focus on God. But for some reason when your feet hit the floor, things change.

You get around people and you're tempted to sin. Your little sister grabs the last waffle at breakfast, which makes you mad. Your cat coughs up a hair ball in your favorite shoes. Your mom asks you to pull weeds in the garden when you wanted to ride bikes with your friends.

At times like that, it's necessary to turn to the Holy Spirit in you and ask him to help you make the correct choices.

Pray:
Ask God's Holy Spirit to help you do what is right.

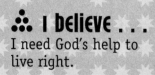

⁖ I believe . . .
I need God's help to live right.

Terry thought he was an expert on everything. So when his friend Randy started skateboarding, Terry decided he could teach Randy a thing or two.

Terry checked out some books from the library, surfed the Internet, and rented a few skateboarding videos. After a few days of research, Terry saw Randy at the skate park. Randy struggled as he tried some basic tricks. Terry walked up to him, feeling confident that he could help.

"You're doing it all wrong," Terry said. "If you want to do an ollie, you need to straighten your back leg and push the tail of the skateboard down."

"How do you know?" Randy asked.

"I read it on-line," Terry said. "Then you have to twist your front foot, jump with your back leg, and use the grip tape on the front of the board to lift it into the air."

"Huh?" Randy said. "I don't get it. Show me."

"I-I can't," Terry admitted. "I've never tried it before, but I know how to do it."

"Sure you do," Randy said sarcastically. "Get lost. I've got to practice."

Check out Ezra 7:10 in the *Young Believer Bible:*

This verse says Ezra was determined to study God's law, obeying it and teaching it to the Israelites.

●●●

Ezra, one of God's prophets, helped the people of Israel turn back to the almighty God. Ezra taught the people God's law and helped them follow God's rules so other nations would see that Israel worshiped the one true God.

But *before* Ezra taught the Israelites God's law, he studied it and obeyed it himself. Ezra is a great example to follow. He had a three-step plan for teaching God's Word.

- **Step One:** Study it. First, you've got to learn it.
- **Step Two:** Do it or obey it. Next, you should practice what you learn. Make sure it works.
- **Step Three:** Teach it. Once you know something and have experienced it, you're better able to teach it.

Pray:

Ask God to help you follow Ezra's example before you try to teach something.

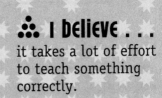

I believe . . .
it takes a lot of effort to teach something correctly.

A new girl just came to our school. She's a Christian who returned home from being a missionary with her family. Everyone thinks she isn't cool because she doesn't wear the right clothes. I want to be her friend, but I'm not sure what my other friends will say. What should I do?
Friendly
Good Hart, Michigan

Dear Friendly,
Your desire to be friends with the new girl is great! Adjusting to a new school can be very difficult, and sometimes the help of one person can make a huge difference. Smiling at her in the hall, asking her to sit with you at lunch, or helping her with an assignment can go a long way in making her feel accepted. And getting over those initial jitters can sometimes be the hardest part for a new student. Going to a new place is scary, especially if the people don't seem friendly. So helping this girl—no matter how she dresses—is the right thing.

As far as your friends go, you need to explain your feelings to them about the new girl. Maybe your friends will understand where you're coming from and want to help too. Even if they don't, you can be positive that your actions are the correct ones.

Check out Galatians 6:10 in the *Young Believer Bible:*

This verse says to do good to all people, especially people who believe in Jesus, whenever we have the opportunity.

●●●

Some kids think the Bible is tricky to read. But the fact is God's Word can be crystal clear—and a lot of times it is. This is one of those cases.

Look around for people in need, or even people you can be nice to for no reason. Maybe you could put your neighbor's newspaper on his porch. Perhaps you can tutor other kids in your class or try to befriend a new girl at church or school. God will give you the opportunities to do good—all you have to do is look for your chances.

Pray:

Ask God to help you recognize opportunities to do good.

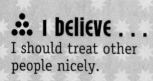

∴ I believe . . .
I should treat other people nicely.

Micah couldn't believe his ears. As he walked past a group of boys in the library, he heard them talking about Robot Town 100. Micah had already created the ultimate robot city on his computer at home and knew everything about the game. He walked back to the table and waited to get involved in their conversation.

"I can't figure out how to put condos by the park," one boy said.

"And I don't know why my city's so unhappy," another boy added. "Maybe I should build an amusement park or another mall."

Finally Micah spoke up.

"It's easy to build condos next to the park," he blurted. "You just need to get a permit by going to a city-council meeting. And your happiness rating isn't based on malls; you need to have better roads, schools, and jobs. The robots love to work!"

Micah took a breath and waited for the boys to thank him for solving their video-game problems.

"What did that kid say?" the first boy asked, totally ignoring Micah.

"I wasn't listening," another boy replied.

Auuggh! Micah thought as he walked away. *Don't they know I have the right answers? Why aren't they listening?*

Check out Ezekiel 2:4-5 in the *Young Believer Bible:*

When God calls Ezekiel, he knows Ezekiel's job won't be easy. So he instructs Ezekiel to say, "This is what the Sovereign Lord says!" That way the people will know God's prophet talked to them, even if they choose not to listen.

• • •

Have you ever felt like Micah? You have all the right answers, but nobody's listening. It can be frustrating to know you're right when other kids don't care about your opinion.

Ezekiel must have felt that way too. He had God's Word—directly from God's mouth—but nobody listened at first.

You also have God's Word—in the Bible. Maybe some friends won't listen and others will make fun of you. But some of the people you tell about God will understand the truth and believe in the Lord. So follow his leading . .. and speak out for God.

Pray:

Ask God to give you the confidence and strength to share his truth with others.

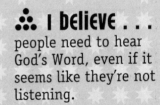

∴ I believe . . .
people need to hear God's Word, even if it seems like they're not listening.

"Thank you very much. Thank you very much. That's the nicest thing that anyone's ever done for me."

Do you recognize those words? You probably do if you've ever seen the musical *Scrooge*. The song is sung a couple of times in the performance. It's kind of fun to sing about being thankful. So many songs seem to be about being sad or discouraged or losing something—or maybe that's just country music: "I lost my dog, my friend doesn't like me, and my truck broke down. La, la, la." Just kidding, country music isn't like that . . . anymore.

But it's not just country music that can be depressing. Blues got its name because it's about sad things. And think about the song "Rock-a-bye, Baby." First the baby's in a tall tree being rocked—there's something plain wrong about that. Then the tree breaks and the baby comes plunging back to the ground. Talk about scary! That's enough to give children nightmares.

Singing about thankfulness is much better. Do you agree? King David probably did.

Check out 1 Chronicles 16:34 in the Young Believer Bible:

David wrote many psalms, which are songs and poems of worship to God. Many of them are in the book of Psalms in the Bible, but this one isn't. Here David says to give thanks to the Lord because he is good. His love lasts forever.

● ● ●

Not only is God good, but he's good to you. What does God's goodness mean in your life?

This is what God's goodness means to me:

_____

_____

_____

Look at everything you listed. You could probably write down enough things to fill this whole book if you had the time. God is *that* good.

Sometimes it's not easy being thankful. It's easier to look at what we don't have, instead of what we have. When those times come, remember that God is good, his love lasts forever . . . and be thankful.

Pray:

Ask God to help you be thankful in all situations.

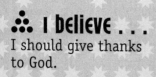

∴ I believe . . .
I should give thanks to God.

"Please cover your left eye and read the third line on the chart," the school nurse tells you.

"Okay. It's *I-N-E-E*—and I think—*D*."

"Very good," the nurse says. "Now cover your other eye, and read the next line down."

"All right," you say. "That's *G-L-A-S*—uhhh—*S-E-S*."

"Hmmm," the nurse says. "I guess you're right. You *do* need glasses, because the letters actually were *E-Y-E-S-A-R-E-G-R-E-A-T*."

⁂

Do you wear glasses? One out of every four children either does or should. And wearing glasses or having corrected vision is in style these days. Some kids and adults wear glasses as a fashion statement, even if they don't need them. With fun frames, different kinds of lenses, and contacts that can change your eye color, wearing glasses and contacts can be cool.

But having good eyesight is even cooler. Seeing clearly can keep you out of danger, make the world appear more beautiful, and help you be a better student. Taking care of your vision and fixing any problems is important. The eye chart doesn't lie: Eyes are great.

Check out Luke 6:42 in the *Young Believer Bible:*

In this verse Jesus encourages us to look at our own lives before telling others how to live. Sometimes a "log" can block our spiritual vision. Jesus wants us to remove anything from our lives that could hinder our vision, so then we can see clearly to help the people around us.

●●●

Going through life with poor vision can cause many problems. You may get more headaches, often feel tired, or suffer from strained eyes. But as crucial as it is to care for your eyes, it's just as important to take care of your spiritual vision.

Jesus says poor spiritual eyes can cause you to make bad judgments about yourself and other people.

These are some things that may be hurting my spiritual vision of God:

_____

_____

_____

Now come up with a plan to remove those things from your spiritual eyes. God wants you to make sure you can see him and his plans for your life clearly.

Pray:

Ask God to help point out anything that may be getting in the way of your view of him.

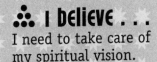

⁂ **I bеlieve . . .**
I need to take care of my spiritual vision.

Kayla couldn't wait for Roman Day at school. She loved dressing up and pretending she lived in a different part of history. Her mom had helped her make the perfect toga, like the ancient Romans wore. It had a belt and flowed all the way to the ground. So when Patti called and said Roman Day was changed to this Friday instead of next Friday, Kayla didn't even think twice. She couldn't wait to wake up and get dressed.

Kayla woke up extra early. She wanted her hair to be just right. Her mom helped her by putting up her dark, long hair. Then Mom used her curling iron so Kayla could have dark ringlets coming down near her face. *Perfect,* Kayla thought as she looked in the mirror.

When Kayla arrived at school, she leapt from the car and rushed to her classroom. She couldn't wait to see what everybody else was wearing. She knew her outfit would be one of the best. But when Kayla opened the door to Mrs. Wright's room, she was shocked . . . she was the only one wearing a toga. Everybody else was wearing normal clothes. Patti turned around in her chair and started to giggle. Kayla felt her cheeks getting hot.

Check out Zephaniah 3:17 in the Young Believer Bible:

This verse says the Lord is with you. He has the power to save you, and he is filled with gladness when he thinks of you. Plus the Lord's love will calm you when you feel fearful.

● ● ●

Has anyone ever played a practical joke on you? Sometimes those jokes don't feel too good and can be very embarrassing.

The great part of having a relationship with Jesus Christ is that a lot of things in this world become less important. It doesn't matter if you're popular, because you have Jesus as your best friend. It doesn't matter if people make fun of you, because God's love never changes. God's opinion of you matters most. You can rest in his love and not worry so much about what other people think of you.

Pray:

Thank God for his incredible love.

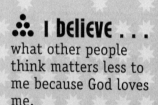

∴ I believe . . .
what other people think matters less to me because God loves me.

November 30

This is the beginning of a special time for some churches. It's the season of Advent, which starts on the Sunday closest to November 30 and ends on Christmas Eve. Everybody is getting ready to celebrate God's Son coming to earth as a baby. The word *advent* means "arrival." Maybe you have an Advent calendar with windows you open up during December as Christmas gets closer. The idea of Advent is to get you excited about Christmas.

There are lots of ways to celebrate Advent. In addition to Advent calendars, some families put Advent wreaths in their homes. The green of the wreath stands for newness in Christ, and the circle shows that God's power never ends. Candles are lit in the wreath to show the light of God—Jesus Christ—coming to earth.

So as the Advent season starts, come up with some ideas on how you can prepare yourself at church and in your home for the excitement of Jesus' birth.

Write down some of those ideas here:

Check out Luke 2:10-11 in the *Young Believer Bible:*
These verses explain the angels' appearance to the shepherds to tell them about Jesus' birth. The angels say they have good news for everyone: Jesus has been born and he is the Lord and Savior. The shepherds immediately run to the village to worship Jesus.

●●●

Opening Christmas presents is awesome. But instead of focusing in on what you want for Christmas, spend some time thinking about how you can make Jesus the center of your celebration. The fact is, no matter how great a gift you get this Christmas (even if it's the newest video game or American Girl doll), it doesn't compare to the gift God gave you when he sent Jesus to make it possible for you to have a relationship with him. That was the most amazing gift of all!

Pray:
Tell God you're going to focus on celebrating his Son this Christmas.

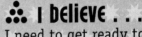

I believe . . .
I need to get ready to celebrate Jesus' birth.

December 1

Have you noticed that some people act like they don't have to pay attention to rules? They glide through life pretending the rules don't apply to them. You know the type:

- Celebrities who think they can take things from a store without paying because they are famous
- Athletes who take drugs to help them perform better in their sport
- People who leave the scene of an accident they caused
- Bullies at school who think they can treat everybody else like dirt
- Politicians who lie and get away with it

The truth is that people's bad actions catch up with them. Even if it appears that a person gets away with something, there are always consequences. God's justice will catch them in the end. His rules don't change, and his laws can't be broken without punishment. The proud are always humbled—especially those who think they're better than everybody else.

Check out Obadiah 1:3-4 in the *Young Believer Bible:*

These verses from the shortest book in the Old Testament talk about the people of Edom. The Edomites thought they were hidden from God and free to do anything they wanted. But they were wrong, and God brought down their kingdom.

●●●

The people of Edom thought they were pretty hot stuff. They thought they were safe from attack and could do anything they wanted because their homes were built high in the rocks. The Edomites rejoiced—and even helped—when other countries fought to destroy God's people.

Have you ever heard the saying "Pride comes before a fall"? That's exactly what happened to Edom. It was proud of its fortress and thought it was above God. But the fact is, nobody is above the Lord. When people break his laws and mock his people, he can humble individuals from the highest heights and bring judgment on the mightiest nation. God's power is absolutely unbeatable. And nothing on earth compares to him.

Pray:

Thank God that he is a fair and right judge who always rules justly.

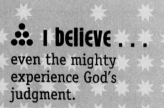

∴ I believe . . .
even the mighty experience God's judgment.

December 2

I love winning. Before every hockey game, I pray that God will help my team win. Is that okay?
Winner
Victoriaville, Quebec

Dear Winner,
Winning is an awesome feeling. But for some kids, winning is everything. They'll do anything to win—even cheat or get into fights. If winning is all you care about, then God isn't first in your life, and that's a problem.

But is praying to win okay? God cares about everything in your life. He wants you to be happy and successful, so praying to win is fine. In fact, there are probably players on the other team praying that their team will win too.

However, God wants you to be like him more than he wants you to win. And sometimes you can learn more by losing than by winning. Next time you lose, you might want to keep that in mind.

Here's an idea: Instead of praying to win, pray that your team plays well, that nobody gets hurt, that the referees make fair calls, and that everybody plays by the rules. Now go hit the ice and do your best!

Check out Philippians 3:14 in the Young Believer Bible:

In this verse the apostle Paul writes that he's determined to win the prize for which God has called him. He knows it will take some effort, but the hard work will be worth it.

●●●

What's more fun: winning a game without even trying or playing hard and defeating a team you never thought you could beat? (This was an easy one, huh?) For some reason, beating the tough opponent is a lot more fun, even though you have to work a lot harder to do it.

The same thing is true in your relationship with Jesus Christ. God's goal for you is to become more like him and understand more about his teachings. But to achieve that goal, you'll have to work hard by reading your Bible, praying, doing devotions, and going to church. And all that hard work will make your success even sweeter.

Pray:

Ask God to give you the strength and determination to live like him.

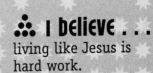

⁘ I believe . . .
living like Jesus is
hard work.

December 3

How often does your family rent movies?

a. every day
b. every week
c. once a month
d. never

Chances are your family falls into the *b* or *c* category. Recent statistics show that Americans spend more than $20 billion a year renting and buying DVDs and VHS tapes—that's just in the United States! All that adds up to hours and hours spent in front of the television.

Did you know the folks in Hollywood specifically target you with their movie making? You probably noticed that a lot of Disney and Nickelodeon television shows have been turned into full-length movies and videos. That's because Hollywood knows if it creates a picture that kids want to see, then a lot of families will plop down the cash to view it. Statistics show the biggest money-making videos and movies are aimed directly at children and have a PG or PG-13 rating.

How does that make you feel? Do you feel powerful? What you watch and buy makes a big difference in the kind of movies that Hollywood produces.

Check out Philippians 4:8 in the
Young Believer Bible:
This verse tells you what God wants you to think about—things that are true, right, pure, lovely, and excellent.

●●●

What kind of movies do you enjoy watching? Action? Comedy? Animated? You have a lot of choices. And each movie has its good and bad parts—even if it's rated G. But since you're getting older, you may have seen a few PG and PG-13 releases too.

As you watch videos, think about Philippians 4:8. Does the movie live up to God's standards? He wants you to have pure, praiseworthy thoughts. He doesn't want your mind to be polluted with frightening images, violent scenes, or bad language. It takes a mature person to make good choices about what to watch.

And as a growing believer in Jesus Christ, you can be that person.

Pray:
Ask God to help guide your entertainment choices.

I believe . . .
I should fill my mind
with good images.

December 4

Do you have any little brothers or sisters? Chances are you do. In the United States, a baby is born every eight seconds. By the time you finish reading this very long, lengthy, huge, massive, boring sentence with lots and lots of commas and extra punctuation(!) thrown in for no reason at all?;, a baby will have been born.

Amazing, huh? And each child is a perfect example of God's workmanship. Every baby is unique and special. Hello!! Another baby has just entered the world. God has a special plan for each and every new life, just like he has a plan for you. You can choose to follow his plan or to steer off the path. But if you stay close to him—oh, good, here comes another baby!—he will stay with you and guide you even when you're old. Even though you might be a great-grandma or great-grandpa someday, you'll always be God's child. Hey, here comes another baby! Wonder what God's plan for him is?

Check out Isaiah 46:4 in the *Young Believer Bible:*
This verse says even when you're old and have white hair, God will be your God. The same God who created you will carry you throughout your life and save you when you're in trouble.

● ● ●

It kind of boggles the mind to think that 10,800 babies will be born in the next 24 hours in the United States. That's enough to fill a small city. Of course, nobody would want to live there with all the crying, spitting up, and stinky diapers. But that's not the point.

The point is, God cares for, loves, and has a special plan for those new lives. Not only that, but God cares for all the other babies born all the time all over the world.

God watches over his children. He rescues them from difficult situations and puts them on the right path.

Be on the lookout for how God has gifted you, because you have the ability to do awesome things for him.

Pray:
Praise God that he made you special and has big plans for your life.

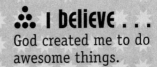

∴ I bELiEVE . . .
God created me to do awesome things.

How does your family celebrate Christmas? Most families have traditions—driving to the Christmas-tree farm together to chop down the perfect tree, baking loads of cookies and holiday goodies to give to friends, or going Christmas caroling through the neighborhood.

Traditions are an important part of Christmas. But why do people keep them? Most traditions have a great story behind them. Did you know that there wasn't even an official celebration of Jesus' birth for more than one hundred years after his death and resurrection? Then in A.D. 137, the bishop of Rome ordered that Jesus' birthday be celebrated with a feast. In A.D. 350, another Roman bishop picked December 25 as that yearly day of celebration. There was already a pagan holiday called Saturnalia around that time, but people began to celebrate Christ's birth instead.

Since then, many Christmas traditions have developed—giving gifts, decorating Christmas trees, and setting up nativity scenes. All of these fun traditions make up the celebration you have today. Even though all of these traditions are great fun, it's important to think how each one can point you to the true meaning of Christmas.

Check out Matthew 1:21 in the *Young Believer Bible:*
This verse explains the real reason we celebrate Christmas. Jesus was born to save us from our sins. He came down from heaven as a human baby so that he could grow up to be the perfect sacrifice for sin.

●●●

Do your holiday traditions show the true meaning of the season? Think of ways you can focus on Jesus as you celebrate this year. When you give gifts, remember the wise men who brought gifts to worship Jesus. When you go caroling, think of how you can share the Good News of salvation. And when you decorate the tree, thank God for giving you the gift of eternal life.

Christmas traditions are especially good when they remind you of why Jesus came and what he's done for you. That's a reason to celebrate!

Here are some things I can do to focus on Jesus this holiday season:

1. _____
2. _____
3. _____

Pray:
Thank God for the gift of his Son.

∴ I believe . . .
Jesus was born to save the world from sin.

Think of something powerful, and write it down:

_____

What did you write? A weight lifter? A Mack truck? Spider-Man? The smell coming from your brother's shoes?

All of those things are powerful. A weight lifter can grab a bar weighing more than three hundred pounds and lift it over his head. Some really big weight lifters can even bench press more than six hundred pounds. Mack trucks are huge pieces of machinery that can pull other huge pieces of machinery. And what can you say about Spider-Man? This make-believe superhero has all kinds of powers. From climbing walls to shooting webs, he's pretty amazing. As far as your brother's shoes go—that's between him and his Odor Eaters.

But God isn't impressed by any of those things (except maybe your brother's shoes . . . oh, never mind). The power that people have and the machines they put together don't amount to anything in his eyes. He knows it's his Spirit who causes everything to happen.

Check out Zechariah 4:6 in the *Young Believer Bible:*

An angel tells Zechariah, a priest and prophet for the Lord, that strength and force don't matter—the Lord's Spirit accomplishes all things.

●●●

Sovereign is a big word that's tough to pronounce (sov-ren). But it's an important one to know, because it's used in the Bible about three hundred times! It means absolute, unlimited, exalted. It means God is the tops, the greatest, unbeatable.

Nothing happens without God knowing about it. He rules over everything that goes on in your life, even the bad stuff. Sometimes that's hard to understand, especially when things aren't going well for you (a parent loses a job, you have to move, your best friend turns against you). But the Bible is clear: Nothing happens without God's Spirit knowing about it and allowing it. Worldly powers or mighty nations can't escape his control. You can trust that everything occurs for a reason, and that the Lord's Spirit uses even the most horrible situations to accomplish his perfect plans.

Pray:

Thank the Lord that he is ultimately powerful and that his Spirit does all things.

I believe . . .
God is sovereign.

December 7

As a Christian, which of the following do you think is most important?

a. spending time expressing your love for God through praise and worship
b. telling God everything and treating him as your best friend
c. learning all you can about God by studying the Bible
d. serving God by helping others, serving in church, or doing missionary work
e. all of the above

If you picked *e*, you have the right idea. At first glance, one action may seem more important than the others, but the Bible says all four are equally important. He doesn't want you to just have an emotional love for him; he wants you also to use your mind and strength to show your love.

Check out Mark 12:30 in the *Young Believer Bible:*

You are carefully made with a heart, soul, mind, and body. God wants you to love him with your whole self and use every gift he's given you for his glory. One part of you is not more important than the others. They all work together to make you a powerful servant for him.

●●●

God created many different people. And because each one is different, there isn't just one best way to love God. Instead, he asks that you love him with your whole being. Maybe you're smart and do well in school. You can love God with your mind by studying his Word and answering people's tough questions about the Bible. Maybe you're naturally loving and caring. God enjoys the praise you give him. Maybe you have a desire to do things for God and others, and you're always looking for ways to help. Service is another way to love God.

But no matter what your strengths are, you can always find ways to love God with every area of your life.

Here's how I can love God better in each of the areas mentioned in Mark 12:30:

With my heart: _____

With my soul: _____

With my mind: _____

With my strength: _____

Pray:
Ask God to give you new ideas about how you can show him that you love him.

⦂ I believe . . .
I should love God with my heart, soul, mind, and strength.

December 8

If you look around your school you'll probably see lots of kids loaded down with backpacks. You're probably a backpack carrier too. With a bunch of subjects and after-school activities, most kids need to carry backpacks to hold all their stuff. What's inside your backpack right now?

Your backpack probably holds schoolbooks and notebooks. Maybe it also carries art supplies, gym clothes, and your lunch. But a lot of kids carry around CD players, video games, and other things they don't need every day.

What's wrong with that? you're probably asking.

Well, backpacks can be dangerous. More than 12,000 backpack-related injuries are reported every year. Some backpacks are just too heavy. Most doctors say your backpack shouldn't weigh more than 15 percent of your body weight—and less is better. That means if you weigh 100 pounds, your fully loaded backpack shouldn't weigh more than 15 pounds.

Other backpack injuries can come from jamming your finger trying to grab a book, tripping over your backpack, or having your backpack fall on you. So watch out!

As silly as it sounds, backpacks can be a real pain in the . . . hand, shoulder, foot, and back.

Check out Matthew 11:28-30 in the *Young Believer Bible:*

Jesus says to come to him when you need rest. You can learn from him without carrying a heavy burden on your shoulders. Being a believer in Jesus Christ is actually easy.

● ● ●

Some kids carry *everything* with them and end up with a supersized weight on their backs, which is just an accident waiting to happen.

When it comes to life's problems, hurts, and fears, God doesn't expect you or want you to carry those things around with you all the time. He wants you to give your heavy burdens to him. And Jesus says his yoke is light. (A yoke is what joins two horses or oxen together to pull a wagon or plow.) When you're hooked up to Jesus, he helps you follow him. God gives you his Word, plus you have the Holy Spirit to give you strength at all times.

So next time you feel your shoulders droop under a heavy load of troubles, remember that Jesus wants to give you rest. Go ahead and hand over your burdens to him.

Pray:

Praise Jesus that he makes it easy to follow him.

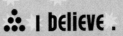

∴ I believe . . .

following Jesus doesn't have to be backbreaking.

Zac Gomez is a real kid. He lives in Texas with his mom and little brother. He has to share a room with his brother, but he doesn't complain. Zac knows he has a lot more than many kids around the world. And Zac has experienced what it means to live without a lot of stuff.

You see, when Zac was little, he lived with his brother and mom in a shelter for six months. Although it's been quite a while since he lived there, he hasn't forgotten the kindness of the shelter workers and how they looked after the needs of the people who stayed there. That's why when his Cub Scout leader challenged his den to donate a blanket, Zac decided to do a whole lot more.

He called local businesses and radio and television stations to take part in a city-wide fund-raiser. Zac encouraged people to give clothes, toys, food, coats, blankets, and other items. And people responded. In just three weeks, he collected enough stuff to fill a 20-foot trailer.

Things went so well the first year that Zac decided to make a tradition of it. Now Zac celebrates his birthday every year by gathering toys and blankets to give to others.

Check out Matthew 25:40 in the *Young Believer Bible:*

Jesus is telling a story to teach a lesson. In this verse Jesus says whatever you do for people in need, you do for him.

●●●

If you're reading this book, you probably have more than most kids in the world. You have an education—you're able to read. You have enough to eat. And you have a warm place to sleep.

Will you think about helping other people because of how generous God has been to you? Look in your closet and dresser, and hunt through all your stuff in the basement, attic, and garage. Find toys and clothes that are still in good shape but that you don't use anymore. Then ask a parent to help you donate them to a shelter or the Salvation Army. Maybe you can even save your money to buy something for a needy child. Whenever you help people in need, you're actually giving to Jesus.

Pray:

Ask God to help you be more giving.

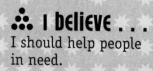

⠿ I bELievE . . .

I should help people in need.

December 10

Picture yourself alone in the mountains of Switzerland. It's winter. It's cold. Snow surrounds you. You have no idea where you are and no clue how to get home. You're lost. Of course, it's easy to get lost in the Swiss Alps. People do it all the time. But that doesn't make you feel better as you shiver in the freezing temperatures.

Suddenly you see a massive mound of fur moving toward you. Could it be a bear? The abominable snowman? A giant Furby? The snow-covered pile of fur keeps moving closer. As it gets within a few feet, you realize you're about to get nose to nose with the largest dog you've ever seen. *Whew. Glad it's not a bear,* you think.

The giant St. Bernard snuggles down beside you. His head is as big as a bowling ball and probably weighs twice as much. His dog breath smells, but that's okay—at least it's warm. His fur radiates heat, and he's carrying survival supplies. The huge dog licks you. That's when you get a peek at his name tag: Barry.

Barry's a good name for dog, you think. *Especially a dog that just saved my life.*

Check out Psalm 37:40 in the *Young Believer Bible:*
This verse says the Lord saves you and shelters you from harm.

●●●

Unless you've been stuck alone in a fierce snowstorm, you had to imagine being saved by Barry at the beginning of this story. But Barry wasn't make-believe. He was real. Barry the St. Bernard saved 40 people when he worked with rescuers in the Swiss Alps—that's the most lives ever saved by one dog.

Saving 40 people is pretty amazing. But that's nothing compared to what Jesus has done. Jesus has saved millions of people. And he doesn't just save their lives on earth. Jesus Christ saves them forever. When he comes into your life, you never die. Instead you live with God and praise him forever in heaven. Now that's some impressive lifesaving!

Pray:
Thank Jesus for being such an awesome Savior.

I believe . . .
Jesus saves people.

December 11

Tree lights. Presents. Santa. During this season, the Christmas story can be overlooked in the hustle and bustle of Christmas shopping, cookie baking, and holiday parties.

Twelve-year-old Kelsey says, "I celebrate Christmas because it's Jesus' birthday, but some of my friends celebrate it just to get all the gifts. Then they make fun of me for celebrating it for the real reason. What should I do?"

Have you ever felt like Kelsey? Maybe you feel like you're the only one who knows that the true meaning of Christmas isn't getting the latest video-game system or cool clothes. Do you ever feel alone, like no one understands where you're coming from? The Bible explains the reason Christians sometimes feel that way.

Check out John 12:40 in the *Young Believer Bible:*

Even though Jesus performed a lot of miracles and fulfilled many Old Testament prophecies, many people in his day didn't believe in him. But God knew that would happen, and the prophet Isaiah even said it would.

●●●

If your unsaved friends are blinded to the truth that Jesus wants to save them, what can you do about it? First, you can pray that the Holy Spirit will work in their hearts and open their eyes.

Christmas is a great opportunity to witness to your friends! But your unbelieving friends may not know the true meaning of Christmas. You could ask your parents to let you have a party with your friends to share the good news about Jesus' birth. You could send out invitations, play fun games, and tell a story about Jesus. Then you might pass out treats and Christmas cards that share the joy of Christ's birth. Take time to focus on Jesus this Christmas. And use this holiday season as an opportunity to shine some light into a dark world!

Here's a list of people I can invite to a "birthday party for Jesus":

1. _____
2. _____
3. _____
4. _____
5. _____

Pray:

Ask God to give you opportunities to share his love with others this Christmas and all through the year.

⁙ I believe . . .

some people have blind eyes and dead hearts when it comes to understanding God's truth.

December 12

Gerty never had enough. At breakfast she always griped that her brother had more granola. When someone brought a treat to school, Gerty would grasp and grab to get the biggest one. And when her grandparents came to visit, she would greet them with "Did you get me anything?"

Gradually, Gerty grew so greedy that no one wanted to share anything with her. Her friends would groan when they saw her coming and grimace when she got grabby. Gerty noticed her friends were grumpy and asked them why.

"It's because you're so greedy, Gerty," Greta said. Gerty gritted her teeth. She had to get a grip and grow up!

"I'm not going to be greedy anymore," she said.

Gerty's friends grinned. "This is great," they said. "After all, it's better to give than to grab!"

Have you ever known someone like Gerty? Maybe you are like her sometimes. The Bible says greed isn't good. In fact, it distracts you from God and keeps you from serving him.

Check out Luke 12:15 in the *Young Believer Bible:*

Jesus tells us to watch out for greed. It's a dangerous sin because it makes us focus on ourselves. The most important thing in life is our relationship with God, not the things we have.

●●●

Have you ever struggled with greed? Maybe you've caught yourself complaining too much when your brother got something you didn't. Perhaps you've hoarded candy without sharing it with others. Or maybe you have a hard time being generous and sharing what you have. People are naturally selfish, so it's easy to become greedy.

Greed causes a person to say by her actions, "I'm number one, and my needs are most important." But the Bible says just the opposite. We should always put others first and not worry about getting our fair share.

That's easier said than done. When you're tempted to get greedy, try concentrating on making other people happy and you'll naturally forget about yourself. When you focus on God and the needs of others, you'll be happier too. Remember, there's no need for greed.

Pray:

Ask God to help you avoid being greedy.

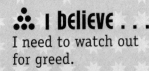

∴ I believe . . .
I need to watch out for greed.

December 13

Do you have a friend who talks all the time? Sometimes you're just hoping for a pause so you can get in a couple of words. If you have any talkative friends, this conversation may sound familiar:

You: How's it going?

Your friend: It's going great. Well, not really. I mean, it was going great this morning. I woke up extra early so I could get ready and play some video games. I didn't start out so well. But I got a new record in my second game. It was awesome! I couldn't believe it. But then my mom yelled downstairs that I was late for school. I had to run upstairs, brush my teeth, and bolt out the door. I felt totally unprepared. Then in science class Mr. Adam gave us a pop quiz. I got, like, none right. At least lunch is coming up. Mom packed me tuna fish. . . .

Wow! All those details. Who needs 'em? With some friends it would probably be nice to have a remote control with a mute button, so you could hit it and make them be quiet.

Isn't it nice to know that God never feels that way?

Check out Ephesians 6:18 in the Young Believer Bible:

In this verse Paul tells believers in Jesus Christ to pray at all times with persistence. But we should be especially on the lookout for ways to pray for other Christians.

●●●

Anything is worth praying about. God cares about all areas of your life. No request is too small, and you're never going to be a bother to him.

But God doesn't want to just hear about *your* life. He deeply cares for you and desires for you to care about the people around you. That's why he loves it when you tell him about other people's needs too. You have a special responsibility to pray for your family and friends. Ask God to bless them and help them follow him.

When it comes to prayer, God wants you to pray often, pray about everything, and pray for other people.

Pray:

Thank God that you can tell him anything at any time.

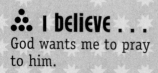

∴ I believe . . .

God wants me to pray to him.

How do you find a friend?

Maybe you're great at making friends. You join a basketball team, and suddenly you have eight new pals. You go to a park and instantly find somebody to play with.

Perhaps you don't make friends as easily. Maybe you are shy or don't know how to strike up a conversation.

Kids are drawn into friendships in many different ways. Here are a few:

- **Similar interests.** Whether you're homeschooled, enjoy soccer, or play the piano, you can find friends who enjoy the same activities.
- **Same age.** A lot of your friends are probably close in age to you or are in your class in school.
- **Close location.** Many kids make friends with neighbors or people who live close by.
- **Shared beliefs.** Church is a great place to find friends who also believe in Jesus.

But no matter how many things you have in common with somebody, you can't *make* that person be your friend. Both of you have to agree that you want to have a friendship—otherwise you're not friends at all.

Check out Amos 3:3 in the *Young Believer Bible:*

God used Amos, a shepherd, to give his message to Israel. This verse says two people who don't agree on where they are going can't walk together.

● ● ●

Your friends can greatly affect who you are. It's natural to pick up habits from kids you spend time with. If you have friends who use bad language or listen to music with wrong messages, you could start talking like them or liking their musical tastes. Friends can also influence your spiritual beliefs. That's what happened to the Israelites. Instead of rejecting false gods and staying close to the one true God, they wandered from him and followed false teachings. They agreed to follow along with evil people, so God judged them.

On the other hand, friends who encourage you to make good decisions can help your relationship with Christ. Do you seek out friends who share your beliefs and values?

Pray:

Ask God to bring good friends into your life.

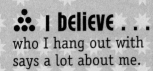

∴ I believe . . .
who I hang out with
says a lot about me.

December 15

Everyone likes a good mystery. First you look for clues. Then you put the pieces together to find out what really happened. Then you use all the information you've gathered to solve the mystery!

Thousands of years ago there was a great mystery. From the time Adam sinned in the Garden of Eden, God promised he would send a Savior who would free people from their sin. All through the Old Testament, God reminded the people of his promise. And hundreds of years before Jesus was born, God's writers wrote clues in the Bible so people would recognize Jesus when he came. Through these clues, people could know that Jesus was the Messiah. The Old Testament contains more than four hundred clues, called prophecies, and every single one came true.

When a detective is solving a crime, the clues are most important. He uses them to discover the truth. You can be a Bible detective by studying what the prophets said about the coming Messiah. All the clues point to Jesus Christ.

Check out Luke 24:44 in the *Young Believer Bible:*

In this verse, Jesus claims that He will fulfill all the prophecies about the Messiah found in the Old Testament. Even though some people didn't believe him, Jesus perfectly fulfilled every prophecy.

• • •

Many years before Jesus came, God used men to write down prophecies that only the true Messiah would fulfill when he came. They said Jesus would be born in Bethlehem (Micah 5:2), be born of a virgin (Isaiah 7:14) and be a descendant of David (Isaiah 16:5). All these things, plus many more, came true. Because of Bible clues, we can know for sure that Jesus is the Savior, and that's really good news!

Here are the prophecies I found in these passages:

1. Isaiah 9:6 _____

2. Isaiah 53 _____

Now take a look at the Gospels, and see if you can find the fulfillments of these prophecies.

Pray:

Thank God for giving us clues to point us to the Savior.

⸪ I believe . . .
Jesus fulfills Old
Testament prophecy.

December 16

Have you ever seen a television show or movie with a character who seems really nice at first but turns out to be the bad guy in the end? Or maybe you've known somebody like that in real life. They seem sugary sweet on the outside, but inside they're nasty and mean. That's one of the reasons parents tell their kids not to talk with strangers. Just because someone appears nice doesn't mean he is.

It's too bad some people act this way. It'd be a lot easier if everybody was totally honest all the time. It certainly would make the world a simpler and safer place to live. Instead of cheating off your test in school, your classmate would turn to you and say, "You should cover your paper better, because I'm trying to cheat off you."

But that's not the way life is. People often try to hide their real intentions. And it's been happening for a long time.

Check out Matthew 2:7-8, 12 in the Young Believer Bible:

In these verses King Herod tells the wise men to find the baby Jesus and report back to him so he can also worship Jesus. But God warns the magi in a dream not to tell the king anything, so they go home a different way.

●●●

Do you think King Herod really wanted to worship Jesus?

If you've read the Christmas story, you know King Herod was lying. He really planned to kill Jesus. When the king's priests and religious teachers told him that prophets a long time ago had predicted that a ruler would be born in Bethlehem, Herod got mad. He didn't want anybody to rule but him.

But as much as Herod wanted to kill Jesus, God had a different plan for his Son. First God warned the wise men in a dream about the king's real plan. Then he warned Jesus' parents to get out of Bethlehem and take Jesus to Egypt. And the same God who protected Jesus still protects his children today.

Pray:

Thank God for his protection, and ask him to give you the wisdom to stay safe.

I believe . . .
God protects me from evil people.

December 17

Holiday quiz time. (Circle only one correct answer per question. No cheating!)

Question 1: Why do we celebrate Christmas?
- Q. To give large, bearded guys good jobs
- R. To help boost the economy through toy sales
- S. To celebrate Jesus' birth

Question 2: What is the reason for the season?
- A. God's Son coming to Earth
- B. An occasion to encourage families to get together and eat large meals
- C. The Earth's tilt and rotation in relation to its orbit around the Sun causes the seasons

Question 3: What is the purpose of Christmas?
- D. To worship Jesus Christ
- E. To celebrate your grandma's pie recipe
- F. To see how many lights you can hang from your house

The test is over. You can relax and stop sweating and untie the knots from your stomach. Please put your pencils down and get ready to grade your own paper.

The answers are *S-A-D,* because it would be *sad* if anybody missed one of these questions.

Check out Matthew 2:9-11 in the Young Believer Bible:

This is the end of the wise men's search for the baby Jesus. These verses tell that the star led the wise men to Jesus. When they saw the child with his mother, Mary, the wise men bowed down and worshiped him.

●●●

A lot of things will try to pull your attention away from Jesus this Christmas. There will be tests at school, holiday programs, family gatherings, shopping for presents, preparing a wish list, and baking cookies. And don't forget that round, white-bearded guy dressed in red and white (no, it's not your uncle Joe).

As you can see, distractions come up a lot during the holidays. Despite all of these things, it's important to keep your eyes on Jesus. He's the reason for Christmas. A believer's number-one goal should be to stay focused on him.

To get back to the basics of what Christmas is all about, all you have to do is look at the wise men. The ultimate goal of Christmas is to worship Christ the King!

⁂ I believe . . .
the purpose of Christmas is worshiping Jesus.

Pray:
Commit to God that you're going to focus on worshiping him this Christmas.

You're getting to the age when a lot of kids start trying to figure out where they fit in and how they should act. Some kids decide they're athletically gifted and begin to act and look like other athletes. They usually wear cross-training shoes, T-shirts, and sweats. Others follow a path into drama and the arts. They decide to participate in all the school productions and sing at church. The mechanical kids are the ones who can take anything apart and put it back together. And the high-tech kids love all the new gadgets and gizmos and are computer whizzes.

But while you try to find your place, always keep in mind what's most important—and it's not fitting in with a certain group of kids at school. As you decide how you should act, remember that your actions represent Jesus Christ.

As a believer in Jesus, you have the responsibility to reflect your Savior in your life—no matter what group you decide to be part of.

Check out 2 John 1:6 in the *Young Believer Bible:*

This verse tells you how you can show God and other people that you love them. All you have to do is obey God's commands. When you follow God's rules, you walk in God's love.

●●●

What are God's commands? It's good to figure out what God is asking you to do *before* you jump in and try to be like him.

These are some things I know God wants me to do:

1. Consider other people's needs ahead of mine.

2. Love the people around me like I want to be loved.

3. _____

4. _____

5. _____

6. _____

7. _____

Look at your list. Do you think if you followed God's commands other kids would see Jesus in you? They definitely would. Your love would be contagious, and people would be drawn to you. But it's not always easy to live as Jesus wants you to. Sometimes your feelings or difficult situations will get in the way. Like all of us, you're going to need his help.

Pray:

Ask God to help you walk in love.

∴ I believe . . .
I show love when I obey God's commands.

You can find out what's important to you by looking at how you spend your time and money. What did you do with most of your time yesterday? Go to school? Play video games? Read the Bible? Write down the top five ways that you use your time:

1. _____   4. _____

2. _____   5. _____

3. _____

Now think about your spending habits. Where does your money go: candy, movies, clothes, video games, the church? Jot down the top five things you did with your money last month:

1. _____   4. _____

2. _____   5. _____

3. _____

Look at what's number one on each of your lists. Is it something that honors God? Where does God's work fall on your lists?

The wonderful thing about God is that he doesn't expect to get all of your money—but he does ask you to give part of it, both generously and cheerfully. And he doesn't expect that you'll spend a majority of your time reading his Word, because he knows you have other responsibilities. But God does want to be the top priority in your life.

Check out Haggai 1:4 in the *Young Believer Bible:*

In this verse the Lord speaks through the prophet Haggai and challenges God's people about his temple. The Lord asks his people if it's good that they live in nice houses while his house is in ruins. The obvious answer: No.

●●●

God's people neglected him and worried more about being comfortable. They used their time and money to build themselves houses, instead of building God's house.

Does that sound familiar? It's easy to get caught in the "comfort trap," where we think of ourselves first and put God second. That's why God sent Haggai—to remind his people about what's most important.

If God is the most important thing in your life, it should be reflected in how you spend your time and money. If you're honoring God, then he can see that what's important to him is important to you.

⁂ I believe . . .

what's important to God should be important to me.

Pray:

Tell God you want him as your number-one priority in life and that you'll use your skills, talents, time, and money to honor him.

December 20

Who would you trust the most to tell you the truth about God?

a. a pastor
b. a teacher
c. a parent

d. a Sunday school teacher
e. a friend
f. a stranger

Whom did you choose? A pastor? A teacher? A parent? You probably have a different level of trust for each person on the list. Most likely you wouldn't ask a stranger an important question about God. And you'd probably trust your pastor's answer more than one your friend gave you.

God gives you parents and teachers so that you can learn and grow. But even the godliest person doesn't have all the answers. And sometimes a person teaching God's Word may accidentally give his own opinion rather than explaining what's really in the Bible.

So how can you know what's really true? Go straight to the source: the Bible. Compare everything you hear to what God says in Scripture. You can study God's Word to see what it says, which is exactly what he wants you to do!

Check out Acts 17:11 in the *Young Believer Bible:*

Luke praised the Bereans because they didn't accept everything Paul said without comparing his words to the Scripture. They were excited to learn from Paul, but they also studied the Bible on their own to make sure that what he was teaching was true.

●●●

God gives you spiritual leaders like pastors and teachers to help you understand the Bible. Accepting what they teach is one way to learn to be more like Christ. But no human is perfect. That's why it's important to look at the Scriptures for yourself to make sure what you're being taught is correct. Plus you can ask the Holy Spirit to help you understand.

Get in the habit of searching God's Word today. When you read the Bible, ask yourself these three questions:

1. What does this verse say?
2. What does it mean?
3. What do I need to do to obey?

Don't believe everything you hear! Check out God's Word first, and the Holy Spirit will keep you on the right path.

Pray:

Ask God to help you be like the Bereans and study his Word.

∴ I believe . . .
I should study God's Word for myself to know what's true.

December 21

You see a lot about angels these days. There are television shows, comic books, best-selling novels, beautiful pieces of art, popular songs, and movies that feature these heavenly beings. Believing in angels is kind of popular too. You can buy necklaces, charms, and bracelets with angels on them. It seems most everyone believes in angels.

What do you picture when you think about an angel?

a. a person with wings, dressed all in white, strumming a harp, and sitting on a cloud
b. a newborn baby brother or sister who looks like a little angel
c. a person who dies and goes to heaven
d. none of the above

The best answer is *d* because none of these ideas is totally accurate. Most people don't know a lot about angels. They might picture cute little babies or a flying person with a bow and arrow. The truth is angels are awesome beings that would frighten the daylights out of you if you ever saw one. They are powerful beings created by God for a specific purpose.

Check out Luke 1:30-31 in the *Young Believer Bible:*
This is where an angel appears to Mary. The angel tells her that God loves her and that she's going to have a baby.

●●●

It's got to be freaky to meet an angel, because most of the time when one appears in the Bible the first thing it says is, "Don't be afraid."

Angels appear a lot in God's Word. You can read about them in both the Old and New Testaments. And they always have a job to do. In the beginning of Luke, an angel appears to Mary to tell her that she's going to give birth to Jesus. Once Jesus is born, a group of angels appears to the shepherds to announce the birth of God's Son. Angels in the Old Testament brought death and destruction to God's enemies.

As you can see, angels are powerful, and they have a lot of different jobs to do.

Pray:
Thank God that he uses mighty angels to accomplish his plans.

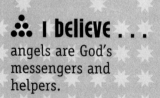

⁂ I believe . . .
angels are God's messengers and helpers.

December 22

Have you ever stood at the top of a really tall building, such as the Sears Tower in Chicago, Illinois? The view can be amazing. On a clear day you can see for miles. Boats that look tiny from way up on the top floors of the building cruise around Lake Michigan. Puny little cars drive into the city on the highway. Row after row of miniature houses sit off in the distance. It's like you're standing on top of the world. Everything looks smaller. Even the tiny little ants scurrying around on the ground look smaller.

Oh, wait, those aren't ants. They're people. An ant couldn't be seen from the top of the Sears Tower. A person is recognizable. Well, sort of.

What's the point? You'll see.

Check out Ephesians 2:8-9 in the
Young Believer Bible:

These verses say salvation isn't a reward for doing good things. Going to heaven is a gift from God to people who believe in him. We can't earn our way to heaven.

●●●

Okay, you'll need to use your imagination for this one. Picture the top of the Sears Tower as heaven. God's sitting up there looking down at us.

A lot of people just walk around on the sidewalk, not thinking about God. But other folks think if they do some good things, then they can earn their way to heaven. These people don't cheat on tests, and they help old ladies cross the street. And let's say those actions help them climb to the third floor. Some people are really good. They give their whole lives to helping sick people in far-off lands. And maybe that allows them to get to the eighth floor. But from the top of the building, everybody still looks the same.

The point is there's nothing a person can do to climb to the top of the building. It's impossible for any human because we're sinful through and through—even if we seem like really good people. But a person can pray a simple prayer and ask Jesus to forgive her sins and help her get to heaven. Then Jesus himself will make sure that she makes it to God the Father in heaven.

Pray:

Thank Jesus for being the only way into heaven.

I believe . . .
I can't work my way to heaven.

Jenny knew everything about Mandy Moviestar. She'd seen all of Mandy's films and had posters and pictures of her on her bedroom walls. Jenny thought Mandy was the best person in the world because her characters in the movies always saved the day. Sometimes Jenny dreamed of being exactly like Mandy.

Then something amazing happened. One morning when Jenny was listening to the radio, she heard the DJ announce a contest. The winner would get to go to the premiere of Mandy's upcoming movie. "Just be the seventh caller to win," the DJ said.

Jenny ran to the phone and dialed.

Busy signal.

She dialed again.

Ring, ring. "Congratulations, you're the big winner!" said the voice on the other end of the phone.

Two weeks later Jenny found herself standing behind the ropes next to the red carpet at Mandy's movie premiere. A huge limousine pulled up, and Mandy stepped out.

"Over here! Over here!" Jenny shouted. "I'm your biggest fan."

Mandy peered at Jenny through her sunglasses. She walked over, looked down her nose at Jenny, and said, "Sorry, I don't know you. I've never talked to you. You're nobody to me."

Then Mandy tossed her hair and walked off.

Check out Philippians 3:8 in the *Young Believer Bible:*
Paul says that everything else is worthless compared to knowing Jesus.

● ● ●

Some people know *about* Jesus, but they don't *know* him. They might have heard that Jesus is a good teacher or that he died on a cross. But just like Jenny had never met Mandy, they've never talked to Jesus. Have you talked to Jesus in prayer? Have you asked him to forgive your sins and come into your life? Have you read what he's told you through the Bible? Do you know him, or do you just know *about* him?

Paul says it's worth losing everything to know Jesus. And unlike someone like Mandy, Jesus will never disappoint you.

Pray:
If you haven't before, pray and ask Jesus to forgive your sins and come into your life. Tell him that you want to know him and have a relationship with him.

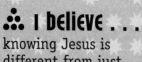

∴ I believe . . .
knowing Jesus is different from just knowing about him.

You've probably been singing a lot of Christmas carols during the last few weeks. Remember "Santa Claus Is Coming to Town"? It says, "You better watch out. You better not cry. You better not pout. I'm telling you why: Santa Claus is coming to town."

But do you know what comes next? Sure you do. "He sees you when you're sleeping. He knows when you're awake. He knows when you've been bad or good, so be good for goodness sake."

And what happens to boys and girls who've been bad? They don't get any presents, right?

Well, you've probably gained some wisdom over the years and figured out that Santa isn't real. Christmas actually lets you celebrate Jesus Christ's birthday. But there are more differences between Santa and Jesus than just the fact that Jesus was a real person and Santa was made up (though he was based on a real person). One of the biggest differences is that Santa only brings toys to kids whose behavior has been good. Jesus, on the other hand, wants to give gifts to everybody.

Check out Ephesians 2:6-7 in the
Young Believer Bible:

These verses talk about God's most precious gift to you: his Son. They say that, because of Jesus, God raises you up to be seated with him. And in the future you'll understand the riches of God's grace given to you in Jesus.

● ● ●

God wants to give you things you don't deserve. That's just who he is. He wants to have a relationship with you. He wants you to enjoy a great life. He wants you to live with him forever in heaven. He wants to bless you.

You don't deserve these things—nobody does. But God gives them anyway. God doesn't expect you to be perfect. In fact, he expects the opposite. He knows you're going to mess up. However, when you mess up, he wants you to pray and ask him to forgive you.

God's willingness to forgive and his desire to bless you is called grace. And that one gift from God makes you one of the richest people on earth.

Pray:

Thank God for his grace.

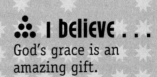

⁂ I believe . . .
God's grace is an amazing gift.

It's Christmas Day. Hooray!

While you enjoy a few weeks off from school, presents, cookies, and time with family, don't forget why you're celebrating. And it's not because of the food—although that's pretty good too. The real reason for the season is Jesus Christ.

You might be thinking . . . *duh?* But it's important to know why Jesus' birth is worth celebrating.

Quiz time. Who was Jesus?

a. God as a human
b. the only child ever born of a virgin
c. the only person to live a sinless life
d. the Savior of the world—the only way to have eternal life in heaven
e. all of the above

If you've taken a few multiple-choice tests before, you know the answer is *e:* all of the above.

Jesus is the most unique man to ever walk the earth. He was 100 percent man. He knows how you feel. But he also is God's only Son. He's 100 percent God. He was around when God the Father formed the universe. He raised the dead, cast out demons, healed the blind, and calmed the storms. Without Jesus' life and death, there would be no forgiveness of sins.

Check out Ephesians 1:7 in the *Young Believer Bible:*
This verse says that because of God's kindness and Jesus' death on a cross, we can be forgiven of all the bad things we do.

●●●

Christ's birth gives everybody the chance for salvation—spiritual rebirth. All you have to do is pray and ask Jesus to forgive your sins and make you a new creation. If you haven't done so before, you can say this prayer.

"Dear God, please forgive me. I know I am a sinner, and I believe Jesus Christ died and rose to heaven so I could be forgiven of my sins and live forever with you. I accept your gift of forgiveness. Thank you for loving me. From this day, I'll do everything I can to follow you. Amen."

If you just prayed, tell your youth pastor or parents. You're a young believer! Time to get a Bible and start reading. And, oh yeah, have a merry Christmas.

Pray:
Thank God for sending his Son to earth.

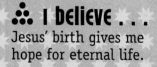

⁂ I believe . . .
Jesus' birth gives me hope for eternal life.

December 26

Have you ever seen those stories on the news about the first baby born in the new year? Usually they're broadcast in big cities such as New York, Chicago, Houston, Denver, or Los Angeles, where lots of babies are born all the time.

Did you ever think what the kid did to deserve all the attention? He just happened to be born after midnight on a certain day of the year, and all of the sudden he's a celebrity (not that he knows he's famous). It seems that if you want to make a big splash in the world, probably the best time and place to be born is in a big city moments after New Year's Eve.

But that's not what God's Son did. He was born in a little town, just as had been predicted hundreds of years beforehand. And he was basically unknown. All he did was make the population go up by one. Sure some shepherds visited him on his birthday, but Jesus' entry into the world didn't bring him a lot of attention.

Check out Micah 5:2 in the *Young Believer Bible:*

This verse predicts the birth of Jesus about 700 years or so before it happened. The prophet says that out of Bethlehem will come a ruler over Israel who has been around since ancient times.

●●●

When was God's Son born?

All right, that was a trick question. You probably said God's Son was born in Bethlehem in about A.D. 0. Good try. The baby Jesus did come to earth about two thousand years ago—that's true. But God's Son actually was alive before he was "born." He has existed forever with God. Another name for Jesus is the Word. John 1:1 says, "In the beginning the Word already existed. He was with God, and he was God."

Jesus has been with God since the beginning. He's 100 percent God. He *is* God. He's the supreme ruler over God's people—and that deserves some attention.

Pray:

Ask God to help you focus on Jesus' power this season.

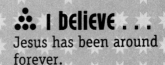

∴ I believe . . .
Jesus has been around forever.

What do you think of when you hear the word *pure*? (Circle all answers that apply.)

- a kitten
- Ivory soap (the commercials say it's more than 99 percent pure)
- a perfectly white baby lamb
- 24-carat gold
- Jesus Christ
- a person who never does anything wrong
- drinking water from a mountain stream
- freshly fallen snow
- a person who messes up, confesses those sins to Jesus, and asks for forgiveness

Pure can mean a lot of different things. Maybe you have additional ideas about the word. When a lot of kids think about the word *pure*, they picture somebody who doesn't do bad things. One mistake, and that's it for purity. It's lost forever. It's like when you get spaghetti sauce on a white T-shirt—it's not coming out. That stain is on there forever.

But that's not how God looks at purity.

Check out Psalm 51:10 in the *Young Believer Bible:*

In this verse David asks God to make his heart pure and to give him the desire to always follow after him.

●●●

David messed up . . . a lot. But he also knew the only way to be pure was to rely on God.

Of the things on the above list, God might say the only two that show real purity are Jesus Christ and a person who messes up, confesses those sins to Jesus, and asks for forgiveness. To God, purity isn't about the sins you don't do. He looks at the heart.

These are some thoughts, attitudes, or actions that might be getting in the way of me having a pure heart in God's eyes:

1. _____

2. _____

3. _____

David was known as a man after God's heart. In other words, he had a pure heart. You can have a pure heart too. All you need to do is ask God to remove the stains of your sin and give you the strength to always follow him.

Pray:
Thank God that he can remove any stain from your heart and make it clean again.

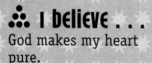

⁙ I believe . . .
God makes my heart pure.

Billy loved the new Sandblaster 4000 video game. He'd played it in the store, but there was no way he was going to lay down $50 to buy it. Billy purchased games at Mr. Mollner's used-game store. He'd been in the store so often that he'd gotten to know Mr. Mollner pretty well.

"How are you doing, Billy?" Mr. Mollner said one afternoon when Billy walked in.

"Hey, Mr. Mollner," Billy answered. "Do you have Sandblaster 4000 yet?"

"Sorry, Billy," Mr. Mollner said. "Nobody's brought one in. But when I get a copy, I'll put your name on it."

"Thanks, Mr. Mollner."

Weeks went by with no call. Finally, Mr. Mollner called and left a message that he had the game.

Todd, a new employee, was behind the counter when Billy walked in. Todd found Sandblaster 4000 and gave it to Billy to inspect. The price tag read $28.00.

"That will be $2.98 including tax," Todd said.

Billy blinked. He quickly handed Todd $3 and left the store.

It wasn't my fault the new salesperson made a mistake, Billy thought. *Besides, I buy stuff from Mr. Mollner all the time. I'm sure God doesn't mind that I got a special deal.*

Check out Luke 16:10 in the *Young Believer Bible:*

In this verse Jesus says if we prove to be faithful with the little things, then we'll be trustworthy with bigger things. But if we cheat even a little, we'll be dishonest in larger matters.

● ● ●

Do you think Billy was being honest? Of course not. The honest thing would have been to point out the cashier's mistake. But that's no big deal, right?

Jesus said if you cheat in the little things, you'll cheat in the big things. In other words, God doesn't look at things as big and little. He sees only right and wrong. Billy's decision wasn't the right one. When it comes to God, your character always counts.

Pray:

Ask God to help you make the right decisions in all situations . . . even when they seem like no big deal.

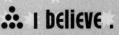 **I believe . . .**
the small things in life matter a lot to God.

Have you ever looked at photos of your parents when they were your age? Pretty funny, huh? It's hard to imagine that your parents went from what they looked like back then to how they appear today.

But guess what? You're going to change too. What you look like today could be very different from what you'll see in the mirror in 10 years. This is such an exciting time in your life. You're growing every day. Perhaps your parents have a place in the house to record your growth. It may make you proud to see how you're getting taller all the time. And it's funny to think that as you grow your parents will shrink. Someday you might even be looking down on them—literally.

You're not only changing in height. You're getting stronger, learning more, and becoming more mature.

And this is only the beginning! In a few years, your body will kick into high gear. Your voice may change, you may grow half a foot in just a few months, and you'll outeat your dad. But at the end of it all, you'll have a good idea of the adult you'll eventually become.

Check out 2 Peter 3:17-18 in the
Young Believer Bible:

These verses encourage you not to be misled by other people's errors or follow bad teaching when it comes to your relationship with Jesus. Instead, you should grow in special favor and your knowledge of the Lord.

●●●

Just as your body is hitting a time of rapid growth, you can commit yourself to grow closer to God. Different temptations (like parties) and obstacles (such as pimples) may enter your life soon. The more you know about Jesus and his will for you, the better you'll be able to handle the tough stuff.

But with growth there is pain. You may experience growing pains as your body sprouts up. And you may have similar feelings as you work to learn more about Jesus. Know that God will reward your efforts as you mature into the person he wants you to be.

Pray:

Ask God to help you grow in your knowledge of him.

⁂ I believe . . .

I need to grow in my knowledge of Jesus Christ.

The Hubble Space Telescope allows scientists to peer deep into the universe and see things they had only dreamed about. The Hubble has helped prove the existence of black holes and has discovered new galaxies.

Zooming 380 miles above Earth, the Hubble travels at five miles per second. It circles this planet about every hour and a half! But even at that speed, the Hubble takes crystal-clear photos of faraway planets and stars. That's because the Hubble is one of the largest and most complex satellites ever built.

About 20 years of research went into building the Hubble Space Telescope, and it's been flying above Earth since 1990. The telescope weighs as much as two adult elephants and is as big as a school bus. But the key to the telescope is a mirror eight feet in diameter that's protected in a long tube from the Sun's glare. Scientists on Earth can look through the Hubble and see the surface of Pluto or watch comets hit Jupiter. Now that's far out!

Check out 2 Chronicles 16:9 in the *Young Believer Bible:*

This verse shows God's power. It says the Lord looks all over Earth for people who are fully committed to him. And when he finds them, he strengthens them.

●●●

God's always watching you. And he doesn't need a high-tech telescope to do it. It's neat to think about God searching Earth for people who are fully committed to him. Can't you just picture God in heaven staring down at Earth with a smile on his face because you love him with all your heart? Well, you can do more than think about it or imagine it. You can *know* it—because it's true.

God strengthens you when you believe in him. God expects you to do great things, but he doesn't expect you to do them alone. He's with you. He'll give you the strength to accomplish whatever he asks you to do.

Pray:

Praise God that he has his eyes on all believers and that he gives you strength.

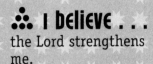

I believe . . . the Lord strengthens me.

You've probably studied time in school. Time is something you can always rely on. It just keeps ticking along. Steady. Always forward. Never stopping. Because you've studied time, you most likely know these basics:

• 60 seconds = 1 minute
• 60 minutes = 1 hour
• 24 hours = 1 day
• 365 days = 1 year

That's not too hard to remember. And because time never changes, there's nothing more to know . . . or is there?

Did you know that some minutes have just 59 seconds and other minutes might take 61 seconds to complete? That's because of something known as *leap seconds*. You've heard of a leap year, right? Every four years it takes 366 days to make a year. The same is true for leap seconds. Most of the time minutes take 60 seconds. But occasionally the Central Bureau of the International Earth Rotation Service in Paris, France, adds or subtracts a second. December 31 is a popular date to do so.

A second is so short that most people don't even know they've lost or gained one. Watches don't even need to be adjusted. But now that you know about it, you also know that time isn't always the same.

Check out Hebrews 13:8 in the *Young Believer Bible:*
This verse gets right to the point. It says that Jesus Christ is the same yesterday, today, and forever.

● ● ●

Time may change, but Jesus Christ never does. He's been around since before time started. God even created time. And Jesus will be around until the end of time. When you learn something about Jesus in Sunday school, from a parent, or by reading the Bible, you can know that it's true and that it will always be true.

These are some things about God that I know will never change:

1. _____
2. _____
3. _____
4. _____

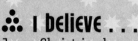

∴ I believe . . .
Jesus Christ is always the same.

The things you wrote down will never change. God is constant. He's totally trustworthy. He's always the same. And you can always count on him. Believe it!

Pray:
Thank God that he never changes.

Index of Scripture References

Genesis 1:1 *October 22*
Genesis 1:16 *October 4*
Genesis 1:20-25 *February 25*
Genesis 1:27 *January 23*
Genesis 1:28 *August 17*
Genesis 2:7 *May 10*
Genesis 50:20 *February 26*
Exodus 13:21 *February 28*
Exodus 20:3 *August 4*
Exodus 20:7 *July 25*
Exodus 20:17 *May 18*
Leviticus 19:11 *March 30*
Leviticus 27:30 *April 13*
Numbers 23:19 *May 28*
Deuteronomy 6:4-5 *May 11*
Deuteronomy 6:14-15 *October 13*
Deuteronomy 8:10 *February 13*
Deuteronomy 22:4 *August 22*
Deuteronomy 31:6 *June 9*
Deuteronomy 32:4 *July 18*
Joshua 1:7 *August 2*
Joshua 1:8 *May 24*
Joshua 22:20 *October 19*
Joshua 23:14 *February 17*
Judges 6:14-16 *May 2*
Ruth 1:16-17 *April 14*
1 Samuel 2:2 *May 31*
1 Samuel 2:8 *January 24*
1 Samuel 10:5-7 *August 23*
1 Samuel 16:7 *February 1*
1 Samuel 17:4-7, 33, 48-51 *September 22*
2 Samuel 22:51 *May 9*
1 Kings 18:21 *October 29*
2 Kings 19:15 *August 10*
1 Chronicles 16:34 *November 27*
2 Chronicles 16:9 *December 30*
Ezra 7:10 *November 24*
Nehemiah 9:6 *March 23*
Esther 4:14 *July 16*
Job 9:10 *July 12*
Job 10:8 *March 10*
Job 37:15-16 *March 2*
Psalm 1:2-3 *June 21*
Psalm 4:4 *June 5*
Psalm 8:3-4 *February 8*
Psalm 12:7 *October 3*
Psalm 16:11 *August 7*
Psalm 19:7 *June 11*

Psalm 19:9-10 *February 3*
Psalm 27:1 *August 21*
Psalm 32:7 *October 12*
Psalm 33:6-8 *November 3*
Psalm 37:4 *May 8*
Psalm 37:8 *May 5*
Psalm 37:40 *December 10*
Psalm 40:5 *November 22*
Psalm 42:1-2 *January 9*
Psalm 46:10 *July 21*
Psalm 51:10 *December 27*
Psalm 52:2-4 *February 27*
Psalm 55:16-17 *September 18*
Psalm 63:8 *January 12*
Psalm 68:3 *October 15*
Psalm 73:23-24 *September 8*
Psalm 90:2-4 *October 23*
Psalm 90:12 *June 6*
Psalm 91:1-2 *January 2*
Psalm 108:1 *July 19*
Psalm 116:1 *March 29*
Psalm 118:6-7 *January 5*
Psalm 119:9-16 *January 14*
Psalm 119:97-98 *August 31*
Psalm 119:105 *April 8*
Psalm 121:2 *July 23*
Psalm 125:1-2 *March 11*
Psalm 127:3 *June 14*
Psalm 130:5 *September 17*
Psalm 139:13-14 *January 20*
Psalm 141:8 *September 13*
Psalm 145:17-20 *October 7*
Proverbs 2:8 *June 30*
Proverbs 3:5-6 *April 22*
Proverbs 3:11-12 *August 20*
Proverbs 9:10 *February 23*
Proverbs 11:13 *July 6*
Proverbs 12:18 *January 27*
Proverbs 13:20 *July 31*
Proverbs 14:23 *November 6*
Proverbs 15:1 *August 12*
Proverbs 15:3 *April 11*
Proverbs 15:22 *March 22*
Proverbs 15:29 *February 9*
Proverbs 16:13 *April 21*
Proverbs 18:24 *June 4*
Proverbs 20:9 *March 24*
Proverbs 22:4 *September 6*

Proverbs 22:6 *May 6*
Proverbs 26:11 *April 1*
Proverbs 26:17 *August 16*
Proverbs 27:6 *March 3*
Proverbs 27:17 *May 29*
Proverbs 29:18 *July 24*
Proverbs 30:5 *May 15*
Ecclesiastes 3:1 *March 6*
Ecclesiastes 3:12 *April 4*
Ecclesiastes 4:9 *January 21*
Ecclesiastes 4:10 *April 29*
Ecclesiastes 7:8 *January 13*
Song of Songs 2:15 *February 29*
Isaiah 1:18 *November 21*
Isaiah 12:2 *August 29*
Isaiah 25:8 *April 19*
Isaiah 38:17-18 *May 17*
Isaiah 40:28 *August 1*
Isaiah 40:31 *September 10*
Isaiah 41:10 *April 5*
Isaiah 43:1 *June 3*
Isaiah 45:11-12 *February 19*
Isaiah 46:4 *December 4*
Isaiah 53:3-5 *April 16*
Isaiah 63:7 *March 25*
Isaiah 64:8 *November 1*
Jeremiah 15:16 *May 4*
Jeremiah 17:14 *January 28*
Jeremiah 23:24 *February 22*
Jeremiah 29:11 *April 24*
Jeremiah 32:17 *October 1*
Lamentations 3:22-23 *June 7*
Ezekiel 2:4-5 *November 26*
Daniel 2:27-28 *September 30*
Daniel 6:22 *September 15*
Daniel 12:3 *January 11*
Hosea 10:12 *June 1*
Hosea 14:2 *October 6*
Joel 2:12-13 *July 9*
Amos 3:3 *December 14*
Obadiah 1:3-4 *December 1*
Jonah 4:10-11 *November 17*
Micah 5:2 *December 26*
Micah 6:8 *August 14*
Micah 7:7 *July 20*
Nahum 1:3 *July 30*
Habakkuk 3:2 *July 15*
Zephaniah 2:3 *October 11*
Zephaniah 3:17 *November 29*
Haggai 1:4 *December 19*
Zechariah 4:6 *December 6*
Malachi 2:10 *September 28*

Matthew 1:21 *December 5*
Matthew 2:7-8, 12 *December 16*
Matthew 2:9-11 *December 17*
Matthew 2:11 *January 6*
Matthew 4:19 *July 11*
Matthew 5:4 *September 1*
Matthew 5:14-16 *January 17*
Matthew 5:34-37 *October 26*
Matthew 5:39-44 *September 20*
Matthew 6:6 *January 8*
Matthew 6:19-20 *June 15*
Matthew 6:24 *June 20*
Matthew 6:25 *August 8*
Matthew 6:33 *September 25*
Matthew 7:7 *June 27*
Matthew 7:9-10 *April 2*
Matthew 7:14 *March 1*
Matthew 7:24-27 *July 3*
Matthew 10:24 *September 16*
Matthew 10:30 *November 5*
Matthew 11:11 *June 2*
Matthew 11:28-30 *December 8*
Matthew 17:20 *January 15*
Matthew 18:10 *May 12*
Matthew 18:19-20 *September 14*
Matthew 20:26-28 *June 8*
Matthew 21:28-31 *April 12*
Matthew 25:14-29 *August 15*
Matthew 25:34-36 *November 15*
Matthew 25:40 *December 9*
Matthew 28:19 *April 18*
Mark 5:19-20 *November 19*
Mark 9:35 *October 24*
Mark 10:25-27 *February 16*
Mark 11:15-17 *February 20*
Mark 12:30 *December 7*
Mark 12:33 *July 29*
Mark 16:15 *October 5*
Luke 1:30-31 *December 21*
Luke 2:10-11 *November 30*
Luke 2:52 *August 5*
Luke 6:40 *July 5*
Luke 6:42 *November 28*
Luke 8:24 *August 24*
Luke 12:15 *December 12*
Luke 16:10 *December 28*
Luke 21:1-4 *November 2*
Luke 24:44 *December 15*
John 1:12-13 *June 10*
John 1:29 *April 10*
John 6:40 *August 30*
John 8:12 *January 29*

9. I should run from temptation.
10. God created me and can do what he wants with me.
11. trusting in God makes me strong—like a mountain.
12. the devil tries to trick me with little things.
13. eternity is forever.
14. Jesus' mercy—not my actions—has made me perfect in his sight.
15. I shouldn't be shy about my relationship with Jesus.
16. my body belongs to God.
17. God gives me the ultimate victory— victory over sin and death.
18. I should fix my eyes on Jesus.
19. God reveals special secrets to believers.
20. Jesus is God.
21. Jesus has power over death.
22. sometimes it's good to ask others for godly advice.
. God created the stars, the earth, and everything living.
Jesus lived a perfect life.
God deserves my praise and thanksgiving.
Jesus is all-powerful, all-seeing, and verywhere.
d forgave me instead of destroying me.
us is my teacher.
communicate with God through
er.
ving somebody is just like lying.
has blinded the eyes of those who
elieve.

n't want me to be a fool.
sense of humor.
t Jesus, the Lion of the tribe of
trol my life.
ne to be happy.
through challenges.
erything about me.
eed a lot of evidence before
Jesus.
the Bible.
e afraid of death.
of God.
.
act like a Christian, not

13. I should give some of my money to God.
14. God wants me to show loyalty.
15. money won't make me happy.
16. Jesus' life has greater purpose than many people realize.
17. the things I say should build up others.
18. God wants me to tell other people about him.
19. Jesus destroys death.
20. Jesus is coming again.
21. honesty is important in relationships.
22. true understanding comes from God.
23. the Holy Spirit helps me in stressful times.
24. God has big dreams for me.
25. God is always close by.
26. there's only one way to have eternal life.
27. God wants me to have patience.
28. doing the right thing will be rewarded eventually.
29. I should surround myself with good friends.
30. God is shaping me to be more like Jesus.

May

1. God is the boss of people who boss me.
2. Jesus can change the world through ordinary people.
3. God will give me courage to do what's right.
4. God's Word feeds my relationship with him.
5. anger can be harmful.
6. my parents want the best for me.
7. God can use my gifts, service, and work in his kingdom.
8. God will give me the desires of my heart.
9. God's kindness helps me to be kind to others.
10. God does awesome things with his creations.
11. I should totally love the one true God.
12. angels are God's servants who protect humans.
13. Jesus tells me all about his Father.
14. when God calls, I must move.
15. evidence exists that proves the Bible is true.
16. I can trust God with every area of my life.
17. there are consequences for sin, but God also offers forgiveness.

John 8:35 *August 18*
John 8:44 *October 10*
John 10:14 *June 18*
John 10:30 *March 20*
John 11:25-26 *March 21*
John 12:40 *December 11*
John 13:14-15 *March 28*
John 14:2-3 *March 8*
John 14:26 *February 7*
John 15:5 *January 19*
John 15:15 *May 13*
John 15:26 *September 12*
John 16:13-14 *October 14*
John 20:29 *April 7*
Acts 2:42 *October 25*
Acts 5:14-15 *February 2*
Acts 9:13-15 *October 30*
Acts 16:31 *October 27*
Acts 17:11 *December 20*
Acts 17:24-27 *April 25*
Romans 1:16 *March 15*
Romans 2:7 *July 14*
Romans 3:22-25 *March 27*
Romans 4:25 *October 18*
Romans 5:3-4 *September 23*
Romans 5:8 *July 27*
Romans 5:12 *July 13*
Romans 6:1-2 *March 5*
Romans 8:14 *July 7*
Romans 8:28 *September 4*
Romans 8:34 *June 24*
Romans 8:38-39 *May 30*
Romans 12:4-8 *February 4*
Romans 13:1 *May 1*
Romans 13:3 *January 16*
Romans 13:8 *September 21*
Romans 14:12 *January 25*
Romans 15:13 *May 16*
1 Corinthians 1:9 *June 23*
1 Corinthians 1:30-31 *June 29*
1 Corinthians 2:6-7, 10 *March 19*
1 Corinthians 2:12 *April 23*
1 Corinthians 2:13-14 *February 10*
1 Corinthians 6:19 *March 16*
1 Corinthians 10:13 *June 28*
1 Corinthians 12:4-6 *May 7*
1 Corinthians 12:12-14 *May 27*
1 Corinthians 12:27 *November 8*
1 Corinthians 15:33 *September 5*
1 Corinthians 15:57 *March 17*
1 Corinthians 15:58 *October 28*
1 Corinthians 16:13 *May 3*

2 Corinthians 1:3 *August 3*
2 Corinthians 4:4 *March 31*
2 Corinthians 4:6 *July 4*
2 Corinthians 5:14-15 *August 19*
2 Corinthians 5:20 *June 12*
2 Corinthians 9:7 *November 20*
2 Corinthians 12:7-9 *February 21*
2 Corinthians 12:10 *November 7*
2 Corinthians 13:13 *February 18*
2 Corinthians 13:7 *July 2*
Galatians 5:14 *February 14*
Galatians 6:10 *November 25*
Ephesians 1:4 *January 30*
Ephesians 1:7 *December 25*
Ephesians 2:6-7 *December 24*
Ephesians 2:8-9 *December 22*
Ephesians 2:18 *May 23*
Ephesians 3:12 *September 3*
Ephesians 4:2 *April 27*
Ephesians 4:29 *April 17*
Ephesians 4:31-32 *February 6*
Ephesians 5:1-2 *January 22*
Ephesians 5:15-17 *October 2*
Ephesians 6:10 *January 18*
Ephesians 6:18 *December 13*
Philippians 1:6 *April 30*
Philippians 1:27 *November 16*
Philippians 2:3 *January 10*
Philippians 2:9-10 *January 31*
Philippians 2:14-15 *February 24*
Philippians 3:8 *December 23*
Philippians 3:14 *December 2*
Philippians 4:8 *December 3*
Philippians 4:13 *October 21*
Colossians 1:16 *July 17*
Colossians 1:18 *August 26*
Colossians 2:6-7 *August 13*
Colossians 2:8 *May 21*
Colossians 3:5-6 *February 5*
Colossians 3:9-10 *September 7*
Colossians 3:23 *August 27*
Colossians 4:6 *November 18*
1 Thessalonians 4:7 *May 14*
1 Thessalonians 4:17 *March 13*
1 Thessalonians 5:5-6 *October 31*
1 Thessalonians 5:15 *September 24*
1 Thessalonians 5:21 *June 13*
1 Thessalonians 5:24 *July 28*
2 Thessalonians 1:3-4 *August 11*
2 Thessalonians 1:7 *June 26*
2 Thessalonians 1:11-12 *July 10*
1 Timothy 4:4 *May 25*

1 Timothy 4:8 *May 20*
1 Timothy 4:12 *September 11*
1 Timothy 5:8 *July 22*
1 Timothy 6:10 *April 15*
1 Timothy 6:11 *August 6*
1 Timothy 6:18 *August 9*
2 Timothy 1:7 *January 1*
2 Timothy 2:6 *April 28*
2 Timothy 2:15 *November 14*
2 Timothy 2:22 *March 9*
2 Timothy 3:16-17 *July 1*
Titus 3:5 *March 14*
Philemon 1:6 *February 12*
Hebrews 2:11 *November 13*
Hebrews 2:14-15 *April 9*
Hebrews 2:18 *November 23*
Hebrews 4:15 *October 8*
Hebrews 6:18 *November 4*
Hebrews 6:19 *June 17*
Hebrews 10:14 *August 28*
Hebrews 10:25 *May 26*
Hebrews 12:1 *January 4*
Hebrews 12:2 *March 18*
Hebrews 13:1 *October 20*
Hebrews 13:3 *November 10*
Hebrews 13:5 *June 16*
Hebrews 13:8 *December 31*
Hebrews 13:17 *October 17*
James 1:12-14 *November 9*
James 1:19 *July 26*
James 1:23-24 *September 2*

James 4:7 *August 25*
James 4:10 *October 9*
1 Peter 1:6-7 *June 19*
1 Peter 2:11 *January 7*
1 Peter 2:13-14 *September 29*
1 Peter 2:20-21 *November 11*
1 Peter 3:10 *October 16*
1 Peter 4:16 *July 8*
1 Peter 5:2 *June 25*
1 Peter 5:8 *March 12*
2 Peter 1:19-21 *March 4*
2 Peter 3:17-18 *December 29*
1 John 1:8-9 *January 3*
1 John 2:1 *May 19*
1 John 3:20 *April 6*
1 John 4:4 *January 26*
1 John 4:4-5 *September 26*
1 John 4:16 *February 15*
1 John 4:19 *March 7*
1 John 4:21 *May 22*
1 John 5:12 *April 26*
2 John 1:6 *December 18*
3 John 1:11 *September 27*
Jude 1:22-23 *September 9*
Revelation 1:8 *November 12*
Revelation 3:20 *February 11*
Revelation 5:5 *April 3*
Revelation 5:6 *March 26*
Revelation 7:17 *September 19*
Revelation 15:3 *June 22*
Revelation 19:11-14 *April 20*

Index of "I Believe" Statements

I believe . . .

January

1. God wants me to be bold.
2. God keeps me safe.
3. God forgives my sins.
4. living for God is a long, exciting race.
5. God helps me overcome my fears.
6. the gifts that the wise men gave Jesus tell me a lot about his life.
7. I'm an alien on earth.
8. prayer is important.
9. I have to work on my relationship with Jesus.
10. God wants me to put others first.
11. I should share Jesus with my friends.
12. I need to stay close to God.
13. making time for God every day is important.
14. I should follow God's instructions in the Bible.
15. God can change the world through me.
16. I can live for Jesus at school.
17. I am a light for God.
18. God is my ultimate power source.
19. I need to live for an audience of One.
20. all people are God's handiwork.
21. great things are accomplished when people work together.
22. to live like God means I need to love others.
23. God created people and patterned them after himself.
24. God is a God of order.
25. it's my responsibility to learn about God.
26. the Holy Spirit gives me power to win over sin.
27. my words make a difference.
28. God is the Great Physician.
29. when it comes to God, I'm not shooting in the dark.
30. God loves me exactly as I am.
31. Jesus is the name above all others.

February

1. God cares about my heart.
2. my life, like a shadow, reflects an image to others.

3. the Bible is precious . . . and sweet.
4. I'm an important part of God's family.
5. I should protect my mind.
6. I need to forgive other people when they make mistakes.
7. the Holy Spirit is my helper.
8. things of beauty are God's gift to me.
9. I shouldn't do wicked things.
10. the Holy Spirit makes God's wisdom understandable.
11. only God holds the keys to true freed
12. I need to tell my friends about Jesus
13. God provides for my needs.
14. other people need to see that I l
15. God is love.
16. nothing is impossible with Go
17. God makes promises and alw them.
18. God is three persons in O
19. God created people.
20. it's okay to get angry things.
21. God created me per
22. I can't hide what
23. God gives me wi
24. God wants me complaining.
25. God created
26. I grow str tough ti
27. I shoul
28. God
29. I ne m

M

April

1. God does
2. God has
3. I should l Judah, co
4. God wants
5. God helps
6. God knows e
7. some people they believe i
8. I should follow
9. I don't need to
10. Jesus is the Lam
11. God is everywher
12. Jesus wants me to just talk like one.

18. God wants me to be content with what I have.
19. Jesus is my advocate.
20. godliness is important.
21. listening to harmful ideas can pull me away from Jesus.
22. God can help me love people.
23. the Holy Spirit connects me to God.
24. I should memorize Scripture and think about it often.
25. all of God's creations are good.
26. I should get together with other Christians at church.
27. I have a special job as part of the body of Christ.
28. God is totally believable and trustworthy.
29. I will be a stronger Christian if I spend time with other believers.
30. nothing can separate me from God's love.
31. God is the Rock.

June

1. I should try doing new things for God.
2. I can be like John the Baptist.
3. God doesn't want me to be afraid.
4. God will never let me down.
5. God wants me to control my anger.
6. God wants me to make the most of my time on earth.
7. I should treat my relationship with God like it's new every day.
8. serving makes me great.
9. God is with me in times of change.
10. all believers belong to God's family.
11. the Bible can show me something new every time I open it.
12. I need to let other people know I'm a Christian.
13. some things are worth holding on to.
14. God wants me to have a good relationship with my parents.
15. I can work hard for heavenly rewards.
16. God gives me what I need.
17. I should anchor my life to Jesus.
18. Jesus is the Good Shepherd.
19. my suffering has a purpose.
20. the most important thing in life is to be Jesus' disciple.
21. I am a tree for God.
22. God can do amazing things.

23. God wants a relationship with me all the time.
24. Jesus defends me.
25. God will use my willingness.
26. Jesus is coming back.
27. God never wants me to stop knocking on his door.
28. when I'm tempted, God provides a way out.
29. I shouldn't brag that I know God.
30. God is my bodyguard.

July

1. reading the Bible is a priority, not an option.
2. I should live my life aiming to hit God's target.
3. I should build my life on God's foundation.
4. I should let my light shine like a star that lasts, not a firework that disappears.
5. there's no shortcut for training.
6. God doesn't want me to gossip.
7. the Spirit of God leads me.
8. being picked on because I'm a Christian is actually a good thing.
9. no matter what I do, I can return to God.
10. having the name *Christian* is the most important thing.
11. God wants me to fish for people.
12. God performs miracles.
13. sin entered the world through Adam.
14. I have only one life with which to please God.
15. God deserves his great reputation.
16. God places me in specific situations to do his work.
17. I can trust God because he made me.
18. God is perfect.
19. my life can make a beautiful sound for God.
20. sometimes God wants me to wait.
21. being quiet to think about God draws me closer to him.
22. treating my family well is a good idea.
23. I can ask God for help.
24. I should obey God's law.
25. God's name is special and should be treated that way.
26. I shouldn't let my emotions get the best of me.

27. God loved me first.
28. God will help me do his work.
29. I show God my love by spending time with him.
30. God always punishes the guilty.
31. God wants me to choose my friends wisely.

August

1. God exists forever.
2. following God's Word will make my life exciting.
3. Jesus comforts people who mourn.
4. God wants me to put him first in my life.
5. Jesus was a kid like me.
6. God will help me avoid the trap of sin.
7. God fills me with joy.
8. I shouldn't worry about what I'm wearing.
9. God wants me to share with others.
10. only God is over all the earth.
11. genuine faith increases when I go through trials.
12. being careful about what I do and say is important.
13. I need to grow in my relationship with Jesus.
14. God is my guide.
15. God rewards me when I put the things he gives me to good use.
16. I shouldn't take on my friends' problems as my own.
17. God provides food for me.
18. my family is forever.
19. I live for Jesus.
20. God disciplines me because he loves me.
21. I don't have to be afraid.
22. I can do great things to help people.
23. the Holy Spirit gives me power to serve God.
24. Jesus can control the weather.
25. I need to trust God and resist the devil.
26. the church is everyone who believes in Jesus as Savior.
27. I should work like I'm doing the job for God.
28. Jesus is the perfect sacrifice.
29. I should put my total trust in God.
30. when I die, my soul will go to heaven to live with Jesus forever.
31. I should hide God's Word in my heart.

September

1. God is my comforter.
2. God's Word is a mirror for my life.
3. I am free to come to God with confidence.
4. God works all things for good.
5. being myself is the best option.
6. my character matters more than my career.
7. I shouldn't lie.
8. Jesus holds my hand.
9. I should work to save other people from the flames.
10. when I'm tied into Jesus my life can soar.
11. age doesn't hold me back from doing things for God.
12. the Holy Spirit is my Counselor.
13. when things get tough, I can hide in God.
14. God shows up when Christians get together.
15. angels watch over me.
16. I need to respect my teachers.
17. God is there for me in the bad times.
18. God hears every one of my prayers.
19. my life should revolve around Jesus Christ.
20. I should pray for bullies.
21. if I borrow something, I should pay it back right away.
22. God uses small people to be heroes.
23. trials and problems produce character.
24. God wants me to show kindness to others.
25. I should seek God and not worry what other people think of me.
26. God's team is the best team.
27. I should do what is good in my relationships.
28. God is the one and only God.
29. I should obey the rules.
30. God reveals special secrets to people who believe in him.

October

1. God is more powerful than anything.
2. only God's opinion counts.
3. I can turn to Jesus for protection.
4. God created space—and everything in it.
5. God wants me to share his Good News.
6. God knows my sins . . . and still forgives me.
7. the Bible tells me what God is like.
8. Jesus was tempted, but he never sinned.

9. God blesses humility.
10. Satan is a liar.
11. my relationship with Jesus takes effort.
12. God protects me from harm.
13. God is a jealous God.
14. I can rely on the Holy Spirit to guide me.
15. I don't have a good reason to be grouchy.
16. I should watch what I say.
17. God wants me to submit to authority.
18. Jesus died so I could have something beautiful.
19. my sin affects others.
20. I show God's love when I care for other believers.
21. I can do all things with God.
22. God works, so I should work too.
23. time holds no power over God.
24. God wants me to put others first.
25. God wants me to make going to church a priority.
26. I should keep my word—without swearing to it.
27. I am saved because I believe in Jesus.
28. what I do for God is always important.
29. I should make up my mind to follow only God.
30. God can use anybody to spread his Word.
31. I am a child of the light.

November
1. God is the molder of my life.
2. God appreciates and understands my sacrifices.
3. I should respect the size of God's creation.
4. God does not lie.
5. God knows everything about me.
6. I should work hard, not just talk about it.
7. God can use my weakness.
8. I am a necessary part of the church.
9. when I overcome temptations, my faith grows stronger.
10. God wants me to remember persecuted Christians.
11. I should follow Jesus' footsteps no matter what.
12. God has always been and always will be.
13. Jesus likes being my brother.
14. God wants me to do my best for him.
15. when I help those in need, I help Jesus.
16. my manners matter.
17. God wants me to be concerned about other people.
18. I should choose words of truth and grace.
19. talking about Jesus helps me understand him better.
20. I should be giving because God has given me so much.
21. the Lord makes my sin as white as snow.
22. God has reasons for everything he does.
23. I need God's help to live right.
24. it takes a lot of effort to teach something correctly.
25. I should treat other people nicely.
26. people need to hear God's Word, even if it seems like they're not listening.
27. I should give thanks to God.
28. I need to take care of my spiritual vision.
29. what other people think matters less to me because God loves me.
30. I need to get ready to celebrate Jesus' birth.

December
1. even the mighty experience God's judgment.
2. living like Jesus is hard work.
3. I should fill my mind with good images.
4. God created me to do awesome things.
5. Jesus was born to save the world from sin.
6. God is sovereign.
7. I should love God with my heart, soul, mind, and strength.
8. following Jesus doesn't have to be backbreaking.
9. I should help people in need.
10. Jesus saves people.
11. some people have blind eyes and dead hearts when it comes to understanding God's truth.
12. I need to watch out for greed.
13. God wants me to pray to him.
14. who I hang out with says a lot about me.
15. Jesus fulfills Old Testament prophecy.
16. God protects me from evil people.
17. the purpose of Christmas is worshiping Jesus.
18. I show love when I obey God's commands.
19. what's important to God should be important to me.
20. I should study God's Word for myself to know what's true.

21. angels are God's messengers and helpers.
22. I can't work my way to heaven.
23. knowing Jesus is different from just knowing about him.
24. God's grace is an amazing gift.
25. Jesus' birth gives me hope for eternal life.
26. Jesus has been around forever.
27. God makes my heart pure.
28. the small things in life matter a lot to God.
29. I need to grow in my knowledge of Jesus Christ.
30. the Lord strengthens me.
31. Jesus Christ is always the same.

Author Information

Jesse Florea has worked for Focus on the Family for more than ten years and has been the editor of *Clubhouse* magazine for over half of that time. He loves children, has two of his own, works with them at church, and wants kids to know the excitement of living for Jesus Christ. He earned bachelor's and master's degrees in communications from Wheaton College in Illinois and has written professionally for more than eighteen years. He lives with his wife and kids in Colorado Springs.

Stephen Arterburn has a heart for children—especially his 12-year-old daughter, Madeline—and has worked extensively to develop their faith in Christ through quality Christian products. He cocreated two kids' fiction series: the Lily series (Zondervan) with Nancy Rue and Camp Wanna Banana (WaterBrook) with Becky Freeman. In addition to these children's projects, he was also the senior editor of the best-selling *Life Recovery Bible* and the Gold Medallion Award–winning *Spiritual Renewal Bible*. He is also known for his best-selling Every Man's Battle series. Finally, he is the founder of Women of Faith and New Life Ministries and host of the daily radio show *New Life Live!*